S0-ARC-339

Learning Processing

A Beginner's Guide to Programming Images, Animation, and Interaction

The Morgan Kaufmann Series in Computer Graphics

Learning Processing

A Beginner's Guide to Programming Images, Animation, and Interaction

Daniel Shiffman

AMSTERDAM • BOSTON • HEIDELBERG • LONDON
NEW YORK • OXFORD • PARIS • SAN DIEGO
SAN FRANCISCO • SINGAPORE • SYDNEY • TOKYO

Morgan Kaufmann Publishers is an imprint of Elsevier

Morgan Kaufmann Publishers is an imprint of Elsevier
30 Corporate Drive, Suite 400, Burlington, MA 01803, USA

Copyright © 2008, Elsevier Inc. All rights reserved.

Designations used by companies to distinguish their products are often claimed as trademarks or registered trademarks. In all instances in which Morgan Kaufmann Publishers is aware of a claim, the product names appear in initial capital or all capital letters. All trademarks that appear or are otherwise referred to in this work belong to their respective owners. Neither Morgan Kaufmann Publishers nor the authors and other contributors of this work have any relationship or affiliation with such trademark owners nor do such trademark owners confirm, endorse, or approve the contents of this work. Readers, however, should contact the appropriate companies for more information regarding trademarks and any related registrations.

No part of this publication may be reproduced, stored in a retrieval system, or transmitted in any form or by any means—electronic, mechanical, photocopying, scanning, or otherwise—without prior written permission of the publisher.

Permissions may be sought directly from Elsevier's Science & Technology Rights Department in Oxford, UK: phone: (+44) 1865 843830, fax: (+44) 1865 853333, E-mail: permissions@elsevier.com. You may also complete your request online via the Elsevier homepage (http://www.elsevier.com) by selecting "Support & Contact" then "Copyright and Permission" and then "Obtaining Permissions."

Library of Congress Cataloging-in-Publication Data
Application submitted.

ISBN: 978-0-12-373602-4

For information on all Morgan Kaufmann publications, visit our
Web site at *www.mkp.com* or *www.books.elsevier.com*

Typset by Charon Tec Ltd., A Macmillan Company (www.macmillansolutions.com).

Printed in the United States of America.

08 09 10 11 12   5 4 3 2 1

Working together to grow
libraries in developing countries

www.elsevier.com | www.bookaid.org | www.sabre.org

ELSEVIER   BOOK AID
International   Sabre Foundation

Contents

Acknowledgments

In the fall of 2001, I wandered into the Interactive Telecommunications Program in the Tisch School of the Arts at New York University having not written a line of code since some early 80's experiments in BASIC on an Apple II+. There, in a first semester course entitled Introduction to Computational Media, I discovered programming. Without the inspiration and support of ITP, my home since 2001, this book would have never been written.

Red Burns, the department's chair and founder, has supported and encouraged me in my work for the last seven years. Dan O'Sullivan has been my teaching mentor and was the first to suggest that I try a course in *Processing* at ITP, giving me a reason to start putting together programming tutorials. Shawn Van Every sat next to me in the office throughout the majority of the writing of this book, providing helpful suggestions, code, and a great deal of moral support along the way. Tom Igoe's work with physical computing provided inspiration for this book, and he was particularly helpful as a resource while putting together examples on network and serial communication. And it was Clay Shirky who I can thank for one day stopping me in the hall to tell me I should write a book in the first place. Clay also provided a great deal of feedback on early drafts.

All of my fellow computational media teachers at ITP have provided helpful suggestions and feedback along the way: Danny Rozin (the inspiration behind Chapters 15 and 16), Amit Pitaru (who helped in particular with the chapter on sound), Nancy Lewis, James Tu, Mark Napier, Chris Kairalla, and Luke Dubois. ITP faculty members Marianne Petit, Nancy Hechinger, and Jean-Marc Gauthier have provided inspiration and support throughout the writing of this book. The rest of the faculty and staff at ITP have also made this possible: George Agudow, Edward Gordon, Midori Yasuda, Megan Demarest, Robert Ryan, John Duane, Marlon Evans, and Tony Tseng.

The students of ITP, too numerous to mention, have been an amazing source of feedback throughout this process, having used much of the material in this book in trial runs for various courses. I have stacks of pages with notes scrawled along the margins as well as a vast archive of e-mails with corrections, comments, and generous words of encouragement.

I am also indebted to the energetic and supportive community of *Processing* programmers and artists. I'd probably be out of a job if it weren't for Casey Reas and Benjamin Fry who created *Processing*. I've learned half of what I know simply from reading through the *Processing* source code; the elegant simplicity of the *Processing* language, web site, and IDE has made programming accessible and fun for all of my students. I've received advice, suggestions, and comments from many *Processing* programmers including Tom Carden, Marius Watz, Karsten Schmidt, Robert Hodgin, Ariel Malka, Burak Arikan, and Ira Greenberg. The following teachers were also helpful test driving early versions of the book in their courses: Hector Rodriguez, Keith Lam, Liubo Borissov, Rick Giles, Amit Pitaru, David Maccarella, Jeff Gray, and Toshitaka Amaoka.

Peter Kirn and Douglas Edric Stanley provided extraordinarily detailed comments and feedback during the technical review process and the book is a great deal better than it would have been without their efforts. Demetrie Tyler did a tremendous job working on the visual design of the cover and interior of this book, making me look much cooler than I am. And a thanks to David Hindman, who worked on helping me organize the screenshots and diagrams.

I'd also like to thank everyone at Morgan Kaufmann/Elsevier who worked on producing the book: Gregory Chalson, Tiffany Gasbarrini, Jeff Freeland, Danielle Monroe, Matthew Cater, Michele Cronin, Denise Penrose, and Mary James.

Finally, and most important, I'd like to thank my wife, Aliki Caloyeras, who graciously stayed awake whenever I needed to talk through the content of this book (and even when I felt the need to practice material for class) my parents, Doris and Bernard Shiffman; and my brother, Jonathan Shiffman, who all helped edit some of the very first pages of this book, even while on vacation.

Introduction

What is this book?

This book tells a story. It is a story of liberation, of taking the first steps toward understanding the foundations of computing, writing your own code, and creating your own media without the bonds of existing software tools. This story is not reserved for computer scientists and engineers. This story is for you.

Who is this book for?

This book is for the beginner. If you have never written a line of code in your life, you are in the right place. No assumptions are made, and the fundamentals of programming are covered slowly, one by one, in the first nine chapters of this book. You do not need any background knowledge besides the basics of operating a computer—turning it on, browsing the web, launching an application, that sort of thing.

Because this book uses *Processing* (more on *Processing* in a moment), it is especially good for someone studying or working in a visual field, such as graphic design, painting, sculpture, architecture, film, video, illustration, web design, and so on. If you are in one of these fields (at least one that involves using a computer), you are probably well versed in a particular software package, possibly more than one, such as Photoshop, Illustrator, AutoCAD, Maya, After Effects, and so on. The point of this book is to release you, at least in part, from the confines of existing tools. What can you make, what can you design if, instead of using someone else's tools, you write your own? If this question interests you, you are in the right place.

If you have some programming experience, but are interested in learning about *Processing*, this book could also be useful. The early chapters will provide you with a quick refresher (and solid foundation) for the more advanced topics found in the second half of the book.

What is *Processing*?

Let's say you are taking Computer Science 101, perhaps taught with the Java programming language. Here is the output of the first example program demonstrated in class:

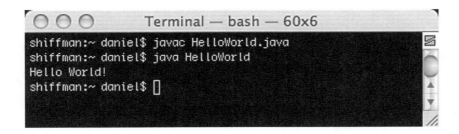

Traditionally, programmers are taught the basics via command line output:

1. TEXT IN → You write your code as text.
2. TEXT OUT → Your code produces text output on the command line.
3. TEXT INTERACTION → The user can enter text on the command line to interact with the program.

The output "Hello, World!" of this example program is an old joke, a programmer's convention where the text output of the first program you learn to write in any given language says "Hello, World!" It first appeared in a 1974 Bell Laboratories memorandum by Brian Kernighan entitled "Programming in C: A Tutorial."

The strength of learning with *Processing* is its emphasis on a more intuitive and visually responsive environment, one that is more conducive to artists and designers learning programming.

1. TEXT IN → You write your code as text.
2. VISUALS OUT → Your code produces visuals in a window.
3. MOUSE INTERACTION → The user can interact with those visuals via the mouse (and more as we will see in this book!).

Processing's "Hello, World!" might look something like this:

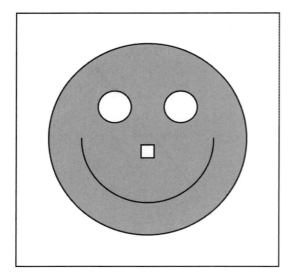

Hello, Shapes!

Though quite friendly looking, it is nothing spectacular (both of these first programs leave out #3: interaction), but neither is "Hello, World!" However, the focus, learning through immediate visual feedback, is quite different.

Processing is not the first language to follow this paradigm. In 1967, the Logo programming language was developed by Daniel G. Bobrow, Wally Feurzeig, and Seymour Papert. With Logo, a programmer writes instructions to direct a turtle around the screen, producing shapes and designs. John Maeda's *Design By Numbers* (1999) introduced computation to visual designers and artists with a simple, easy to use syntax.

While both of these languages are wonderful for their simplicity and innovation, their capabilities are limited.

Processing, a direct descendent of *Logo* and *Design by Numbers*, was born in 2001 in the "Aesthetics and Computation" research group at the Massachusetts Institute of Technology Media Lab. It is an open source initiative by Casey Reas and Benjamin Fry, who developed *Processing* as graduate students studying with John Maeda.

> *"Processing is an open source programming language and environment for people who want to program images, animation, and sound. It is used by students, artists, designers, architects, researchers, and hobbyists for learning, prototyping, and production. It is created to teach fundamentals of computer programming within a visual context and to serve as a software sketchbook and professional production tool. Processing is developed by artists and designers as an alternative to proprietary software tools in the same domain."*
> *— www.processing.org*

To sum up, *Processing* is awesome. First of all, it is free. It doesn't cost a dime. Secondly, because *Processing* is built on top of the Java programming language (this is explored further in the last chapter of this book), it is a fully functional language without some of the limitations of *Logo* or *Design by Numbers*. There is very little you can't do with *Processing*. Finally, *Processing* is open source. For the most part, this will not be a crucial detail of the story of this book. Nevertheless, as you move beyond the beginning stages, this philosophical principle will prove invaluable. It is the reason that such an amazing community of developers, teachers, and artists come together to share work, contribute ideas, and expand the features of *Processing*.

A quick surf-through of the *processing.org* Web site reveals this vibrant and creative community. There, code is shared in an open exchange of ideas and artwork among beginners and experts alike. While the site contains a complete reference as well as a plethora of examples to get you started, it does not have a step-by-step tutorial for the true beginner. This book is designed to give you a jump start on joining and contributing to this community by methodically walking you through the fundamentals of programming as well as exploring some advanced topics.

It is important to realize that, although without *Processing* this book might not exist, this book is not a *Processing* book per se. The intention here is to teach you programming. We are choosing to use *Processing* as our learning environment, but the focus is on the core computational concepts, which will carry you forward in your digital life as you explore other languages and environments.

But shouldn't I be Learning _____ ?

You know you want to. Fill in that blank. You heard that the next big thing is that programming language and environment Flibideeflobidee. Sure it sounds made up, but that friend of yours will not stop talking about how awesome it is. How it makes everything soooo easy. How what used to take you a whole day to program can be done in five minutes. And it works on a Mac. And a PC! And a toaster oven! And you can program your pets to speak with it. In Japanese!

Here's the thing. That magical language that solves all your problems does not exist. No language is perfect, and *Processing* comes with its fair share of limitations and flaws. *Processing*, however, is an excellent place to start (and stay). This book teaches you the fundamentals of programming so that you can apply them throughout your life, whether you use *Processing*, Java, Actionscript, C, PHP, or some other language.

It is true that for some projects, other languages and environments can be better. But *Processing* is really darn good for a lot of stuff, especially media-related and screen-based work. A common misconception is that *Processing* is just for fiddling around; this is not the case. People (myself included) are out there using *Processing* from day number 1 to day number 365 of their project. It is used for web applications, art projects in museums and galleries, and exhibits and installations in public spaces. Most recently, I used *Processing* to develop a real-time graphics video wall system (*http://www.mostpixelsever.com*) that can display content on a 120 by 12 foot (yes, feet!) video wall in the lobby of InterActive Corps' New York City headquarters.

Not only is *Processing* great for actually doing stuff, but for learning, there really isn't much out there better. It is free and open source. It is simple. It is visual. It is fun. It is object-oriented (we will get to this later.) And it does actually work on Macs, PCs, and Linux machines (no talking dogs though, sorry).

So I would suggest to you that you stop worrying about what it is you should be using and focus on learning the fundamentals with *Processing*. That knowledge will take you above and beyond this book to any language you want to tackle.

Write in this book!

Let's say you are a novelist. Or a screenwriter. Is the only time you spend writing the time spent sitting and typing at a computer? Or (gasp) a typewriter? Most likely, this is not the case. Perhaps ideas swirl in your mind as you lie in bed at night. Or maybe you like to sit on a bench in the park, feed the pigeons, and play out dialogue in your head. And one late night, at the local pub, you find yourself scrawling out a brilliant plot twist on a napkin.

Well, writing software, programming, and creating code is no different. It is really easy to forget this since the work itself is so inherently tied to the computer. But you must find time to let your mind wander, think about logic, and brainstorm ideas away from the chair, the desk, and the computer. Personally, I do all my best programming while jogging.

Sure, the actual typing on the computer part is pretty important. I mean, you will not end up with a life-changing, working application just by laying out by the pool. But thinking you always need to be hunched over the glare of an LCD screen will not be enough.

Writing all over this book is a step in the right direction, ensuring you will practice thinking through code away from the keyboard. I have included many exercises in the book that incorporate a "fill in the blanks" approach. (All of these fill in the blanks exercises have answers on the book's Web site, *http://www.learningprocessing.com,* so you can check your work.) Use these pages! When an idea inspires you, make a note and write it down. Think of the book as a workbook and sketchbook for your computational ideas. (You can of course use your own sketchbook, too.)

I would suggest you spend half your time reading this book away from the computer and the other half, side by side with your machine, experimenting with example code along the way.

How should I read this book?

It is best to read this book in order. Chapter 1, Chapter 2, Chapter 3, and so on. You can get a bit more relaxed about this after the end of Chapter 9 but in the beginning it is pretty important.

The book is designed to teach you programming in a linear fashion. A more advanced text might operate more like a reference where you read bits and pieces here and there, moving back and forth throughout the book. But here, the first half of the book is dedicated to making one example, and building the features of that example one step at a time (more on this in a moment). In addition, the fundamental elements of computer programming are presented in a particular order, one that comes from several years of trial and error with a group of patient and wonderful students in New York University's Interactive Telecommunications Program ("ITP") at the Tisch School of the Arts (*http://itp.nyu.edu*).

The chapters of the book (23 total) are grouped into lessons (10 total). The first nine chapters introduce computer graphics, and cover the fundamental principles behind computer programming. Chapters 10 through 12 take a break from learning new material to examine how larger projects are developed with an incremental approach. Chapters 13 through 23 expand on the basics and offer a selection of more advanced topics ranging from 3D, to incorporating live video, to data visualization.

The "Lessons" are offered as a means of dividing the book into digestible chunks. The end of a lesson marks a spot at which I suggest you take a break from reading and attempt to incorporate that lesson's chapters into a project. Suggestions for these projects are offered (but they are really just that: suggestions).

Is this a textbook?

This book is designed to be used either as a textbook for an introductory level programming course or for self-instruction.

I should mention that the structure of this book comes directly out of the course "Introduction to Computational Media" at ITP. Without the help my fellow teachers of this class (Dan O'Sullivan, Danny Rozin, Chris Kairalla, Shawn Van Every, Nancy Lewis, Mark Napier, and James Tu) and hundreds of students (I wish I could name them all here), I don't think this book would even exist.

To be honest, though, I am including a bit more material than can be taught in a beginner level one semester course. Out of the 23 chapters, I probably cover about 18 of them in detail in my class (but make reference to everything in the book at some point). Nevertheless, whether or not you are reading the book for a course or learning on your own, it is reasonable that you could consume the book in a period of a few months. Sure, you can read it faster than that, but in terms of actually writing code and developing projects that incorporate all the material here, you will need a fairly significant amount of time. As tempting as it is to call this book "Learn to Program with 10 Lessons in 10 Days!" it is just not realistic.

Here is an example of how the material could play out in a 14 week semester course.

Week 1	Lesson 1: Chapters 1–3
Week 2	Lesson 2: Chapters 4–6
Week 3	Lesson 3: Chapters 7–8
Week 4	Lesson 4: Chapter 9
Week 5	Lesson 5: Chapter 10–11
Week 6	Midterm! (Also, continue Lesson 5: Chapter 12)

Week 7	Lesson 6: Chapter 13–14
Week 8	Lesson 7: Chapter 15–16
Week 9	Lesson 8: Chapters 17–19
Week 10	Lesson 9: Chapters 20–21
Week 11	Lesson 10: Chapters 22–23
Week 12	Final Project Workshop
Week 13	Final Project Workshop
Week 14	Final Project Presentations

Will this be on the test?

A book will only take you so far. The real key is practice, practice, practice. Pretend you are 10 years old and taking violin lessons. Your teacher would tell you to practice every day. And that would seem perfectly reasonable to you. Do the exercises in this book. Practice every day if you can.

Sometimes when you are learning, it can be difficult to come up with your own ideas. These exercises are there so that you do not have to. However, if you have an idea for something you want to develop, you should feel free to twist and tweak the exercises to fit with what you are doing.

A lot of the exercises are tiny little drills that can be answered in a few minutes. Some are a bit harder and might require up to an hour. Along the way, however, it is good to stop and work on a project that takes longer, a few hours, a day, or a week. As I just mentioned, this is what the "lesson" structure is for. I suggest that in between each lesson, you take a break from reading and work on making something in *Processing*. A page with project suggestions is provided for each lesson.

All of the answers to all of the exercises can be found on this book's web site. Speaking of which …

Do you have a web site?

The Web site for this book is: *http://www.learningprocessing.com*

There you will find the following things:

- Answers to all exercises in the book.
- Downloadable versions of all code in the book.
- Online versions of the examples (that can be put online) in the book.
- Corrections of any errors in the book.
- Additional tips and tutorials beyond material in the book.
- Questions and comments page.

Since many of the examples in this book use color and are animated, the black and white, static screenshots provided in the pages here will not give you the whole picture. As you are reading, you can refer to the web site to view the examples running in your browser as well as download them to run locally on your computer.

This book's web site is not a substitute for the amazing resource that is the official *Processing* web site: *http://www.processing.org*. There, you will find the *Processing* reference, many more examples, and a lively forum.

Take It One Step at a Time

The Philosophy of Incremental Development

There is one more thing we should discuss before we embark on this journey together. It is an important driving force behind the way I learned to program and will contribute greatly to the style of this book. As coined by a former professor of mine, it is called the "philosophy of incremental development." Or perhaps, more simply, the "one-step-at-a-time approach."

Whether you are a total novice or a coder with years of experience, with any programming project, it is crucial not to fall into the trap of trying to do too much all at once. Your dream might be to create the uber-*Processing* program that, say, uses Perlin noise to procedurally generate textures for 3D vertex shapes that evolve via the artificial intelligence of a neural network that crawls the web mining for today's news stories, displaying the text of these stories onscreen in colors taken from a live video feed of a viewer in front of the screen who can control the interface with live microphone input by singing.

There is nothing wrong with having grand visions, but the most important favor you can do for yourself is to learn how to break those visions into small parts and attack each piece slowly, one at a time. The previous example is a bit silly; nevertheless, if you were to sit down and attempt to program its features all at once, I am pretty sure you would end up using a cold compress to treat your pounding headache.

To demonstrate, let's simplify and say that you aspire to program the game Space Invaders (see: *http://en.wikipedia.org/wiki/Space_Invaders*). While this is not explicitly a game programming book, the skills to accomplish this goal will be found here. Following our newfound philosophy, however, we know we need to develop one step at a time, breaking down the problem of programming Space Invaders into small parts. Here is a quick attempt:

1. Program the spaceship.
2. Program the invaders.
3. Program the scoring system.

Great, we divided our program into three steps! Nevertheless, we are not at all finished. The key is to divide the problem into the *smallest pieces possible*, to the point of absurdity, if necessary. You will learn to scale back into larger chunks when the time comes, but for now, the pieces should be so small that they seem ridiculously oversimplified. After all, if the idea of developing a complex game such as Space Invaders seems overwhelming, this feeling will go away if you leave yourself with a list of steps to follow, each one simple and easy.

With that in mind, let's try a little harder, breaking Step 1 from above down into smaller parts. The idea here is that you would write six programs, the first being the simplest: *display a triangle*. With each step, we add a small improvement: *move the triangle*. As the program gets more and more advanced, eventually we will be finished.

1.1   Draw a triangle onscreen. The triangle will be our spaceship.
1.2   Position the triangle at the bottom of the screen.
1.3   Position the triangle slightly to the right of where it was before.
1.4   Animate the triangle so that it moves from position left to right.
1.5   Animate the triangle from left to right only when the right-arrow key is pressed.
1.6   Animate the triangle right to left when the left-arrow key is pressed.

Of course, this is only a small fraction of all of the steps we need for a full Space Invaders game, but it demonstrates a vital way of thinking. The benefits of this approach are not simply that it makes programming easier (which it does), but that it also makes "debugging" easier.

Debugging[1] refers to the process of finding defects in a computer program and fixing them so that the program behaves properly. You have probably heard about bugs in, say, the Windows operating system: miniscule, arcane errors deep in the code. For us, a bug is a much simpler concept: a mistake. Each time you try to program something, it is very likely that *something* will not work as you expected, if at all. So if you start out trying to program everything all at once, it will be very hard to find these bugs. The one-step-at-a-time methodology, however, allows you to tackle these mistakes one at a time, squishing the bugs.

In addition, incremental development lends itself really well to *object-oriented programming*, a core principle of this book. Objects, which will be introduced in Lesson 3, Chapter 8, will help us to develop projects in modular pieces as well as provide an excellent means for organizing (and sharing) code. Reusability will also be key. For example, if you have programmed a spaceship for Space Invaders and want to start working on asteroids, you can grab the parts you need (i.e., the moving spaceship code), and develop the new pieces around them.

Algorithms

When all is said and done, computer programming is all about writing *algorithms*. An algorithm is a sequential list of instructions that solves a particular problem. And the philosophy of incremental development (which is essentially an algorithm for you, the human being, to follow) is designed to make it easier for you to write an algorithm that implements your idea.

As an exercise, before you get to Chapter 1, try writing an algorithm for something you do on a daily basis, such as brushing your teeth. Make sure the instructions seem comically simple (as in "Move the toothbrush one centimeter to the left").

Imagine that you had to provide instructions on how to accomplish this task to someone entirely unfamiliar with toothbrushes, toothpaste, and teeth. That is how it is to write a program. A computer is nothing more than a machine that is brilliant at following precise instructions, but knows nothing about the world at large. And this is where we begin our journey, our story, our new life as a programmer. We begin with learning how to talk to our friend, the computer.

---

[1] The term "debugging" comes from the apocryphal story of a moth getting stuck in the relay circuits of one of computer scientist Grace Murray Hopper's computers.

Introductory Exercise: Write instructions for brushing your teeth.

Some suggestions:

- Do you do different things based on conditions? How might you use the words "if" or "otherwise" in your instructions? (For example: if the water is too cold, increase the warm water. Otherwise, increase cold water.)
- Use the word "repeat" in your instructions. For example: Move the brush up and down. Repeat 5 times.

Also, note that we are starting with Step # 0. In programming, we often like to count starting from 0 so it is good for us to get used to this idea right off the bat!

How to brush your teeth by _____

Step 0. _____

Step 1. _____

Step 2. _____

Step 3. _____

Step 4. _____

Step 5. _____

Step 6. _____

Step 7. _____

Step 8. _____

Step 9. _____

Lesson One

The Beginning

1 Pixels

"A journey of a thousand miles begins with a single step."
—Lao-tzu

In this chapter:
– Specifying pixel coordinates.
– Basic shapes: point, line, rectangle, ellipse.
– Color: grayscale, "RGB."
– Color transparency.

Note that we are not doing any programming yet in this chapter! We are just dipping our feet in the water and getting comfortable with the idea of creating onscreen graphics with text-based commands, that is, "code"!

1.1 Graph Paper

This book will teach you how to program in the context of computational media, and it will use the development environment *Processing* (*http://www.processing.org*) as the basis for all discussion and examples. But before any of this becomes relevant or interesting, we must first channel our eighth grade selves, pull out a piece of graph paper, and draw a line. The shortest distance between two points is a good old fashioned line, and this is where we begin, with two points on that graph paper.

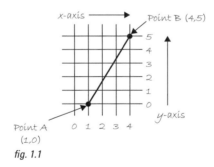

fig. 1.1

Figure 1.1 shows a line between point A (1,0) and point B (4,5). If you wanted to direct a friend of yours to draw that same line, you would give them a shout and say "draw a line from the point one-zero to the point four-five, please." Well, for the moment, imagine your friend was a computer and you wanted to instruct this digital pal to display that same line on its screen. The same command applies (only this time you can skip the pleasantries and you will be required to employ a precise formatting). Here, the instruction will look like this:

```
line(1,0,4,5);
```

Congratulations, you have written your first line of computer code! We will get to the precise formatting of the above later, but for now, even without knowing too much, it should make a fair amount of sense. We are providing a *command* (which we will refer to as a "function") for the machine to follow entitled "line." In addition, we are specifying some *arguments* for how that line should be drawn, from point

A (0,1) to point B (4,5). If you think of that line of code as a sentence, the *function* is a *verb* and the *arguments* are the *objects* of the sentence. The code sentence also ends with a semicolon instead of a period.

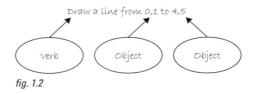

fig. 1.2

The key here is to realize that the computer screen is nothing more than a *fancier* piece of graph paper. Each pixel of the screen is a coordinate—two numbers, an "*x*" (horizontal) and a "*y*" (vertical)—that determine the location of a point in space. And it is our job to specify what shapes and colors should appear at these pixel coordinates.

Nevertheless, there is a catch here. The graph paper from eighth grade ("Cartesian coordinate system") placed (0,0) in the center with the *y*-axis pointing up and the *x*-axis pointing to the right (in the positive direction, negative down and to the left). The coordinate system for pixels in a computer window, however, is reversed along the *y*-axis. (0,0) can be found at the top left with the positive direction to the right horizontally and down vertically. See Figure 1.3.

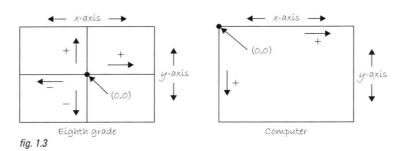

fig. 1.3

Exercise 1-1: Looking at how we wrote the instruction for line "line(1,0,4,5);" how would you guess you would write an instruction to draw a rectangle? A circle? A triangle? Write out the instructions in English and then translate it into "code."

English: _____

Code: _____

English: _____

Code: _____

English: _____

Code: _____

Come back later and see how your guesses matched up with how Processing *actually works.*

1.2 Simple Shapes

The vast majority of the programming examples in this book will be visual in nature. You may ultimately learn to develop interactive games, algorithmic art pieces, animated logo designs, and (insert your own category here) with *Processing*, but at its core, each visual program will involve setting pixels. The simplest way to get started in understanding how this works is to learn to draw primitive shapes. This is not unlike how we learn to draw in elementary school, only here we do so with code instead of crayons.

Let's start with the four primitive shapes shown in Figure 1.4.

fig. 1.4

For each shape, we will ask ourselves what information is required to specify the location and size (and later color) of that shape and learn how *Processing* expects to receive that information. In each of the diagrams below (Figures 1.5 through 1.11), assume a window with a width of 10 pixels and height of 10 pixels. This isn't particularly realistic since when we really start coding we will most likely work with much larger windows (10 × 10 pixels is barely a few millimeters of screen space). Nevertheless for demonstration purposes, it is nice to work with smaller numbers in order to present the pixels as they might appear on graph paper (for now) to better illustrate the inner workings of each line of code.

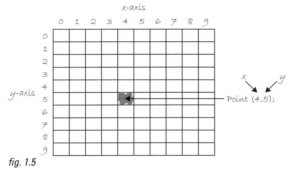

fig. 1.5

A point is the easiest of the shapes and a good place to start. To draw a point, we only need an *x* and *y* coordinate as shown in Figure 1.5. A line isn't terribly difficult either. A line requires two points, as shown in Figure 1.6.

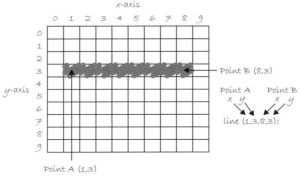

fig. 1.6

Once we arrive at drawing a rectangle, things become a bit more complicated. In *Processing*, a rectangle is specified by the coordinate for the top left corner of the rectangle, as well as its width and height (see Figure 1.7).

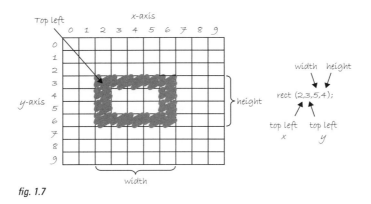

fig. 1.7

However, a second way to draw a rectangle involves specifying the centerpoint, along with width and height as shown in Figure 1.8. If we prefer this method, we first indicate that we want to use the "CENTER" mode before the instruction for the rectangle itself. Note that *Processing* is case-sensitive. Incidentally, the default mode is "CORNER," which is how we began as illustrated in Figure 1.7.

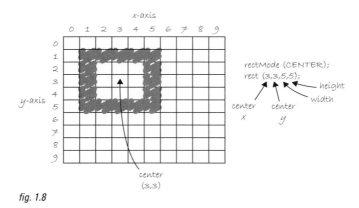

fig. 1.8

Finally, we can also draw a rectangle with two points (the top left corner and the bottom right corner). The mode here is "CORNERS" (see Figure 1.9).

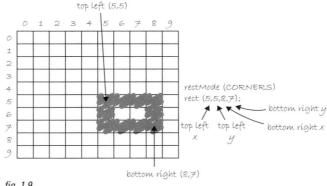

fig. 1.9

Once we have become comfortable with the concept of drawing a rectangle, an ellipse is a snap. In fact, it is identical to *rect()* with the difference being that an ellipse is drawn where the bounding box[1] (as shown in Figure 1.11) of the rectangle would be. The default mode for *ellipse()* is "CENTER", rather than "CORNER" as with *rect()*. See Figure 1.10.

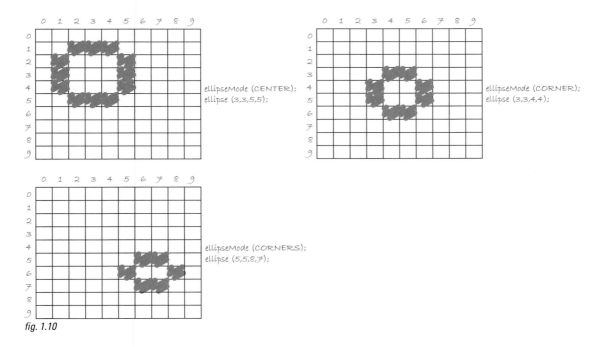

fig. 1.10

It is important to acknowledge that in Figure 1.10, the ellipses do not look particularly circular. *Processing* has a built-in methodology for selecting which pixels should be used to create a circular shape. Zoomed in like this, we get a bunch of squares in a circle-like pattern, but zoomed out on a computer screen, we get a nice round ellipse. Later, we will see that *Processing* gives us the power to develop our own

---

[1]A bounding box of a shape in computer graphics is the smallest rectangle that includes all the pixels of that shape. For example, the bounding box of a circle is shown in Figure 1.11.

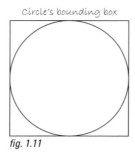

Circle's bounding box

fig. 1.11

algorithms for coloring in individual pixels (in fact, we can already imagine how we might do this using "point" over and over again), but for now, we are content with allowing the "ellipse" statement to do the hard work.

Certainly, point, line, ellipse, and rectangle are not the only shapes available in the *Processing* library of functions. In Chapter 2, we will see how the *Processing* reference provides us with a full list of available drawing functions along with documentation of the required arguments, sample syntax, and imagery. For now, as an exercise, you might try to imagine what arguments are required for some other shapes (Figure 1.12):

triangle()
arc()
quad()
curve()

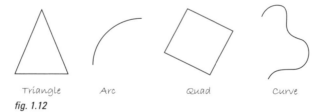

Triangle   Arc   Quad   Curve
fig. 1.12

Exercise 1-2: Using the blank graph below, draw the primitive shapes specified by the code.

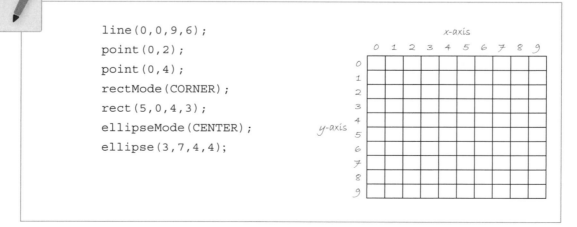

```
line(0,0,9,6);
point(0,2);
point(0,4);
rectMode(CORNER);
rect(5,0,4,3);
ellipseMode(CENTER);
ellipse(3,7,4,4);
```

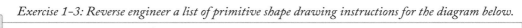

Exercise 1-3: Reverse engineer a list of primitive shape drawing instructions for the diagram below.

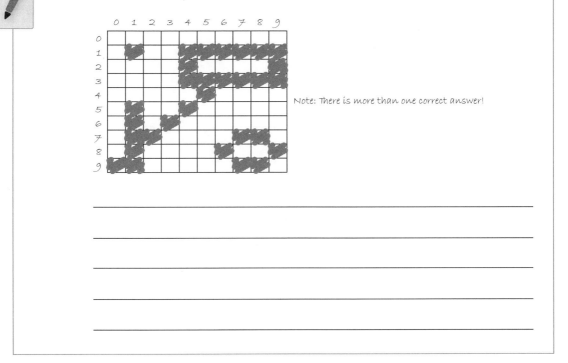

Note: There is more than one correct answer!

_____

_____

_____

_____

_____

1.3 Grayscale Color

As we learned in Section 1.2, the primary building block for placing shapes onscreen is a pixel coordinate. You politely instructed the computer to draw a shape at a specific location with a specific size. Nevertheless, a fundamental element was missing—color.

In the digital world, precision is required. Saying "Hey, can you make that circle bluish-green?" will not do. Therefore, color is defined with a range of numbers. Let's start with the simplest case: *black and white* or *grayscale*. In grayscale terms, we have the following: 0 means black, 255 means white. In between, every other number—50, 87, 162, 209, and so on—is a shade of gray ranging from black to white. See Figure 1.13.

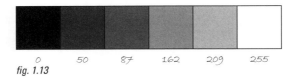

fig. 1.13

Does 0–255 seem arbitrary to you?

Color for a given shape needs to be stored in the computer's memory. This memory is just a long sequence of 0's and 1's (a whole bunch of on or off switches.) Each one of these switches is a *bit*, eight of them together is a *byte*. Imagine if we had eight bits (one byte) in sequence—how many ways can we configure these switches? The answer is (and doing a little research into binary numbers will prove this point) 256 possibilities, or a range of numbers between 0 and 255. We will use eight bit color for our grayscale range and 24 bit for full color (eight bits for each of the red, green, and blue color components; see Section 1.4).

Understanding how this range works, we can now move to setting specific grayscale colors for the shapes we drew in Section 1.2. In *Processing*, every shape has a **stroke()** or a **fill()** or both. The **stroke()** is the outline of the shape, and the **fill()** is the interior of that shape. Lines and points can only have **stroke()**, for obvious reasons.

If we forget to specify a color, *Processing* will use black (0) for the **stroke()** and white (255) for the **fill()** by default. Note that we are now using more realistic numbers for the pixel locations, assuming a larger window of size 200 × 200 pixels. See Figure 1.14.

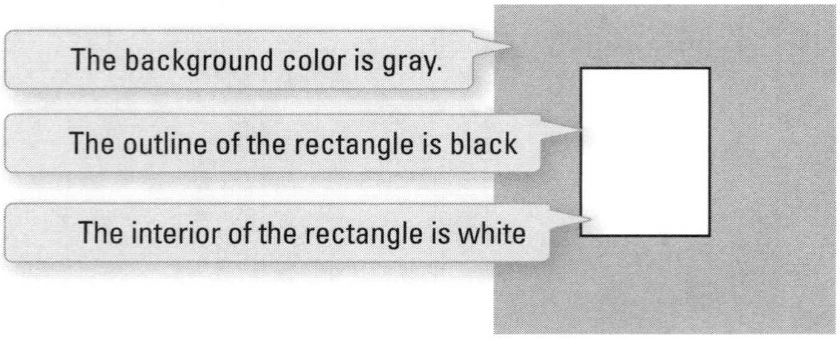

> The background color is gray.
>
> The outline of the rectangle is black
>
> The interior of the rectangle is white

fig. 1.14

```
rect(50,40,75,100);
```

By adding the **stroke()** and **fill()** functions *before* the shape is drawn, we can set the color. It is much like instructing your friend to use a specific pen to draw on the graph paper. You would have to tell your friend *before* he or she starting drawing, not after.

There is also the function **background()**, which sets a background color for the window where shapes will be rendered.

Example 1-1: Stroke and fill

```
background(255);
stroke(0);
fill(150);
rect(50,50,75,100);
```

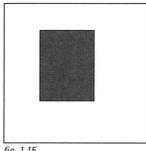

fig. 1.15

stroke() or **fill()** can be eliminated with the **noStroke()** or **noFill()** functions. Our instinct might be to say "**stroke(0)**" for no outline, however, it is important to remember that 0 is not "nothing", but rather denotes the color black. Also, remember not to eliminate both—with **noStroke()** and **noFill()**, nothing will appear!

Example 1-2: *noFill ()*

```
background(255);
stroke(0);
noFill();
ellipse(60,60,100,100);
```

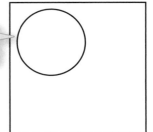

nofill( ) leaves the shape with only an outline

If we draw two shapes at one time, *Processing* will always use the most recently specified *stroke()* and *fill()*, reading the code from top to bottom. See Figure 1.17.

fig. 1.16

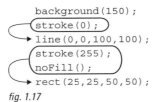

```
background(150);
stroke(0);
line(0,0,100,100);
stroke(255);
noFill();
rect(25,25,50,50);
```

fig. 1.17

Exercise 1–4: Try to guess what the instructions would be for the following screenshot.

1.4 RGB Color

A nostalgic look back at graph paper helped us learn the fundamentals for pixel locations and size. Now that it is time to study the basics of digital color, we search for another childhood memory to get us started. Remember finger painting? By mixing three "primary" colors, any color could be generated. Swirling all colors together resulted in a muddy brown. The more paint you added, the darker it got.

Digital colors are also constructed by mixing three primary colors, but it works differently from paint. First, the primaries are different: red, green, and blue (i.e., "RGB" color). And with color on the screen, you are mixing light, not paint, so the mixing rules are different as well.

- Red   + green   = yellow
- Red   + blue   = purple
- Green   + blue   = cyan (blue-green)
- Red   + green   +   blue   = white
- No colors   = black

This assumes that the colors are all as bright as possible, but of course, you have a range of color available, so some red plus some green plus some blue equals gray, and a bit of red plus a bit of blue equals dark purple.

While this may take some getting used to, the more you program and experiment with RGB color, the more it will become instinctive, much like swirling colors with your fingers. And of course you can't say "Mix some red with a bit of blue," you have to provide an exact amount. As with grayscale, the individual color elements are expressed as ranges from 0 (none of that color) to 255 (as much as possible), and they are listed in the order R, G, and B. You will get the hang of RGB color mixing through experimentation, but next we will cover some code using some common colors.

Note that this book will only show you black and white versions of each *Processing* sketch, but everything is documented online in full color at *http://www.learningprocessing.com* with RGB color diagrams found specifically at: *http://learningprocessing.com/color*.

Example 1-3: RGB color

```
background(255);
noStroke();

fill(255,0,0);          Bright red
ellipse(20,20,16,16);

fill(127,0,0);          Dark red
ellipse(40,20,16,16);

fill(255,200,200);      Pink (pale red).
ellipse(60,20,16,16);
```

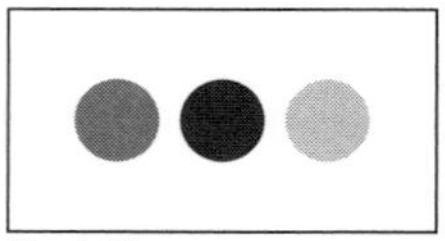

fig. 1.18

Processing also has a color selector to aid in choosing colors. Access this via TOOLS (from the menu bar) → COLOR SELECTOR. See Figure 1.19.

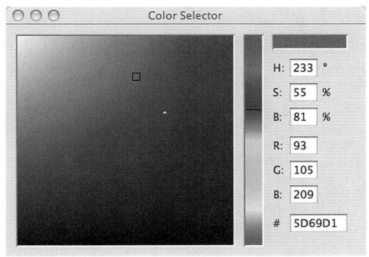

fig. 1.19

Exercise 1-5: Complete the following program. Guess what RGB values to use (you will be able to check your results in Processing *after reading the next chapter). You could also use the color selector, shown in Figure 1.19.*

```
fill(_____,_____,_____);        Bright blue
ellipse(20,40,16,16);

fill(_____,_____,_____);        Dark purple
ellipse(40,40,16,16);

fill(_____,_____,_____);        Yellow
ellipse(60,40,16,16);
```

Exercise 1-6: What color will each of the following lines of code generate?

```
fill(0,100,0);         _____

fill(100);             _____

stroke(0,0,200);       _____

stroke(225);           _____

stroke(255,255,0);     _____

stroke(0,255,255);     _____

stroke(200,50,50);     _____
```

1.5 Color Transparency

In addition to the red, green, and blue components of each color, there is an additional optional fourth component, referred to as the color's "alpha." Alpha means transparency and is particularly useful when you want to draw elements that appear partially see-through on top of one another. The alpha values for an image are sometimes referred to collectively as the "alpha channel" of an image.

It is important to realize that pixels are not literally transparent, this is simply a convenient illusion that is accomplished by blending colors. Behind the scenes, *Processing* takes the color numbers and adds a percentage of one to a percentage of another, creating the optical perception of blending. (If you are interested in programming "rose-colored" glasses, this is where you would begin.)

Alpha values also range from 0 to 255, with 0 being completely transparent (i.e., 0% opaque) and 255 completely opaque (i.e., 100% opaque). Example 1-4 shows a code example that is displayed in Figure 1.20.

Example 1-4: Alpha transparency

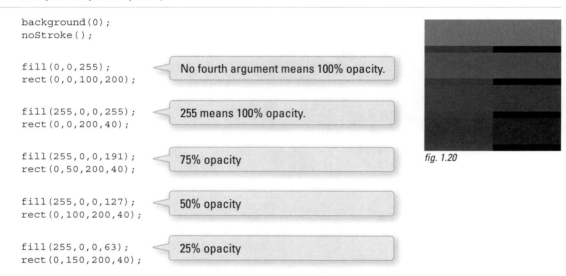

```
background(0);
noStroke();

fill(0,0,255);          No fourth argument means 100% opacity.
rect(0,0,100,200);

fill(255,0,0,255);      255 means 100% opacity.
rect(0,0,200,40);

fill(255,0,0,191);      75% opacity
rect(0,50,200,40);

fill(255,0,0,127);      50% opacity
rect(0,100,200,40);

fill(255,0,0,63);       25% opacity
rect(0,150,200,40);
```

fig. 1.20

1.6 Custom Color Ranges

RGB color with ranges of 0 to 255 is not the only way you can handle color in *Processing*. Behind the scenes in the computer's memory, color is *always* talked about as a series of 24 bits (or 32 in the case of colors with an alpha). However, *Processing* will let us think about color any way we like, and translate our values into numbers the computer understands. For example, you might prefer to think of color as ranging from 0 to 100 (like a percentage). You can do this by specifying a custom *colorMode()*.

```
colorMode(RGB,100);
```
With **colorMode( )** you can set your own color range.

The above function says: "OK, we want to think about color in terms of red, green, and blue. The range of RGB values will be from 0 to 100."

Although it is rarely convenient to do so, you can also have different ranges for each color component:

```
colorMode(RGB,100,500,10,255);
```

Now we are saying "Red values go from 0 to 100, green from 0 to 500, blue from 0 to 10, and alpha from 0 to 255."

Finally, while you will likely only need RGB color for all of your programming needs, you can also specify colors in the HSB (hue, saturation, and brightness) mode. Without getting into too much detail, HSB color works as follows:

- **Hue**—The color type, ranges from 0 to 360 by default (think of 360° on a color "wheel").
- **Saturation**—The vibrancy of the color, 0 to 100 by default.
- **Brightness**—The, well, brightness of the color, 0 to 100 by default.

Exercise 1-7: Design a creature using simple shapes and colors. Draw the creature by hand using only points, lines, rectangles, and ellipses. Then attempt to write the code for the creature, using the Processing *commands covered in this chapter:* **point(), lines(), rect(), ellipse(), stroke(),** *and* **fill()**. *In the next chapter, you will have a chance to test your results by running your code in* Processing.

Example 1-5 shows my version of Zoog, with the outputs shown in Figure 1.21.

Example 1-5: Zoog

```
ellipseMode(CENTER);
rectMode(CENTER);
stroke(0);
fill(150);
rect(100,100,20,100);
fill(255);
ellipse(100,70,60,60);
fill(0);
ellipse(81,70,16,32);
ellipse(119,70,16,32);
stroke(0);
line(90,150,80,160);
line(110,150,120,160);
```

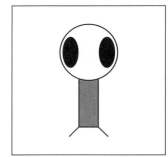

fig. 1.21

The sample answer is my *Processing*-born being, named Zoog. Over the course of the first nine chapters of this book, we will follow the course of Zoog's childhood. The fundamentals of programming will be demonstrated as Zoog grows up. We will first learn to display Zoog, then to make an interactive Zoog and animated Zoog, and finally to duplicate Zoog in a world of many Zoogs.

I suggest you design your own "thing" (note that there is no need to limit yourself to a humanoid or creature-like form; any programmatic pattern will do) and recreate all of the examples throughout the first nine chapters with your own design. Most likely, this will require you to only change a small portion (the shape rendering part) of each example. This process, however, should help solidify your understanding of the basic elements required for computer programs—Variables, Conditionals, Loops, Functions, Objects, and Arrays—and prepare you for when Zoog matures, leaves the nest, and ventures off into the more advanced topics from Chapter 10 on in this book.

2 Processing

"Computers in the future may weigh no more than 1.5 tons."
—*Popular Mechanics, 1949*

"Take me to your leader."
—*Zoog, 2008*

In this chapter:
– Downloading and installing *Processing*.
– Menu options.
– A *Processing* "sketchbook."
– Writing code.
– Errors.
– The *Processing* reference.
– The "Play" button.
– Your first sketch.
– Publishing your sketch to the web.

2.1 *Processing* to the Rescue

Now that we conquered the world of primitive shapes and RGB color, we are ready to implement this knowledge in a real world programming scenario. Happily for us, the environment we are going to use is *Processing*, free and open source software developed by Ben Fry and Casey Reas at the MIT Media Lab in 2001. (See this book's introduction for more about *Processing*'s history.)

Processing's core library of functions for drawing graphics to the screen will provide for immediate visual feedback and clues as to what the code is doing. And since its programming language employs all the same principles, structures, and concepts of other languages (specifically Java), everything you learn with *Processing* is *real* programming. It is not some pretend language to help you get started; it has all the fundamentals and core concepts that all languages have.

After reading this book and learning to program, you might continue to use *Processing* in your academic or professional life as a prototyping or production tool. You might also take the knowledge acquired here and apply it to learning other languages and authoring environments. You may, in fact, discover that programming is not your cup of tea; nonetheless, learning the basics will help you become a better-informed technology citizen as you work on collaborative projects with other designers and programmers.

It may seem like overkill to emphasize the *why* with respect to *Processing*. After all, the focus of this book is primarily on learning the fundamentals of computer programming in the context of computer graphics and design. It is, however, important to take some time to ponder the reasons behind selecting a programming language for a book, a class, a homework assignment, a web application, a software suite, and so forth. After all, now that you are going to start calling yourself a computer programmer at cocktail parties, this question will come up over and over again. I need programming in order to accomplish project *X*, what language and environment should I use?

I say, without a shadow of doubt, that for you, the beginner, the answer is *Processing*. Its simplicity is ideal for a beginner. At the end of this chapter, you will be up and running with your first computational design and ready to learn the fundamental concepts of programming. But simplicity is not where *Processing* ends. A trip through the *Processing* online exhibition (*http://processing.org/exhibition/*) will uncover a wide variety of beautiful and innovative projects developed entirely with *Processing*. By the end of this book, you will have all the tools and knowledge you need to take your ideas and turn them into real world software projects like those found in the exhibition. *Processing* is great both for learning and for producing, there are very few other environments and languages you can say that about.

2.2 How do I get *Processing?*

For the most part, this book will assume that you have a basic working knowledge of how to operate your personal computer. The good news, of course, is that *Processing* is available for free download. Head to *http://www.processing.org/* and visit the download page. If you are a Windows user, you will see two options: "Windows (standard)" and "Windows (expert)." Since you are reading this book, it is quite likely you are a beginner, in which case you will want the standard version. The expert version is for those who have already installed Java themselves. For Mac OS X, there is only one download option. There is also a Linux version available. Operating systems and programs change, of course, so if this paragraph is obsolete or out of date, visit the download page on the site for information regarding what you need.

The *Processing* software will arrive as a compressed file. Choose a nice directory to store the application (usually "c:\Program Files\" on Windows and in "Applications" on Mac), extract the files there, locate the "Processing" executable, and run it.

Exercise 2-1: Download and install Processing.

2.3 The *Processing* Application

The *Processing* development environment is a simplified environment for writing computer code, and is just about as straightforward to use as simple text editing software (such as TextEdit or Notepad) combined with a media player. Each sketch (*Processing* programs are referred to as "sketches") has a filename, a place where you can type code, and some buttons for saving, opening, and running sketches. See Figure 2.1.

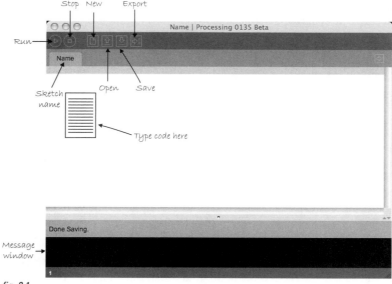

fig. 2.1

To make sure everything is working, it is a good idea to try running one of the *Processing* examples. Go to FILE → EXAMPLES → (pick an example, suggested: Topics → Drawing → ContinuousLines) as shown in Figure 2.2.

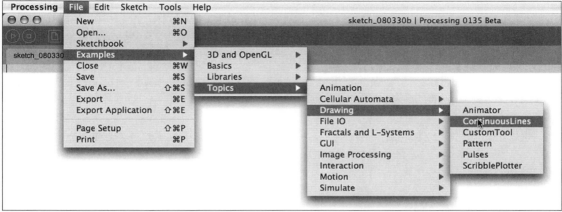

fig. 2.2

Once you have opened the example, click the "run" button as indicated in Figure 2.3. If a new window pops open running the example, you are all set! If this does not occur, visit the online FAQ "Processing won't start!" for possible solutions. The page can be found at this direct link: *http://www.processing.org/faq/bugs.html#wontstart.*

  Exercise 2-2: Open a sketch from the Processing *examples and run it.*

fig. 2.3

Processing programs can also be viewed full-screen (known as "present mode" in *Processing*). This is available through the menu option: Sketch → Present (or by shift-clicking the run button). Present will not resize your screen resolution. If you want the sketch to cover your entire screen, you must use your screen dimensions in *size()*.

2.4 The Sketchbook

Processing programs are informally referred to as *sketches*, in the spirit of quick graphics prototyping, and we will employ this term throughout the course of this book. The folder where you store your sketches is called your "sketchbook." Technically speaking, when you run a sketch in *processing*, it runs as a local application on your computer. As we will see both in this Chapter and in Chapter 18, *Processing* also allows you to export your sketches as web applets (mini-programs that run embedded in a browser) or as platform-specific stand-alone applications (that could, for example, be made available for download).

Once you have confirmed that the *Processing* examples work, you are ready to start creating your own sketches. Clicking the "new" button will generate a blank new sketch named by date. It is a good idea to "Save as" and create your own sketch name. (Note: *Processing* does not allow spaces or hyphens, and your sketch name cannot start with a number.)

When you first ran *Processing*, a default "Processing" directory was created to store all sketches in the "My Documents" folder on Windows and in "Documents" on OS X. Although you can select any directory on your hard drive, this folder is the default. It is a pretty good folder to use, but it can be changed by opening the *Processing* preferences (which are available under the FILE menu).

Each *Processing* sketch consists of a folder (with the same name as your sketch) and a file with the extension "pde." If your *Processing* sketch is named *MyFirstProgram*, then you will have a folder named *MyFirstProgram* with a file *MyFirstProgram.pde* inside. The "pde" file is a plain text file that contains the source code. (Later we will see that *Processing* sketches can have multiple pde's, but for now one will do.) Some sketches will also contain a folder called "data" where media elements used in the program, such as image files, sound clips, and so on, are stored.

 Exercise 2-3: Type some instructions from Chapter 1 into a blank sketch. Note how certain words are colored. Run the sketch. Does it do what you thought it would?

2.5 Coding in *Processing*

It is finally time to start writing some code, using the elements discussed in Chapter 1. Let's go over some basic syntax rules. There are three kinds of statements we can write:

- Function calls
- Assignment operations
- Control structures

For now, every line of code will be a function call. See Figure 2.4. We will explore the other two categories in future chapters. Functions have a name, followed by a set of arguments enclosed in parentheses. Recalling Chapter 1, we used functions to describe how to draw shapes (we just called them "commands" or "instructions"). Thinking of a function call as a natural language sentence, the function name is the verb ("draw") and the arguments are the objects ("point 0,0") of the sentence. Each function call must always end with a semicolon. See Figure 2.5.

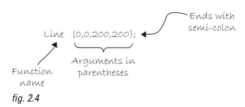

fig. 2.4

We have learned several functions already, including **background(), stroke(), fill(), noFill (), noStroke(), point(), line(), rect(), ellipse(), rectMode(),** and **ellipseMode().** *Processing* will execute a sequence of functions one by one and finish by displaying the drawn result in a window. We forgot to learn one very important function in Chapter 1, however—*size(). size()* specifies the dimensions of the window you want to create and takes two arguments, width and height. The *size()* function should always be first.

```
size(320,240);
```
Opens a window of width 320 and height 240.

Let's write a first example (see Figure 2.5).

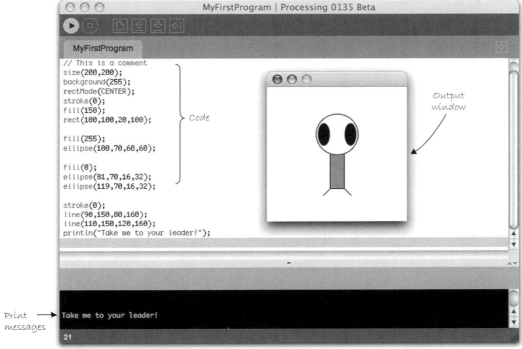

fig. 2.5

There are a few additional items to note.

- The *Processing* text editor will color *known* words (sometimes referred to as "reserved" words or "keywords"). These words, for example, are the drawing functions available in the *Processing* library, "built-in" variables (we will look closely at the concept of *variables* in Chapter 3) and constants, as well as certain words that are inherited from the Java programming language.
- Sometimes, it is useful to display text information in the *Processing* message window (located at the bottom). This is accomplished using the ***println()*** function. ***println()*** takes one argument, a *String* of characters enclosed in quotes (more about *Strings* in Chapter 14). When the program runs, *Processing* displays that *String* in the message window (as in Figure 2.5) and in this case the *String* is "Take me to your leader!" This ability to print to the message window comes in handy when attempting to *debug* the values of variables (see Chapter 12, Debugging).
- The number in the bottom left corner indicates what line number in the code is selected.
- You can write "comments" in your code. Comments are lines of text that *Processing* ignores when the program runs. You should use them as reminders of what the code means, a bug you intend to fix, or a to do list of items to be inserted, and so on. Comments on a single line are created with two forward slashes, //. Comments over multiple lines are marked by /* followed by the comments and ending with */.

```
// This is a comment on one line

/* This is a comment that
spans several lines
of code */
```

A quick word about comments. You should get in the habit right now of writing comments in your code. Even though our sketches will be very simple and short at first, you should put comments in for everything. Code is very hard to read and understand without comments. You do not need to have a comment for every line of code, but the more you include, the easier a time you will have revising and reusing your code later. Comments also force you to understand how code works as you are programming. If you do not know what you are doing, how can you write a comment about it?

Comments will not always be included in the text here. This is because I find that, unlike in an actual program, code comments are hard to read in a book. Instead, this book will often use code "hints" for additional insight and explanations. If you look at the book's examples on the web site, though, comments will always be included. So, I can't emphasize it enough, write comments!

```
//A comment about this code
line(0,0,100,100);
```
A hint about this code!

 Exercise 2-4: Create a blank sketch. Take your code from the end of Chapter 1 and type it in the Processing *window. Add comments to describe what the code is doing. Add a* **println()** *statement to display text in the message window. Save the sketch. Press the "run" button. Does it work or do you get an error?*

2.6 Errors

The previous example only works because we did not make any errors or typos. Over the course of a programmer's life, this is quite a rare occurrence. Most of the time, our first push of the play button will not be met with success. Let's examine what happens when we make a mistake in our code in Figure 2.6.

Figure 2.6 shows what happens when you have a typo—"elipse" instead of "ellipse" on line 9. If there is an error in the code when the play button is pressed, *Processing* will not open the sketch window, and will instead display the error message. This particular message is fairly friendly, telling us that we probably meant to type "ellipse." Not all *Processing* error messages are so easy to understand, and we will continue to look at other errors throughout the course of this book. An Appendix on common errors in Processing is also included at the end of the book.

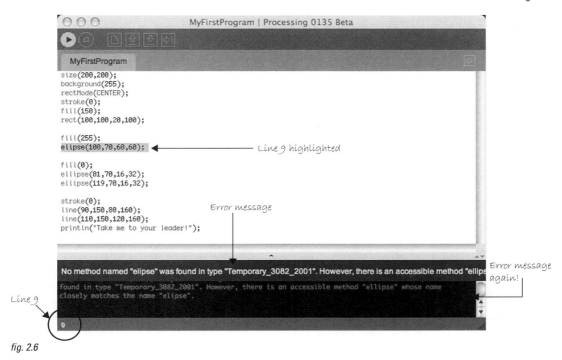

fig. 2.6

Processing *is case sensitive!*

If you type *Ellipse* instead of *ellipse*, that will also be considered an error.

In this instance, there was only one error. If multiple errors occur, *Processing* will only alert you to the first one it finds (and presumably, once that error is corrected, the next error will be displayed at run time). This is somewhat of an unfortunate limitation, as it is often useful to have access to an entire list of errors when fixing a program. This is simply one of the trade-offs we get in a simplified environment such as *Processing*. Our life is made simpler by only having to look at one error at a time, nevertheless we do not have access to a complete list.

This fact only further emphasizes the importance of incremental development discussed in the book's introduction. If we only implement one feature at a time, we can only make one mistake at a time.

 Exercise 2-5: Try to make some errors happen on purpose. Are the error messages what you expect?

Exercise 2-6: Fix the errors in the following code.

```
size(200,200);          _____

background();           _____

stroke 255;             _____

fill(150)               _____

rectMode(center);       _____

rect(100,100,50);       _____
```

2.7 The *Processing* Reference

The functions we have demonstrated—*ellipse(), line(), stroke()*, and so on—are all part of *Processing*'s library. How do we know that "ellipse" isn't spelled "elipse", or that *rect()* takes four arguments (an "*x* coordinate," a "*y* coordinate," a "width," and a "height")? A lot of these details are intuitive, and this speaks to the strength of *Processing* as a beginner's programming language. Nevertheless, the only way to know for sure is by reading the online reference. While we will cover many of the elements from the reference throughout this book, it is by no means a substitute for the reference and both will be required for you to learn *Processing*.

The reference for *Processing* can be found online at the official web site (*http://www.processing.org*) under the "reference" link. There, you can browse all of the available functions by category or alphabetically. If you were to visit the page for *rect()*, for example, you would find the explanation shown in Figure 2.7.

As you can see, the reference page offers full documentation for the function *rect()*, including:

- **Name**—The name of the function.
- **Examples**—Example code (and visual result, if applicable).
- **Description**—A friendly description of what the function does.
- **Syntax**—Exact syntax of how to write the function.
- **Parameters**—These are the elements that go inside the parentheses. It tells you what kind of data you put in (a number, character, etc.) and what that element stands for. (This will become clearer as we explore more in future chapters.) These are also sometimes referred to as "arguments."
- **Returns**—Sometimes a function sends something back to you when you call it (e.g., instead of asking a function to perform a task such as draw a circle, you could ask a function to add two numbers and *return* the answer to you). Again, this will become more clear later.
- **Usage**—Certain functions will be available for *Processing* applets that you publish online ("Web") and some will only be available as you run *Processing* locally on your machine ("Application").
- **Related Methods**—A list of functions often called in connection with the current function. Note that "functions" in Java are often referred to as "methods." More on this in Chapter 6.

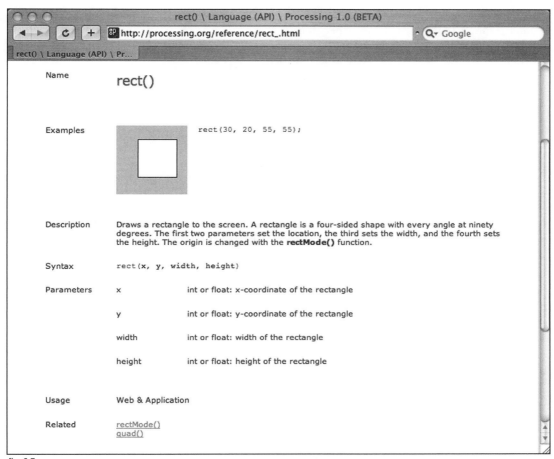

fig. 2.7

Processing also has a very handy "find in reference" option. Double-click on any keyword to select it and go to to HELP → FIND IN REFERENCE (or select the keyword and hit SHIFT+CNTRL+F).

Exercise 2-7: Using the Processing *reference, try implementing two functions that we have not yet covered in this book. Stay within the "Shape" and "Color (setting)" categories.*

Exercise 2-8: Using the reference, find a function that allows you to alter the thickness of a line. What arguments does the function take? Write example code that draws a line one pixel wide, then five pixels wide, then 10 pixels wide.

2.8 The "Play" Button

One of the nice qualities of *Processing* is that all one has to do to run a program is press the "play" button. It is a nice metaphor and the assumption is that we are comfortable with the idea of *playing* animations, movies, music, and other forms of media. *Processing* programs output media in the form of real-time computer graphics, so why not just *play* them too?

Nevertheless, it is important to take a moment and consider the fact that what we are doing here is not the same as what happens on an iPod or TiVo. *Processing* programs start out as text, they are translated into machine code, and then executed to run. All of these steps happen in sequence when the play button is pressed. Let's examine these steps one by one, relaxed in the knowledge that *Processing* handles the hard work for us.

Step 1. Translate to Java. *Processing* is really Java (this will become more evident in a detailed discussion in Chapter 23). In order for your code to run on your machine, it must first be translated to Java code.

Step 2. Compile into Java byte code. The Java code created in Step 1 is just another text file (with the .java extension instead of .pde). In order for the computer to understand it, it needs to be translated into machine language. This translation process is known as compilation. If you were programming in a different language, such as C, the code would compile directly into machine language specific to your operating system. In the case of Java, the code is compiled into a special machine language known as Java byte code. It can run on different platforms (Mac, Windows, cellphones, PDAs, etc.) as long as the machine is running a "Java Virtual Machine." Although this extra layer can sometimes cause programs to run a bit slower than they might otherwise, being cross-platform is a great feature of Java. For more on how this works, visit http://java.sun.com or consider picking up a book on Java programming (after you have finished with this one).

Step 3. Execution. The compiled program ends up in a JAR file. A JAR is a Java archive file that contains compiled Java programs ("classes"), images, fonts, and other data files. The JAR file is executed by the Java Virtual Machine and is what causes the display window to appear.

2.9 Your First Sketch

Now that we have downloaded and installed *Processing*, understand the basic menu and interface elements, and have gotten familiar with the online reference, we are ready to start coding. As I briefly mentioned in Chapter 1, the first half of this book will follow one example that illustrates the foundational elements of programming: *variables, arrays, conditionals, loops, functions,* and *objects.* Other examples will be included along the way, but following just one will reveal how the basic elements behind computer programming build on each other.

The example will follow the story of our new friend Zoog, beginning with a static rendering with simple shapes. Zoog's development will include mouse interaction, motion, and cloning into a population of many Zoogs. While you are by no means required to complete every exercise of this book with your own alien form, I do suggest that you start with a design and after each chapter, expand the functionality of that design with the programming concepts that are explored. If you are at a loss for an idea, then just draw your own little alien, name it Gooz, and get programming! See Figure 2.8.

Example 2-1: Zoog again

```
size(200,200); // Set the size of the window
background(255); // Draw a black background
smooth();


// Set ellipses and rects to CENTER mode
ellipseMode(CENTER);
rectMode(CENTER);


// Draw Zoog's body
stroke(0);
fill(150);
rect(100,100,20,100);


// Draw Zoog's head
fill(255);
ellipse(100,70,60,60);


// Draw Zoog's eyes
fill(0);
ellipse(81,70,16,32);
ellipse(119,70,16,32);


// Draw Zoog's legs
stroke(0);
line(90,150,80,160);
line(110,150,120,160);
```

> The function **smooth()** enables "anti-aliasing" which smooths the edges of the shapes. **no smooth()** disables anti-aliasing.

> Zoog's body.

> Zoog's head.

> Zoog's eyes.

> Zoog's legs.

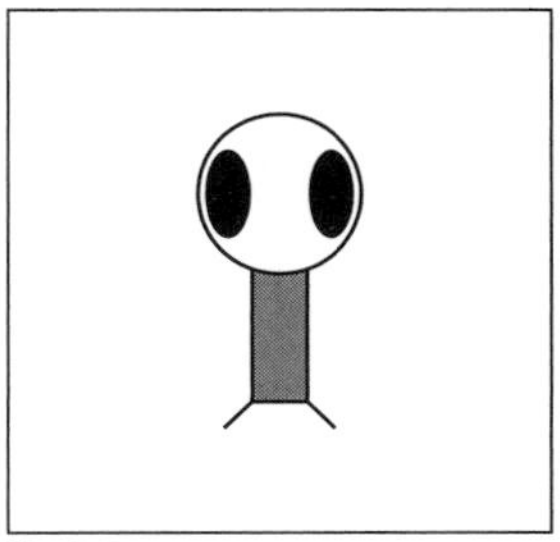

fig. 2.8

Let's pretend, just for a moment, that you find this Zoog design to be so astonishingly gorgeous that you just cannot wait to see it displayed on your computer screen. (Yes, I am aware this may require a fairly significant suspension of disbelief.) To run any and all code examples found in this book, you have two choices:

- Retype the code manually.
- Visit the book's web site (*http://www.learningprocessing.com*), find the example by its number, and copy/paste (or download) the code.

Certainly option #2 is the easier and less time-consuming one and I recommend you use the site as a resource for seeing sketches running in real-time and grabbing code examples. Nonetheless, as you start learning, there is real value in typing the code yourself. Your brain will sponge up the syntax and logic as you type and you will learn a great deal by making mistakes along the way. Not to mention simply running the sketch after entering each new line of code will eliminate any mystery as to how the sketch works.

You will know best when you are ready for copy/paste. Keep track of your progress and if you start running a lot of examples without feeling comfortable with how they work, try going back to manual typing.

*Exercise 2-9: Using what you designed in Chapter 1, implement your own screen drawing, using only 2D primitive shapes—**arc()**, **curve()**, **ellipse()**, **line()**, **point()**, **quad()**, **rect()**, **triangle()**—and basic color functions—**background()**, **colorMode()**, **fill()**, **noFill()**, **noStroke()**, and **stroke()**. Remember to use **size()** to specify the dimensions of your window. Suggestion: Play the sketch after typing each new line of code. Correct any errors or typos along the way.*

2.10 Publishing Your Program

After you have completed a *Processing* sketch, you can publish it to the web as a Java applet. This will become more exciting once we are making interactive, animated applets, but it is good to practice with a simple example. Once you have finished Exercise 2-9 and determined that your sketch works, select FILE → EXPORT.

Note that if you have errors in your program, it will not export properly, so always test by running first!

A new directory named "applet" will be created in the sketch folder and displayed, as shown in Figure 2.9.

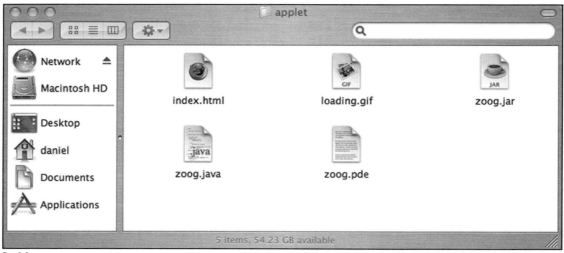

fig. 2.9

You now have the necessary files for publishing your applet to the web.

- **index.html**—The HTML source for a page that displays the applet.
- **loading.gif**—An image to be displayed while the user loads the applet (*Processing* will supply a default one, but you can create your own).
- **zoog.jar**—The compiled applet itself.
- **zoog.java**—The translated Java source code (looks like your *Processing* code, but has a few extra things that Java requires. See Chapter 20 for details.)
- **zoog.pde**—Your *Processing* source.

To see the applet working, double-click the "index.html" file which should launch a page in your default web browser. See Figure 2.10. To get the applet online, you will need web server space and FTP software (or you can also use a *Processing* sketch sharing site such as http://www.openprocessing.org). You can find some tips for getting started at this book's web site.

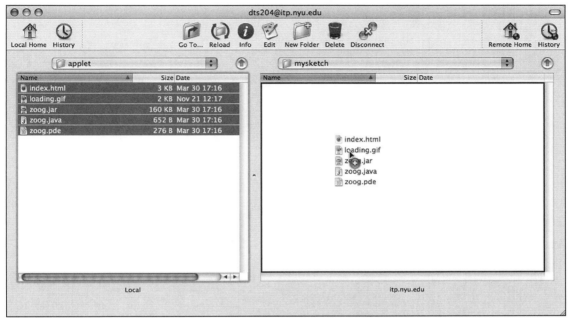

fig. 2.10

 *Exercise 2-10: Export your sketch as an applet. View the sketch in the browser (either locally or by uploading).*0000200002

3 Interaction

"Always remember that this whole thing was started with a dream and a mouse."
—Walt Disney

"The quality of the imagination is to flow and not to freeze."
—Ralph Waldo Emerson

In this chapter:
– The "flow" of a program.
– The meaning behind *setup( )* and *draw( )*.
– Mouse interaction.
– Your first "dynamic" *Processing* program.
– Handling events, such as mouse clicks and key presses.

3.1 Go with the flow.

If you have ever played a computer game, interacted with a digital art installation, or watched a
screensaver at three in the morning, you have probably given very little thought to the fact that the
software that runs these experiences happens over a *period of time*. The game starts, you save princess
so-and-so from the evil lord who-zee-ma-whats-it, achieve a high score, and the game ends.

What I want to focus on in this chapter is that very "flow" over time. A game begins with a set of initial
conditions: you name your character, you start with a score of zero, and you start on level one. Let's think
of this part as the program's *SETUP*. After these conditions are initialized, you begin to play the game.
At every instant, the computer checks what you are doing with the mouse, calculates all the appropriate
behaviors for the game characters, and updates the screen to render all the game graphics. This cycle of
calculating and drawing happens over and over again, ideally 30 or more times per second for a smooth
animation. Let's think of this part as the program's *DRAW*.

This concept is crucial to our ability to move beyond static designs (as in Chapter 2) with
Processing.

> **Step 1.** Set starting conditions for the program one time.
> **Step 2.** Do something over and over and over and over (and over …) again until the program
> quits.

Consider how you might go about running a race.

> **Step 1.** Put on your sneakers and stretch. Just do this once, OK?
> **Step 2.** Put your right foot forward, then your left foot. Repeat this over and over as fast as
> you can.
> **Step 3.** After 26 miles, quit.

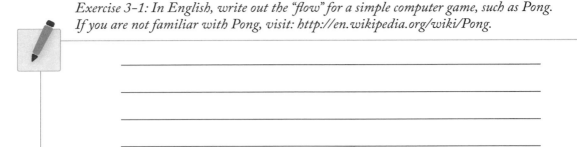

Exercise 3-1: In English, write out the "flow" for a simple computer game, such as Pong. If you are not familiar with Pong, visit: http://en.wikipedia.org/wiki/Pong.

_____

_____

_____

_____

3.2 Our Good Friends, *setup( )* and *draw( )*

Now that we are good and exhausted from running marathons in order to better learn programming, we can take this newfound knowledge and apply it to our first "dynamic" *Processing* sketch. Unlike Chapter 2's static examples, this program will draw to the screen continuously (i.e., until the user quits). This is accomplished by writing two "blocks of code" *setup()* and *draw()*. Technically speaking *setup()* and *draw()* are functions. We will get into a longer discussion of writing our own functions in a later chapter; for now, we understand them to be two sections where we write code.

What is a block of code?

A block of code is any code enclosed within curly brackets.

```
{
  A block of code
}
```

Blocks of code can be nested within each other, too.

```
{
  A block of code
  {
    A block inside a block of code
  }
}
```

This is an important construct as it allows us to separate and manage our code as individual pieces of a larger puzzle. A programming convention is to indent the lines of code within each block to make the code more readable. *Processing* will do this for you via the Auto-Format option (Tools → Auto-Format).

Blocks of code will reveal themselves to be crucial in developing more complex logic, in terms of *variables, conditionals, iteration, objects,* and *functions,* as discussed in future chapters. For now, we only need to look at two simple blocks: *setup()* and *draw()*.

Let's look at what will surely be strange-looking syntax for *setup()* and *draw()*. See Figure 3.1.

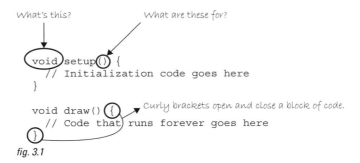

fig. 3.1

Admittedly, there is a lot of stuff in Figure 3.1 that we are not entirely ready to learn about. We have covered that the curly brackets indicate the beginning and end of a "block of code," but why are there parentheses after "setup" and "draw"? Oh, and, my goodness, what is this "void" all about? It makes me feel sad inside! For now, we have to decide to feel comfortable with not knowing everything all at once, and that these important pieces of syntax will start to make sense in future chapters as more concepts are revealed.

For now, the key is to focus on how Figure 3.1's structures control the flow of our program. This is shown in Figure 3.2.

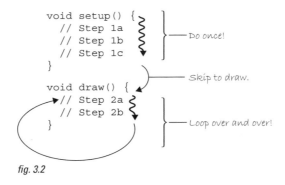

fig. 3.2

How does it work? When we run the program, it will follow our instructions precisely, executing the steps in *setup()* first, and then move on to the steps in *draw()*. The order ends up being something like:

1a, 1b, 1c, 2a, 2b, 2a, 2b, 2a, 2b, 2a, 2b, 2a, 2b, 2a, 2b …

Now, we can rewrite the Zoog example as a dynamic sketch. See Example 3–1.

Example 3-1: Zoog as dynamic sketch

```
void setup(){
  // Set the size of the window
  size(200,200);
}

void draw() {
  // Draw a white background
  background(255);

  // Set CENTER mode
  ellipseMode(CENTER);
  rectMode(CENTER);


  // Draw Zoog's body
  stroke(0);
  fill(150);
  rect(100,100,20,100);


  // Draw Zoog's head
  stroke(0);
  fill(255);
  ellipse(100,70,60,60);


  // Draw Zoog's eyes
  fill(0);
  ellipse(81,70,16,32);
  ellipse(119,70,16,32);


  // Draw Zoog's legs
  stroke(0);
  line(90,150,80,160);
  line(110,150,120,160);
}
```

> **setup()** runs first one time. **size()** should always be first line of **setup()** since *Processing* will not be able to do anything before the window size if specified.

> **draw()** loops continuously until you close the sketch window.

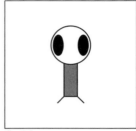

fig. 3.3

Take the code from Example 3-1 and run it in *Processing*. Strange, right? You will notice that nothing in the window changes. This looks identical to a *static* sketch! What is going on? All this discussion for nothing?

Well, if we examine the code, we will notice that nothing in the ***draw()*** function *varies*. Each time through the loop, the program cycles through the code and executes the identical instructions. So, yes, the program is running over time redrawing the window, but it looks static to us since it draws the same thing each time!

Exercise 3-2: Redo the drawing you created at the end of Chapter 2 as a dynamic program. Even though it will look the same, feel good about your accomplishment!

3.3 Variation with the Mouse

Consider this. What if, instead of typing a number into one of the drawing functions, you could type "the mouse's *X* location" or "the mouse's *Y* location."

```
line(the mouse's X location, the mouse's Y location, 100, 100);
```

In fact, you can, only instead of the more descriptive language, you must use the keywords **mouseX** and **mouseY**, indicating the horizontal or vertical position of the mouse cursor.

Example 3-2: *mouseX* and *mouseY*

```
void setup() {
  size(200,200);

}

void draw() {
  background(255);

  // Body
  stroke(0);
  fill(175);
  rectMode(CENTER);
  rect(mouseX,mouseY,50,50);
}
```

> Try moving **background()** to **setup()** and see the difference! (Exercise 3–3)

> **mouseX** is a keyword that the sketch replaces with the horizontal position of the mouse.
> **mouseY** is a keyword that the sketch replaces with the vertical position of the mouse.

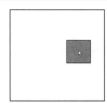

fig. 3.4

 *Exercise 3–3: Explain why we see a trail of rectangles if we move **background()** to **setup()**, leaving it out of **draw()**.*

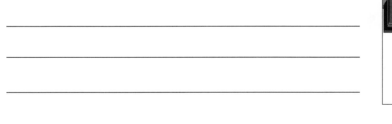

_____

_____

_____

_____

_____

An Invisible Line of Code

If you are following the logic of *setup()* and *draw()* closely, you might arrive at an interesting question: *When does* Processing *actually display the shapes in the window? When do the new pixels appear?*

On first glance, one might assume the display is updated for every line of code that includes a drawing function. If this were the case, however, we would see the shapes appear onscreen one at a time. This would happen so fast that we would hardly notice each shape appearing individually. However, when the window is erased every time *background()* is called, a somewhat unfortunate and unpleasant result would occur: flicker.

Processing solves this problem by updating the window only at the end of every cycle through *draw()*. It is as if there were an invisible line of code that renders the window at the end of the *draw()* function.

```
void draw() {
  // All of your code
  // Update Display Window -- invisible line of code we don't see
}
```

This process is known as *double-buffering* and, in a lower-level environment, you may find that you have to implement it yourself. Again, we take the time to thank *Processing* for making our introduction to programming friendlier and simpler by taking care of this for us.

We could push this idea a bit further and create an example where a more complex pattern (multiple shapes and colors) is controlled by *mouseX* and *mouseY* position. For example, we can rewrite Zoog to follow the mouse. Note that Zoog's body is located at the exact location of the mouse (*mouseX, mouseY*), however, other parts of Zoog's body are drawn relative to the mouse. Zoog's head, for example, is located at (*mouseX, mouseY-30*). The following example only moves Zoog's body and head, as shown in Figure 3.5.

Example 3-3: Zoog as dynamic sketch with variation

```
void setup() {
  size(200,200); // Set the size of the window
  smooth();
}

void draw() {
  background(255); // Draw a white background

  // Set ellipses and rects to CENTER mode
  ellipseMode(CENTER);
  rectMode(CENTER);

  // Draw Zoog's body
  stroke(0);
  fill(175);
  rect(mouseX,mouseY,20,100);          Zoog's body is drawn at the location
                                       (mouseX, mouseY).

  // Draw Zoog's head
  stroke(0);
  fill(255);
  ellipse(mouseX,mouseY-30,60,60);     Zoog's head is drawn above the body
                                       at the location (mouseX, mouseY-30).
```

fig. 3.5

```
// Draw Zoog's eyes
fill(0);
ellipse(81,70,16,32);
ellipse(119,70,16,32);

// Draw Zoog's legs
stroke(0);
line(90,150,80,160);
line(110,150,120,160);
}
```

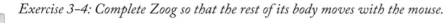

Exercise 3-4: Complete Zoog so that the rest of its body moves with the mouse.

```
// Draw Zoog's eyes
fill(0);
ellipse(_____,_____ ,16,32);

ellipse(_____,_____ ,16,32);

// Draw Zoog's legs
stroke(0);
line(_____,_____,_____,_____);

line(_____,_____,_____,_____);
```

Exercise 3-5: Recode your design so that shapes respond to the mouse (by varying color and location).

In addition to **mouseX** and **mouseY**, you can also use **pmouseX** and **pmouseY**. These two keywords stand for the "previous" mouseX and mouseY locations, that is, where the mouse was the last time we cycled through **draw()**. This allows for some interesting interaction possibilities. For example, let's consider what happens if we draw a line from the previous mouse location to the current mouse location, as illustrated in the diagram in Figure 3.6.

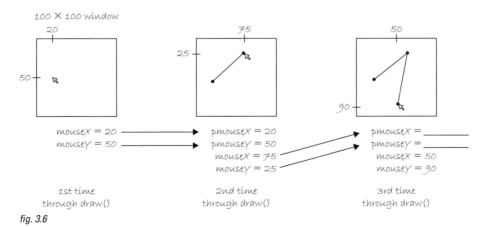

fig. 3.6

Exercise 3-6: Fill in the blank in Figure 3.6.

By connecting the previous mouse location to the current mouse location with a line each time through *draw()*, we are able to render a continuous line that follows the mouse. See Figure 3.7.

Example 3-4: Drawing a continuous line

```
void setup() {
  size(200,200);
  background(255);
  smooth();
}

void draw() {
  stroke(0);
  line(pmouseX,pmouseY,mouseX,mouseY);
}
```

> Draw a line from previous mouse location to current mouse location.

fig. 3.7

*Exercise 3-7: The formula for calculating the speed of the mouse's horizontal motion is the absolute value of the difference between **mouseX** and **pmouseX**. The absolute value of a number is defined as that number without its sign:*

- *The absolute value of −2 is 2.*
- *The absolute value of 2 is 2.*

In Processing, *we can get the absolute value of the number by placing it inside the **abs()** function, that is,*

- abs(−5) → 5

The speed at which the mouse is moving is therefore:

- abs(*mouseX-pmouseX*)

*Update Exercise 3-7 so that the faster the user moves the mouse, the wider the drawn line. Hint: look up **strokeWeight()** in the Processing reference.*

```
stroke(255);
_____    (_____);
line(pmouseX,pmouseY,mouseX,mouseY);
```

3.4 Mouse Clicks and Key Presses

We are well on our way to creating dynamic, interactive *Processing* sketches through the use the ***setup()*** and ***draw()*** framework and the ***mouseX*** and ***mouseY*** keywords. A crucial form of interaction, however, is missing—clicking the mouse!

In order to learn how to have something happen when the mouse is clicked, we need to return to the flow of our program. We know ***setup()*** happens once and ***draw()*** loops forever. When does a mouse click occur? Mouse presses (and key presses) as considered *events* in *Processing*. If we want something to happen (such as "the background color changes to red") when the mouse is clicked, we need to add a third block of code to handle this event.

This event "function" will tell the program what code to execute when an event occurs. As with ***setup()***, the code will occur once and only once. That is, once and only once for each occurrence of the event. An event, such as a mouse click, can happen multiple times of course!

These are the two new functions we need:

- ***mousePressed()***—Handles mouse clicks.
- ***keyPressed()***—Handles key presses.

The following example uses both event functions, adding squares whenever the mouse is pressed and clearing the background whenever a key is pressed.

Example 3-5: *mousePressed( )* and *keyPressed( )*

```
void setup() {
  size(200,200);
  background(255);
}

void draw() {

}

void mousePressed() {
  stroke(0);
  fill(175);
  rectMode(CENTER);
  rect(mouseX,mouseY,16,16);
}

void keyPressed() {
  background(255);
}
```

> Nothing happens in ***draw()*** in this example!

> Whenever a user clicks the mouse the code written inside ***mousePressed()*** is executed.

> Whenever a user presses a key the code written inside ***keyPressed()*** is executed.

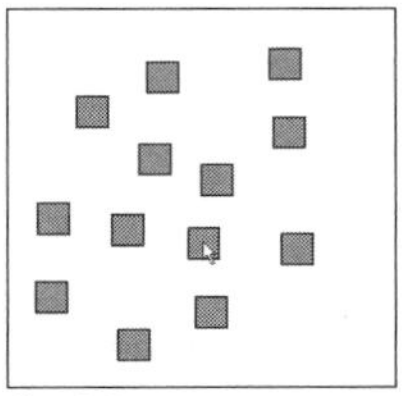

fig. 3.8

In Example 3-5, we have four functions that describe the program's flow. The program starts in ***setup()*** where the size and background are initialized. It continues into ***draw()***, looping endlessly. Since ***draw()*** contains no code, the window will remain blank. However, we have added two new functions: ***mousePressed()*** and *keyPressed()*. The code inside these functions sits and waits. When the user clicks the mouse (or presses a key), it springs into action, executing the enclosed block of instructions once and only once.

*Exercise 3-8: Add "**background(255);**" to the **draw()** function. Why does the program stop working?*

We are now ready to bring all of these elements together for Zoog.

- Zoog's entire body will follow the mouse.
- Zoog's eye color will be determined by mouse location.
- Zoog's legs will be drawn from the previous mouse location to the current mouse location.
- When the mouse is clicked, a message will be displayed in the message window: "Take me to your leader!"

Note the addition in Example 3–6 of the function *frameRate()*. *frameRate()*, which requires an integer between 1 and 60, enforces the speed at which *Processing* will cycle through *draw()*. *frameRate (30)*, for example, means 30 frames per second, a traditional speed for computer animation. If you do not include *frameRate()*, *Processing* will attempt to run the sketch at 60 frames per second. Since computers run at different speeds, *frameRate()* is used to make sure that your sketch is consistent across multiple computers.

This frame rate is just a maximum, however. If your sketch has to draw one million rectangles, it may take a long time to finish the draw cycle and run at a slower speed.

Example 3-6: Interactive Zoog

```
void setup() {
  // Set the size of the window

  size(200,200);
  smooth();
  frameRate(30);
}
```

> The frame rate is set to 30 frames per second.

```
void draw() {
  // Draw a black background
  background(255);

  // Set ellipses and rects to CENTER mode
  ellipseMode(CENTER);
  rectMode(CENTER);

  // Draw Zoog's body
  stroke(0);
  fill(175);
  rect(mouseX,mouseY,20,100);

  // Draw Zoog's head
  stroke(0);
  fill(255);
  ellipse(mouseX,mouseY-30,60,60);
```

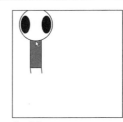

fig. 3.9

```
  // Draw Zoog's eyes
  fill(mouseX,0,mouseY);
  ellipse(mouseX-19,mouseY-30,16,32);
  ellipse(mouseX+19,mouseY-30,16,32);

  // Draw Zoog's legs
  stroke(0);
  line(mouseX-10,mouseY+50,pmouseX-10,pmouseY+60);
  line(mouseX+10,mouseY+50,pmouseX+10,pmouseY+60);
}

void mousePressed() {
  println("Take me to your leader!");
}
```

The eye color is determined by the mouse location.

The legs are drawn according to the mouse location *and the previous mouse location*.

Lesson One Project

(You may have completed much of this project already via the exercises in Chapters 1–3. This project brings all of the elements together. You could either start from scratch with a new design or use elements from the exercises.)

Step 1. Design a static screen drawing using RGB color and primitive shapes.

Step 2. Make the static screen drawing dynamic by having it interact with the mouse. This might include shapes following the mouse, changing their size according to the mouse, changing their color according to the mouse, and so on.

Use the space provided below to sketch designs, notes, and pseudocode for your project.

Lesson Two

Everything You Need to Know

4 Variables

"All of the books in the world contain no more information than is broadcast as video in a single large American city in a single year. Not all bits have equal value."
—*Carl Sagan*

"Believing oneself to be perfect is often the sign of a delusional mind."
—*Lieutenant Commander Data*

In this chapter:
– Variables: What are they?
– Declaring and initializing variables.
– Common uses for variables.
– Variables you get "for free" in *Processing* (AKA "built-in" variables).
– Using random values for variables.

4.1 What is a Variable?

I admit it. When I teach programming, I launch into a diatribe of analogies in an attempt to explain the concept of a variable in an intuitive manner. On any given day, I might say "A variable is like a bucket." You put something in the bucket, carry it around with you, and retrieve it whenever you feel inspired. "A variable is like a storage locker." Deposit some information in the locker where it can live safely, readily available at a moment's notice. "A variable is a lovely, yellow post-it note, on which is written the message: I am a variable. Write your information on me."

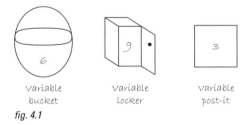

variable
bucket

variable
locker

variable
post-it

fig. 4.1

I could go on. But I won't. I think you get the idea. And I am not entirely sure we really need an analogy since the concept itself is rather simple. Here's the deal.

The computer has memory. Why do we call it memory? Because it is what the computer uses to *remember* stuff it needs.

Technically speaking, a *variable* is a named pointer to a location in the computer's memory ("memory address") where data is stored. Since computers only process information one instruction at a time, a variable allows a programmer to save information from one point in the program and refer back to it at a later time. For a *Processing* programmer, this is incredibly useful; variables can keep track of information related to shapes: color, size, location. Variables are exactly what you need to make a triangle change from blue to purple, a circle fly across the screen, and a rectangle shrink into oblivion.

Out of all the available analogies, I tend to prefer the *piece of paper* approach: *graph paper.*

Imagine that the computer's memory is a sheet of graph paper and each cell on the graph paper has an address. With pixels, we learned how to refer to those cells by column and row numbers. Wouldn't it be nice if we could name those cells? With variables, we can.

Let's name one "Billy's Score" (we will see why we are calling it that in the next section) and give it the value 100. That way, whenever we want to use Billy's score in a program, we do not have to remember the value 100. It is there in memory and we can ask for it by name. See Figure 4.2.

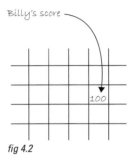

fig 4.2

The power of a variable does not simply rest with the ability to remember a value. The whole point of a variable is that those values *vary*, and more interesting situations arise as we periodically alter that value.

Consider a game of Scrabble between Billy and Jane. To keep track of the score, Jane takes out paper and pencil, and scrawls down two column names: "Billy's Score" and "Jane's Score." As the two play, a running tally is kept of each player's points below the headings. If we imagine this game to be virtual Scrabble programmed on a computer, we suddenly can see the concept of a variable that *varies* emerge. That piece of paper is the computer's memory and on that paper, information is written—"Billy's Score" and "Jane's Score" are variables, locations in memory where each player's total points are stored and that change over time. See Figure 4.3.

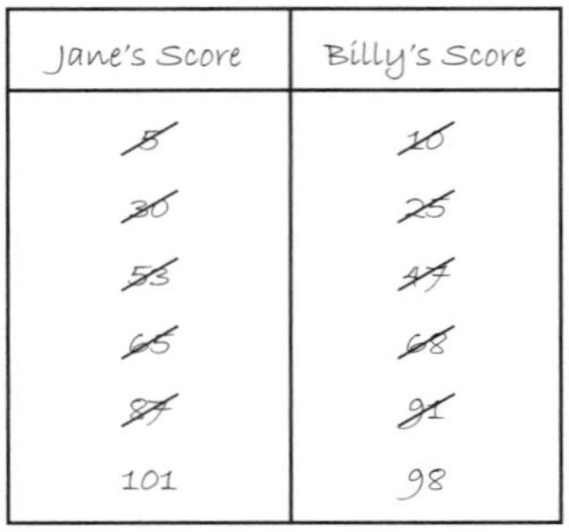

Jane's Score	Billy's Score
15	10
30	25
55	44
65	68
94	91
101	98

fig. 4.3

In our Scrabble example, the variable has two elements—a *name* (e.g., "Jane's Score") and a *value* (e.g., 101). In *Processing*, variables can hold different kinds of values and we are required to explicitly define the *type* of value before we can use a given variable.

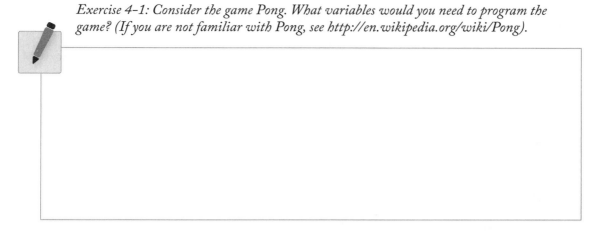

Exercise 4-1: Consider the game Pong. What variables would you need to program the game? (If you are not familiar with Pong, see http://en.wikipedia.org/wiki/Pong).

4.2 Variable Declaration and Initialization

Variables can hold *primitive* values or *references to objects and arrays.* For now, we are just going to worry about primitives—we will get to objects and arrays in a later chapter. Primitive values are the building blocks of data on the computer and typically involve a singular piece of information, like a number or character.

Variables are declared by first stating the type, followed by the name. Variable names must be one word (no spaces) and must start with a letter (they can include numbers, but cannot start with a number). They cannot include any punctuation or special characters, with the exception of the underscore: "_".

A *type* is the kind of data stored in that variable. This could be a whole number, a decimal number, or a character. Here are data types you will commonly use:

- **Whole numbers,** such as 0, 1, 2, 3, −1, −2, and so on are stored as "integers" and the type keyword for integer is "*int*".
- **Decimal numbers,** such as 3.14159, 2.5, and −9.95 are typically stored as "floating point values" and the type keyword for floating point is "*float*".
- **Characters,** such as the letters 'a', 'b', 'c', and so on are stored in variables of type "*char*" and are declared as a letter enclosed in single quotes, that is, '*a*'. Characters are useful when determining what letter on the keyboard has been pressed, and for other uses involving *Strings* of text (see Chapter 17).

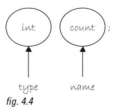

fig. 4.4

In Figure 4.4, we have a variable named "count" of type "int," which stands for integer. Other possible data types are listed below.

Don't Forget

- **Variables must have a type.** Why? This is how the computer knows exactly how much memory should be allocated to store that variable's data.
- **Variables must have a name.**

All Primitive Types

- *boolean*: true or false
- *char*: a character, 'a','b','c', etc.
- *byte*: a small number, −128 to 127
- *short*: a larger number, −32768 to 32767
- *int*: a big number, −2147483648 to 2147483647
- *long*: a really huge number
- *float*: a decimal number, such as 3.14159
- *double*: a decimal number with a lot more decimal places (only necessary for advanced programs requiring mathematical precision).

Once a variable is declared, we can then assign it a value by setting it equal to something. In most cases, if we forget to initialize a variable, *Processing* will give it a default value, such as 0 for integers, 0.0 for floating points, and so on. However, it is good to get into the habit of always initializing variables in order to avoid confusion.

```
int count;
count = 50;
```
> Declare and initialize a variable in two lines of code.

To be more concise, we can combine the above two statements into one.

```
int count = 50;
```
> Declare and initialize a variable in one lines of code.

What's in a name?

Tips for choosing good variable names

- Avoid using words that appear elsewhere in the *Processing* language. In other words, do not call your variable *mouseX*, there already is one!
- Use names that mean something. This may seem obvious, but it is an important point. For example, if you are using a variable to keep track of score, call it "score" and not, say, "cat."
- Start your variable with a lowercase letter and join together words with capitals. Words that start with capitals are reserved for classes (Chapter 8). For example: "frogColor" is good, "Frogcolor" is not. this canTake some gettingUsedTo but it will comeNaturally soonEnough.

A variable can also be initialized by another variable (*x* equals *y*), or by evaluating a mathematical expression (*x* equals *y* plus *z*, etc.). Here are some examples:

Example 4-1: Variable declaration and initialization examples

```
int count = 0;          // Declare an int named count, assigned the value 0
char letter = 'a';      // Declare a char named letter, assigned the value 'a'
double d = 132.32;      // Declare a double named d, assigned the value 132.32
boolean happy = false;  // Declare a boolean named happy, assigned the value false
float x = 4.0;          // Declare a float named x, assigned the value 4.0
float y;                // Declare a float named y (no assignment)
y = x + 5.2;            // Assign the value of x plus 5.2 to the previously declared y
float z = x*y + 15.0;   // Declare a variable named z, assign it the value which
                        // is x times y plus 15.0.
```

Exercise 4-2: Write out variable declaration and initialization for the game Pong.

_____

_____

_____

_____

_____

_____

4.3 Using a Variable

Though it may initially seem more complicated to have words standing in for numbers, variables make our lives easier and more interesting.

Let's take a simple example of a program that draws a circle onscreen.

> In a moment, we'll add variables at the top here.

```
void setup() {
  size(200,200);
}

void draw() {
  background(255);
  stroke(0);
  fill(175);
  ellipse(100,100,50,50);
}
```

In Chapter 3, we learned how to take this simple example one step further, changing the location of a shape to *mouseX, mouseY* in order to assign its location according to the mouse.

```
ellipse(mouseX,mouseY,50,50);
```

Can you see where this is going? *mouseX* and *mouseY* are named references to the horizonal and vertical location of the mouse. They are variables! However, because they are built into the *Processing* environment (note how they are colored red when you type them in your code), they can be used without being declared. Built-in variables (AKA "System" variables) are discussed further in the next section.

What we want to do now is create our own variables by following the syntax for declaring and initializing outlined above, placing the variables at the top of our code. You can declare variables elsewhere in your code and we will get into this later. For now to avoid any confusion, all variables should be at the top.

Rule of Thumb: When to Use a Variable

There are no hard and fast rules in terms of when to use a variable. However, if you find yourself hard-coding in a bunch of numbers as you program, take a few minutes, review your code, and change these values to variables.

Some programmers say that if a number appears three or more times, it should be a variable. Personally, I would say if a number appears once, use a variable. Always use variables!

Example 4-2: Using variables

```
int circleX = 100;
int circleY = 100;

void setup() {
  size(200,200);
}

void draw() {
  background(100);
  stroke(255);
  fill(0);
  ellipse(circleX,circleY,50,50);
}
```

> Declare and initialize two integer variables at the top of the code.

> Use the variables to specify the location of an ellipse.

Running this code, we achieve the same result as in the first example: a circle appears in the middle of the screen. Nevertheless, we should open our hearts and remind ourselves that a variable is not simply a placeholder for one constant value. We call it a variable because it *varies*. To change its value, we write an *assignment operation*, which assigns a new value.

Up until now, every single line of code we wrote called a function: *line(), ellipse(), stroke()*, etc. Variables introduce assignment operations to the mix. Here is what one looks like (it is the same as how we initialize a variable, only the variable does not need to be declared).

   variable name = *expression*

```
x = 5;
x = a + b;
x = y - 10 * 20;
x = x * 5;
```

> Examples of assigning a new value to a variables.

A common example is incrementation. In the above code, circleX starts with a value of 100. If we want to increment circleX by one, we say circleX equals itself plus one. In code, this amounts to "circleX = circleX + 1;".

Let's try adding that to our program (and let's start circle*X* with the value of 0).

Example 4-3: Varying variables

```
int circleX = 0;
int circleY = 100;

void setup() {
  size(200,200);
}

void draw() {
  background(255);
  stroke(0);
  fill(175);
  ellipse(circleX,circleY,50,50);

  circleX = circleX + 1;
}
```

> An assignment operation that increments the value of circleX by 1.

What happens? If you run Example 4-3 in *Processing*, you will notice that the circle moves from left to right. Remember, ***draw()*** loops over and over again, all the while retaining the value of circleX in memory. Let's pretend we are the computer for a moment. (This may seem overly simple and obvious, but it is key to our understanding of the principles of programming motion.)

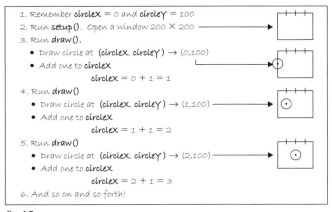

fig. 4.5

Practicing how to follow the code step-by-step will lead you to the questions you need to ask before writing your own sketches. *Be one with the computer.*

- What data do you and the computer need to remember for your sketch?
- How do you and the computer use that data to draw shapes on the screen?
- How do you and the computer alter that data to make your sketch interactive and animated?

Exercise 4-3: Change Example 4-3 so that instead of the circle moving from left to right, the circle grows in size. What would you change to have the circle follow the mouse as it grows? How could you vary the speed at which the circle grows?

```
int circleSize = 0;
int circleX = 100;
int circleY = 100;

void setup() {
  size(200,200);
}

void draw() {
  background(0);
  stroke(255);
  fill(175);

  _____

  _____

}
```

4.4 Many Variables

Let's take the example one step further and use variables for every piece of information we can think of. We will also use floating point values to demonstrate greater precision in adjusting variable values.

Example 4-4: Many variables

```
float circleX = 0;
float circleY = 0;
float circleW = 50;
float circleH = 100;
float circleStroke = 255;
float circleFill = 0;
float backgroundColor = 255;
float change = 0.5;

// Your basic setup
void setup() {
  size(200,200);
  smooth();
}
```

> We've got eight variables now! All of type float.

fig. 4.6

```
void draw() {
  // Draw the background and the ellipse
  background(backgroundColor);
  stroke(circleStroke);
  fill(circleFill);
  ellipse(circleX,circleY,circleW,circleH);

  // Change the values of all variables
  circleX = circleX + change;
  circleY = circleY + change;
  circleW = circleW + change;
  circleH = circleH - change;
  circleStroke = circleStroke - change;
  circleFill = circleFill + change;
}
```

> Variables are used for everything: background, stroke, fill, location, and size.

> The variable change is used to increment and decrement the other variables.

 Exercise 4-4

Step 1: *Write code that draws the following screenshots with hard-coded values. (Feel free to use colors instead of grayscale.)*

Step 2: *Replace all of the hard-coded numbers with variables.*

Step 3: *Write assignment operations in **draw()** that change the value of the variables. For example, "variable1 = variable1 + 2;". Try different expressions and see what happens!*

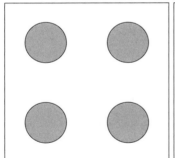 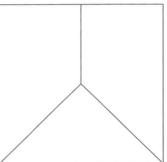 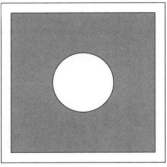

4.5 System Variables

As we saw with **mouseX** and **mouseY**, *Processing* has a set of convenient system variables freely available. These are commonly needed pieces of data associated with all sketches (such as the *width* of the window, the *key* pressed on the keyboard, etc.). When naming your own variables, it is best to avoid system variable names, however, if you inadvertently use one, your variable will become primary and override the system one. Here is a list of commonly used system variables (there are more, which you can find in the *Processing* reference).

- **width**—Width (in pixels) of sketch window.
- **height**—Height (in pixels) of sketch window.
- **frameCount**—Number of frames processed.

- **frameRate**—Rate that frames are processed (per second).
- **screen.width**—Width (in pixels) of entire screen.
- **screen.height**—Height (in pixels) of entire screen.
- **key**—Most recent key pressed on the keyboard.
- **keyCode**—Numeric code for key pressed on keyboard.
- **keyPressed**—True or false? Is a key pressed?
- **mousePressed**—True or false? Is the mouse pressed?
- **mouseButton**—Which button is pressed? Left, right, or center?

Following is an example that makes use of some of the above variables; we are not ready to use them all yet, as we will need some more advanced concepts to make use of many features.

Example 4-5: Using system variables

```
void setup() {
  size(200,200);
  frameRate(30);
}

void draw() {
  background(100);
  stroke(255);
  fill(frameCount/2);          frameCount is used to color a rectangle.
  rectMode(CENTER);
  rect(width/2,height/2,mouseX+10,mouseY+10);
}
                                 The rectangle will always be in the
void keyPressed() {              middle of the window if it is located at
  println(key);                  (width/2, height/2).
}
```

*Exercise 4-5: Using width and height, recreate the following screenshot. Here's the catch: the shapes must resize themselves relative to the window size. (In other words, no matter what you specify for **size()**, the result should look identical.)*

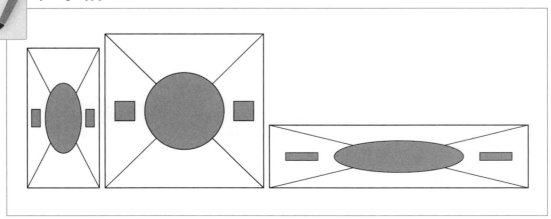

4.6 Random: Variety is the spice of life.

So, you may have noticed that the examples in this book so far are a bit, say, humdrum. A circle here. A square here. A grayish color. Another grayish color.

There is a method to the madness (or lack of madness in this case). It all goes back to the driving principle behind this book: *incremental development*. It is much easier to learn the fundamentals by looking at the individual pieces, programs that do one and only one thing. We can then begin to add functionality on top, step by step.

Nevertheless, we have waited patiently through four chapters and we have arrived at the time where we can begin to have a bit of fun. And this fun will be demonstrated via the use of the function *random()*. Consider, for a moment, Example 4-6, whose output is shown in Figure 4.7.

Example 4-6: Ellipse with variables

```
float r = 100;        Declare and initialize
float g = 150;        your variables
float b = 200;
float a = 200;

float diam = 20;
float x = 100;
float y = 100;
void setup() {
  size(200,200);
  background(255);
  smooth();
}

void draw() {
  // Use those variables to draw an ellipse
  stroke(0);
  fill(r,g,b,a);       Use those variables! (Remember, the fourth
  ellipse(x,y,diam,diam);   argument for a color is transparency).
}
```

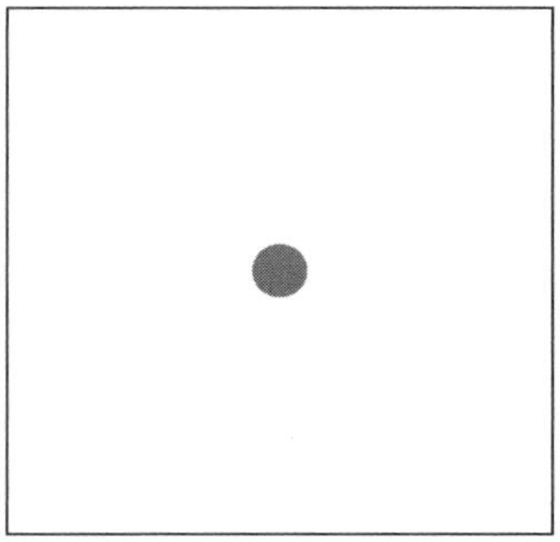

fig. 4.7

There it is, our dreary circle. Sure, we can adjust variable values and move the circle, grow its size, change its color, and so on. However, what if every time through *draw()*, we could make a new circle, one with a random size, color, and position? The *random()* function allows us to do exactly that.

random() is a special kind of function, it is a function that *returns* a value. We have encountered this before. In Exercise 3-7 we used the function *abs()* to calculate the absolute value of a number. The idea of a function that *calculates a value* and *returns it* will be explored fully in Chapter 7, but we are going to take some time to introduce the idea now and let it sink in a bit.

Unlike most of the functions we are comfortable with (e.g., *line()*, *ellipse()*, and *rect()*), *random()* does not draw or color a shape on the screen. Instead, *random()* answers a question; it returns that answer to us. Here is a bit of dialogue. Feel free to rehearse it with your friends.

> *Me*:   Hey random, what's going on? Hope you're well. Listen, I was wondering, could you give me a random number between 1 and 100?
>
> *Random*:   Like, no problem. How about the number 63?
>
> *Me*:   That's awesome, really great, thank you. OK, I'm off. Gotta draw a rectangle 63 pixels wide, OK?

Now, how would this sequence look in our slightly more formal, *Processing* environment? The code below the part of "me" is played by the variable "w".

```
float w = random(1,100);
rect(100,100,w,50);
```
> A random float between 1 and 100.

The *random()* function requires two arguments and returns a random floating point number ranging from the first argument to the second. The second argument must be larger than the first for it to work properly. The function *random()* also works with one argument by assuming a range between zero and that argument.

In addition, *random()* only returns floating point numbers. This is why we declared "w" above as a *float*. However, if you want a random integer, you can convert the result of the random function to an *int*.

```
int w = int(random(1,100));
rect(100,100,w,50);
```
> A random integer between 1 and 100.

Notice the use of nested parentheses. This is a nice concept to get used to as it will be quite convenient to call functions inside of functions as we go. The *random()* function returns a float, which is then passed to the *int()* function that converts it to an integer. If we wanted to go nuts nesting functions, we could even condense the above code into one line:

```
rect(100,100,int(random(1,100)),50);
```

Incidentally, the process of converting one data type to another is referred to as "casting." In Java (which *Processing* is based on) casting a float to an integer can also be written this way:

```
int w = (int) random(1,100);
```
> The result of *random (1,100)* is a float. It can be converted to an integer by "casting."

OK, we are now ready to experiment with *random()*. Example 4-7 shows what happens if we take every variable associated with drawing the ellipse (fill, location, size) and assign it to a random number each cycle through *draw()*. The output is shown in Figure 4.8.

Example 4-7: Filling variables with random values

```
float r;
float g;
float b;
float a;

float diam;
float x;
float y;

void setup() {
  size(200,200);
  background(0);
  smooth();
}

void draw() {
  // Fill all variables with random values
  r = random(255);
  g = random(255);
  b = random(255);
  a = random(255);
  diam = random(20);
  x = random(width);
  y = random(height);

  // Use values to draw an ellipse
  noStroke();
  fill(r,g,b,a);
  ellipse(x,y,diam,diam);
}
```

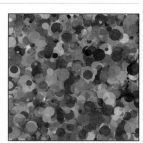

fig. 4.8

> Each time through **draw()**, new random numbers are picked for a new ellipse.

4.7 Variable Zoog

We are now ready to revisit Zoog, our alien friend, who was happily following the mouse around the screen when we last checked in. Here, we will add two pieces of functionality to Zoog.

- **New feature #1**—Zoog will rise from below the screen and fly off into space (above the screen).
- **New feature #2**—Zoog's eyes will be colored randomly as Zoog moves.

Feature #1 is solved by simply taking the previous program that used **mouseX** and **mouseY** and substituting our own variables in their place.

Feature #2 is implemented by creating three additional variables eyeRed, eyeGreen, and eyeBlue that will be used for the *fill()* function before displaying the eye ellipses.

Example 4-8: Variable Zoog

```
float zoogX;
float zoogY;

float eyeR;
float eyeG;
float eyeB;

void setup() {
  size(200,200);
```

> Declaring variables. zoogX and zoogY are for feature #1. eyeR, eyeG, eyeB are for feature #2.

fig. 4.9

```
  zoogX = width/2;      // Zoog always starts in the middle
  zoogY = height + 100; // Zoog starts below the screen
  smooth();
}
```

> Feature #1. zoogX and zoogY are initialized based on the size of the window. Note we cannot initialize these variables before the *size ()* function is called since we are using the built-in variables *width* and *height*.

```
void draw() {

  background(255);

  // Set ellipses and rects to CENTER mode
  ellipseMode(CENTER);
  rectMode(CENTER);

  // Draw Zoog's body
  stroke(0);
  fill(150);
  rect(zoogX,zoogY,20,100);
```

> Feature #1. zoogX and zoogY are used for the shape locations.

```
  // Draw Zoog's head
  stroke(0);
  fill(255);
  ellipse(zoogX,zoogY-30,60,60);

  // Draw Zoog's eyes
  eyeR = random(255);
  eyeG = random(255);
  eyeB = random(255);
  fill(eyeR,eyeG,eyeB);
```

> Feature #2. eyeR, eyeG, and eye B are given random values and used in the *fill()* function.

```
  ellipse(zoogX-19,zoogY-30,16,32);
  ellipse(zoogX+19,zoogY-30,16,32);
  // Draw Zoog's legs
  stroke(150);
  line(zoogX-10,zoogY+50,zoogX-10,height);
  line(zoogX+10,zoogY+50,zoogX+10,height);

  // Zoog moves up
  zoogY = zoogY - 1;
```

> Feature #1. zoogY is decreased by one so that zoog moves upward on the screen.

```
}
```

*Exercise 4-6: Revise Example 4-8 so that Zoog shakes left and right as Zoog moves upward. Hint: this requires the use of **random()** in combination with zoogX.*

zoogX = _____ ;

*Exercise 4-7: Using variables and the **random()** function, revise your design from the Lesson One Project to move around the screen, change color, size, location, and so on.*

5 Conditionals

"That language is an instrument of human reason, and not merely a medium for the expression of thought, is a truth generally admitted."
—*George Boole*

"The way I feel about music is that there is no right and wrong. Only true and false."
—*Fiona Apple*

In this chapter:
– Boolean expressions.
– Conditional statements: How a program produces different results based on varying circumstances.
– *If, Else If, Else.*

5.1 Boolean Expressions

What's your favorite kind of test? Essay format? Multiple choice? In the world of computer programming, we only take one kind of test: a *boolean* test—true or false. A *boolean expression* (named for mathematician George Boole) is an expression that evaluates to either true or false. Let's look at some common language examples:

- I am hungry.   → true
- I am afraid of computer programming.   → false
- This book is a hilarious read.   → false

In the formal logic of computer science, we test relationships between numbers.

- 15 is greater than 20   → false
- 5 equals 5   → true
- 32 is less than or equal to 33   → true

In this chapter, we will learn how to use a variable in a boolean expression, allowing our sketch to take different paths depending on the current value stored in the variable.

- $x > 20$ → depends on current value of x
- $y == 5$ → depends on current value of y
- $z <= 33$ → depends on current value of z

The following operators can be used in a boolean expression.

Relational Operators

>	greater than		<=	less than or equal to
<	less than		==	equality
>=	greater than or equal to		!=	inequality

5.2 Conditionals: If, Else, Else If

Boolean expressions (often referred to as "conditionals") operate within the sketch as questions. Is 15 greater than 20? If the answer is yes (i.e., true), we can choose to execute certain instructions (such as draw a rectangle); if the answer is no (i.e., false), those instructions are ignored. This introduces the idea of branching; depending on various conditions, the program can follow different paths.

In the physical world, this might amount to instructions like so:

If I am hungry then eat some food, otherwise if I am thirsty, drink some water, otherwise, take a nap.

In *Processing*, we might have something more like:

If the mouse is on the left side of the screen, draw a rectangle on the left side of the screen.

Or, more formally, with the output shown in Figure 5.1,

```
if (mouseX < width/2) {
  fill(255);
  rect(0,0,width/2,height);
}
```

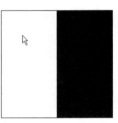

fig. 5.1

The boolean expression and resulting instructions in the above source code is contained within a block of code with the following syntax and structure:

```
if (boolean expression) {
  // code to execute if boolean expression is true
}
```

The structure can be expanded with the keyword *else* to include code that is executed if the boolean expression is false. This is the equivalent of "otherwise, do such and such."

```
if (boolean expression) {
  // code to execute if boolean expression is true
} else {
  // code to execute if boolean expression is false
}
```

For example, we could say the following, with the output shown in Figure 5.2.

If the mouse is on the left side of the screen, draw a white background, otherwise draw a black background.

```
if (mouseX < width/2) {
  background(255);
} else {
  background(0);
}
```

fig. 5.2

Finally, for testing multiple conditions, we can employ an "else if." When an *else if* is used, the conditional statements are evaluated in the order presented. As soon as one boolean expression is found to be true, the corresponding code is executed and the remaining boolean expressions are ignored. See Figure 5.3.

```
if (boolean expression #1) {
   // code to execute if boolean expression #1 is true
} else if (boolean expression #2) {
   // code to execute if boolean expression #2 is true
} else if (boolean expression #n) {
   // code to execute if boolean expression #n is true
} else {
   // code to execute if none of the above
   // boolean expressions are true
}
```

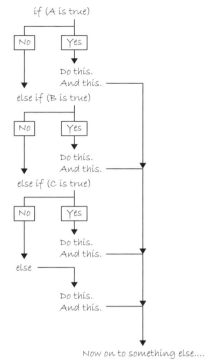

fig. 5.3

Taking our simple mouse example a step further, we could say the following, with results shown in Figure 5.4.

If the mouse is on the left third of the window, draw a white background, if it is in the middle third, draw a gray background, otherwise, draw a black background.

```
if (mouseX < width/3) {
  background(255);
} else if (mouseX < 2*width/3) {
  background(127);
} else {
  background(0);
}
```

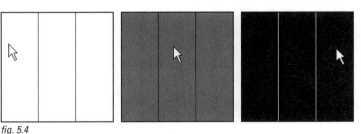

fig. 5.4

Exercise 5-1: Consider a grading system where numbers are turned into letters. Fill in the blanks in the following code to complete the boolean expression.

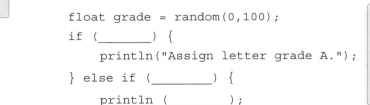

```
float grade = random(0,100);
if (_____) {
    println("Assign letter grade A.");
} else if (_____) {
    println (_____);
```

In one conditional statement, you can only ever have one *if* and one *else*. However, you can have as many *else if*'s as you like!

```
    } else if (_____) {
        println(_____);
    } else if (_____) {
        println(_____);
    } else {
        println(_____);
    }
```

Exercise 5-2: Examine the following code samples and determine what will appear in the message window. Write down your answer and then execute the code in Processing *to compare.*

Problem #1: Determine if a number is between 0 and 25, 26 and 50, or greater than 50.

```
int x = 75;

if (x > 50) {
    println(x + " is greater than
    50!");
} else if (x > 25) {
    println(x + " is greater than
    25!");
} else {
    println(x + " is 25 or
    less!");
}
```

```
int x = 75;

if(x > 25) {
    println(x + " is greater
    than 25!");
} else if (x > 50) {
    println(x + " is greater
    than 50!");
} else {
    println(x + " is 25 or
    less!");
}
```

OUTPUT:_____   **OUTPUT:**_____

Although the syntax is correct, what is problematic about the code in column two above?

Problem #2: If a number is 5, change it to 6. If a number is 6, change it to five.

```
int x = 5;                          int x = 5;

println("x is now: " + x);          println("x is now: " + x);
if (x == 5) {                       if (x == 5) {
  x = 6;                              x = 6;
}                                   } else if (x == 6) {
if (x == 6) {                         x = 5;
  x = 5;                            }
}                                   println("x is now: " + x);
println("x is now: " + x);
```

OUTPUT:_____   OUTPUT:_____

Although the syntax is correct, what is problematic about the code in column one above?

It is worth pointing out that in Exercise 5-2 when we test for equality we must use *two* equal signs. This is because, when programming, asking if something is equal is different from assigning a value to a variable.

```
if (x == y) {
```
"Is *x* equal to *y*?" Use double equals!

```
x = y;
```
"Set *x* equal to *y*." Use single equals!

5.3 Conditionals in a Sketch

Let's look at a very simple example of a program that performs different tasks based on the result of certain conditions. Our pseudocode is below.

Step 1. Create variables to hold on to red, green, and blue color components. Call them r, g, and b.
Step 2. Continuously draw the background based on those colors.
Step 3. If the mouse is on the right-hand side of the screen, increment the value of r, if it is on the left-hand side decrement the value of r.
Step 4. Constrain the value r to be within 0 and 255.

This pseudocode is implemented in *Processing* in Example 5-1.

Example 5-1: Conditionals

```
float r = 150;
float g = 0;
float b = 0;

void setup() {
  size(200,200);
}

void draw() {
  background(r,g,b);
  stroke(255);
  line(width/2,0,width/2,height);

  if(mouseX > width/2) {
    r = r + 1;
  } else {
    r = r - 1;
  }

  if (r > 255) {
    r = 255;
  } else if (r < 0) {
    r = 0;
  }
}
```

1. Variables.

2. Draw stuff.

3. "If the mouse is on the right side of the screen" is equivalent to "if *mouseX* is greater than width divided by 2."

4. If *r* is greater than 255, set it to 255. If *r* is less than 0, set it to 0.

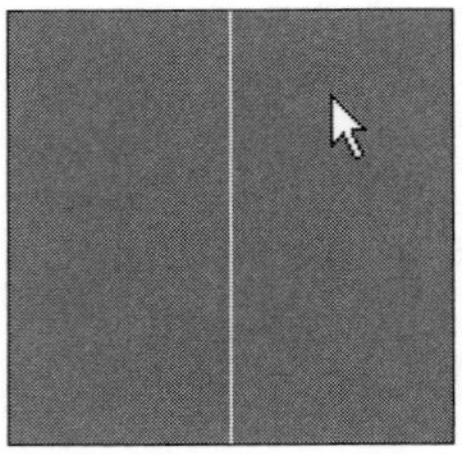

fig. 5.5

Constraining the value of a variable, as in Step 4, is a common problem. Here, we do not want color values to increase to unreasonable extremes. In other examples, we might want to constrain the size or location of a shape so that it does not get too big or too small, or wander off the screen.

While using if statements is a perfectly valid solution to the constrain problem, *Processing* does offer a function entitled ***constrain()*** that will get us the same result in one line of code.

```
if (r > 255) {
  r = 255;
} else if (r < 0) {
  r = 0;
}

r = constrain(r,0,255);
```

Constrain with an "if" statement.

Constrain with the ***constrain()*** function.

constrain() takes three arguments: the value we intend to constrain, the minimum limit, and the maximum limit. The function *returns* the "constrained" value and is assigned back to the variable *r*. (Remember what it means for a function to *return* a value? See our discussion of ***random()***.)

Getting into the habit of *constraining* values is a great way to avoid errors; no matter how sure you are that your variables will stay within a given range, there are no guarantees other than *constrain()* itself. And someday, as you work on larger software projects with multiple programmers, functions such as *constrain()* can ensure that sections of code work well together. Handling errors before they happen in code is emblematic of good style.

Let's make our first example a bit more advanced and change all three color components according to the mouse location and click state. Note the use of *constrain()* for all three variables. The system variable *mousePressed* is true or false depending on whether the user is holding down the mouse button.

Example 5-2: More conditionals

```
float r = 0;
float b = 0;
float g = 0;
```
Three variables for the background color.

```
void setup() {
    size(200,200);
}

void draw() {
  background(r,g,b);
  stroke(0);
```
Color the background and draw lines to divide the window into quadrants.

fig. 5.6

```
  line(width/2,0,width/2,height);
  line(0,height/2,width,height/2);

  if(mouseX > width/2) {
    r = r + 1;
  } else {
    r = r - 1;
  }
```
If the mouse is on the right-hand side of the window, increase red. Otherwise, it is on the left-hand side and decrease red.

```
  if (mouseY > height/2) {
    b = b + 1;
  } else {
    b = b - 1;
  }
```
If the mouse is on the bottom of the window, increase blue. Otherwise, it is on the top and decrease blue.

```
  if (mousePressed) {
    g = g + 1;
  } else {
    g = g - 1;
  }
```
If the mouse is pressed (using the system variable *mousePressed*) increase green.

```
  r = constrain(r,0,255);
  g = constrain(g,0,255);
  b = constrain(b,0,255);
}
```
Constrain all color values to between 0 and 255.

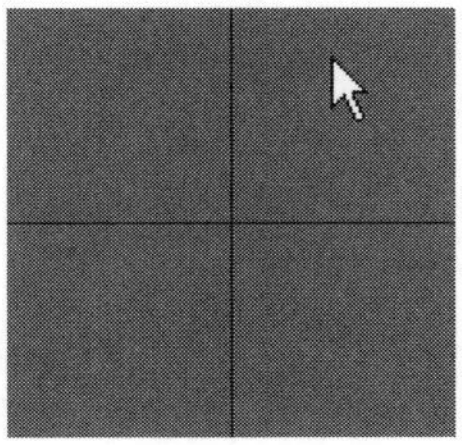

Exercise 5-3: Move a rectangle across a window by incrementing a variable. Start the shape at x coordinate 0 and use an if statement to have it stop at coordinate 100. Rewrite the sketch to use **constrain()** *instead of the if statement. Fill in the missing code.*

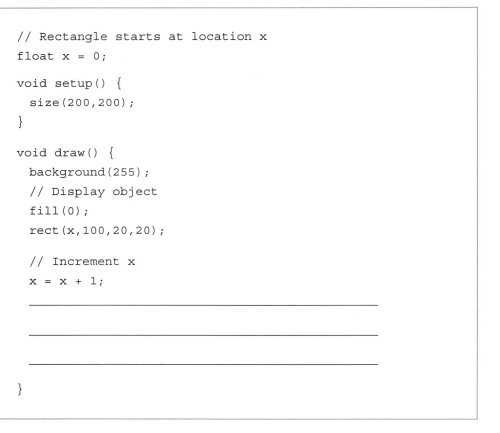

```
// Rectangle starts at location x
float x = 0;

void setup() {
  size(200,200);
}

void draw() {
  background(255);
  // Display object
  fill(0);
  rect(x,100,20,20);

  // Increment x
  x = x + 1;

  _____

  _____

  _____

}
```

5.4 Logical Operators

We have conquered the simple *if* statement:

If my temperature is greater than 98.6, then take me to see the doctor.

Sometimes, however, simply performing a task based on one condition is not enough. For example:

If my temperature is greater than 98.6 **OR** *I have a rash on my arm, take me to see the doctor.*

If I am stung by a bee **AND** *I am allergic to bees, take me to see the doctor.*

We will commonly want to do the same thing in programming from time to time.

If the mouse is on the right side of the screen **AND** *the mouse is on the bottom of the screen, draw a rectangle in the bottom right corner.*

Our first instinct might be to write the above code using a nested if statement, like so:

```
if (mouseX > width/2) {
  if (mouseY > height/2) {
    fill(255);
    rect(width/2,height/2,width/2,height/2);
  }
}
```

In other words, we would have to bypass *two* if statements before we can reach the code we want to execute. This works, yes, but can be accomplished in a simpler way using what we will call a "logical and," written as two ampersands ("&&"). A single ampersand ("&") means something else[1] in *Processing* so make sure you include two!

> || (logical OR)
> && (logical AND)
> ! (logical NOT)

A "logical or" is two vertical bars (AKA two "pipes") "||". If you can't find the pipe, it is typically on the keyboard as shift-backslash.

```
if (mouseX > width/2 && mouseY > height/2) {
  fill(255);
  rect(width/2,height/2,width/2,height/2);
}
```

> If the mouse is on the right side *and* on the bottom.

In addition to && and ||, we also have access to the logical operator "not," written as an exclamation point: !

*If my temperature is **NOT** greater than 98.6, I won't call in sick to work.*

*If I am stung by a bee **AND** I am **NOT** allergic to bees, do not worry!*

A *Processing* example is:

*If the mouse is **NOT** pressed, draw a circle, otherwise draw a square.*

```
if (!mousePressed) {
  ellipse(width/2,height/2,100,100);
} else {
  rect(width/2,height/2,100,100);
}
```

> ! means not. *"mousePressed"* is a *boolean* variable that acts as its own boolean expression. Its value is either true or false (depending on whether or not the mouse is currently pressed). Boolean variables will be explored in greater detail in Section 5.6.

Notice this example could also be written omitting the *not*, saying:

If the mouse is pressed, draw a square, otherwise draw a circle.

---

[1]"&" or "|" are reserved for *bitwise* operations in *Processing*. A bitwise operation compares each bit (0 or 1) of the binary representations of two numbers. It is used in rare circumstances where you require low-level access to bits.

Exercise 5-4: Are the following boolean expressions true or false? Assume variables
x = 5 and y = 6.

```
!(x > 6)        _____

(x==6 && x==5)  _____

(x==6 || x==5)  _____

(x>-1 && y<10)  _____
```

Although the syntax is correct, what is flawed about the following boolean expression?

```
(x > 10  &&  x < 5) _____
```

Exercise 5-5: Write a program that implements a simple rollover. In other words, if the
mouse is over a rectangle, the rectangle changes color. Here is some code to get you started.

```
int x = 50;
int y = 50;
int w = 100;
int h = 75;

void setup() {
  size(200,200);
}

void draw() {
  background(0);

  stroke(255);
  if (_____ && _____ && _____ && _____) {

    _____
  } _____ {

    _____
  }
  rect(x,y,w,h);
}
```

5.5 Multiple Rollovers

Let's solve a simple problem together, a slightly more advanced version of Exercise 5-5. Consider the four screenshots shown in Figure 5.7 from one single sketch. A white square is displayed in one of four quadrants, according to the mouse location.

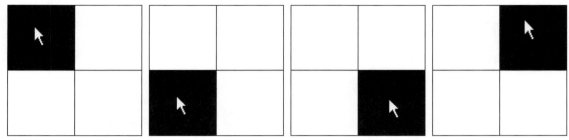

fig. 5.7

Let's first write the logic of our program in pseudocode (i.e., English).

Setup:

1.   Set up a window of 200×200 pixels.

Draw:

1.   Draw a white background.
2.   Draw horizontal and vertical lines to divide the window in four quadrants.
3.   If the mouse is in the top left corner, draw a black rectangle in the top left corner.
4.   If the mouse is in the top right corner, draw a black rectangle in the top right corner.
5.   If the mouse is in the bottom left corner, draw a black rectangle in the bottom left corner.
6.   If the mouse is in the bottom right corner, draw a black rectangle in the bottom right corner.

For instructions 3 through 6, we have to ask ourselves the question: "How do we know if the mouse is in a given corner?" To accomplish this, we need to develop a more specific if statement. For example, we would say: "If the mouse X location is greater than 100 pixels and the mouse Y location is greater than 100 pixels, draw a black rectangle in the bottom right corner. As an exercise, you may want to try writing this program yourself based on the above pseudocode. The answer, for your reference, is given in Example 5-3.

Example 5-3: Rollovers

```
void setup() {
  size(200,200);
}

void draw() {
  background(255);
  stroke(0);
  line(100,0,100,200);
  line(0,100,200,100);
```

```
// Fill a black color
noStroke();
fill(0);

if (mouseX < 100 && mouseY < 100) {
  rect(0,0,100,100);
} else if (mouseX > 100 && mouseY < 100) {
  rect(100,0,100,100);
} else if (mouseX < 100 && mouseY > 100) {
  rect(0,100,100,100);
} else if (mouseX > 100 && mouseY > 100) {
  rect(100,100,100,100);
}
}
```

> Depending on the mouse location, a different rectangle is displayed.

 Exercise 5-6: Rewrite Example 5-3 so that the squares fade from white to black when the mouse leaves their area. Hint: you need four variables, one for each rectangle's color.

5.6 Boolean Variables

The natural next step up from programming a rollover is a button. After all, a button is just a rollover that responds when clicked. Now, it may feel ever so slightly disappointing to be programming rollovers and buttons. Perhaps you are thinking: "Can't I just select 'Add Button' from the menu or something?" For us, right now, the answer is no. Yes, we are going to eventually learn how to use code from a library (and you might use a library to make buttons in your sketches more easily), but there is a lot of value in learning how to program GUI (graphical user interface) elements from scratch.

For one, practicing programming buttons, rollovers, and sliders is an excellent way to learn the basics of variables and conditionals. And two, using the same old buttons and rollovers that every program has is not terribly exciting. If you care about and are interested in developing new interfaces, understanding how to build an interface from scratch is a skill you will need.

OK, with that out of the way, we are going to look at how we use a *boolean variable* to program a button. A boolean variable (or a variable of type boolean) is a variable that can only be true or false. Think of it as a switch. It is either on or off. Press the button, turn the switch on. Press the button again, turn it off. We just used a boolean variable in Example 5-2: the built-in variable ***mousePressed***. ***mousePressed*** is true when the mouse is pressed and false when the mouse is not.

And so our button example will include one boolean variable with a starting value of false (the assumption being that the button starts in the off state).

```
boolean button = false;
```

> A boolean variables is either true of false.

In the case of a rollover, any time the mouse hovered over the rectangle, it turned white. Our sketch will turn the background white when the button is pressed and black when it is not.

```
if (button) {
  background(255);
} else {
  background(0);
}
```

> If the value of button is true, the background is white. If it is false, black.

We can then check to see if the mouse location is inside the rectangle and if the mouse is pressed, setting the value of button to true or false accordingly. Here is the full example:

Example 5-4: Hold down the button

```
boolean button = false;

int x = 50;
int y = 50;
int w = 100;
int h = 75;

void setup() {
  size(200,200);
}

void draw() {
  if (mouseX > x && mouseX < x+w && mouseY > y && mouseY < y+h && mousePressed) {
    button = true;
  } else {
    button = false;
  }

  if (button) {
    background(255);
    stroke(0);
  } else {
    background(0);
    stroke(255);
  }

  fill(175);
  rect(x,y,w,h);
}
```

> The button is pressed if *(mouseX, mouseY)* is inside the rectangle and *mousePressed* is true.

This example simulates a button connected to a light that is only on when the button is pressed. As soon as you let go, the light goes off. While this might be a perfectly appropriate form of interaction for some instances, it is not what we are really going for in this section. What we want is a button that operates like a switch; when you flip the switch (press the button), if the light is off, it turns on. If it is on, it turns off.

For this to work properly, we must check to see if the mouse is located inside the rectangle inside *mousePressed()* rather than as above in *draw()*. By definition, when the user clicks the mouse, the code inside *mousePressed()* is executed once and only once (see Section 3.4). When the mouse is clicked, we want the switch to turn on or off (once and only once).

We now need to write some code that "toggles" the switch, changes its state from on to off, or off to on. This code will go inside *mousePressed()*.

If the variable "button" equals true, we should set it to false. If it is false, we should set it to true.

```
if (button) {
  button = false;
} else {
  button = true;
}
```

> The explicit way to toggle a boolean variable. If the value of button is true, set it equal to false. Otherwise, it must be false, so set it equal to true.

There is a simpler way to go which is the following:

```
button = !button;
```

> Not true is false. Not false is true!

Here, the value of button is set to "not" itself. In other words, if the button is true then we set set it to *not true* (false). If it is false then we set it to *not false* (true). Armed with this odd but effective line of code, we are ready to look at the button in action in Example 5-5.

Example 5-5: Button as switch

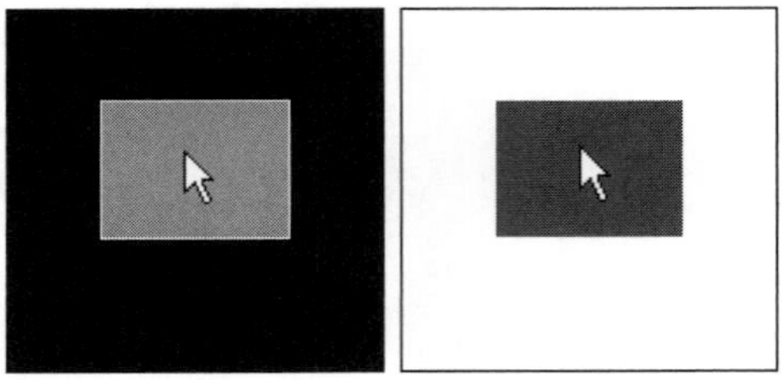

```
boolean button = false;

int x = 50;
int y = 50;
int w = 100;
int h = 75;

void setup() {
  size(200,200);
}

void draw() {
  if (button) {
    background(255);
    stroke(0);
  } else {
    background(0);
    stroke(255);
  }

  fill(175);
  rect(x,y,w,h);
}

void mousePressed() {
  if (mouseX > x && mouseX < x+w && mouseY > y && mouseY < y+h){
    button = !button;
  }
}
```

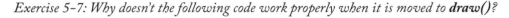

fig. 5.8

> When the mouse is pressed, the state of the button is toggled. Try moving this code to *draw()* like in the rollover example. (See Exercise 5–7.)

*Exercise 5-7: Why doesn't the following code work properly when it is moved to **draw()**?*

```
if (mouseX > x && mouseX < x+w && mouseY > y && mouseY < y+h &&
mousePressed) {

  button = !button;

}
```

Exercise 5-8: Example 4-3 in the previous chapter moved a circle across the window. Change the sketch so that the circle only starts moving once the mouse has been pressed. Use a boolean variable.

```
boolean _____ = _____;

int circleX = 0;
int circleY = 100;

void setup() {
  size(200,200);
}

void draw() {
  background(100);
  stroke(255);
  fill(0);
  ellipse(circleX,circleY,50,50);

  _____

  _____

  _____

}

void mousePressed() {

  _____

}
```

5.7 A Bouncing Ball

It is time again to return to our friend Zoog. Let's review what we have done so far. First, we learned to draw Zoog with shape functions available from the *Processing* reference. Afterward, we realized we could use variables instead of hard-coded values. Having these variables allowed us move Zoog. If Zoog's location is *X*, draw it at *X*, then at *X* + 1, then at *X* + 2, and so on.

It was an exciting, yet sad moment. The pleasure we experienced from discovering the motion was quickly replaced by the lonely feeling of watching Zoog leave the screen. Fortunately, conditional statements are here to save the day, allowing us to ask the question: *Has Zoog reached the edge of the screen? If so, turn Zoog around!*

To simplify things, let's start with a simple circle instead of Zoog's entire pattern.

Write a program where Zoog (a simple circle) moves across the screen horizontally from left to right. When it reaches the right edge it reverses direction.

From the previous chapter on variables, we know we need global variables to keep track of Zoog's location.

```
int x = 0;
```

Is this enough? No. In our previous example Zoog always moved one pixel.

```
x = x + 1;
```

This tells Zoog to move to the right. But what if we want it to move to the left? Easy, right?

```
x = x - 1;
```

In other words, sometimes Zoog moves with a speed of "+1" and sometimes "−1." The speed of Zoog *varies*. Yes, bells are ringing. In order to switch the direction of Zoog's speed, we need another *variable*: speed.

```
int x = 0;
int speed = 1;
```

> A variable for Zoog's speed. When speed is positive Zoog moves to the right, when speed is negative Zoog moves to the left.

Now that we have our variables, we can move on to the rest of the code. Assuming *setup()* sets the size of the window, we can go directly to examining the steps required inside of *draw()*. We can also refer to Zoog as a ball in this instance since we are just going to draw a circle.

```
background(0);
stroke(255);
fill(100);
ellipse(x,100,32,32);
```

> For simplicity, Zoog is just a circle.

Elementary stuff. Now, in order for the ball to move, the value of its *x* location should change each cycle through *draw()*.

```
x = x + speed;
```

If we ran the program now, the circle would start on the left side of the window, move toward the right, and continue off the edge of the screen—this is the result we achieved in Chapter 4. In order for it to turn around, we need a conditional statement.

If the ball goes off the edge, turn the ball around.

Or more formally. . .

If x is greater than width, reverse speed.

```
if (x > width) {
    speed = speed * -1;
}
```

> Multiplying by −1 reverses the speed.

Reversing the Polarity of a Number

When we want to reverse the polarity of a number, we mean that we want a positive number to become negative and a negative number to become positive. This is achieved by multiplying by –1. Remind yourself of the following:

- `-5 * -1 = 5`
- `-5 * -1 = -5`
- `-1 * 1 = -1`
- `-1 * -1 = 1`

Running the sketch, we now have a circle that turns around when it reaches the right-most edge, but runs off the left-most edge of the screen. We'll need to revise the conditional slightly.

If the ball goes off either the right or left edge, turn the ball around.

Or more formally. . .

If x is greater than width or if x is less than zero, reverse speed.

```
if ((x > width) || (x < 0)) {
  speed = speed * -1;
}
```

> Remember, ‖ means "or".

Example 5-6 puts it all together.

Example 5-6: Bouncing ball

```
int x = 0;
int speed = 1;

void setup() {
  size(200,200);
  smooth();
}

void draw() {
  background(255);

  x = x + speed;

  if ((x > width) || (x < 0)){
    speed = speed * -1;
  }

  // Display circle at x location
  stroke(0);
  fill(175);
  ellipse(x,100,32,32);
}
```

> Add the current speed to the *x* location.

> If the object reaches either edge, multiply speed by −1 to turn it around.

Exercise 5-9: Rewrite Example 5-6 so that the ball not only moves horizontally, but vertically as well. Can you implement additional features, such as changing the size or color of the ball based on certain conditions? Can you make the ball speed up or slow down in addition to changing direction?

The "bouncing ball" logic of incrementing and decrementing a variable can be applied in many ways beyond the motion of shapes onscreen. For example, just as a square moves from left to right, a color can go from less red to more red. Example 5-7 takes the same bouncing ball algorithm and applies it to changing color.

Example 5-7: "Bouncing" color

```
float c1 = 0;
float c2 = 255;

float c1dir = 0.1;
float c2dir = -0.1;

void setup() {
  size(200,200);
}

void draw() {
  noStroke();

  // Draw rectangle on left
  fill(c1,0,c2);
  rect(0,0,100,200);

  // Draw rectangle on right
  fill(c2,0,c1);
  rect(100,0,100,200);

  // Adjust color values
  c1 = c1 + c1dir;
  c2 = c2 + c2dir;

  // Reverse direction of color change
  if (c1 < 0 || c1 > 255) {
    c1dir *=  -1;
  }

  if (c2 < 0 || c2 > 255) {
    c2dir *=  -1;
  }
}
```

> Two variables for color.

> Start by incrementing c1.
> Start by decrementing c2.

fig. 5.9

> Instead of reaching the edge of a window, these variables reach the "edge" of color: 0 for no color and 255 for full color. When this happens, just like with the bouncing ball, the direction is reversed.

Having the conditional statement in our collection of programming tools allows for more complex motion. For example, consider a rectangle that follows the edges of a window.

One way to solve this problem is to think of the rectangle's motion as having four possible states, numbered 0 through 3. See Figure 5.10.

- State #0: left to right.
- State #1: top to bottom.
- State #2: right to left.
- State #3: bottom to top.

We can use a variable to keep track of the state number and adjust the *x, y* coordinate of the rectangle according to the state. For example: "If the state is 2, *x* equals *x* minus 1."

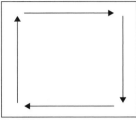

fig. 5.10

Once the rectangle reaches the endpoint for that state, we can change the state variable. "If the state is 2: (a) *x* equals *x* minus 1. (b) if *x* less than zero, the state equals 3."

The following example implements this logic.

Example 5-8: Square following edge, uses a "state" variable

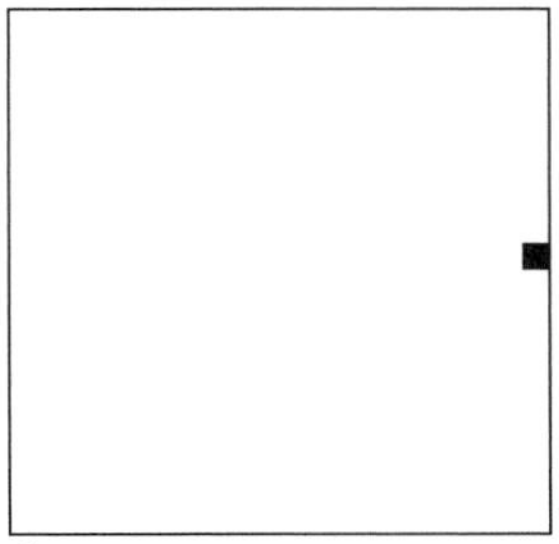

```
int x = 0; // x location of square
int y = 0; // y location of square

int speed = 5; // speed of square

int state = 0;
```

> A variable to keep track of the square's "state." Depending on the value of its state, it will either move right, down, left, or up.

```
void setup() {
  size(200,200);
}
```

fig. 5.11

```
void draw(){
  background(100);

  // Display the square
  noStroke();
  fill(255);
  rect(x,y,10,10);
  if (state == 0) {
    x = x + speed;
    if (x > width-10) {
      x = width-10;
      state = 1;
    }
  } else if (state == 1) {
    y = y + speed;
    if (y > height-10) {
      y = height-10;
      state = 2;
    }
```

> If the state is 0, move to the right.

> If, while the state is 0, it reaches the right side of the window, change the state to 1.
> Repeat this same logic for all states!

```
  } else if (state == 2) {
    x = x - speed;
    if (x < 0) {
      x = 0;
      state = 3;
    }
  } else if (state == 3) {
    y = y - speed;
    if (y < 0) {
      y = 0;
      state = 0;
    }
  }
}
```

5.8 Physics 101

For me, one of the happiest moments of my programming life was the moment I realized I could code gravity. And in fact, armed with variables and conditionals, you are now ready for this moment.

The bouncing ball sketch taught us that an object moves by altering its location according to speed.

location = location + speed

Gravity is a force of attraction between all masses. When you drop a pen, the force of gravity from the earth (which is overwhelmingly larger than the pen) causes the pen to accelerate toward the ground. What we must add to our bouncing ball is the concept of "acceleration" (which is caused by gravity, but could be caused by any number of forces). Acceleration increases (or decreases) speed. In other words, acceleration is the rate of change of speed. And speed is the rate of change of location. So we just need another line of code:

speed = speed + acceleration

And now we have a simple gravity simulation.

Example 5-9: Simple gravity

```
float x = 100; // x location of square
float y = 0;   // y location of square

float speed = 0; // speed of square
float gravity = 0.1;

void setup() {
  size(200,200);

}

void draw() {
  background(255);
```

A new variable, for gravity (i.e., acceleration). We use a relatively small number (0.1) because this acceleration accumulates over time, increasing the speed. Try changing this number to 2.0 and see what happens.

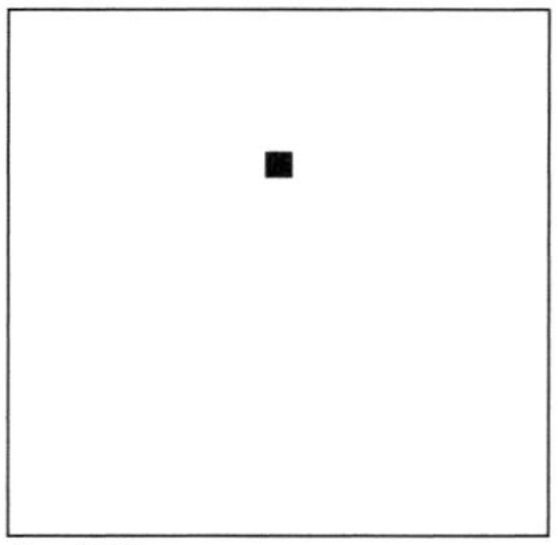

fig. 5.12

```
// Display the square
fill(0);
noStroke();
rectMode(CENTER);
rect(x,y,10, 10);

y = y + speed;
```
> Add speed to location.

```
speed = speed + gravity;
```
> Add gravity to speed.

```
// If square reaches the bottom
// Reverse speed
if (y > height) {
  speed = speed * -0.95;
}
}
```
> Multiplying by −0.95 instead of −1 slows the square down each time it bounces (by decreasing speed). This is known as a "dampening" effect and is a more realistic simulation of the real world (without it, a ball would bounce forever).

Exercise 5-10: Continue with your design and add some of the functionality demonstrated in this chapter. Some options:

- Make parts of your design rollovers that change color when the mouse is over certain areas.
- Move it around the screen. Can you make it bounce off all edges of the window?
- Fade colors in and out.

Here is a simple version with Zoog.

Example 5-10: Zoog and conditionals

```
float x = 100;
float y = 100;
float w = 60;
float h = 60;
float eyeSize = 16;

float xspeed = 3;
float yspeed = 1;
```
> Zoog has variables for speed in the horizontal and vertical direction.

```
void setup() {
  size(200,200);
  smooth();
}

void draw() {
  // Change the location of Zoog by speed
  x = x + xspeed;
  y = y + yspeed;
```

```
if ((x > width) || (x < 0)) {
  xspeed = xspeed * -1;
}
```

> An **IF** statements with a logical **OR** determines if Zoog has reached either the right or left edges of the screen. When this is true, we multiply the speed by −1, reversing Zoog's direction!

```
if ((y > height) || (y < 0)) {
  yspeed = yspeed * -1;
}
```

> Identical logic is applied to the *y* direction as well.

```
background(0);
ellipseMode(CENTER);
rectMode(CENTER);
noStroke();

// Draw Zoog's body
fill(150);
rect(x,y,w/6,h*2);

// Draw Zoog's head
fill(255);
ellipse(x,y-h/2,w,h);

// Draw Zoog's eyes
fill(0);
ellipse(x-w/3,y-h/2,eyeSize,eyeSize*2);
ellipse(x+w/3,y-h/2,eyeSize,eyeSize*2);

// Draw Zoog's legs
stroke(150);
line(x-w/12,y+h,x-w/4,y+h+10);
line(x+w/12,y+h,x+w/4,y+h+10);
}
```

6 Loops

"Repetition is the reality and the seriousness of life."
—*Soren Kierkegaard*

"What's the key to comedy? Repetition. What's the key to comedy? Repetition."
—*Anonymous*

In this chapter:
- The concept of iteration.
- Two types of loops: "while," and "for." When do we use them?
- Iteration in the context of computer graphics.

6.1 What is iteration? I mean, what is iteration? Seriously, what is iteration?

Iteration is the generative process of repeating a set of rules or steps over and over again. It is a fundamental concept in computer programming and we will soon come to discover that it makes our lives as coders quite delightful. Let's begin.

For the moment, think about legs. Lots and lots of legs on our little Zoog. If we had only read Chapter 1 of this book, we would probably write some code as in Example 6-1.

Example 6-1: Many lines

```
size(200,200);
background(255);

// Legs
stroke(0);
line(50,60,50,80);
line(60,60,60,80);
line(70,60,70,80);
line(80,60,80,80);
line(90,60,90,80);
line(100,60,100,80);
line(110,60,110,80);
line(120,60,120,80);
line(130,60,130,80);
line(140,60,140,80);
line(150,60,150,80);
```

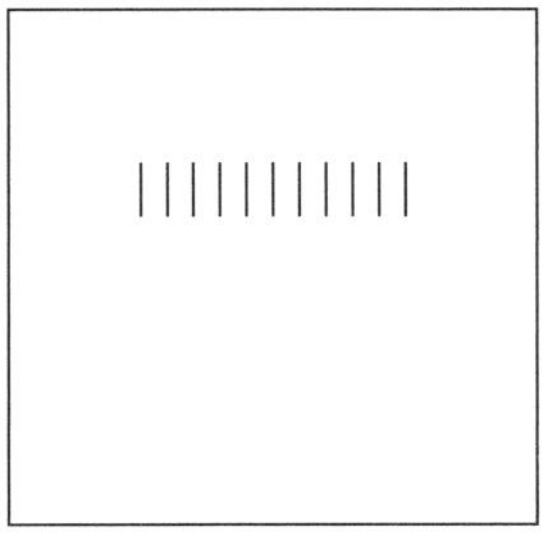

fig. 6.1

In the above example, legs are drawn from $x = 50$ pixels all the way to $x = 150$ pixels, with one leg every 10 pixels. Sure, the code accomplishes this, however, having learned variables in Chapter 4, we can make some substantial improvements and eliminate the hard-coded values.

First, we set up variables for each parameter of our system: the legs' x, y locations, length, and the spacing between the legs. Note that for each leg drawn, only the x value changes. All other variables stay the same (but they could change if we wanted them to!).

Example 6-2: Many lines with variables

```
size(200,200);
background(0);

// Legs
stroke(255);

int y = 80;          // Vertical location of each line
int x = 50;          // Initial horizontal location for first line
int spacing = 10;    // How far apart is each line
int len = 20;        // Length of each line

line(x,y,x,y+len);        Draw the first leg.


x = x + spacing;
line(x,y,x,y+len);        Add spacing so the next leg
                          appears 10 pixels to the right.

x = x + spacing;
line(x,y,x,y+len);

x = x + spacing;
line(x,y,x,y+len);        Continue this process for
                          each leg, repeating it over
                          and over.
x = x + spacing;
line(x,y,x,y+len);

x = x + spacing;
line(x,y,x,y+len);

x = x + spacing;
line(x,y,x,y+len);

x = x + spacing;
line(x,y,x,y+len);

x = x + spacing;
line(x,y,x,y+len);

x = x + spacing;
line(x,y,x,y+len);

x = x + spacing;
line(x,y,x,y+len);
```

Not too bad, I suppose. Strangely enough, although this is technically more efficient (we could adjust the spacing variable, for example, by changing only one line of code), we have taken a step backward, having produced twice as much code! And what if we wanted to draw 100 legs? For every leg, we need two lines of code. That's 200 lines of code for 100 legs! To avoid this dire, carpal-tunnel inducing problem, we want to be able to say something like:

Draw one line one hundred times.

Aha, only one line of code!

Obviously, we are not the first programmers to reach this dilemma and it is easily solved with the very commonly used *control structure*—the *loop*. A loop structure is similar in syntax to a conditional (see Chapter 5). However, instead of asking a yes or no question to determine whether a block of code should be executed one time, our code will ask a yes or no question to determine *how many times* the block of code should be *repeated*. This is known as iteration.

6.2 "WHILE" Loop, the Only Loop You Really Need

There are three types of loops, the *while* loop, the *do-while* loop, and the *for* loop. To get started, we are going to focus on the *while* loop for a little while (sorry, couldn't resist). For one thing, the only loop you really need is *while*. The *for* loop, as we will see, is simply a convenient alternative, a great shorthand for simple counting operations. *Do-while*, however, is rarely used (not one example in this book requires it) and so we will ignore it.

Just as with conditional (*if/else*) structures, a *while* loop employs a boolean test condition. If the test evaluates to true, the instructions enclosed in curly brackets are executed; if it is false, we continue on to the next line of code. The difference here is that the instructions inside the *while* block continue to be executed over and over again until the test condition becomes false. See Figure 6.2.

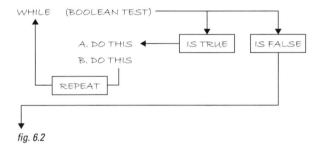

fig. 6.2

Let's take the code from the legs problem. Assuming the following variables...

```
int y = 80;              // Vertical location of each line
int x = 50;              // Initial horizontal location for first line
int spacing = 10;        // How far apart is each line
int len = 20;            // Length of each line
```

... we had to manually repeat the following code:

```
stroke(255);
line(x,y,x,y+len);       // Draw the first leg

x = x + spacing;         // Add "spacing" to x
line(x,y,x,y+len);       // The next leg is 10 pixels to the right

x = x + spacing;         // Add "spacing" to x
line(x,y,x,y+len);       // The next leg is 10 pixels to the right

x = x + spacing;         // Add ''spacing" to x
line(x,y,x,y+len);       // The next leg is 10 pixels to the right

// etc. etc. repeating with new legs
```

Now, with the knowledge of the existence of *while* loops, we can rewrite the code as in Example 6-3, adding a variable that tells us when to stop looping, that is, at what pixel the legs stop.

Example 6-3: While loop

```
int endLegs = 150;

stroke(0);
while (x <= endLegs) {
  line(x,y,x,y+len);
  x = x + spacing;
}
```

> A variable to mark where the legs end.

> Draw each leg inside a *while* loop.

fig. 6.3

Instead of writing "*line(x,y,x,y+len);*" many times as we did at first, we now write it only *once inside of the while loop*, saying "as long as *x* is less than 150, draw a line at *x*, all the while incrementing *x*." And so what took 21 lines of code before, now only takes four!

In addition, we can change the spacing variable to generate more legs. The results are shown in Figure 6.4.

```
int spacing = 4;



while (x <= endLegs) {
  line(x,y,x,y+len); // Draw EACH leg
  x = x + spacing;
}
```

> A smaller spacing value results in legs closer together.

fig. 6.4

Let's look at one more example, this time using rectangles instead of lines, as shown in Figure 6.5, and ask three key questions.

fig. 6.5

1. What is the initial condition for your loop? Here, since the first rectangle is at *y* location 10, we want to start our loop with *y* = 10.

   ```
   int y = 10;
   ```

2. When should your loop stop? Since we want to display rectangles all the way to the bottom of the window, the loop should stop when *y* is greater than height. In other words, we want the loop to keep going *as long as y is less than height.*

```
while (y < 100) {
  // Loop!
}
```

3. What is your loop operation? In this case, each time through the loop, we want to draw a new rectangle below the previous one. We can accomplish this by calling the **rect()** function and incrementing y by 20.

```
rect(100,y,100,10);
y = y + 20;
```

Putting it all together:

```
int y = 10;
```
> Initial condition.

```
while (y < height) {
  rect(100,y,100,10);
```
> The loop continues while the boolean expression is true. Therefore, the loop stops when the boolean expression is false.

```
  y = y + 20;
}
```
> We increment y each time through the loop, drawing rectangle after rectangle until y is no longer less than height.

 Exercise 6-1: Fill in the blanks in the code to recreate the following screenshots.

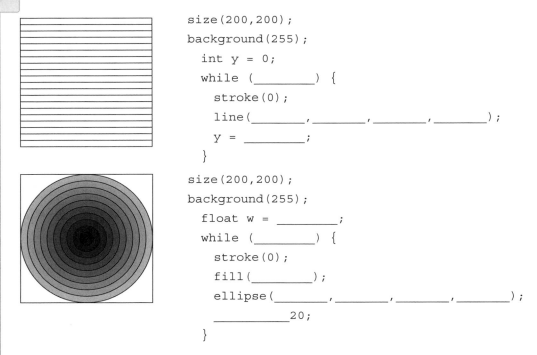

```
size(200,200);
background(255);
  int y = 0;
  while (_____) {
    stroke(0);
    line(_____,_____,_____,_____);
    y = _____;
  }
```

```
size(200,200);
background(255);
  float w = _____;
  while (_____) {
    stroke(0);
    fill(_____);
    ellipse(_____,_____,_____,_____);
    _____20;
  }
```

6.3 "Exit" Conditions

Loops, as you are probably starting to realize, are quite handy. Nevertheless, there is a dark, seedy underbelly in the world of loops, where nasty things known as *infinite loops* live. See Figure 6.6.

fig. 6.6

Examining the "legs" in Example 6-3, we can see that as soon as *x* is greater than 150, the loop stops. And this always happens because *x* increments by "spacing", which is always a positive number. This is not an accident; whenever we embark on programming with a loop structure, we must make sure that the exit condition for the loop will eventually be met!

Processing will not give you an error should your exit condition never occur. The result is Sisyphean, as your loop rolls the boulder up the hill over and over and over again to infinity.

Example 6-4: Infinite loop. Don't do this!

```
int x = 0;
while (x < 10){
  println(x);
  x = x - 1;
}
```

> Decrementing *x* results in an infinite loop here because the value of *x* will never be 10 or greater. Be careful!

For kicks, try running the above code (make sure you have saved all your work and are not running some other mission-critical software on your computer). You will quickly see that *Processing* hangs. The only way out of this predicament is probably to force-quit *Processing*. Infinite loops are not often as obvious as in Example 6-4. Here is another flawed program that will *sometimes* result in an infinite loop crash.

Example 6-5: Another infinite loop. Don't do this!

```
int y = 80;              // Vertical location of each line
int x = 0;               // Horizontal location of first line
int spacing = 10;        // How far apart is each line
int len = 20;            // Length of each line
int endLegs = 150;       // Where should the lines stop?

void setup() {
  size(200,200);
}

void draw() {
  background(0);
  stroke(255);

  x = 0;
  spacing = mouseX/2;
}
```

> The spacing variable, which sets the distance in between each line, is assigned a value equal to *mouseX* divided by two.

```
while (x <= endLegs) {
  line(x,y,x,y+len);

  x = x + spacing;
}
}
```

> Exit Condition — when *x* is greater than ***endlegs.***

> Incrementation of *x*. *x* always increases by the value of spacing. What is the range of possible value for spacing?

Will an infinite loop occur? We know we will be stuck looping forever if *x* never is greater than 150. And since *x* increments by spacing, if spacing is zero (or a negative number) *x* will always remain the same value (or go down in value.)

Recalling the ***constrain()*** function described in Chapter 4, we can guarantee no infinite loop by constraining the value of spacing to a positive range of numbers:

```
int spacing = constrain(mouseX/2, 1, 100);
```

> Using ***constrain()*** to ensure the exit condition is met.

Since spacing is directly linked with the necessary exit condition, we enforce a specific range of values to make sure no infinite loop is ever reached. In other words, in pseudocode we are saying: *"Draw a series of lines spaced out by N pixels where N can never be less than 1!"*

This is also a useful example because it reveals an interesting fact about ***mouseX***. You might be tempted to try putting ***mouseX*** directly in the incrementation expression as follows:

```
while (x <= endLegs) {
  line(x,y,x,y+len);
  x = x + mouseX / 2;
}
```

> Placing ***mouseX*** inside the loop is not a solution to the infinite loop problem.

Wouldn't this solve the problem, since even if the loop gets stuck as soon as the user moves the mouse to a horizontal location greater than zero, the exit condition would be met? It is a nice thought, but one that is sadly quite flawed. ***mouseX*** and ***mouseY*** are updated with new values at the beginning of each cycle through ***draw()***. So even if the user moves the mouse to *X* location 50 from location 0, ***mouseX*** will never know this new value because it will be stuck in its infinite loop and not able to get to the next cycle through ***draw()***.

6.4 "FOR" Loop

A certain style of ***while*** loop where one value is incremented repeatedly (demonstrated in Section 6.2) is particularly common. This will become even more evident once we look at arrays in Chapter 9. The *for* loop is a nifty shortcut for commonly occurring ***while*** loops. Before we get into the details, let's talk through some common loops you might write in *Processing* and how they are written as a *for* loop.

Start at 0 and count up to 9.	`for (int i = 0; i < 10; i = i + 1)`
Start at 0 and count up to 100 by 10.	`for (int i = 0; i < 101; i = i + 10)`
Start at 100 and count down to 0 by 5.	`for (int i = 100; i >= 0; i = i - 5)`

Looking at the above examples, we can see that a *for* loop consists of three parts:

- **Initialization**—Here, a variable is declared and initialized for use within the body of the loop. This variable is most often used inside the loop as a counter.
- **Boolean Test**—This is exactly the same as the boolean tests found in conditional statements and *while* loops. It can be any expression that evaluates to true or false.
- **Iteration Expression**—The last element is an instruction that you want to happen with each loop cycle. Note that the instruction is executed at the end of each cycle through the loop. (You can have multiple iteration expressions, as well as variable initializations, but for the sake of simplicity we will not worry about this now.)

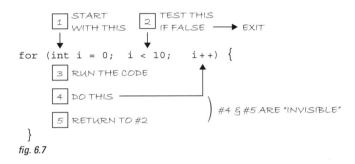

fig. 6.7

In English, the above code means: repeat this code 10 times. Or to put it even more simply: count from zero to nine!

To the machine, it means the following:

- Declare a variable *i*, and set its initial value to 0.
- While *i* is less than 10, repeat this code.
- At the end of each iteration, add one to *i*.

> A *for* loop can have its own variable just for the purpose of counting. A variable not declared at the top of the code is called a *local variable*. We will explain and define it shortly.

Increment/Decrement Operators

The shortcut for adding or subtracting one from a variable is as follows:

x++;   is equivalent to: x = x + 1;   meaning: "increment *x* by 1" or "add 1 to the current value of *x*"

x−−;   is equivalent to: x = x − 1;

We also have:
x += 2;   same as x = x + 2;
x *= 3;   same as x = x*3;
and so on.

The same exact loop can be programmed with the *while* format:

```
int i = 0;
while (i < 10) {
  i++;
  //lines of code to execute here
}
```

> This is the translation of the *for* loop, using a *while* loop.

Rewriting the leg drawing code to use a *for* statement looks like this:

Example 6-6: Legs with a *for* loop

```
int y = 80;                  // Vertical location of each line
int spacing = 10;            // How far apart is each line
int len = 20;                // Length of each line

for (int x = 50; x <= 150; x += spacing) {
  line(x,y,x,y+len);
}
```

> Translation of the legs *while* loop to a *for* loop.

*Exercise 6-2: Rewrite Exercise 6-1 using a **for** loop.*

```
size(200,200);
background(255);

  for (int y =_____;_____;_____) {
    stroke(0);
     line(_____,_____,_____,_____);
  }
```

```
size(200,200);
background(255);
  for (_____;_____;_____-=20) {
    stroke(0);
    fill(_____);
     ellipse(_____,_____,_____,
        _____);
     ellipse(_____,_____,_____,
        _____);
  }
```

Exercise 6-3: Following are some additional examples of loops. Match the appropriate screenshot with the loop structure. Each example assumes the same four lines of initial code.

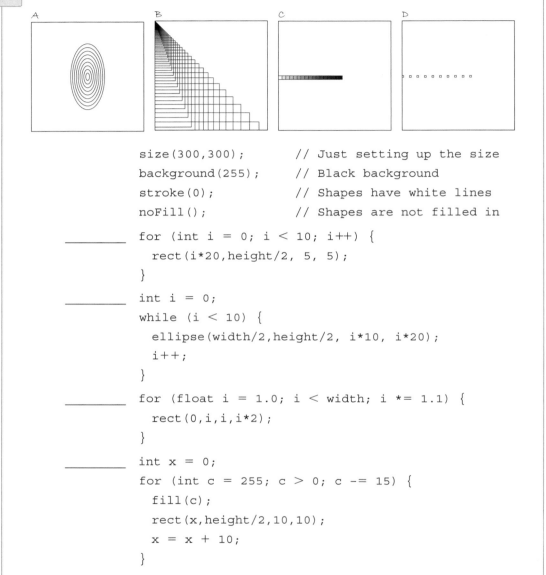

```
size(300,300);        // Just setting up the size
background(255);       // Black background
stroke(0);            // Shapes have white lines
noFill();             // Shapes are not filled in
```

_____
```
for (int i = 0; i < 10; i++) {
  rect(i*20,height/2, 5, 5);
}
```

_____
```
int i = 0;
while (i < 10) {
  ellipse(width/2,height/2, i*10, i*20);
  i++;
}
```

_____
```
for (float i = 1.0; i < width; i *= 1.1) {
  rect(0,i,i,i*2);
}
```

_____
```
int x = 0;
for (int c = 255; c > 0; c -= 15) {
  fill(c);
  rect(x,height/2,10,10);
  x = x + 10;
}
```

6.5 Local vs. Global Variables (AKA "Variable Scope")

Up until this moment, any time that we have used a variable, we have declared it at the top of our program above *setup()*.

```
int x = 0;
void setup() {

}
```
> We have always declared our variables at the top of our code.

This was a nice simplification and allowed us to focus on the fundamentals of declaring, initializing, and using variables. Variables, however, can be declared anywhere within a program and we will now look at what it means to declare a variable somewhere other than the top and how we might go about choosing the right location for declaring a variable.

Imagine, for a moment, that a computer program is running your life. And in this life, variables are pieces of data written on post-its that you need to remember. One post-it might have the address of a restaurant for lunch. You write it down in the morning and throw it away after enjoying a nice turkey burger. But another post-it might contain crucial information (such as a bank account number), and you save it in a safe place for years on end. This is the concept of *scope*. Some variables exist (i.e., are accessible) throughout the entire course of a program's life—*global variables*—and some live temporarily, only for the brief moment when their value is required for an instruction or calculation—*local variables*.

In *Processing*, global variables are declared at the top of the program, outside of both ***setup()*** and ***draw()***. These variables can be used in any line of code anywhere in the program. This is the easiest way to use a variable since you do not have to remember when you can and cannot use that variable. You can *always* use that variable (and this is why we started with global variables only).

Local variables are variables declared within a block of code. So far, we have seen many different examples of blocks of code: ***setup()***, ***draw()***, ***mousePressed()***, and ***keyPressed()***, *if* statements, and *while* and *for* loops.

A local variable declared within a block of code is only available for use inside that specific block of code where it was declared. If you try to access a local variable outside of the block where it was declared, you will get this error:

> "*No accessible field named* "variableName" *was found*"

This is the same exact error you would get if you did not bother to declare the variable "variableName" at all. *Processing* does not know what it is because no variable with that name exists within the block of code you happen to be in.

Here is an example where a local variable is used inside of ***draw()*** for the purpose of executing a *while* loop.

Example 6-7: Local variable

```
void setup() {
  size(200,200);
}
void draw() {
  background(0);
```

> *X* is not available! It is local to the ***draw()*** block of code.

```
  int x = 0;
  while (x < width) {
    stroke(255);
    line(x,0,x,height);
    x += 5;
  }
}
```

> *X* is available! Since it is declared within the ***draw()*** block of code, it is available here. Notice, however, that it is not available inside ***draw()*** above where it is declared. Also, it is available inside the ***while*** block of code because *while* is inside of ***draw ()***.

```
void mousePressed() {
  println("The mouse was pressed!");
}
```

> *X* is not available! It is local to the ***draw()*** block of code.

Why bother? Couldn't we just have declared *x* as a global variable? While this is true, since we are only using *x* within the ***draw()*** function, it is wasteful to have it as a global variable. It is more efficient and ultimately less confusing when programming to declare variables only within the scope of where they are necessary. Certainly, many variables *need* to be global, but this is not the case here.

A *for* loop offers up a spot for a local variable within the "initialization" part:

```
for (int i = 0; i < 100; i+=10) {     i is only available inside the for loop.
  stroke(255);
  fill(i);
  rect(i,0,10,height);
}
```

It is not required to use a local variable in the *for* loop, however, it is usually convenient to do so.

It is theoretically possible to declare a local variable with the same name as a global variable. In this case, the program will use the local variable within the current scope and the global variable outside of that scope. As a general rule, it is better to never declare multiple variables with the same name in order to avoid this type of confusion.

Exercise 6–4: Predict the results of the following two programs. Test your theory by running them.

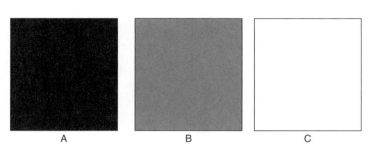

A   B   C

```
//SKETCH #1: Global          //SKETCH #2: Local
"count"                       "count"
int count = 0;               void setup() {
                               size(200,200);
                             }
void setup() {
  size(200,200);             void draw() {
}                              int count = 0;
                               count = count = 1;
void draw() {                  background(count);
  count = count + 1;         }
  background(count);
}
```

_____   _____

6.6 Loop Inside the Main Loop

The distinction between local and global variables moves us one step further toward successfully integrating a loop structure into Zoog. Before we finish this chapter, I want to take a look at one of the most common points of confusion that comes with writing your first loop in the context of a "dynamic" *Processing* sketch.

Consider the following loop (which happens to be the answer to Exercise 6-2). The outcome of the loop is shown in Figure 6.8.

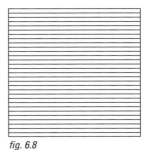

```
for (int y = 0; y < height; y+=10) {
  stroke(0);
  line(0,y,width,y);
}
```

fig. 6.8

Let's say we want to take the above loop and display each line one at a time so that we see the lines appear animated from top to bottom. Our first thought might be to take the above loop and bring it into a dynamic *Processing* sketch with **setup()** and **draw()**.

```
void setup() {
  size(200,200);
}

void draw() {
  background(255);
  for (int y = 0; y < height; y+=10) {
    stroke(0);
    line(0,y,width,y);
  }
}
```

If we read the code, it seems to make sense that we would see each line appear one at a time. "Set up a window of size 200 by 200 pixels. Draw a black background. Draw a line at *y* equals 0. Draw a line at *y* equals 10. Draw a line at *y* equals 20."

Referring back to Chapter 2, however, we recall that *Processing* does not actually update the display window until the end of **draw()** is reached. This is crucial to remember when using **while** and **for** loops. These loops serve the purpose of repeating something in the context of *one cycle* through **draw()**. They are a loop inside of the sketch's main loop, **draw()**.

Displaying the lines one at a time is something we can do with a global variable in combination with the very looping nature of **draw()** itself

Example 6-8: Lines one at a time

```
int y = 0;                    No for loop here. Instead, a global variable.

void setup() {
  size(200,200);
  background(0);
  frameRate(5);               Slowing down the frame rate so we can
}                             easily see the effect.
```

```
void draw() {
  // Draw a line
  stroke(255);
  line(0,y,width,y);
  // Increment y
  y += 10;
}
```

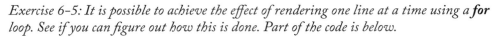

Only one line is drawn each time through **draw( )**.

The logic of this sketch is identical to Example 4-3, our first motion sketch with variables. Instead of moving a circle across the window horizontally, we are moving a line vertically (but not clearing the background for each frame).

*Exercise 6-5: It is possible to achieve the effect of rendering one line at a time using a **for** loop. See if you can figure out how this is done. Part of the code is below.*

```
int endY;

void setup() {
  size(200,200);
  frameRate(5);
  endY = _____;
}

void draw() {
  background(0);
  for (int y = _____; _____; _____) {
    stroke(255);
    line(0,y,width,y);
  }
  _____;
}
```

Using a loop inside **draw()** also opens up the possibility of interactivity. Example 6-9 displays a series of rectangles (from left to right), each one colored with a brightness according to its distance from the mouse.

Example 6-9: Simple while loop with interactivity

```
void setup() {
  size(255,255);
  background(0);
}

void draw() {
  background(0);
  // Start with i as 0
  int i = 0;
  // While i is less than the width of the window
  while (i < width) {
    noStroke();
```

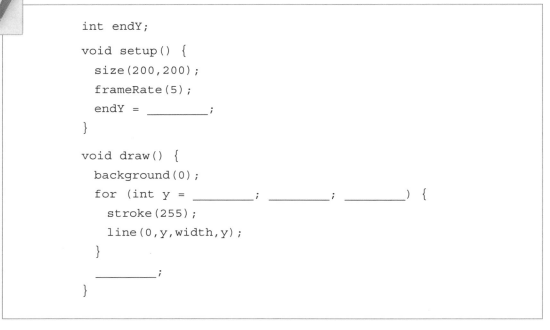

fig. 6.9

```
        float distance = abs(mouseX - i);
```

> The distance between the current rectangle and the mouse is equal to the absolute value of the difference between *i* and **mouseX**.

```
        fill(distance);
        rect(i,0,10,height);
```

> That distance is used to fill the color of a rectangle at horizontal location *i*.

```
        // Increase i by 10
        i += 10;
    }
}
```

*Exercise 6-6: Rewrite Example 6-9 using a **for** loop.*

6.7 Zoog grows arms.

We last left Zoog bouncing back and forth in our *Processing* window. This new version of Zoog comes with one small change. Example 6-10 uses a *for* loop to add a series of lines to Zoog's body, resembling arms.

Example 6-10: Zoog with arms

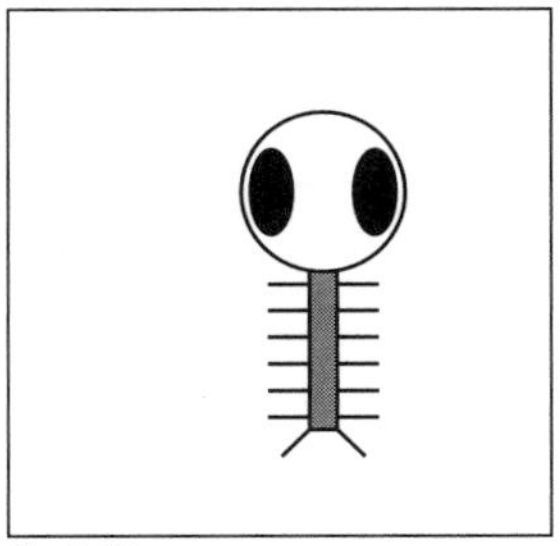

```
int x = 100;
int y = 100;
int w = 60;
int h = 60;
int eyeSize = 16;
int speed = 1;

void setup() {

  size(200,200);
  smooth();
}

void draw(){

  // Change the x location of Zoog by speed
  x = x + speed;

  // If we've reached an edge, reverse speed (i.e. multiply it by -1)
  //(Note if speed is a + number, square moves to the right,- to the left)
  if ((x > width)||(x < 0)) {
    speed = speed * -1;
  }

  background(255); // Draw a white background

  // Set ellipses and rects to CENTER mode
  ellipseMode(CENTER);
  rectMode(CENTER);

  // Draw Zoog's arms with a for loop
  for (int i = y+5; i < y + h; i+=10) {
    stroke(0);
    line(x-w/3,i,x+w/3,i);
  }
```

fig. 6.10

> Arms are incorporated into Zoog's design with a *for* loop drawing a series if lines.

```
// Draw Zoog's body
stroke(0);
fill(175);
rect(x,y,w/6,h*2);

// Draw Zoog's head
fill(255);
ellipse(x,y-h/2,w,h);

// Draw Zoog's eyes
fill(0);
ellipse(x-w/3,y-h/2,eyeSize,eyeSize*2);
ellipse(x+w/3,y-h/2,eyeSize,eyeSize*2);

// Draw Zoog's legs
stroke(0);
line(x-w/12,y+h,x-w/4,y+h+10);
line(x+w/12,y+h,x+w/4,y+h+10);
}
```

We can also use a loop to draw multiple instances of Zoog by placing the code for Zoog's body inside of a *for* loop. See Example 6–11.

Example 6-11: Multiple Zoogs

```
int w = 60;
int h = 60;
int eyeSize = 16;

void setup() {
  size(400,200);
  smooth();
}

void draw() {
background(255);
ellipseMode(CENTER);
rectMode(CENTER);

int y = height/2;

// Multiple versions of Zoog
for (int x = 80; x < width; x+= 80) {
  // Draw Zoog's body
  stroke(0);
  fill(175);
  rect(x,y,w/6,h*2);

  // Draw Zoog's head
  fill(255);
  ellipse(x,y-h/2,w,h);

  // Draw Zoog's eyes
  fill(0);
  ellipse(x-w/3,y-h/2,eyeSize,eyeSize*2);
  ellipse(x+w/3,y-h/2,eyeSize,eyeSize*2);
```

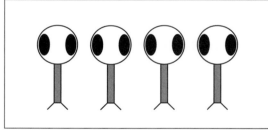

fig. 6.11

> The variable x is now included in a ***for*** loop, in order to iterate and display multiple Zoogs!

```
// Draw Zoog's legs
stroke(0);
line(x-w/12,y+h,x-w/4,y+h+10);
line(x+w/12,y+h,x+w/4,y+h+10); }
}
```

 *Exercise 6-7: Add something to your design using a **for** or **while** loop. Is there anything you already have which could be made more efficient with a loop?*

 *Exercise 6-8: Create a grid of squares (each colored randomly) using a **for** loop. (Hint: You will need two **for** loops!) Recode the same pattern using a "while" loop instead of "for."*

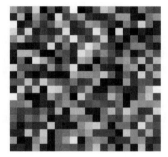

Lesson Two Project

Step 1. Take your Lesson One design and rewrite it with variables instead of hard-coded values. Consider using a *for* loop in the creation of your design.

Step 2. Write a series of assignment operations that alter the values of those variables and make the design dynamic. You might also use system variables, such as *width*, *height*, *mouseX*, and *mouseY*.

Step 3. Using conditional statements, alter the behavior of your design based on certain conditions. What happens if it touches the edge of the screen, or if it grows to a certain size? What happens if you move the mouse over elements in your design?

Use the space provided below to sketch designs, notes, and pseudocode for your project.

Lesson Three

Organization

7 Functions

8 Objects

7 Functions

"When it's all mixed up, better break it down."
—Tears for Fears

In this chapter:
– Modularity.
– Declaring and defining a function.
– Calling a function.
– Parameter passing.
– Returning a value.
– Reusability.

7.1 Break It Down

The examples provided in Chapters 1 through 6 are short. We probably have not looked at a sketch with more than 100 lines of code. These programs are the equivalent of writing the opening paragraph of this chapter, as opposed to the whole chapter itself.

Processing is great because we can make interesting visual sketches with small amounts of code. But as we move forward to looking at more complex projects, such as network applications or image processing programs, we will start to have hundreds of lines of code. We will be writing essays, not paragraphs. And these large amounts of code can prove to be unwieldy inside of our two main blocks—*setup()* and *draw().*

Functions are a means of taking the parts of our program and separating them out into modular pieces, making our code easier to read, as well as to revise. Let's consider the video game Space Invaders. Our steps for *draw()* might look something like:

- Erase background.
- Draw spaceship.
- Draw enemies.
- Move spaceship according to user keyboard interaction.
- Move enemies.

What's in a name?

Functions are often called other things, such as "Procedures" or "Methods" or "Subroutines." In some programming languages, there is a distinction between a procedure (performs a task) and a function (calculates a value). In this chapter, I am choosing to use the term function for simplicity's sake. Nevertheless, the technical term in the Java programming language is "method" (related to Java's object-oriented design) and once we get into objects in Chapter 8, we will use the term "method" to describe functions inside of objects.

Before this chapter on functions, we would have translated the above pseudocode into actual code, and placed it inside **draw()**. Functions, however, will let us approach the problem as follows:

```
void draw() {
  background(0);
  drawSpaceShip();        We are calling functions we made up inside of draw()!
  drawEnemies();
  moveShip();
  moveEnemies();
}
```

The above demonstrates how functions will make our lives easier with clear and easy to manage code. Nevertheless, we are missing an important piece: the function *definitions*. Calling a function is old hat. We do this all the time when we write **line()**, **rect()**, **fill()**, and so on. Defining a new "made-up" function is going to be hard work.

Before we launch into the details, let's reflect on why writing our own functions is so important:

- **Modularity**—Functions break down a larger program into smaller parts, making code more manageable and readable. Once we have figured out how to draw a spaceship, for example, we can take that chunk of spaceship drawing code, store it away in a function, and call upon that function whenever necessary (without having to worry about the details of the operation itself).
- **Reusability**—Functions allow us to reuse code without having to retype it. What if we want to make a two player Space Invaders game with two spaceships? We can *reuse* the **drawSpaceShip()** function by calling it multiple times without having to repeat code over and over.

In this chapter, we will look at some of our previous programs, written without functions, and demonstrate the power of modularity and reusability by incorporating functions. In addition, we will further emphasize the distinctions between local and global variables, as functions are independent blocks of code that will require the use of local variables. Finally, we will continue to follow Zoog's story with functions.

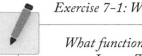

Exercise 7-1: Write your answers below.

What functions might you write for your Lesson Two Project?	*What functions might you write in order to program the game Pong?*

7.2 "User Defined" Functions

In *Processing*, we have been using functions all along. When we say "line(0,0,200,200);" we are calling the function *line()*, a built-in function of the *Processing* environment. The ability to draw a line by calling the function *line()* does not magically exist. Someone, somewhere defined (i.e., wrote the underlying code for) how *Processing* should display a line. One of *Processing*'s strengths is its library of available functions, which we have started to explore throughout the first six chapters of this book. Now it is time to move beyond the built-in functions of *Processing* and write our own *user-defined (AKA "made-up") functions*.

7.3 Defining a Function

A function definition (sometimes referred to as a "declaration") has three parts:

- Return type.
- Function name.
- Arguments.

It looks like this:

returnType   functionName (arguments) {
   // Code body of function
}

Deja vu?

Remember when in Chapter 3 we introduced the functions *setup()* and *draw()*? Notice that they follow the same format we are learning now.

setup() and *draw()* are functions we define and are called automatically by *Processing* in order to run the sketch. All other functions we write have to be called by us.

For now, let's focus solely on the functionName and code body, ignoring "returnType" and "arguments".

Here is a simple example:

Example 7-1: Defining a function

```
void drawBlackCircle() {
  fill(0);
  ellipse(50,50,20,20);
}
```

This is a simple function that performs one basic task: drawing an ellipse colored black at coordinate (50,50). Its name—***drawBlackCircle()***—is arbitrary (we made it up) and its code body consists of two instructions (we can have as much or as little code as we choose). It is also important to remind ourselves that this is only the definition of the function. The code will never happen unless the function is actually called from a part of the program that is being executed. This is accomplished by referencing the function name, that is, calling a function, as shown in Example 7-2.

Example 7-2: Calling a function

```
void draw() {
  background(255);
  drawBlackCircle();
}
```

*Exercise 7-2: Write a function that displays Zoog (or your own design). Call that function from within **draw()**.*

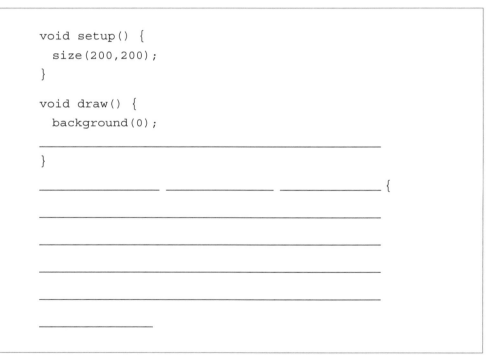

```
void setup() {
  size(200,200);
}

void draw() {
  background(0);

  _____

}

_____ _____ _____ {

  _____

  _____

  _____

  _____

  _____
```

7.4 Simple Modularity

Let's examine the bouncing ball example from Chapter 5 and rewrite it using functions, illustrating one technique for breaking a program down into modular parts. Example 5-6 is reprinted here for your convenience.

Example 5-6: Bouncing ball

```
// Declare global variables
int x = 0;
int speed = 1;

void setup() {
  size(200,200);
  smooth();
}

void draw() {
  background(255);
```

```
// Change x by speed
x = x + speed;
```
◁ Move the ball!

```
// If we've reached an edge, reverse speed
if ((x > width) || (x < 0)) {
speed = speed * -1;
}
```
◁ Bounce the ball!

```
// Display circle at x location
stroke(0);
fill(175);
ellipse(x,100,32,32);
```
◁ Display the ball!

```
}
```

Once we have determined how we want to divide the code up into functions, we can take the pieces out of *draw()* and insert them into function definitions, calling those functions inside *draw()*. Functions typically are written below *draw()*.

Example 7-3: Bouncing ball with functions

```
// Declare all global variables (stays the same)
int x = 0;
int speed = 1;

// Setup does not change
void setup() {
  size(200,200);
  smooth();
}

void draw() {
  background(255);
  move();
  bounce();
  display();
}
```

Instead of writing out all the code about the ball is *draw()*, we simply call three functions. How do we know the names of these functions? We made them up!

```
// A function to move the ball
void move() {
  // Change the x location by speed
x = x + speed;
}


// A function to bounce the ball
void bounce() {
  // If we've reached an edge, reverse speed
  if ((x > width) || (x < 0)) {
    speed = speed * -1;
  }
}


// A function to display the ball
void display() {
  stroke(0);
  fill(175);
  ellipse(x,100,32,32);
}
```

> Where should functions be placed?

> You can define your functions anywhere in the code outside of *setup()* and *draw()*.

> However, the convention is to place your function definitions below *draw()*.

Note how simple *draw()* has become. The code is reduced to function *calls*; the detail for how variables change and shapes are displayed is left for the function *definitions*. One of the main benefits here is the programmer's sanity. If you wrote this program right before leaving on a two-week vacation in the Caribbean, upon returning with a nice tan, you would be greeted by well-organized, readable code. To change how the ball is rendered, you only need to make edits to the *display()* function, without having to search through long passages of code or worrying about the rest of the program. For example, try replacing *display()* with the following:

```
void display() {
  background(255);
  rectMode(CENTER);
  noFill();
  stroke(0);
  rect(x,y,32,32);
  fill(255);
  rect(x-4,y-4,4,4);
  rect(x+4,y-4,4,4);
  line(x-4,y+4,x+4,y+4);
}
```

> If you want to change the appearance of the shape, the *display()* function can be rewritten leaving all the other features of the sketch intact.

Another benefit of using functions is greater ease in debugging. Suppose, for a moment, that our bouncing ball function was not behaving appropriately. In order to find the problem, we now have the option of turning on and off parts of the program. For example, we might simply run the program with *display()* only, by commenting out *move()* and *bounce()*:

```
void draw() {
  background(0);
  // move();
  // bounce();
  display();
}
```

> Functions can be commented out to determine if they are causing a bug or not.

The function definitions for *move()* and *bounce()* still exist, only now the functions are not being called. By adding function calls one by one and executing the sketch each time, we can more easily deduce the location of the problematic code.

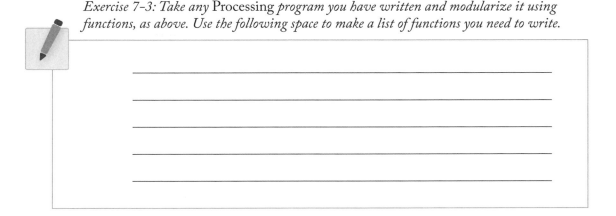

Exercise 7-3: Take any Processing *program you have written and modularize it using functions, as above. Use the following space to make a list of functions you need to write.*

7.5 Arguments

Just a few pages ago we said "Let's ignore **ReturnType** and **Arguments**." We did this in order to ease into functions by sticking with the basics. However, functions possess greater powers than simply breaking a program into parts. One of the keys to unlocking these powers is the concept of *arguments* (AKA "parameters").

Arguments are values that are "passed" into a function. You can think of them as conditions under which the function should operate. Instead of merely saying "Move," a function might say "Move *N* number of steps," where "*N*" is the argument.

When we display an ellipse in *Processing*, we are required to specify details about that ellipse. We can't just say draw an ellipse, we have to say draw an ellipse *at this location* and *with this size*. These are the *ellipse()* function's *arguments* and we encountered this in Chapter 1 when we learned to call functions for the first time.

Let's rewrite *drawBlackCircle()* to include an argument:

```
void drawBlackCircle(int diameter) {
  fill(0);
  ellipse(50,50, diameter, diameter);
}
```
"diameter" is an arguments to the function *drawBlackCircle()*.

An argument is simply a variable declaration inside the parentheses in the function definition. This variable is a *local variable* (Remember our discussion in Chapter 6?) to be used in that function (and only in that function). The white circle will be sized according to the value placed in parentheses.

```
drawBlackCircle(16);  // Draw the circle with a diameter of 16
drawBlackCircle(32);  // Draw the circle with a diameter of 32
```

Looking at the bouncing ball example, we could rewrite the *move()* function to include an argument:

```
void move(int speedFactor) {
  x = x + (speed * speedFactor);
}
```
The argument "speedFactor" affects how fast the circle moves.

In order to move the ball twice as fast:

```
move(2);
```

Or by a factor of 5:

```
move(5);
```

We could also pass another variable or the result of a mathematical expression (such as *mouseX* divided by 10) into the function. For example:

```
move(mouseX/10);
```

Arguments pave the way for more flexible, and therefore reusable, functions. To demonstrate this, we will look at code for drawing a collection of shapes and examine how functions allow us to draw multiple versions of the pattern without retyping the same code over and over.

Leaving Zoog until a bit later, consider the following pattern resembling a car (viewed from above as shown in Figure 7.1):

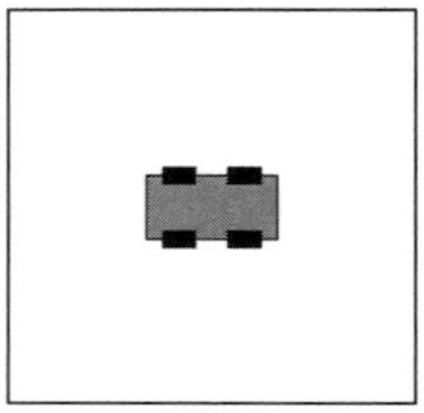

```
size(200,200);
background(255);
int x = 100;            // x location
int y = 100;            // y location
int thesize = 64;       // size
int offset = thesize/4; // position of wheels relative to car

// draw main car body (i.e. a rect)
rectMode(CENTER);
stroke(0);
fill(175);
rect(x,y,thesize,thesize/2);

// draw four wheels relative to center
fill(0);
rect(x-offset,y-offset,offset,offset/2);
rect(x+offset,y-offset,offset,offset/2);
rect(x-offset,y+offset,offset,offset/2);
rect(x+offset,y+offset,offset,offset/2);
```

fig. 7.1

> The car shape is five rectangles, one large rectangle in the center and four wheels on the outside.

To draw a second car, we repeat the above code with different values, as shown in Figure 7.2.

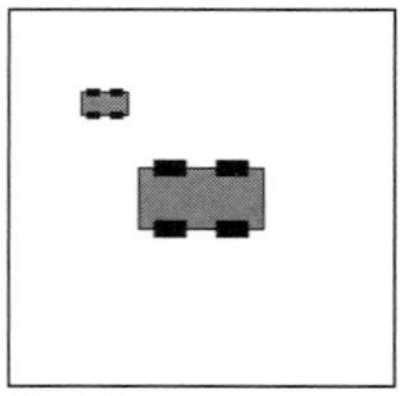

```
x = 50;                 // x location
y = 50;                 // y location
thesize = 24;           // size
offset = thesize/4;     // position of wheels relative to car

// draw main car body (i.e. a rect)
rectMode(CENTER);
stroke(0);
fill(175);
rect(x,y,thesize,thesize/2);

// draw four wheels relative to center
fill(0);
rect(x-offset,y-offset,offset,offset/2);
rect(x+offset,y-offset,offset,offset/2);
rect(x-offset,y+offset,offset,offset/2);
rect(x+offset,y+offset,offset,offset/2);
```

fig. 7.2

> Every single line of code is repeated to draw the second car.

It should be fairly apparent where this is going. After all, we are doing the same thing twice, why bother repeating all that code? To escape this repetition, we can move the code into a function that displays the car according to several arguments (position, size, and color).

```
void drawcar(int x, int y, int thesize, color c) {
    // Using a local variable "offset"
    int offset = thesize/4;
    // Draw main car body
    rectMode(CENTER);
    stroke(200);
    fill(c);
    rect(x,y,thesize,thesize/2);
    // Draw four wheels relative to center
    fill(200);
    rect(x-offset,y-offset,offset,offset/2);
    rect(x+offset,y-offset,offset,offset/2);
    rect(x-offset,y+offset,offset,offset/2);
    rect(x+offset,y+offset,offset,offset/2);
}
```

> Local variables can be declared and used in a function!

> This code is the *function definition*. The function ***drawCar()*** draws a car shape based on four arguments: horizontal location, vertical location, size, and color.

In the ***draw()*** function, we then call the ***drawCar()*** function three times, passing four *parameters* each time. See the output in Figure 7.3.

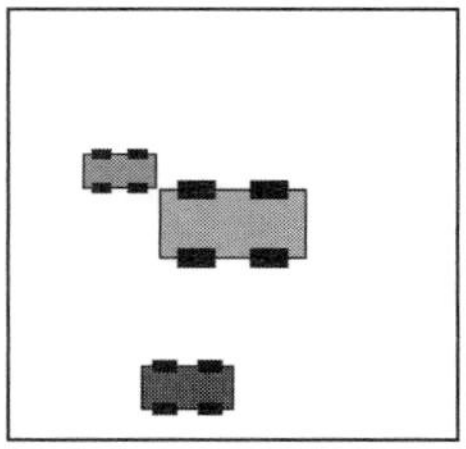

```
void setup() {
    size(200,200);
}

void draw() {
    background(0);
    drawCar(100,100,64,color(200,200,0));
    drawCar(50,75,32,color(0,200,100));
    drawCar(80,175,40,color(200,0,0));
}
```

fig. 7.3

> This code ***calls the function*** three times, with the exact number of parameters in the right order.

Technically speaking, *arguments* are the variables that live inside the parentheses in the function definition, that is, "*void drawCar(int x, int y, int thesize, color c).*" *Parameters* are the values passed into the function when it is called, that is, "*drawCar(80,175,40,color (100,0,100));*". The semantic difference between arguments and parameters is rather trivial and we should not be terribly concerned if we confuse the use of the two words from time to time.

The concept to focus on is this ability to *pass* parameters. We will not be able to advance our programming knowledge unless we are comfortable with this technique.

Let's go with the word *pass*. Imagine a lovely, sunny day and you are playing catch with a friend in the park. You have the ball. You (the main program) call the function (your friend) and pass the ball

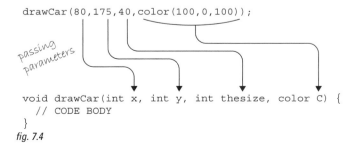

fig. 7.4

(the argument). Your friend (the function) now has the ball (the argument) and can use it however he or she pleases (the code itself inside the function) See Figure 7.4.

Important Things to Remember about Passing Parameters

- You must pass the same number of parameters as defined in the function.
- When a parameter is passed, it must be of the same *type* as declared within the arguments in the function definition. An integer must be passed into an integer, a floating point into a floating point, and so on.
- The value you pass as a parameter to a function can be a literal value (20, 5, 4.3, etc.), a variable (*x*, *y*, etc.), or the result of an expression (8 + 3, 4 * *x*/2, random(0,10), etc.)
- Arguments act as local variables to a function and are only accessible within that function.

Exercise 7–4: The following function takes three numbers, adds them together, and prints the sum to the message window.

```
void sum(int a, int b, int c) {
  int total = a + b + c;
  println(total);
}
```

Looking at the function definition above, write the code that calls the function.

_____

Exercise 7-5: OK, here is the opposite problem. Here is a line of code that assumes a function that takes two numbers, multiplies them together, and prints the result to a message window. Write the function definition that goes with this function call.

```
multiply(5.2,9.0);
```

_____

_____

_____

_____

*Exercise 7-6: Here is the bouncing ball from Example 5-6 combined with the **drawCar()** function. Fill in the blanks so that you now have a bouncing car with parameter passing! (Note that the global variables are now named globalX and globalY to avoid confusion with the local variables x and y in **drawCar()**).*

```
int globalX = 0;
int globalY = 100;
int speed = 1;

void setup() {
  size(200,200);
  smooth();
}

void draw() {
  background(0);

  _____

  _____


  _____

}

void move() {
  // Change the x location by speed
  globalX = globalX + speed;
}

void bounce() {
  if ((globalX > width) || (globalX < 0)) {
    speed = speed * -1;
  }
}

void drawCar(int x, int y, int thesize, color c) {
  int offset = thesize / 4;
  rectMode(CENTER);
  stroke(200);
  fill(c);
  rect(x,y,thesize,thesize/2);
  fill(200);
```

```
            rect(x-offset,y-offset,offset,offset/2);
            rect(x+offset,y-offset,offset,offset/2);
            rect(x-offset,y+offset,offset,offset/2);
            rect(x+offset,y+offset,offset,offset/2);
        }
```

7.6 Passing a Copy

There is a slight problem with the "playing catch" analogy. What I really should have said is the following. Before tossing the ball (the argument), you make a copy of it (a second ball), and pass it to the receiver (the function).

Whenever you pass a primitive value (integer, float, char, etc.) to a function, you do not actually pass the value itself, but a copy of that variable. This may seem like a trivial distinction when passing a hard-coded number, but it is not so trivial when passing a variable.

The following code has a function entitled *randomizer()* that receives one argument (a floating point number) and adds a random number between −2 and 2 to it. Here is the pseudocode.

- **num** is the number 10.
- **num** is displayed: **10**
- **A copy of num** is passed into the argument **newnum** in the function *randomizer()*.
- In the function *randomizer()*:
  - a random number is added to **newnum**.
  - **newnum** is displayed: **10.34232**
- **num** is displayed again: **Still 10! A copy was sent into newnum so num has not changed.**

And here is the code:

```
void setup() {
  float num = 10;
  println("The number is: " + num);
  randomizer(num);
  println("The number is: " + num);
}

void randomizer(float newnum) {
  newnum = newnum + random(-2,2);
  println("The new number is: " + newnum);
}
```

Even though the variable **num** was passed into the variable **newnum**, which then quickly changed values, the original value of the variable **num** was not affected because a copy was made.

I like to refer to this process as "pass by copy," however, it is more commonly referred to as "pass by value." This holds true for all primitive data types (the only kinds we know about so far: integer, float, etc.), but will not be the case when we learn about *objects* in the next chapter.

This example also gives us a nice opportunity to review the *flow* of a program when using a function. Notice how the code is executed in the order that the lines are written, but when a function is called, the code leaves its current line, executes the lines inside of the function, and then comes back to where it left off. Here is a description of the above example's flow:

1. Set num equal to 10.
2. Print the value of num.
3. Call the function randomizer.
   a. Set newnum equal to newnum plus a random number.
   b. Print the value of newnum.
4. Print the value of num.

Exercise 7-7: Predict the output of this program by writing out what would appear in the message window.

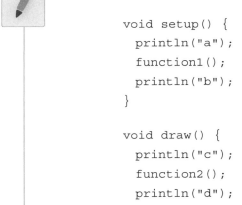

```
void setup() {
  println("a");
  function1();
  println("b");
}

void draw() {
  println("c");
  function2();
  println("d");
  function1();
  noLoop();
}

void function1() {
  println("e");
  println("f");
}

void function2() {
  println("g");
  function1();
  println("h");
}
```

Output:
_____
_____
_____
_____
_____
_____
_____
_____
_____
_____
_____
_____
_____
_____
_____
_____

New! **noLoop()** is a built-in function in *Processing* that stops **draw()** from looping. In this case, we can use it to ensure that **draw()** only executes one time. We could restart it at some other point in the code by calling the function **loop()**.

It is perfectly reasonable to call a function from within a function. In fact, we do this all the time whenever we call any function from inside of **setup()** or **draw()**.

7.7 Return Type

So far we have seen how functions can separate a sketch into smaller parts, as well as incorporate arguments to make it reusable. There is one piece missing still, however, from this discussion and it is the answer to the question you have been wondering all along: "What does *void* mean?"

As a reminder, let's examine the structure of a function definition again:

ReturnType   FunctionName   (Arguments) {
   //code body of function
}

OK, now let's look at one of our functions:

```
// A function to move the ball
void move(int speedFactor) {
  // Change the x location of organism by speed multiplied by speedFactor
  x = x + (speed * speedFactor);
}
```

"move" is the **FunctionName**, "speedFactor" is an **Argument** to the function and "void" is the **ReturnType**. All the functions we have defined so far did not have a return type; this is precisely what "void" means: no return type. But what is a return type and when might we need one?

Let's recall for a moment the *random()* function we examined in Chapter 4. We asked the function for a random number between 0 and some value, and *random()* graciously heeded our request and gave us back a random value within the appropriate range. The *random()* function *returned* a value. What type of a value? A floating point number. In the case of *random()*, therefore, its *return type* is a *float*.

The *return type* is the data type that the function returns. In the case of *random()*, we did not specify the return type, however, the creators of *Processing* did, and it is documented on the reference page for *random()*.

> *Each time the **random()** function is called, it returns an unexpected value within the specified range. If one parameter is passed to the function it will return a float between zero and the value of the parameter. The function call **random(5)** returns values between 0 and 5. If two parameters are passed, it will return a float with a value between the parameters. The function call **random(-5, 10.2)** returns values between -5 and 10.2.*
>
> *—From http://www.processing.org/reference/random.html*

If we want to write our own function that returns a value, we have to specify the type in the function definition. Let's create a trivially simple example:

```
int sum(int a, int b, int c) {
  int total = a + b + c;
  return total;
}
```

> This function, which adds three numbers together, has a return type — *int*.

> A return statement is required! A function with a return type must always return a value of that type.

Instead of writing *void* as the return type as we have in previous examples, we now write *int*. This specifies that the function must return a value of type integer. In order for a function to return a value, a *return statement* is required. A return statement looks like this:

return valueToReturn;

If we did not include a return statement, *Processing* would give us an error:

> *The method "int sum(int a, int b, int c);" must contain a return statement with an expression compatible with type "int."*

As soon as the return statement is executed, the program exits the function and sends the returned value back to the location in the code where the function was called. That value can be used in an assignment operation (to give another variable a value) or in any appropriate expression. See the illustration in Figure 7.5. Here are some examples:

```
int x = sum(5,6,8);
int y = sum(8,9,10) * 2;
int z = sum(x,y,40);
line(100,100,110,sum(x,y,z));
```

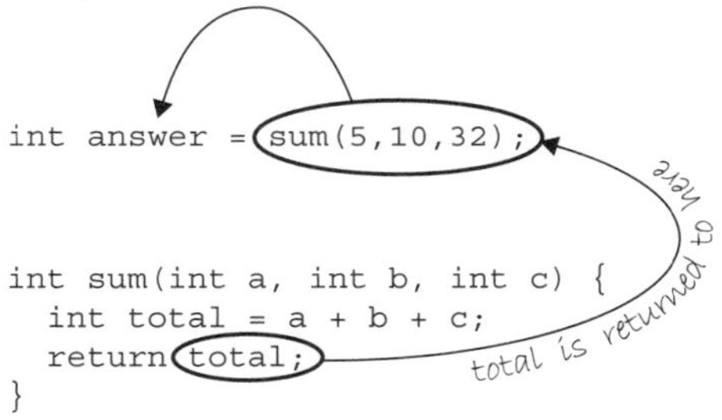

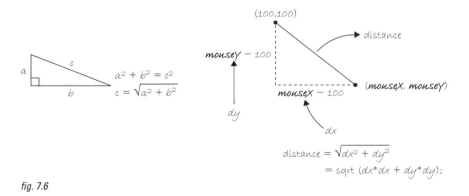

```
int answer = sum(5,10,32);

int sum(int a, int b, int c) {
  int total = a + b + c;
  return total;
}
```
total is returned a value here

fig. 7.5

I hate to bring up playing catch in the park again, but you can think of it as follows. You (*the main program*) throw a ball to your friend (*a function*). After your friend catches that ball, he or she thinks for a moment, puts a number inside the ball (*the return value*) and passes it back to you.

Functions that return values are traditionally used to perform complex calculations that may need to be performed multiple times throughout the course of the program. One example is calculating the distance between two points: (*x1,y1*) and (*x2,y2*). The distance between pixels is a very useful piece of information in interactive applications. *Processing*, in fact, has a built-in distance function that we can use. It is called ***dist()***.

```
float d = dist(100, 100, mouseX, mouseY);
```

> Calculating the distance between (100,100) and *(mouseX,mouseY)*.

This line of code calculates the distance between the mouse location and the point (100,100). For the moment, let's pretend *Processing* did not include this function in its library. Without it, we would have to calculate the distance manually, using the Pythagorean Theorem, as shown in Figure 7.6.

$a^2 + b^2 = c^2$

$c = \sqrt{a^2 + b^2}$

(100,100)

distance

$mouseY - 100$

dy

$mouseX - 100$

(mouseX, mouseY)

dx

$distance = \sqrt{dx^2 + dy^2}$

$= sqrt (dx*dx + dy*dy);$

fig. 7.6

```
float dx = mouseX - 100;
float dy = mouseY - 100;
float d = sqrt(dx*dx + dy*dy);
```

If we wanted to perform this calculation many times over the course of a program, it would be easier to move it into a function that returns the value *d*.

```
float distance(float x1, float y1, float x2, float y2) {
  float dx = x1 - x2;
  float dy = y1 - y2;
  float d = sqrt(dx*dx + dy*dy);
  return d;
}
```

> Our version of *Processing's* **dist()** function.

Note the use of the return type *float*. Again, we do not have to write this function because *Processing* supplies it for us. But since we did, we can now look at an example that makes use of this function.

Example 7-4: Using a function that returns a value, distance

```
void setup() {
  size(200,200);
}


void draw() {
background(0);
stroke(0);

// Top left square
fill(distance(0,0,mouseX,mouseY));
rect(0,0,width/2-1,height/2-1);


// Top right square
fill(distance(width,0,mouseX,mouseY));
rect(width/2,0,width/2-1,height/2-1);


// Bottom left square
fill(distance(0,height,mouseX,mouseY));
rect(0,height/2,width/2-1,height/2-1);


// Bottom right square
fill(distance(width,height,mouseX,mouseY));
rect(width/2,height/2,width/2-1,height/2-1);
}


float distance(float x1, float y1, float x2, float y2)
{
  float dx = x1 - x2;
  float dy = y1 - y2;
  float d = sqrt(dx*dx + dy*dy);
  return d;
}
```

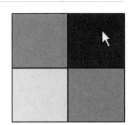

fig. 7.7

> Our distance function is used to calculate a brightness value for each quadrant. We could use the built-in function **dist()** instead, but we are learning how to write our own functions.

Exercise 7-8: Write a function that takes one argument—F for Fahrenheit—and computes the result of the following equation (converting the temperature to Celsius).

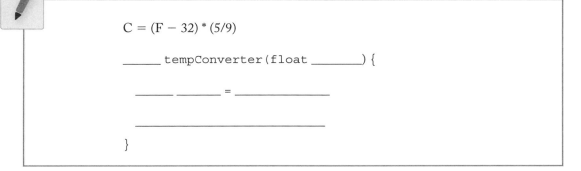

$$C = (F - 32) * (5/9)$$

_____ tempConverter(float _____) {

_____ _____ = _____

_____

}

7.8 Zoog Reorganization

Zoog is now ready for a fairly major overhaul.

- Reorganize Zoog with two functions: *drawZoog()* and *jiggleZoog()*. Just for variety, we are going to have Zoog jiggle (move randomly in both the *x* and *y* directions) instead of bouncing back and forth.
- Incorporate arguments so that Zoog's jiggliness is determined by the *mouseX* position and Zoog's eye color is determined by Zoog's distance to the mouse.

Example 7-5: Zoog with functions

```
float x = 100;
float y = 100;
float w = 60;
float h = 60;
float eyeSize = 16;
void setup() {
  size(200,200);
  smooth();
}

void draw() {
  background(255);   // Draw a black background

  // mouseX position determines speed factor for moveZoog function
  // float factor = constrain(mouseX/10,0,5);
  jiggleZoog(factor);

  // pass in a color to drawZoog
  // function for eye's color
  float d = dist(x,y,mouseX,mouseY);
  color c = color(d);
  drawZoog(c);
}
```

fig. 7.8

The code for changing the variables associated with Zoog and displaying Zoog is moved outside of *draw()* and into functions called here. The functions are given arguments, such as "Jiggle Zoog by the following factor" and "draw Zoog with the following eye color."

```
void jiggleZoog(float speed) {
  // Change the x and y location of Zoog randomly
  x = x + random(-1,1)*speed;
  y = y + random(-1,1)*speed;

  // Constrain Zoog to window
  x = constrain(x,0,width);
  y = constrain(y,0,height);
}

void drawZoog(color eyeColor) {
  // Set ellipses and rects to CENTER mode
  ellipseMode(CENTER);
  rectMode(CENTER);

// Draw Zoog's arms with a for loop
  for (float i = y-h/3; i < y + h/2; i += 10) {
    stroke(0);
    line(x-w/4,i,x+w/4,i);
  }

// Draw Zoog's body
  stroke(0);
  fill(175);
  rect(x,y,w/6,h);

// Draw Zoog's head
  stroke(0);
  fill(255);
  ellipse(x,y-h,w,h);

// Draw Zoog's eyes
  fill(eyeColor);
  ellipse(x-w/3,y-h,eyeSize,eyeSize*2);
  ellipse(x+w/3,y-h,eyeSize,eyeSize*2);

// Draw Zoog's legs
  stroke(0);
  line(x-w/12,y+h/2,x-w/4,y+h/2+10);
  line(x+w/12,y+h/2,x+w/4,y+h/2+10);
}
```

Exercise 7-9: Following is a version of Example 6–11 ("multiple Zoogs") that calls a function to draw Zoog. Write the function definition that completes this sketch. Feel free to redesign Zoog in the process.

```
void setup() {
  size(400,200);  // Set the size of the window
  smooth();       // Enables Anti-Aliasing (smooth edges on
                        shapes)
}
```

```
void draw() {
  background(0);  // Draw a black background
  int y = height/2;
  // Multiple versions of Zoog are displayed by using a for loop
  for (int x = 80; x < width; x += 80) {
    drawZoog(x,100,60,60,16);
  }
}
```

_____

_____

_____

_____

_____

_____

_____

_____

Exercise 7-10: Rewrite your Lesson Two Project using functions. Still 10! A copy was sent into newnum so num has not changed.

8 Objects

"No object is so beautiful that, under certain conditions, it will not look ugly."
—Oscar Wilde

In this chapter:
– Data and functionality, together at last.
– What is an object?
– What is a class?
– Writing your own classes.
– Creating your own objects.
– Processing "tabs."

8.1 I'm down with OOP.

Before we begin examining the details of how object-oriented programming (OOP) works in *Processing*, let's embark on a short conceptual discussion of "objects" themselves. It is important to understand that we are not introducing any new programming fundamentals: objects use everything we have already learned: variables, conditional statements, loops, functions, and so on. What is entirely new, however, is a way of thinking, a way of structuring and organizing everything we have already learned.

Imagine you were not programming in *Processing*, but were instead writing out a program for your day, a list of instructions, if you will. It might start out something like:

- Wake up.
- Drink coffee (or tea).
- Eat breakfast: cereal, blueberries, and soy milk.
- Ride the subway.

What is involved here? Specifically, what *things* are involved? First, although it may not be immediately apparent from how we wrote the above instructions, the main thing is *you*, a human being, a person. You exhibit certain properties. You look a certain way; perhaps you have brown hair, wear glasses, and appear slightly nerdy. You also have the ability to do stuff, such as wake up (presumably you can also sleep), eat, or ride the subway. An object is just like you, a thing that has properties and can do stuff.

So how does this relate to programming? The properties of an object are variables; and the stuff an object can do are functions. Object-oriented programming is the marriage of everything we have learned in Chapters 1 through 7, data and functionality, all rolled into one *thing*.

Let's map out the data and functions for a very simple human object:

Human data

- Height.
- Weight.
- Gender.

- Eye color.
- Hair color.

Human functions

- Sleep.
- Wake up.
- Eat.
- Ride some form of transportation.

Now, before we get too much further, we need to embark on a brief metaphysical digression. The above structure is not a human being itself; it simply describes the idea, or the concept, behind a human being. It describes what it is to be human. To be human is to have height, hair, to sleep, to eat, and so on. This is a crucial distinction for programming objects. This human being template is known as a *class*. A *class* is different from an *object*. You are an object. I am an object. That guy on the subway is an object. Albert Einstein is an object. We are all people, real world *instances* of the idea of a human being.

Think of a cookie cutter. A cookie cutter makes cookies, but it is not a cookie itself. The cookie cutter is the *class*, the cookies are the *objects*.

Exercise 8-1: Consider a car as an object. What data would a car have? What functions would it have?

Car data

_____

_____

_____

_____

_____

Car functions

_____

_____

_____

_____

_____

8.2 Using an Object

Before we look at the actual writing of a *class* itself, let's briefly look at how using objects in our main program (i.e., **setup()** and **draw()**) makes the world a better place.

Returning to the car example from Chapter 7, you may recall that the pseudocode for the sketch looked something like this:

Data (Global Variables):

Car color.
Car *x* location.
Car *y* location.
Car *x* speed.

Setup:

> Initialize car color.
> Initialize car location to starting point.
> Initialize car speed.

Draw:

> Fill background.
> Display car at location with color.
> Increment car's location by speed.

In Chapter 7, we defined global variables at the top of the program, initialized them in ***setup()***, and called *functions* to move and display the car in ***draw()***.

Object-oriented programming allows us to take all of the variables and functions out of the main program and store them inside a car object. A car object will know about its data—*color*, *location*, *speed*. That is part one. Part two of the car object is the stuff it can do, the methods (functions inside an object). The car can *move* and it can be *displayed*.

Using object-oriented design, the pseudocode improves to look something like this:

Data (Global Variables):

> Car object.

Setup:

> Initialize car object.

Draw:

> Fill background.
> Display car object.
> Move car object.

Notice we removed all of the global variables from the first example. Instead of having separate variables for car color, car location, and car speed, we now have only one variable, a ***Car*** variable! And instead of initializing those three variables, we initialize one thing, the ***Car*** object. Where did those variables go? They still exist, only now they live inside of the ***Car*** object (and will be defined in the ***Car*** class, which we will get to in a moment).

Moving beyond pseudocode, the actual body of the sketch might look like:

```
Car myCar;            An object in Processing.

void setup() {
  myCar = new Car();
}

void draw() {
  background(0);
  myCar.move();
  myCar.display();
}
```

We are going to get into the details regarding the previous code in a moment, but before we do so, let's take a look at how the Car *class* itself is written.

8.3 Writing the Cookie Cutter

The simple Car example above demonstrates how the use of object in *Processing* makes for clean, readable code. The hard work goes into writing the object template, that is the *class* itself. When you are first learning about object-oriented programming, it is often a useful exercise to take a program written without objects and, not changing the functionality at all, rewrite it using objects. We will do exactly this with the car example from Chapter 7, recreating exactly the same look and behavior in an object-oriented manner. And at the end of the chapter, we will remake Zoog as an object.

All classes must include four elements: *name*, *data*, *constructor*, and *methods*. (Technically, the only actual required element is the class name, but the point of doing object-oriented programming is to include all of these.)

Here is how we can take the elements from a simple non-object-oriented sketch (a simplified version of the solution to Exercise 7-6) and place them into a Car class, from which we will then be able to make Car objects.

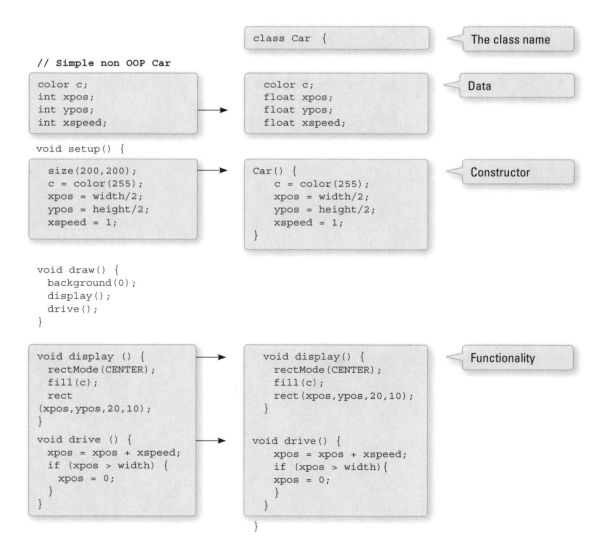

```
                                                    class Car {              The class name

// Simple non OOP Car

color c;                           color c;                                  Data
int xpos;                          float xpos;
int ypos;                          float ypos;
int xspeed;                        float xspeed;

void setup() {

  size(200,200);                   Car() {                                   Constructor
  c = color(255);                    c = color(255);
  xpos = width/2;                    xpos = width/2;
  ypos = height/2;                   ypos = height/2;
  xspeed = 1;                        xspeed = 1;
}                                  }

void draw() {
  background(0);
  display();
  drive();
}

void display () {                  void display() {                         Functionality
  rectMode(CENTER);                  rectMode(CENTER);
  fill(c);                           fill(c);
  rect                               rect(xpos,ypos,20,10);
(xpos,ypos,20,10);                 }
}

void drive () {                    void drive() {
  xpos = xpos + xspeed;              xpos = xpos + xspeed;
  if (xpos > width) {                if (xpos > width){
    xpos = 0;                          xpos = 0;
  }                                  }
}                                  }

                                   }
```

- **The Class Name**—The name is specified by "class WhateverNameYouChoose". We then enclose all of the code for the class inside curly brackets after the name declaration. Class names are traditionally capitalized (to distinguish them from variable names, which traditionally are lowercase).
- **Data**—The data for a class is a collection of variables. These variables are often referred to as *instance* variables since each *instance* of an object contains this set of variables.
- **A Constructor**—The constructor is a special function inside of a class that creates the instance of the object itself. It is where you give the instructions on how to set up the object. It is just like *Processing*'s **setup()** function, only here it is used to create an individual object within the sketch, whenever a **new** object is created from this *class*. It always has the same name as the class and is called by invoking the **new** operator: "**Car myCar = new Car();**".
- **Functionality**—We can add functionality to our object by writing methods. These are done in the same way as described in Chapter 7, with a return type, name, arguments, and a body of code.

This code for a *class* exists as its own block and can be placed anywhere outside of **setup()** and **draw()**.

A Class Is a New Block of Code!

```
void setup() {

}
void draw() {

}
class Car {

}
```

---

*Exercise 8-2: Fill in the blanks in the following Human class definition. Include a function called **sleep()** or make up your own function. Follow the syntax of the Car example. (There are no right or wrong answers in terms of the actual code itself; it is the structure that is important.)*

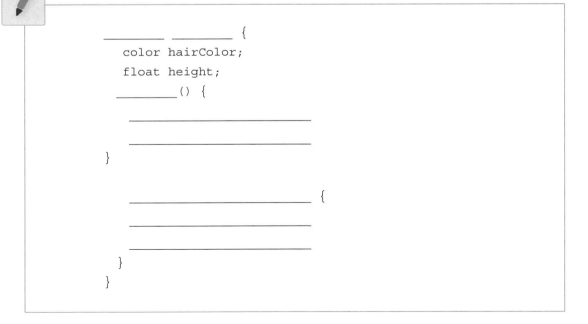

```
_____ _____ {
    color hairColor;
    float height;
    _____ () {

        _____

        _____
    }


    _____ {

        _____

        _____
    }
}
```

8.4 Using an Object: The Details

In Section 8.2, we took a quick peek at how an object can greatly simplify the main parts of a *Processing* sketch (***setup()*** and ***draw()***).

```
Car myCar;                          Step 1. Declare an object.

void setup() {
  myCar = new Car();                Step 2. Initialize object.
}

void draw() {
  background(0);
  myCar.move();                     Step 3. Call methods on the object.
  myCar.display();
}
```

Let's look at the details behind the above three steps outlining how to use an object in your sketch.

Step 1. Declaring an object variable.

If you flip back to Chapter 4, you may recall that a variable is declared by specifying a *type* and a *name*.

```
// Variable Declaration
int var;   // type name
```

The above is an example of a variable that holds onto *a primitive*, in this case an integer. As we learned in Chapter 4, primitive data types are singular pieces of information: an integer, a float, a character. Declaring a variable that holds onto an object is quite similar. The difference is that here the type is the class name, something we will make up, in this case "Car." Objects, incidentally, are not primitives and are considered *complex* data types. (This is because they store multiple pieces of information: data and functionality. Primitives only store data.)

Step 2. Initializing an object.

Again, you may recall from Chapter 4 that in order to initialize a variable (i.e., give it a starting value), we use an assignment operation—variable equals something.

```
// Variable Initialization
var = 10;   // var equals 10
```

Initializing an object is a bit more complex. Instead of simply assigning it a primitive value, like an integer or floating point number, we have to construct the object. An object is made with the ***new*** operator.

```
// Object Initialization
myCar = new Car();        The new operator is used to make a new object.
```

In the above example, "myCar" is the object variable name and "=" indicates we are setting it equal to something, that something being a ***new*** instance of a Car object. What we are really doing here is initializing a Car object. When you initialize a primitive variable, such as an integer, you just set it equal to a number. But an object may contain multiple pieces of data. Recalling the Car class from the previous section, we see that this line of code calls the *constructor*, a special function named ***Car()*** that initializes all of the object's variables and makes sure the Car object is ready to go.

One other thing; with the primitive integer "var," if you had forgotten to initialize it (set it equal to 10), *Processing* would have assigned it a default value, zero. An object (such as "myCar"), however, has no default value. If you forget to initialize an object, *Processing* will give it the value *null*. *null* means *nothing*. Not zero. Not negative one. Utter nothingness. Emptiness. If you encounter an error in the message window that says "***NullPointerException***" (and this is a pretty common error), that error is most likely caused by having forgotten to initialize an object. (See the Appendix for more details.)

Step 3. Using an object

Once we have successfully declared and initialized an object variable, we can use it. Using an object involves calling functions that are built into that object. A human object can eat, a car can drive, a dog can bark. Functions that are inside of an object are technically referred to as "methods" in Java so we can begin to use this nomenclature (see Section 7.1). Calling a method inside of an object is accomplished via dot syntax:

> **variableName.objectMethod(Method Arguments);**

In the case of the car, none of the available functions has an argument so it looks like:

```
myCar.draw();
myCar.display();
```
> Functions are called with the "dot syntax".

*Exercise 8-3: Assume the existence of a Human class. You want to write the code to declare a Human object as well as call the function **sleep()** on that human object. Write out the code below:*

Declare and initialize the Human object: _____

Call the ***sleep()*** function: _____

8.5 Putting It Together with a Tab

Now that we have learned how to define a class and use an object born from that class, we can take the code from Sections 8.2 and 8.3 and put them together in one program.

Example 8-1: A Car class and a Car object

```
Car myCar;

void setup() {
  size(200,200);

  // Initialize Car object
  myCar = new Car();
}

void draw() {
  background(0);
  // Operate Car object.
  myCar.move();
  myCar.display();
}
```
> Declare car object as a globle variable.

> Initialize car object in ***setup()*** by calling constructor.

> Operate the car object in ***draw()*** by calling object methods using the dots syntax.

```
class Car {

  color c;
  float xpos;
  float ypos;
  float xspeed;

  Car() {
    c = color(255);
    xpos = width/2;
    ypos = height/2;
    xspeed = 1;
  }

  void display() {
    // The car is just a square
    rectMode(CENTER);
    fill(c);
    rect(xpos,ypos,20,10);
  }

  void move() {
    xpos = xpos + xspeed;
    if (xpos > width) {
      xpos = 0;
    }
  }
}
```

Define a class below the rest of the program.

Variables.

A constructor.

Function.

Function.

You will notice that the code block that contains the Car class is placed below the main body of the program (under *draw()*). This spot is identical to where we placed user-defined functions in Chapter 7. Technically speaking, the order does not matter, as long as the blocks of code (contained within curly brackets) remain intact. The Car class could go above *setup()* or it could even go between *setup()* and *draw()*. Though any placement is technically correct, when programming, it is nice to place things where they make the most logical sense to our human brains, the bottom of the code being a good starting point. Nevertheless, *Processing* offers a useful means for separating blocks of code from each other through the use of tabs.

In your *Processing* window, look for the arrow inside a square in the top right-hand corner. If you click that button, you will see that it offers the "New Tab" option shown in Figure 8.1.

Upon selecting "New Tab," you will be prompted to type in a name for the new tab, as shown in Figure 8.2.

Although you can pick any name you like, it is probably a good idea to name the tab after the *class* you intend to put there. You can then type the main body of code on one tab (entitled "objectExample" in Figure 8.2) and type the code for your class in another (entitled "Car").

Toggling between the tabs is simple, just click on the tab name itself, as shown in Figure 8.3. Also, it should be noted that when a new tab is created, a new .pde file is created inside the sketch folder, as shown in Figure 8.4. The program has both an objectExample.pde file and Car.pde file.

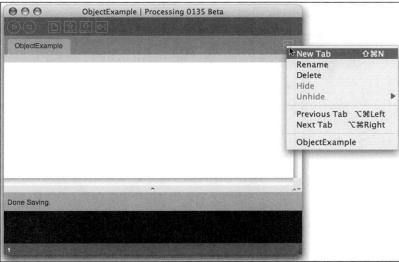

fig. 8.1

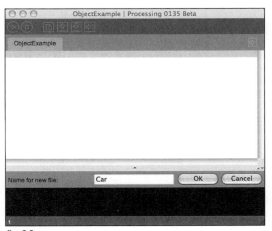

fig. 8.2

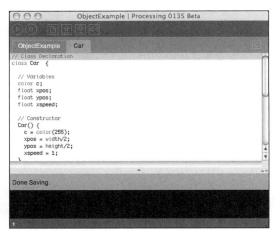

fig. 8.3

fig. 8.4

Exercise 8-4: Create a sketch with multiple tabs. Try to get the Car example to run without any errors.

8.6 Constructor Arguments

In the previous examples, the car object was initialized using the **new** operator followed by the *constructor* for the class.

```
Car myCar = new Car();
```

This was a useful simplification while we learned the basics of OOP. Nonetheless, there is a rather serious problem with the above code. What if we wanted to write a program with two car objects?

```
// Creating two car objects
Car myCar1 = new Car();
Car myCar2 = new Car();
```

This accomplishes our goal; the code will produce two car objects, one stored in the variable myCar1 and one in myCar2. However, if you study the Car class, you will notice that these two cars will be identical: each one will be colored white, start in the middle of the screen, and have a speed of 1. In English, the above reads:

Make a new car.

We want to instead say:

Make a new red car, at location (0,10) with a speed of 1.

So that we could also say:

Make a new blue car, at location (0,100) with a speed of 2.

We can do this by placing arguments inside of the constructor method.

```
Car myCar = new Car(color(255,0,0),0,100,2);
```

The constructor must be rewritten to incorporate these arguments:

```
Car(color tempC, float tempXpos, float tempYpos, float tempXspeed) {
  c = tempC;
  xpos = tempXpos;
  ypos = tempYpos;
  xspeed = tempXspeed;
}
```

In my experience, the use of constructor arguments to initialize object variables can be somewhat bewildering. Please do not blame yourself. The code is strange-looking and can seem awfully redundant: "For every single variable I want to initialize in the constructor, I have to duplicate it with a temporary argument to that constructor?"

Nevertheless, this is quite an important skill to learn, and, ultimately, is one of the things that makes object-oriented programming powerful. But for now, it may feel painful. Let's briefly revisit parameter passing again to understand how it works in this context. See Figure 8.5.

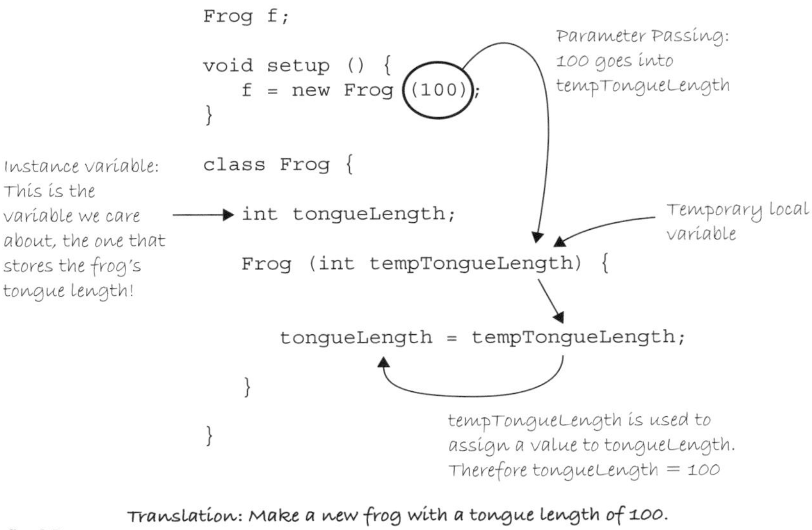

```
Frog f;

void setup () {
    f = new Frog ((100));
}

class Frog {

    int tongueLength;

    Frog (int tempTongueLength) {

        tongueLength = tempTongueLength;

    }

}
```

Parameter Passing: 100 goes into tempTongueLength

Instance variable: This is the variable we care about, the one that stores the frog's tongue length!

Temporary local variable

tempTongueLength is used to assign a value to tongueLength. Therefore tongueLength = 100

Translation: Make a new frog with a tongue length of 100.

fig. 8.5

Arguments are local variables used inside the body of a function that get filled with values when the function is called. In the examples, they have *one purpose only*, to initialize the variables inside of an object. These are the variables that count, the car's actual car, the car's actual *x* location, and so on. The constructor's arguments are just *temporary*, and exist solely to pass a value from where the object is made into the object itself.

This allows us to make a variety of objects using the same constructor. You might also just write the word *temp* in your argument names to remind you of what is going on (c vs. tempC). You will also see programmers use an underscore (c vs. c_) in many examples. You can name these whatever you want, of course. However, it is advisable to choose a name that makes sense to you, and also to stay consistent.

We can now take a look at the same program with multiple object instances, each with unique properties.

Example 8-2: Two Car objects

```
Car myCar1;
Car myCar2;

void setup() {
  size(200,200);

  myCar1 = new Car(color(255,0,0),0,100,2);
  myCar2 = new Car(color(0,0,255),0,10,1);
}

void draw() {
  background(255);
```

Two objects!

Parameters go inside the parentheses when the object is constructed.

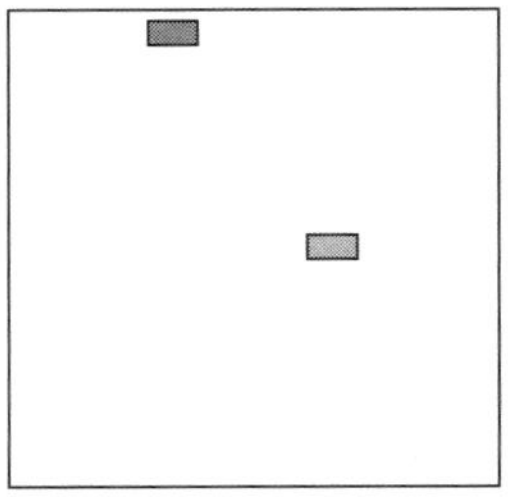

fig. 8.6

```
    myCar1.move();
    myCar1.display();
    myCar2.move();
    myCar2.display();
}

class Car {

    color c;
    float xpos;
    float ypos;
    float xspeed;

    Car(color tempC, float tempXpos, float tempYpos, float tempXspeed) {
        c = tempC;
        xpos = tempXpos;
        ypos = tempYpos;
        xspeed = tempXspeed;
    }

    void display() {
        stroke(0);
        fill(c);
        rectMode(CENTER);
        rect(xpos,ypos,20,10);
    }

    void move() {
        xpos = xpos + xspeed;
        if (xpos > width) {
            xpos = 0;
        }
    }
}
```

> Even though there are *multiple* objects, we still only need *one* class. No matter how many cookies we make, only one cookie cutter is needed. Isn't object-oriented programming swell?

> The Constructor is defined with arguments.

Exercise 8-5: Rewrite the gravity example from Chapter 5 using objects with a Ball class. Include two instances of a Ball object. The original example is included here for your reference with a framework to help you get started.

```
    _____ _____;
    Ball ball2;


    float grav = 0.1;


    void setup() {
        size(200,200);
        ball1 = new _____(50,0,16);
        _____(100,50,32);
    }
```

```
void draw() {
  background(100);
  ball1.display();

  _____

  _____

  _____
}

_____ {

  float x;

  _____

  float speed;
  float w;

  _____(_____,_____,_____) {

    x = _____;

    _____

    _____

    speed = 0;
  }
  void _____() {

    _____

    _____

    _____

  }

  _____

  _____

  _____

  _____

  _____

  _____

}
```

```
// Simple gravity
float x = 100;        // x
location
float y = 0;          // y
location

float speed = 0;      // speed
float gravity = 0.1;// gravity

void setup() {
  size(200,200);
}

void draw() {
  background(100);

  // display the square
  fill(255);
  noStroke();
  rectMode(CENTER);
  rect(x,y,10,10);

  // Add speed to y location
  y = y + speed;
  // Add gravity to speed
  speed = speed + gravity;

  // If square reaches the bottom
  // Reverse speed
  if (y > height) {
    speed = speed * -0.95;
  }
}
```

8.7 Objects are data types too!

This is our first experience with object-oriented programming, so we want to take it easy. The examples in this chapter all use just one class and make, at most, two or three objects from that class. Nevertheless, there are no actual limitations. A *Processing* sketch can include as many classes as you feel like writing. If you were programming the Space Invaders game, for example, you might create a *Spaceship* class, an *Enemy* class, and a *Bullet* class, using an object for each entity in your game.

In addition, although not *primitive*, classes are data types just like integers and floats. And since classes are made up of data, an object can therefore contain other objects! For example, let's assume you had just finished programming a *Fork* and *Spoon* class. Moving on to a *PlaceSetting* class, you would likely include variables for both a *Fork* object and a *Spoon* object inside that class itself. This is perfectly reasonable and quite common in object-oriented programming.

```
class PlaceSetting {

  Fork fork;                    A class can include other objects among its variables.
  Spoon spoon;

  PlaceSetting() {
    fork = new Fork();
    spoon = new Spoon();
  }
}
```

Objects, just like any data type, can also be passed in as arguments to a function. In the Space Invaders game example, if the spaceship shoots the bullet at the enemy, we would probably want to write a function inside the Enemy class to determine if the Enemy had been hit by the bullet.

```
void hit(Bullet b) {        A function can have an object as its argument.
// Code to determine if
// the bullet struck the enemy
}
```

In Chapter 7, we showed how when a primitive value (integer, float, etc.) is passed in a function, a copy is made. With objects, this is not the case, and the result is a bit more intuitive. If changes are made to an object after it is passed into a function, those changes will affect that object used anywhere else throughout the sketch. This is known as *pass by reference* since instead of a copy, a reference to the actual object itself is passed into the function.

As we move forward through this book and our examples become more advanced, we will begin to see examples that use multiple objects, pass objects into functions, and more. The next chapter, in fact, focuses on how to make lists of objects. And Chapter 10 walks through the development of a project that includes multiple classes. For now, as we close out the chapter with Zoog, we will stick with just one class.

8.8 Object-Oriented Zoog

Invariably, the question comes up: "When should I use object-oriented programming?" For me, the answer is *always*. Objects allow you to organize the concepts inside of a software application into modular, reusable packages. You will see this again and again throughout the course of this book. However, it is not always convenient or necessary to start out every project using object-orientation, especially while you are learning. *Processing* makes it easy to quickly "sketch" out visual ideas with non object-oriented code.

For any *Processing* project you want to make, my advice is to take a step-by-step approach. You do not need to start out writing classes for everything you want to try to do. Sketch out your idea first by writing code in *setup()* and *draw()*. Nail down the logic of what you want to do as well as how you want it to look. As your project begins to grow, take the time to reorganize your code, perhaps first with functions, then with objects. It is perfectly acceptable to dedicate a significant chunk of your time to this reorganization process (often referred to as *refactoring*) without making any changes to the end result, that is, what your sketch looks like and does on screen.

This is exactly what we have been doing with cosmonaut Zoog from Chapter 1 until now. We sketched out Zoog's look and experimented with some motion behaviors. Now that we have something, we can take the time to *refactor* by making Zoog into an object. This process will give us a leg up in programming Zoog's future life in more complex sketches.

And so it is time to take the plunge and make a Zoog class. Our little Zoog is almost all grown up. The following example is virtually identical to Example 7-5 (Zoog with functions) with one major difference. All of the variables and all of the functions from Example 7-5 are now incorporated into the Zoog class with *setup()* and *draw()* containing barely any code.

Example 8-3

```
Zoog zoog;                                      Zoog is an object!

void setup() {
  size(200,200);
  smooth();
  zoog = new Zoog(100,125,60,60,16);            Zoog is given initial properties via the constructor.
}

void draw() {
  background(255);
  // mouseX position determines speed factor
  float factor = constrain(mouseX/10,0,5);
  zoog.jiggle(factor);
  zoog.display();                               Zoog can do stuff with functions!
}

class Zoog {
  // Zoog's variables
  float x,y,w,h,eyeSize;

  // Zoog constructor
  Zoog(float tempX, float tempY, float tempW, float tempH, float tempEyeSize) {
    x = tempX;
    y = tempY;
    w = tempW;                                  Everything about Zoog is contained in this one class.
    h = tempH;                                  Zoog has properties (location, with , height, eye size)
    eyeSize = tempEyeSize;                      and Zoog has abilities (jiggle, display).
  }
```

```
// Move Zoog
void jiggle(float speed) {
  // Change the location of Zoog randomly
  x = x + random(-1,1)*speed;
  y = y + random(-1,1)*speed;

  // Constrain Zoog to window
  x = constrain(x,0,width);
  y = constrain(y,0,height);
}

// Display Zoog
void display() {
  // Set ellipses and rects to CENTER mode
  ellipseMode(CENTER);
  rectMode(CENTER);

  // Draw Zoog's arms with a for loop
  for (float i = y - h/3; i < y + h/2; i += 10) {
    stroke(0);
    line(x-w/4,i,x+w/4,i);
  }

  // Draw Zoog's body
  stroke(0);
  fill(175);
  rect(x,y,w/6,h);

  // Draw Zoog's head
  stroke(0);
  fill(255);
  ellipse(x,y-h,w,h);

  // Draw Zoog's eyes
  fill(0);
  ellipse(x-w/3,y-h,eyeSize,eyeSize*2);
  ellipse(x+w/3,y-h,eyeSize,eyeSize*2);

  // Draw Zoog's legs
  stroke(0);
  line(x-w/12,y+h/2,x-w/4,y+h/2+10);
  line(x+w/12,y+h/2,x+w/4,y+h/2+10);

  }
}
```

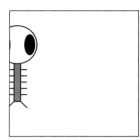

fig. 8.7

Exercise 8-6: Rewrite Example 8-3 to include two Zoogs. Can you vary their appearance? Behavior? Consider adding color as a Zoog variable.

Lesson Three Project

Step 1. Take your Lesson Two Project and reorganize the code using functions.

Step 2. Reorganize the code one step further using a class and an object variable.

Step 3. Add arguments to the Constructor of your class and try making two or three objects with different variables.

Use the space provided below to sketch designs, notes, and pseudocode for your project.

Lesson Four

More of the Same

9 Arrays

9 Arrays

*"I might repeat to myself slowly and soothingly, a list of quotations beautiful
from minds profound—if I can remember any of the damn things."*
—Dorothy Parker

In this chapter:
– What is an array?
– Declaring an array.
– Initialization.
– Array operations—using the "for" loop with an array.
– Arrays of objects.

9.1 Arrays, why do we care?

Let's take a moment to revisit the car example from the previous chapter on object-oriented
programming. You may remember we spent a great deal of effort on developing a program that contained
multiple instances of a class, that is, two objects.

```
Car myCar1;
Car myCar2;
```

This was indeed an exciting moment in the development of our lives as computer programmers. It is
likely you are contemplating a somewhat obvious question. How could I take this further and write a
program with 100 car objects? With some clever copying and pasting, you might write a program with
the following beginning:

```
Car myCar1
Car myCar2
Car myCar3
Car myCar4
Car myCar5
Car myCar6
Car myCar7
Car myCar8
Car myCar9
Car myCar10
Car myCar11
Car myCar12
Car myCar13
Car myCar14
Car myCar15
Car myCar16
Car myCar17
Car myCar18
Car myCar19
Car myCar20
Car myCar21
```

```
Car myCar22
Car myCar23
Car myCar24
Car myCar25
Car myCar26
Car myCar27
Car myCar28
Car myCar29
Car myCar30
Car myCar31
Car myCar32
Car myCar33
Car myCar34
Car myCar35
Car myCar36
Car myCar37
Car myCar38
Car myCar39
Car myCar40
Car myCar41
Car myCar42
Car myCar43
Car myCar44
Car myCar45
Car myCar46
Car myCar47
Car myCar48
Car myCar49
Car myCar50
Car myCar51
Car myCar52
Car myCar53
Car myCar54
Car myCar55
Car myCar56
Car myCar57
Car myCar58
Car myCar59
Car myCar60
Car myCar61
Car myCar62
Car myCar63
Car myCar64
Car myCar65
Car myCar66
Car myCar67
Car myCar68
Car myCar69
Car myCar70
Car myCar71
Car myCar72
Car myCar73
Car myCar74
Car myCar75
Car myCar76
Car myCar77
Car myCar78
Car myCar79
```

```
Car myCar80
Car myCar81
Car myCar82
Car myCar83
Car myCar84
Car myCar85
Car myCar86
Car myCar87
Car myCar88
Car myCar89
Car myCar90
Car myCar91
Car myCar92
Car myCar93
Car myCar94
Car myCar95
Car myCar96
Car myCar97
Car myCar98
Car myCar99
Car myCar100
```

If you really want to give yourself a headache, try completing the rest of the program modeled after the above start. It will not be a pleasant endeavor. I am certainly not about to leave you any workbook space in this book to practice.

An array will allow us to take these 100 lines of code and put them into one line. Instead of having 100 variables, an array is *one* thing that contains a *list* of variables.

Any time a program requires multiple instances of similar data, it might be time to use an array. For example, an array can be used to store the scores of four players in a game, a selection of 10 colors in a design program, or a list of fish objects in an aquarium simulation.

Exercise 9-1: Looking at all of the sketches you have created so far, do any merit the use of an array? Why?

_____

_____

_____

_____

_____

9.2 What is an array?

From Chapter 4, you may recall that a variable is a named pointer to a location in memory where data is stored. In other words, variables allow programs to keep track of information over a period of time. An array is exactly the same, only instead of pointing to one singular piece of information, an array points to multiple pieces. See Figure 9.1.

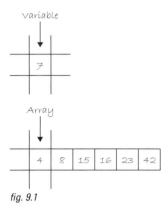

fig. 9.1

You can think of an array as a list of variables. A list, it should be noted, is useful for two important reasons. Number one, the list keeps track of the elements in the list themselves. Number two, the list keeps track of *the order* of those elements (which element is the first in the list, the second, the third, etc.). This is a crucial point since in many programs, the order of information is just as important as the information itself.

In an array, each element of the list has a unique *index,* an integer value that designates its position in the list (element #1, element #2, etc.). In all cases, the name of the array refers to the list as a whole, while each element is accessed via its position.

Notice how in Figure 9.2, the indices range from 0 to 9. The array has a total of 10 elements, but the first element number is 0 and the last element is 9. We might be tempted to stomp our feet and complain: "Hey, why aren't the elements numbered from 1 to 10? Wouldn't that be easier?"

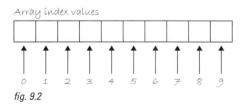

fig. 9.2

While at first, it might intuitively seem like we should start counting at one (and some programming languages do), we start at zero because technically the first element of the array is located at the start of the array, a distance of zero from the beginning. Numbering the elements starting at 0 also makes many *array operations* (the process of executing a line of code for every element of the list) a great deal more convenient. As we continue through several examples, you will begin to believe in the power of counting from zero.

Exercise 9-2: If you have an array with 1,000 elements, what is the range of index values for that array?

Answer: _____ through _____

9.3 Declaring and Creating an Array

In Chapter 4, we learned that all variables must have a name and a data type. Arrays are no different. The declaration statement, however, does look different. We denote the use of an array by placing empty square brackets ("[]") after the type declaration. Let's start with an array of primitive values, for example, integers. (We can have arrays of any data type, and we will soon see how we can make an array of objects.) See Figure 9.3.

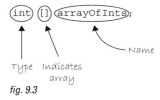

Type   Indicates
       array

fig. 9.3

The declaration in Figure 9.3 indicates that "arrayOfInts" will store a list of integers. The array name "arrayOfInts" can be absolutely anything you want it to be (we only include the word "array" here to illustrate what we are learning).

One fundamental property of arrays, however, is that they are of fixed size. Once we define the size for an array, it can never change. A list of 10 integers can never *go to 11*. But where in the above code is the size of the array defined? It is not. The code simply declares the array; we must also make sure we *create* the actual instance of the array with a specified size.

To do this, we use the ***new*** operator, in a similar manner as we did in calling the constructor of an object. In the object's case, we are saying "Make a *new* Car" or "Make a *new* Zoog." With an array, we are saying "Make a *new* array of integers," or "Make a *new* array of Car objects," and so on. See array declaration in Figure 9.4.

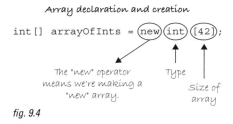

fig. 9.4

The array declaration in Figure 9.4 allows us to specify the array size: how many elements we want the array to hold (or, technically, how much memory in the computer we are asking for to store our beloved data). We write this statement as follows: the new operator, followed by the data type, followed by the size of the array enclosed in brackets. This size must be an integer. It can be a hard-coded number, a variable (of type integer), or an expression that evaluates to an integer (like 2 + 2).

Example 9-1: Additional array declaration and creation examples

```
float[] scores = new float[4];              // A list of 4 floating point numbers
Human[] people = new Human[100];            // A list of 100 Human objects
int num = 50;
Car[] cars = new Car[num];                  // Using a variable to specify size
Spaceship[] ships = new Shapeship[num*2 + 3]; // Using an expression to
                                               specify size
```

Exercise 9-3: Write the declaration statements for the following arrays:

30 integers	
100 floating point numbers	
56 Zoog objects	

Exercise 9-4: Which of the following array declarations are valid and which are invalid (and why)?

`int[] numbers = new int[10];`	
`float[] numbers = new float[5+6];`	
`int num = 5;` `float[] numbers = new int[num];`	
`float num = 5.2;` `Car[] cars = new Car[num];`	

`int num = (5 * 6)/2;`
`float[] numbers = new`
`float[num = 5];`	

`int num = 5;` `Zoog[] zoogs = new Zoog[num * 10];`	

Things are looking up. Not only did we successfully declare the existence of an array, but we have given it a size and allocated physical memory for the stored data. A major piece is missing, however: the data stored in the array itself!

9.4 Initializing an Array

One way to fill an array is to hard-code the values stored in each spot of the array.

Example 9-2: Initializing the elements of an array one at a time

```
int[] stuff = new int[3];

stuff[0] = 8;    // The first element of the array equals 8
stuff[1] = 3;    // The second element of the array equals 3
stuff[2] = 1;    // The third element of the array equals 1
```

As you can see, we refer to each element of the array individually by specifying an index, starting at 0. The syntax for this is the name of the array, followed by the index value enclosed in brackets.

arrayName[INDEX]

A second option for initializing an array is to manually type out a list of values enclosed in curly braces and separated by commas.

Example 9-3: Initializing the elements of an array all at once

```
int[] arrayOfInts = {1, 5, 8, 9, 4, 5};
float[] floatArray = {1.2, 3.5, 2.0, 3.4123, 9.9};
```

Exercise 9-5: Declare an array of three Zoog objects. Initialize each spot in the array with a Zoog object via its index.

Zoog__ zoogs = new _____ [_____];

_____[_____] = _____ _____(100, 100, 50, 60, 16);

_____[_____] = _____ _____(_____);

_____[_____] = _____ _____(_____);

Both of these approaches are not commonly used and you will not see them in most of the examples throughout the book. In fact, neither initialization method has really solved the problem posed at the beginning of the chapter. Imagine initializing each element individually with a list of 100 or (gasp) 1,000 or (gasp gasp!) 1,000,000 elements.

The solution to all of our woes involves a means for *iterating* through the elements of the array. Ding ding ding. Hopefully a loud bell is ringing in your head. Loops! (If you are lost, revisit Chapter 6.)

9.5 Array Operations

Consider, for a moment, the following problem:

> *(A) Create an array of 1,000 floating point numbers. (B) Initialize every element of that array with a random number between 0 and 10.*

Part A we already know how to do.

```
float[] values = new float[1000];
```

What we want to avoid is having to do this for Part B:

```
values[0] = random(0,10);
values[1] = random(0,10);
values[2] = random(0,10);
values[3] = random(0,10);
values[4] = random(0,10);
values[5] = random(0,10);
etc. etc.
```

Let's describe in English what we want to program:

> For every number n from 0 to 99, initialize the nth element stored in array as a random value between 0 and 10. Translating into code, we have:

```
int n = 0;
values[n]   = random(0,10);
values[n+1] = random(0,10);
values[n+2] = random(0,10);
values[n+3] = random(0,10);
values[n+4] = random(0,10);
values[n+5] = random(0,10);
```

Unfortunately, the situation has not improved. We have, nonetheless, taken a big leap forward. By using a variable (n) to describe an index in the array, we can now employ a *while* loop to initialize every n element.

Example 9-4: Using a *while* loop to initialize all elements of an array

```
int n = 0;
while (n < 1000) {
  values[n] = random(0,10);
  n = n + 1;
}
```

A *for* loop allows us to be even more concise, as Example 9-5 shows.

Example 9-5: Using a *for* loop to initialize all elements of an array

```
for (int n = 0; n < 1000; n++) {
  values[n] = random(0,10);
}
```

What was once 1,000 lines of code is now three!

We can exploit the same technique for any type of array operation we might like to do beyond simply initializing the elements. For example, we could take the array and double the value of each element (we will use *i* from now on instead of *n* as it is more commonly used by programmers).

Example 9-6: An array operation

```
for (int i = 0; i < 1000; i++) {
  values[i] = values[i] * 2;
}
```

There is one problem with Example 9-6: the use of the hard-coded value 1,000. Striving to be better programmers, we should always question the existence of a hard-coded number. In this case, what if we wanted to change the array to have 2,000 elements? If our program was very long with many array operations, we would have to make this change everywhere throughout our code. Fortunately for us, *Processing* gives us a nice means for accessing the size of an array dynamically, using the dot syntax we learned for objects in Chapter 8. *length* is a property of every array and we can access it by saying:

arrayName dot length

Let's use *length* while clearing an array. This will involve resetting every value to 0.

Example 9-7: An array operation using dot length

```
for (int i = 0; i < values.length; i++) {
  values[i] = 0;
}
```

Exercise 9-6: Assuming an array of 10 integers, that is,

```
int[] nums = {5,4,2,7,6,8,5,2,8,14};
```

write code to perform the following array operations (Note that the number of clues vary, just because a [____] is not explicitly written in does not mean there should not be brackets).

Square each number (i.e., multiply each by itself)	`for (int i ___; i < _____; i++) {`
	`    _____[i] = _____*_____;`
	`}`

Add a random number between zero and 10 to each number.	_____ _____ += int (_____) ; __

Add to each number the number that follows in the array. Skip the last value in the array.	```for (int i = 0; i < _____; i++) {```
	
	 ```_____ += _____ [____];```
	
	 ```}```

Calculate the sum of all the numbers.	_____ _____ = ____ ;
	 ```for (int i = 0; i < nums.length; i++)```
	 ```{```
	
	 _____ += _____ ;
	
	 ```}```

9.6 Simple Array Example: The Snake

A seemingly trivial task, programming a trail following the mouse, is not as easy as it might initially appear. The solution requires an array, which will serve to store the history of mouse locations. We will use two arrays, one to store horizontal mouse locations, and one for vertical. Let's say, arbitrarily, that we want to store the last 50 mouse locations.

First, we declare the two arrays.

```
int[] xpos = new int[50];
int[] ypos = new int[50];
```

Second, in *setup()*, we must initialize the arrays. Since at the start of the program there has not been any mouse movement, we will just fill the arrays with 0's.

```
for (int i = 0; i < xpos.length; i++) {
  xpos[i] = 0;
  ypos[i] = 0;
}
```

Each time through the main *draw()* loop, we want to update the array with the current mouse location. Let's choose to put the current mouse location in the last spot of the array. The length of the array is 50, meaning index values range from 0–49. The the last spot is index 49, or the length of the array minus one.

```
xpos[xpos.length-1] = mouseX;
ypos[ypos.length-1] = mouseY;
```

The last spot in an array is length minus one.

Now comes the hard part. We want to keep only the last 50 mouse locations. By storing the current mouse location at the end of the array, we are overwriting what was previously stored there. If the mouse is at (10,10) during one frame and (15,15) during another, we want to put (10,10) in the second to last spot and (15,15) in the last spot. The solution is to shift all of the elements of the array down one spot before updating the current location. This is shown in Figure 9.5.

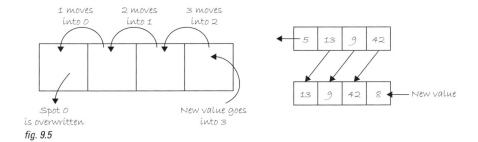

fig. 9.5

Element index 49 moves into spot 48, 48 moves into spot 47, 47 into 46, and so on. We can do this by looping through the array and setting each element index *i* to the value of element *i plus one*. Note we must stop at the second to last value since for element 49 there is no element 50 (49 plus 1). In other words, instead of having an exit condition

i < *xpos.length;*

we must instead say:

i < *xpos.length – 1;*

The full code for performing this array shift is as follows:

```
for (int i = 0; i < xpos.length-1; i++) {
  xpos[i] = xpos[i+1];
  ypos[i] = ypos[i+1];
}
```

Finally, we can use the history of mouse locations to draw a series of circles. For each element of the xpos array and ypos array, draw an ellipse at the corresponding values stored in the array.

```
for (int i = 0; i < xpos.length; i++) {
  noStroke();
  fill(255);
  ellipse(xpos[i],ypos[i],32,32);
}
```

Making this a bit fancier, we might choose to link the brightness of the circle as well as the size of the circle to the location in the array, that is, the earlier (and therefore older) values will be bright and small and the later (newer) values will be darker and bigger. This is accomplished by using the counting variable *i* to evaluate color and size.

```
for (int i = 0; i < xpos.length; i++) {
  noStroke();
  fill(255-i*5);
  ellipse(xpos[i],ypos[i],i,i);
}
```

Putting all of the code together, we have the following example, with the output shown in Figure 9.6.

Example 9-8: A snake following the mouse

```
// x and y positions
int[] xpos = new int[50];          Declare two arrays with 50 elemets.
int[] ypos = new int[50];

void setup() {
  size(200,200);
  smooth();

  // Initialize
  for (int i = 0; i < xpos.length; i++)
    xpos[i] = 0;                    Initialize all elements of each array to zero.
    ypos[i] = 0;
  }
}


void draw() {
  background(255);

  // Shift array values
  for (int i = 0; i < xpos.length-1; i++) {
    xpos[i] = xpos[i+1];
    ypos[i] = ypos[i+1];           Shift all elements down one spot.
  }                                 xpos[0] = xpos[1], xpos[1] = xpos = [2], and so on.
                                    Stop at the second to last element.

  // New location
  xpos[xpos.length-1] = mouseX;
  ypos[ypos.length-1] = mouseY;    Update the last spot in the array with the
                                    mouse location.

  // Draw everything
  for (int i = 0; i < xpos.length; i++) {
  noStroke();
    fill(255-i*5);
    ellipse(xpos[i],ypos[i],i,i);  Draw an ellipse for each element in the arrays.
  }                                 Color and size are tied to the loop's counter: i.
}
```

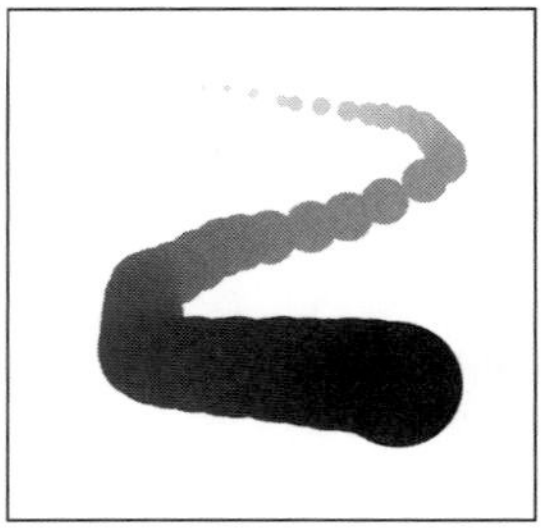

fig. 9.6

Exercise 9-7: Rewrite the snake example in an object-oriented fashion with a Snake class. Can you make snakes with slightly different looks (different shapes, colors, sizes)? (For an advanced problem, create a Point class that stores an x and y coordinate as part of the sketch. Each snake object will have an array of Point objects, instead of two separate arrays of x and y values. This involves arrays of objects, covered in the next section.)

9.7 Arrays of Objects

I know, I know. I still have not fully answered the question. How can we write a program with 100 car objects?

One of the nicest features of combining object-oriented programming with arrays is the simplicity of transitioning a program from one object to 10 objects to 10,000 objects. In fact, if we have been careful, we will not have to change the Car *class* whatsoever. A *class* does not care how many objects are made from it. So, assuming we keep the identical Car class code, let's look at how we expand the main program to use an array of objects instead of just one.

Let's revisit the main program for one Car object.

```
Car myCar;

void setup() {
  myCar = new Car(color(255,0,0),0,100,2);
}

void draw() {
  background(255);
  myCar.move();
  myCar.display();
}
```

There are three steps in the above code and we need to alter each one to account for an array.

BEFORE

Declare the Car
```
Car myCar;
```

Initialize the Car
```
myCar = new Car(color(255),0,100,2);
```

Run the Car by Calling Methods
```
myCar.move();
myCar.display();
```

AFTER

Declare the Car Array
```
Car[] cars = new Car[100];
```

Initialize each element of the Car Array
```
for (int i = 0; i < cars.length; i++) {
  cars[i] = new Car(color(i*2),0,i*2,i);
}
```

Run each element of the Car Array
```
for (int i = 0; i < cars.length; i++) {
  cars[i].move();
  cars[i].display();
}
```

This leaves us with Example 9–9. Note how changing the number of cars present in the program requires only altering the array definition. Nothing else anywhere has to change!

Example 9-9: An array of Car objects

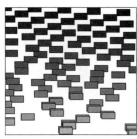

fig. 9.7

```
Car[] cars = new Car[100];          ← An array of 100 Car objects!

void setup() {
  size(200,200);
  smooth();

  for (int i = 0; i < cars.length; i++) {
    cars[i] = new Car(color(i*2),0,i*2,i/20.0);
  }
}
                              Initialize each Car using a for loop.
void draw() {
  background(255);
  for (int i = 0; i < cars.length; i++) {
    cars[i].move();
    cars[i].display();
  }                           Run each Car using a for loop.
}

class Car {                   The Car class does not change
  color c;                    whether we are making one
  float xpos;                 car, 100 cars or 1,000 cars!
  float ypos;
  float xspeed;

  Car(color c_, float xpos_, float ypos_, float xspeed_) {
    c = c_;
    xpos = xpos_;
    ypos = ypos_;
    xspeed = xspeed_;
  }

  void display() {
    rectMode(CENTER);
    stroke(0);
    fill(c);
    rect(xpos,ypos,20,10);
  }

  void move() {
    xpos = xpos + xspeed;
    if (xpos > width) {
      xpos = 0;
    }
  }
}
```

9.8 Interactive Objects

When we first learned about variables (Chapter 4) and conditionals (Chapter 5), we programmed a simple rollover effect. A rectangle appears in the window and is one color when the mouse is on top and another color when the mouse is not. The following is an example that takes this simple idea and puts it into a "Stripe" object. Even though there are 10 stripes, each one individually responds to the mouse by having its own *rollover()* function.

```
void rollover(int mx, int my) {
  if (mx > x && mx < x + w) {
    mouse = true;
  } else {
    mouse = false;
  }
}
```

This function checks to see if a point (*mx*, *my*) is contained within the vertical stripe. Is it greater than the left edge and less than the right edge? If so, a boolean variable "mouse" is set to true. When designing your classes, it is often convenient to use a boolean variable to keep track of properties of an object that resemble a switch. For example, a Car object could be running or not running. Zoog could be happy or not happy.

This boolean variable is used in a conditional statement inside of the Stripe object's *display()* function to determine the Stripe's color.

```
void display() {
  if (mouse) {
    fill(255);
  } else {
    fill(255,100);
  }
  noStroke();
  rect(x,0,w,height);
}
```

When we call the *rollover()* function on that object, we can then pass in *mouseX* and *mouseY* as arguments.

```
stripes[i].rollover(mouseX,mouseY);
```

Even though we could have accessed *mouseX* and *mouseY* directly inside of the *rollover ()* function, it is better to use arguments. This allows for greater flexibility. The Stripe object can check and determine if any *x,y* coordinate is contained within its rectangle. Perhaps later, we will want the Stripe to turn white when another object, rather than the mouse, is over it.

Here is the full "interactive stripes" example.

Example 9-10: Interactive stripes

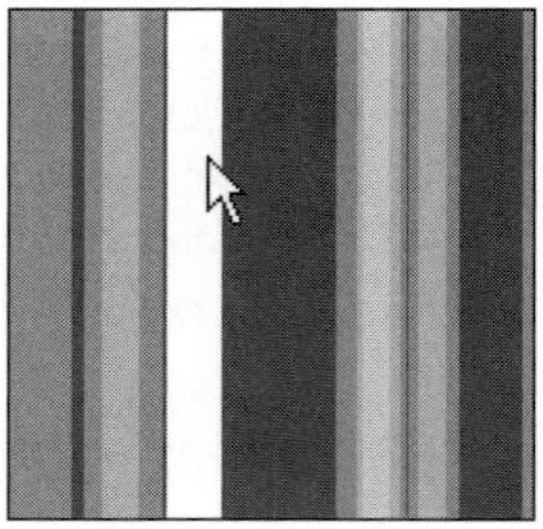

```
// An array of stripes
Stripe[] stripes = new Stripe[10];

void setup() {
  size(200,200);
  // Initialize all "stripes"
  for (int i = 0; i < stripes.length; i++) {
    stripes[i] = new Stripe();
  }
}
```

fig. 9.8

```
void draw() {
  background(100);
  // Move and display all "stripes"
  for (int i = 0; i < stripes.length; i++) {
    // Check if mouse is over the Stripe
    stripes[i].rollover(mouseX,mouseY);
    stripes[i].move();
    stripes[i].display();
  }
}
```

> Passing the mouse coordinates into an object.

```
class Stripe {
  float x;        // horizontal location of stripe
  float speed;    // speed of stripe
  float w;        // width of stripe
  boolean mouse;  // state of stripe (mouse is over or not?)
```

> A boolean variable keeps track of the object's state.

```
  Stripe() {
    x = 0;              // All stripes start at 0
    speed = random(1);  // All stripes have a random positive speed
    w = random(10,30);
    mouse = false;
  }

  // Draw stripe
  void display() {
    if (mouse) {
      fill(255);
    } else {
      fill(255,100);
    }
    noStroke();
    rect(x,0,w,height);
  }
```

> Boolean variable determines Stripe color.

```
  // Move stripe
  void move() {
    x += speed;
    if (x > width+20) x = -20;
  }
```

```
                                            ┌─────────────────────────┐
    // Check if point is inside of Stripe   │ Check to see if point (mx,my) is │
    void rollover(int mx, int my) {         │ inside the Stripe.      │
      // Left edge is x, Right edge is x+w   └─────────────────────────┘
      if (mx > x && mx < x + w) {
        mouse = true;
      } else {
        mouse = false;
      }
    }
}
```

Exercise 9-8: Write a Button class (see Example 5-5 for a non-object-oriented button). The button class should register when a mouse is pressed over the button and change color. Create button objects of different sizes and locations using an array. Before writing the main program, sketch out the Button class. Assume the button is off when it first appears. Here is a code framework:

```
class Button {
  float x;
  float y;
  float w;
  float h;
  boolean on;

  Button(float tempX, float tempY, float tempW, float tempH) {
    x = tempX;
    y = tempY;
    w = tempW;
    h = tempH;
    on = _____;
  }
```

_____

_____

_____

_____

_____

_____

_____

_____

```
        _____

        _____

        _____

        _____

        _____

    }
```

9.9 *Processing's* Array Functions

OK, so I have a confession to make. I lied. Well, sort of. See, earlier in this chapter, I made a very big point of emphasizing that once you set the size of an array, you can never change that size. Once you have made 10 Button objects, you can't make an 11th.

And I stand by those statements. Technically speaking, when you allocate 10 spots in an array, you have told *Processing* exactly how much space in memory you intend to use. You can't expect that block of memory to happen to have more space next to it so that you can expand the size of your array.

However, there is no reason why you couldn't just make a new array (one that has 11 spots in it), copy the first 10 from your original array, and pop a new Button object in the last spot. *Processing*, in fact, offers a set of array functions that manipulate the size of an array by managing this process for you. They are: *shorten(), concat(), subset(), append(), splice(),* and *expand().* In addition, there are functions for changing the order in an array, such as *sort()* and *reverse().*

Details about all of these functions can be found in the reference. Let's look at one example that uses *append()* to expand the size of an array. This example (which includes an answer to Exercise 8-5) starts with an array of one object. Each time the mouse is pressed, a new object is created and appended to the end of the original array.

Example 9-11: Resizing an array using *append()*

```
Ball[] balls = new Ball[1];          We start with an array
float gravity = 0.1;                 with just one element.

void setup() {
  size(200,200);
  smooth();
  frameRate(30);
  // Initialize ball index 0
  balls[0] = new Ball(50,0,16);
}                                    Whatever the length of
                                     that array, update and
void draw() {                        display all of the objects.
  background(100);
  // Update and display all balls
  for (int i = 0; i < balls.length; i++) {
```

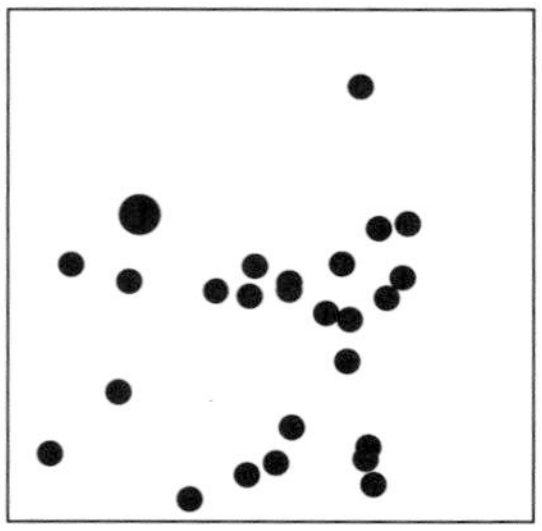

fig. 9.9

```
      balls[i].gravity();
      balls[i].move();
      balls[i].display();
    }
}

void mousePressed() {
  // A new ball object
  Ball b = new Ball(mouseX,mouseY,10);

  // Append to array
  balls = (Ball[]) append(balls,b);
}

class Ball {
  float x;
  float y;
  float speed;
  float w;

  Ball(float tempX, float tempY, float tempW) {
    x = tempX;
    y = tempY;
    w = tempW;
    speed = 0;
  }

  void gravity() {
    // Add gravity to speed
    speed = speed + gravity;
  }

  void move() {
    // Add speed to y location
    y = y + speed;
    // If square reaches the bottom
    // Reverse speed
    if (y > height) {
      speed = speed * -0.95;
      y = height;
    }
  }

  void display() {
    // Display the circle
    fill(255);
    noStroke();
    ellipse(x,y,w,w);
  }
}
```

Make a new object at the mouse location.

Here, the function, *append()* adds an element to the end of the array. *append()* takes two arguments. The first is the array you want to append to, and the second is the thing you want to append.

You have to reassign the result of the *append()* function to the original array. In addition, the *append()* function requires that you explicitly state the type of data in the array again by putting the array data type in parentheses: "(Ball[])". This is known as casting.

Another means of having a resizable array is through the use of a special object known as an *ArrayList*, which will be covered in Chapter 23.

9.10 One Thousand and One Zoogs

It is time to complete Zoog's journey and look at how we move from one Zoog object to many. In the same way that we generated the Car array or Stripe array example, we can simply copy the exact Zoog class created in Example 8-3 and implement an array.

Example 9-12: 200 Zoog objects in an array

```
Zoog[] zoogies = new Zoog[200];

void setup() {
  size(400,400);
  smooth();
  for (int i = 0; i < zoogies.length; i++) {
    zoogies[i] = new Zoog(random(width),random(height),30,30,8);
  }
}
```

> The only difference between this example and the previous chapter (Example 8-3) is the use of an array for multiple Zoog objects.

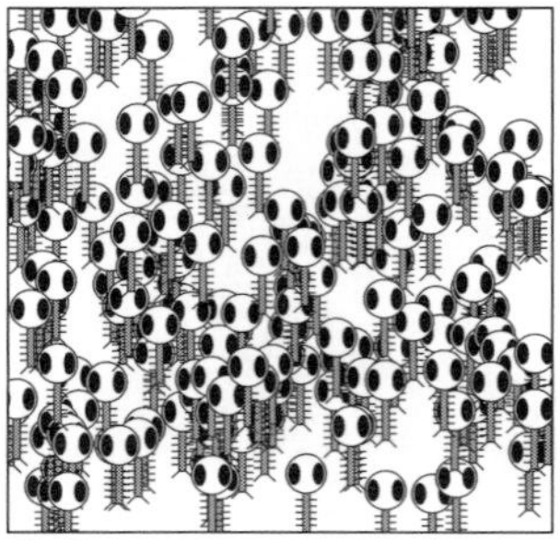

```
void draw() {
  background(255); // Draw a black background
  for (int i = 0; i < zoogies.length; i++) {
    zoogies[i].display();
    zoogies[i].jiggle();
  }
}

class Zoog {
  // Zoog's variables
  float x,y,w,h,eyeSize;

  // Zoog constructor
  Zoog(float tempX, float tempY, float tempW, float tempH, float tempEyeSize) {
    x = tempX;
    y = tempY;
    w = tempW;
    h = tempH;
    eyeSize = tempEyeSize;
  }

  // Move Zoog
  void jiggle() {
    // Change the location
    x = x + random(-1,1);
    y = y + random(-1,1);

    // Constrain Zoog to window
    x = constrain(x,0,width);
    y = constrain(y,0,height);
  }

  // Display Zoog
  void display() {
    // Set ellipses and rects to CENTER mode
    ellipseMode(CENTER);
    rectMode(CENTER);
```

fig. 9.10

> For simplicity we have also removed the "speed" argument from the *jiggle()* function. Try adding it back in as an exercise.

```
// Draw Zoog's arms with a for loop
for (float i = y-h/3; i < y + h/2; i+=10) {
  stroke(0);
  line(x-w/4,i,x+w/4,i);
}

// Draw Zoog's body
stroke(0);
fill(175);
rect(x,y,w/6,h);

// Draw Zoog's head
stroke(0);
fill(255);
ellipse(x,y-h,w,h);

// Draw Zoog's eyes
fill(0);
ellipse(x-w/3,y-h,eyeSize,eyeSize*2);
ellipse(x+w/3,y-h,eyeSize,eyeSize*2);

// Draw Zoog's legs
stroke(0);
line(x-w/12,y+h/2,x-w/4,y+h/2+10);
line(x+w/12,y+h/2,x+w/4,y+h/2+10);
  }
}
```

Lesson Four Project

Step 1. Take the Class you made in Lesson Three and make an array of objects from that class.

Step 2. Can you make the objects react to the mouse? Try using the *dist()* function to determine the object's proximity to the mouse. For example, could you make each object jiggle more the closer it is to the mouse?

How many objects can you make before the sketch runs too slow?

Use the space provided below to sketch designs, notes, and pseudocode for your project.

Lesson Five

Putting It All Together

10 Algorithms

"Lather. Rinse. Repeat."
— Unknown

10.1 Where have we been? Where are we going?

Our friend Zoog had a nice run. Zoog taught us the basics of the shape drawing libraries in *Processing*. From there, Zoog advanced to interacting with the mouse, to moving autonomously via variables, changing direction with conditionals, expanding its body with a loop, organizing its code with functions, encapsulating its data and functionality into an object, and finally duplicating itself with an array. It is a good story, and one that treated us well. Nonetheless, it is highly unlikely that all of the programming projects you intend to do after reading this book will involve a collection of alien creatures jiggling around the screen (if they do, you are one lucky programmer!). What we need to do is pause for a moment and consider what we have learned and how it can apply to what *you want to do*. What is your idea and how can variables, conditionals, loops, functions, objects, and arrays help you?

In earlier chapters we focused on straightforward "one feature" programming examples. Zoog would jiggle and only jiggle. Zoog didn't suddenly start hopping. And Zoog was usually all alone, never interacting with other alien creatures along the way. Certainly, we could have taken these early examples further, but it was important at the time to stick with basic functionality so that we could really learn the fundamentals.

In the real world, software projects usually involve many moving parts. This chapter aims to demonstrate how a larger project is created out of many smaller "one feature" programs like the ones we are starting to feel comfortable making. You, the programmer, will start with an overall vision, but must learn how to break it down into individual parts to successfully execute that vision.

We will start with an idea. Ideally, we would pick a sample "idea" that could set the basis for any project you want to create after reading this book. Sadly, there is no such thing. Programming your own software is terrifically exciting because of the immeasurable array of possibilities for creation. Ultimately, you will have to make your own way. However, just as we picked a simple creature for learning the fundamentals, knowing we will not really be programming creatures all of our lives, we can attempt to make a generic choice, one that will hopefully serve for learning about the process of developing larger projects.

Our choice will be a simple game with interactivity, multiple objects, and a goal. The focus will not be on good game design, but rather on good *software design*. How do you go from thought to code? How do you implement your own algorithm to realize your ideas? We will see how a larger project divides into four mini-projects and attack them one by one, ultimately bringing all parts together to execute the original idea.

We will continue to emphasize object-oriented programming, and each one of these parts will be developed using a *class*. The payoff will be seeing how easy it then is to create the final program by bringing the self-contained, fully functional classes together. Before we get to the idea and its parts, let's review the concept of an *algorithm* which we'll need for steps 2a and 2b.

Our Process

1. **Idea**—Start with an idea.
2. **Parts**—Break the idea down into smaller parts.
   a. **Algorithm Pseudocode**—For each part, work out the algorithm for that part in pseudocode.
   b. **Algorithm Code**—Implement that algorithm with code.
   c. **Objects**—Take the data and functionality associated with that algorithm and build it into a class.
3. **Integration**—Take all the classes from Step 2 and integrate them into one larger algorithm.

10.2 Algorithm: Dance to the beat of your own drum.

An algorithm is a procedure or formula for solving a problem. In computer programming, an algorithm is the sequence of steps required to perform a task. Every single example we have created so far in this book involved an algorithm.

An algorithm is not too far off from a recipe.

1. Preheat oven to 400°F.
2. Place four boneless chicken breasts in a baking dish.
3. Spread mustard evenly over chicken.
4. Bake at 400°F for 30 min.

The above is a nice algorithm for cooking mustard chicken. Clearly we are not going to write a *Processing* program to cook chicken. Nevertheless, if we did, the above pseudocode might turn into the following code.

```
preheatOven(400);
placeChicken(4,"baking dish"167);
spreadMustard();
bake(400,30);
```

An example that uses an algorithm to solve a math problem is more relevant to our pursuits. Let's describe an algorithm to evaluate the sum of a sequence of numbers 1 through N.

$$SUM(N) = 1+2+3+ \ ... \ +N$$

where N is any given whole number greater than zero.

1. Set SUM = 0 and a counter $I = 1$
2. Repeat the following steps while I is less than or equal to N.
   a. Calculate SUM + I and save the result in SUM.
   b. Increase the value of I by 1.
3. The solution is now the number saved in SUM.

Translating the preceding algorithm into code, we have:

```
int sum = 0;
int n = 10;
int i = 0;

while (i <= n) {
  sum = sum + i;
  i++;
}

print ln(sum);
```

Step 1. Set sum equal to 0 and counter $i = 0$.

Step 2. Repeat while $i <= n$.
Step 2a. Increment sum.
Step 2b. Increment i.

Step 3. The solution is in sum. Print sum!

Traditionally, programming is thought of as the process of (1) developing an idea, (2) working out an algorithm to implement that idea, and (3) writing out the code to implement that algorithm. This is what we have accomplished in both the chicken and summation examples. Some ideas, however, are too large to be finished in one fell swoop. And so we are going to revise these three steps and say programming is the process of (1) developing an idea, (2) breaking that idea into smaller manageable parts, (3) working out the algorithm for each part, (4) writing the code for each part, (5) working out the algorithm for all the parts together, and (6) integrating the code for all of the parts together.

This does not mean to say one shouldn't experiment along the way, even altering the original idea completely. And certainly, once the code is finished, there will almost always remain work to do in terms of cleaning up code, bug fixes, and additional features. It is this thinking process, however, that should guide you from idea to code. If you practice developing your projects with this strategy, creating code that implements your ideas will hopefully feel less daunting.

10.3 From Idea to Parts

To practice our development strategy, we will begin with the idea, a very simple game. Before we can get anywhere, we should describe the game in paragraph form.

Rain Game

The object of this game is to catch raindrops before they hit the ground. Every so often (depending on the level of difficulty), a new drop falls from the top of the screen at a random horizontal location with a random vertical speed. The player must catch the raindrops with the mouse with the goal of not letting any raindrops reach the bottom of the screen.

Exercise 10.1: Write out an idea for a project you want to create. Keep it simple, just not too simple. A few elements, a few behaviors will do.

Now let's see if we can take the "Rain Game" idea and break it down into smaller parts. How do we do this? For one, we can start by thinking of the elements in the game: the raindrops and the catcher. Secondly, we should think about these elements' behaviors. For example, we will need a timing mechanism so that the drops fall "every so often". We will also need to determine when a raindrop is "caught." Let's organize these parts more formally.

Part 1. Develop a program with a circle controlled by the mouse. This circle will be the user-controlled "rain catcher."

Part 2. Write a program to test if two circles intersect. This will be used to determine if the rain catcher has caught a raindrop.

Part 3. Write a timer program that executes a function every N seconds.

Part 4. Write a program with circles falling from the top of the screen to the bottom. These will be the raindrops.

Parts 1 through 3 are simple and each can be completed in one fell swoop. However, with Part 4, even though it represents one piece of the larger project, it is complex enough that we will need to complete this exact exercise by breaking it down into smaller steps and building it back up.

 Exercise 10-2: Take your idea from Exercise 10-1 and write out the individual parts. Try to make the parts as simple as possible (almost to the point that it seems absurd). If the parts are too complex, break them down even further.

Sections 10.4 to 10.7 will follow the process of Steps 2a, 2b, and 2c (see breakout box on p. 166) for each individual part. For each part, we will first work out the algorithm in pseudocode, then in actual code, and finish with an object-oriented version. If we do our job correctly, all of the functionality needed will be built into a class which can then be easily copied into the final project itself when we get to Step 3 (integration of all parts).

10.4 Part 1: The Catcher

This is the simplest part to construct and requires little beyond what we learned in Chapter 3. Having pseudocode that is only two lines long is a good sign, indicating that this step is small enough to handle and does not need to be made into even smaller parts.

Pseudocode:
- Erase background.
- Draw an ellipse at the mouse location.

Translating it into code is easy:

```
void setup() {
  size(400,400);
  smooth();
}
```

```
void draw() {
  background(255);
  stroke(0);
  fill(175);
  ellipse(mouseX,mouseY,64,64);
}
```

This is good step, but we are not done. As stated, our goal is to develop the rain catcher program in an object-oriented manner. When we take this code and incorporate it into the final program, we will want to have it separated out into a class so that we can make a "catcher" object. Our pseudocode would be revised to look like the following.

Setup:

- Initialize catcher object.

Draw:

- Erase background.
- Set catcher location to mouse location.
- Display catcher.

Example 10-1 shows the code rewritten assuming a Catcher object.

Example 10-1: Catcher

```
Catcher catcher;

void setup() {
  size(400,400);
  catcher = new Catcher(32);
  smooth();
}

void draw() {
  background(255);
  catcher.setLocation(mouseX,mouseY);
  catcher.display();
}
```

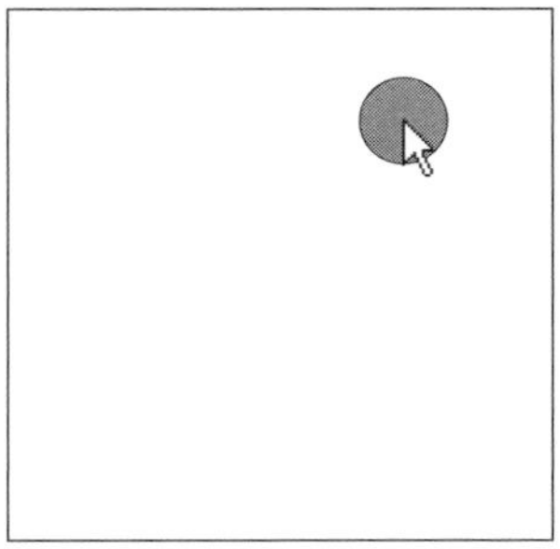

fig. 10.1

The Catcher class itself is rather simple, with variables for location and size, and two functions, one to set the location and one to display.

```
class Catcher {
  float r;        // radius
  float x,y;      // location

  Catcher(float tempR) {
    r = tempR;
    x = 0;
    y = 0;
  }
```

```
void setLocation(float tempX, float tempY) {
  x = tempX;
  y = tempY;
}

void display() {
  stroke(0);
  fill(175);
  ellipse(x,y,r*2,r*2);
}
}
```

10.5 Part 2: Intersection

Part 2 of our list requires us to determine when the catcher and a raindrop intersect. Intersection *functionality* is what we want to focus on developing in this step. We will start with a simple bouncing ball class (which we saw in Example 5-6) and work out how to determine when two bouncing circles intersect. During the "integration" process, this ***intersect()*** function will be incorporated into the Catcher class to catch raindrops.

Here is our algorithm for this intersection part.

Setup:

- Create two ball objects.

Draw:

- Move balls.
- If ball #1 intersects ball #2, change color of both balls to white. Otherwise, leave color gray.
- Display balls.

Certainly the hard work here is the intersection test, which we will get to in a moment. First, here is what we need for a simple bouncing "Ball" class without an intersection test.

Data:

- *X* and *Y* location.
- Radius.
- Speed in *X* and *Y* directions.

Functions:

- Constructor.
  - Set radius based on argument
  - Pick random location.
  - Pick random speed.
- Move.
  - Increment *X* by speed in *X* direction.
  - Increment *Y* by speed in *Y* direction.
  - If Ball hits any edge, reverse direction.
- Display.
  - Draw a circle at *X* and *Y* location.

We are now ready to translate this into code.

Example 10-2: Bouncing ball class

```
class Ball {
  float r;  // radius
  float x,y;       // location
  float xspeed,yspeed; // speed

  // Constructor
  Ball(float tempR) {
    r = tempR;
    x = random(width);
    y = random(height);
    xspeed = random(-5,5);
    yspeed = random(-5,5);
  }

  void move() {
    x += xspeed;  // Increment x
    y += yspeed;  // Increment y

    // Check horizontal edges
    if (x > width || x < 0) {
      xspeed *=   -1;
    }

    //Check vertical edges
    if (y > height || y < 0) {
      yspeed *= -1;
    }
  }

  // Draw the ball
  void display() {
    stroke(255);
    fill(100,50);
    ellipse(x,y,r*2,r*2);
  }
}
```

From here, it is pretty easy to create a sketch with two ball objects. Ultimately, in the final sketch, we'll need an array for many raindrops, but for now, two ball variables will be simpler.

Example 10-2 Catcher (Cont.): Two ball objects

```
// Two ball variables
Ball ball1;
Ball ball2;

void setup() {
  size(400,400);
  smooth();
  // Initialize balls
  ball1 = new Ball(64);
  ball2 = new Ball(32);
}

void draw() {
  background(0);
```

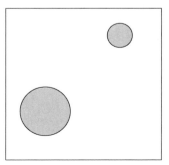

fig. 10.2

```
  // Move and display balls
  ball1.move();
  ball2.move();
  ball1.display();
  ball2.display();
}
```

Now that we have set up our system for having two circles moving around the screen, we need to develop an algorithm for determining if the circles intersect. In *Processing*, we know we can calculate the distance between two points using the **dist()** function (see Chapter 7). We also have access to the radius of each circle (the variable *r* inside each object). The diagram in Figure 10.3 shows how we can compare the distance between the circles and the sum of the radii to determine if the circles overlap.

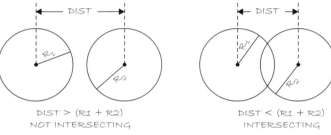

fig. 10.3

OK, so assuming the following:
- x_1,y_1: coordinates of circle one
- x_2,y_2: coordinates of circle two
- r_1: radius of circle one
- r_2: radius of circle two

We have the statement:

If the distance between (x_1,y_1) and (x_2,y_2) is less than the sum of r_1 and r_2, circle one intersects circle two.

Our job now is to write a function that returns true or false based on the above statement.

```
  // A function that returns true or false based on whether two circles intersect
  // If distance is less than the sum of radii the circles touch
  boolean intersect(float x1, float y1, float x2, float y2, float r1, float r2) {
    float distance = dist(x1,y2,x2,y2); // Calculate distance
    if (distance < r1 + r2) {           // Compare distance to r1 + r2
      return true;
    } else {
      return false;
    }
  }
```

Now that the function is complete, we can test it with data from ball1 and ball2.

```
boolean intersecting = intersect(ball1.x,ball1.y,ball2.x,ball2.y,ball1.r,ball2.r);
if (intersecting) {
  println("The circles are intersecting!");
}
```

The above code is somewhat awkward and it will be useful to take the function one step further, incorporating it into the ball class itself. Let's first look at the entire main program as it stands.

```
// Two ball variables
Ball ball1;
Ball ball2;

void setup() {
  size(400,400);
  framerate(30);
  smooth();
  // Initialize balls
  ball1 = new Ball(64);
  ball2 = new Ball(32);
}

void draw() {
  background(0);
  // Move and display balls
  ball1.move();
  ball2.move();
  ball1.display();
  ball2.display();
  boolean intersecting = intersect(ball1.x,ball1.y,ball2.x,ball2.y,ball1.r,ball2.r);
  if (intersecting) {
    println("The circles are intersecting!");
  }
}

// A function that returns true or false based on whether two circles intersect
// If distance is less than the sum of radii the circles touch
boolean intersect(float x1, float y1, float x2, float y2, float r1, float r2) {
  float distance = dist(x1,y2,x2,y2);      // Calculate distance
  if (distance < r1 + r2) {                // Compare distance to r1 + r2
    return true;
  } else {
    return false;
  }
}
```

Since we have programmed the balls in an object-oriented fashion, it is not terribly logical to suddenly have an ***intersect()*** function that lives outside of the ball class. A ball object should know how to test if it is intersecting another ball object. Our code can be improved by incorporating the intersect logic into the class itself, saying "***ball1.intersect (ball2);***" or, does Ball 1 intersect Ball 2?

```
void draw() {
  background(0);
  // Move and display balls
  ball1.move();
  ball2.move();
  ball1.display();
  ball2.display();
```

```
    boolean intersecting = ball1.intersect(ball2);
    if (intersecting) {
      println("The circles are intersecting!");
    }
  }
}
```

> Assumes a function *intersect()* inside the Ball class that returns true or false.

Following this model and the algorithm for testing intersection, here is a function for inside the ball class itself. Notice how the function makes use of both its own location (*x* and *y*) as well as the other ball's location (*b.x* and *b.y*).

```
// A function that returns true or false based on whether two Ball objects intersect
// If distance is less than the sum of radii the circles touch
boolean intersect(Ball b) {
  float distance = dist(x,y,b.x,b.y);  // Calculate distance
  if (distance < r + b.r) {            // Compare distance to sum of radii
    return true;
  } else {
    return false;
  }
}
```

Putting it all together, we have the code in Example 10-3.

Example 10-3: Bouncing ball with intersection

```
// Two ball variables
Ball ball1;
Ball ball2;

void setup() {
  size(400,400);
  smooth();
  // Initialize balls
  ball1 = new Ball(64);
  ball2 = new Ball(32);
}

void draw() {
  background(255);
  // Move and display balls
  ball1.move();
  ball2.move();
  if (ball1.intersect(ball2)) {
    ball1.highlight();
    ball2.highlight();
  }
  ball1.display();
  ball2.display();
}

class Ball {
  float r; // radius
  float x,y;
  float xspeed,yspeed;
  color c = color(100,50);
```

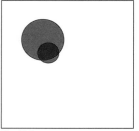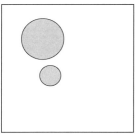

fig. 10.4

> New! An object can have a function that takes another object as an argument. This is one way to have objects communicate. In this case they are checking to see if they intersect.

```
// Constructor
Ball(float tempR) {
  r = tempR;
  x = random(width);
  y = random(height);
  xspeed = random(-5,5);
  yspeed = random(-5,5);
}

void move() {
  x += xspeed;  // Increment x
  y += yspeed;  // Increment y

  // Check horizontal edges
  if (x > width || x < 0) {
    xspeed *= -1;
  }
  // Check vertical edges
  if (y > height || y < 0) {
    yspeed *= -1;
  }
}

void highlight() {
  c = color(0,150);
}
```

> Whenever the balls are touching, this **highlight()** function is called and the color is darkened.

```
// Draw the ball
void display() {
  stroke(0);
  fill(c);
  ellipse(x,y,r*2,r*2);
  c = color(100,50);
}
```

> After the ball is displayed, the color is reset back to a darker gray.

```
// A function that returns true or false based on whether two circles intersect
// If distance is less than the sum of radii the circles touch
boolean intersect(Ball b) {
  float distance = dist(x,y,b.x,b.y);  // Calculate distance
  if (distance < r + b.r) {            // Compare distance to
                                       //    sum of radii

    return true;
  } else {
    return false;
  }
}
}
```

> Objects can be passed into functions as arguments too!

10.6 Part 3: The Timer

Our next task is to develop a timer that executes a function every *N* seconds. Again, we will do this in two steps, first just using the main body of a program and second, taking the logic and putting it into a Timer class. *Processing* has the functions *hour()*, *second()*, *minute()*, *month()*, *day()*, and *year()* to deal with time. We could conceivably use the *second()* function to determine how much time has passed. However, this is not terribly convenient, since *second()* rolls over from 60 to 0 at the end of every minute.

For creating a timer, the function *millis()* is best. First of all, *millis()*, which returns the number of milliseconds since a sketch started, allows for a great deal more precision. One millisecond is one one-thousandth of a second (1,000 ms = 1 s). Secondly, *millis()* never rolls back to zero, so asking for the milliseconds at one moment and subtracting it from the milliseconds at a later moment will always result in the amount of time passed.

Let's say we want an applet to change the background color to red 5 seconds after it started. Five seconds is 5,000 ms, so it is as easy as checking if the result of the *millis()* function is greater than 5,000.

```
if (millis() > 5000) {
  background(255,0,0);
}
```

Making the problem a bit more complicated, we can expand the program to change the background to a new random color every 5 seconds.

Setup:

- Save the time at startup (note this should always be zero, but it is useful to save it in a variable anyway). Call this "savedTime".

Draw:

- Calculate the time passed as the current time (i.e., *millis()*) minus savedTime. Save this as "passedTime".
- If passedTime is greater than 5,000, fill a new random background and *reset savedTime to the current time.* This step will restart the timer.

Example 10-4 translates this into code.

Example 10-4: Implementing a timer

```
int savedTime;
int totalTime = 5000;

void setup() {
  size(200,200);
  background(0);
  savedTime = millis();
}

void draw() {

  // Calculate how much time has passed
  int passedTime = millis() - savedTime;
  // Has five seconds passed?
  if (passedTime > totalTime) {
    println("5 seconds have passed!");
    background(random(255));  // Color a new background
    savedTime = millis();  // Save the current time to restart the timer!
  }
}
```

With the above logic worked out, we can now move the timer into a class. Let's think about what data is involved in the timer. A timer must know the time at which it started (*savedTime*) and how long it needs to run (*totalTime*).

Data:

- savedTime
- totalTime

The timer must also be able to *start* as well as check and see if it *is finished*.

Functions:

- ***start()***
- ***isFinished()***—returns true or false

Taking the code from the non-object-oriented example and building it out with the above structure, we have the code shown in Example 10-5.

Example 10-5: Object-oriented timer

```
Timer timer;

void setup() {
  size(200,200);
  background(0);
  timer = new Timer(5000);
  timer.start();
}

void draw() {
  if (timer.isFinished()) {
    background(random(255));
    timer.start();
  }
}

class Timer {

  int savedTime;  // When Timer started
  int totalTime;  // How long Timer should last

  Timer(int tempTotalTime) {
    totalTime = tempTotalTime;
  }

  // Starting the timer
  void start() {
    savedTime = millis();
  }

  boolean isFinished() {
    // Check how much time has passed
    int passedTime = millis() - savedTime;
    if (passedTime > totalTime) {
      return true;
    } else {
      return false;
    }
  }
}
```

> When the timer starts it stores the current time in milliseconds.

> The function ***isFinished()*** returns true if 5,000 ms have passed. The work of the timer is farmed out to this method.

10.7 Part 4: Raindrops

We are almost there. We have created a catcher, we know how to test for intersection, and we have completed the timer object. The final piece of the puzzle is the raindrops themselves. Ultimately, we want an array of Raindrop objects falling from the top of the window to the bottom. Since this step involves creating an array of objects that move, it is useful to approach this fourth part as a series of even smaller steps, subparts of Part 4, thinking again of the individual elements and behaviors we will need.

Part 4 Subparts:
> **Part 4.1.** A single moving raindrop.
> **Part 4.2.** An array of raindrop objects.
> **Part 4.3.** Flexible number of raindrops (appearing one at a time).
> **Part 4.4.** Fancier raindrop appearance.

Part 4.1, creating the motion of a raindrop (a simple circle for now) is easy—Chapter 3 easy.

- Increment raindrop *y* value.
- Display raindrop.

Translating into code we have *Part 4.1—A single moving raindrop*, shown in Example 10-6.

Example 10-6: Simple raindrop behavior

```
float x,y; // Variables for drop location

void setup() {
  size(400,400);
  background(0);
  x = width/2;
  y = 0;
}

void draw() {
  background(255);
  // Display the drop
  fill(50,100,150);
  noStroke();
  ellipse(x,y,16,16);
  // Move the drop
  y++;
}
```

Again, however, we need to go a step further and make a Drop class—after all we will ultimately want an array of drops. In making the class, we can add a few more variables, such as speed and size, as well as a function to test if the raindrop reaches the bottom of the screen, which will be useful later for scoring the game.

```
class Drop {

  float x,y;    // Variables for location of raindrop
  float speed;  // Speed of raindrop
  color c;
  float r;      // Radius of raindrop
```

> A raindrop object has a location, speed, color, and size.

```
Drop() {
  r = 8;                    // All raindrops are the same size
  x = random(width);        // Start with a random x location
  y = -r*4;                 // Start a little above the window
  speed = random(1,5);      // Pick a random speed
  c = color(50,100,150);    // Color
}


//Move the raindrop down
void move() {
  y += speed;     // Increment by speed
}


// Check if it hits the bottom
boolean reachedBottom() {
  // If we go a little past the bottom
  if (y > height+r*4) {
    return true;
  } else {
    return false;
  }
}


// Display the raindrop
void display() {
  // Display the drop
  fill(50,100,150);
  noStroke();
  ellipse(x,y,r*2,r*2);
}
}
```

> Incrementing *y* is now in the ***move()*** function.

> In addition, we have a function that determines if the drop leaves the window.

Before we move on to Part 4.3, the array of drops, we should make sure that a singular Drop object functions properly. As an exercise, complete the code in Exercise 10-3 that would test a single drop object.

Exercise 10-3: Fill in the blanks below completing the "test Drop" sketch.

```
Drop drop;

void setup() {
  size(200,200);

  _____;

}

void draw() {
  background(255);
  drop. _____;

  _____;

}
```

Now that this is complete, the next step is to go from one drop to an array of drops—**Part 4.2**. This is exactly the technique we perfected in Chapter 9.

```
// An array of drops
Drop[] drops = new Drop[50];                    Instead of one Drop object, an array of 50.

void setup() {
  size(400,400);
  smooth();
  // Initialize all drops
  for (int i = 0; i < drops.length; i++) {      Using a loop to initialize all drops.
    drops[i] = new Drop();
  }
}

void draw() {
  background(255);
  // Move and display all drops
  for (int i = 0; i < drops.length; i++) {      Move and display all drops.
    drops[i].move();
    drops[i].display();
  }
}
```

The problem with the above code is that the raindrops appear all at once. According to the specifications we made for our game, we want to have the raindrops appear one at a time, every *N* seconds—we are now at **Part 4.3—Flexible number of raindrops (appearing one at a time)**. We can skip worrying about the timer for now and just have one new raindrop appear every frame. We should also make our array much larger, allowing for many more raindrops.

To make this work, we need a new variable to keep track of the total number of drops—"totalDrops". Most array examples involve walking through the entire array in order to deal with the entire list. Now, we want to access a portion of the list, the number stored in totalDrops. Let's write some pseudocode to describe this process:

Setup:

- Create an array of drops with 1,000 spaces in it.
- Set totalDrops = 0.

Draw:

- Create a new drop in the array (at the location totalDrops). Since totalDrops starts at 0, we will first create a new raindrop in the first spot of the array.
- Increment totalDrops (so that the next time we arrive here, we will create a drop in the next spot in the array).
- If totalDrops exceeds the array size, reset it to zero and start over.
- Move and display all available drops (i.e., totalDrops).

Example 10-7 translates the above pseudocode into code.

Example 10-7: Drops one at a time

```
// An array of drops
Drop[] drops = new Drop[1000];

int totalDrops = 0;

void setup() {
  size(400,400);
  smooth();
  background(0);
}

void draw() {
  background(255);

  // Initialize one drop
  drops[totalDrops] = new Drop();
  // Increment totalDrops
  totalDrops++;
  // If we hit the end of the array
  if (totalDrops >= drops.length) {
  totalDrops = 0; //Start over
  }

  // Move and display drops
  for (int i = 0; i < totalDrops; i++) {
    drops[i].move();
    drops[i].display();
  }
}
```

New variable to keep track of total number of drops we want to use!

New! We no longer move and display all drops, but rather only the "totalDrops" that are currently present in the game.

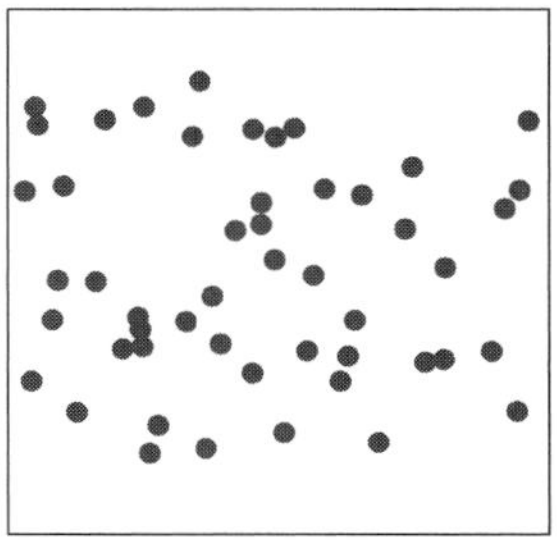

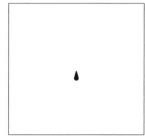

fig. 10.5

We have taken the time to figure out how we want the raindrop to move, created a class that exhibits that behavior, and made an array of objects from that class. All along, however, we have just been using a circle to display the drop. The advantage to this is that we were able to delay worrying about the drawing code and focus on the motion behaviors and organization of data and functions. Now we can focus on how the drops look—*Part 4.4—Finalize raindrop appearance.*

One way to create a more "drop-like" look is to draw a sequence of circles in the vertical direction, starting small, and getting larger as they move down.

Example 10-8: Fancier looking raindrop

```
background(255);
for (int i=2; i<8; i++) {
  noStroke();
  fill(0);
  ellipse(width/2,height/2+i*4,i*2,i*2);
}
```

We can incorporate this algorithm in the raindrop class from Example 10-7, using *x* and *y* for the start of the ellipse locations, and the raindrop radius as the maximum value for *i* in the for loop. The output is shown in Figure 10.7.

fig. 10.6

```
// Display the raindrop
void display() {
  // Display the drop
  noStroke();
  fill(c);
  for (int i = 2; i < r; i++) {
    ellipse(x,y+i*4,i*2,i*2);
  }
}
```

fig. 10.7

10.8 Integration: Puttin' on the Ritz

It is time. Now that we have developed the individual pieces and confirmed that each one works properly, we can assemble them together in one program. The first step is to create a new *Processing* sketch that has four tabs, one for each of our classes and one main program, as shown in Figure 10.8.

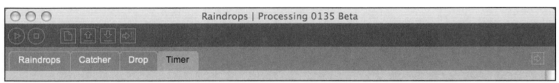

fig. 10.8

The first step is to copy and paste the code for each class into each tab. Individually, they will not need to change, so there is no need for us to revisit the code. What we do need to revisit is the main program—what goes in *setup()* and *draw()*. Referring back to the original game description and knowing how the pieces were assembled, we can write the pseudocode algorithm for the entire game.

Setup:

- Create Catcher object.
- Create array of drops.
- Set totalDrops equal to 0.
- Create Timer object.
- Start timer.

Draw:

- Set Catcher location to mouse location.
- Display Catcher.
- Move all available Drops.
- Display all available Drops.
- If the Catcher intersects any Drop.
  - Remove Drop from screen.
- If the timer is finished:
  - Increase the number of drops.
  - Restart timer.

Notice how every single step in the above program has already been worked out previously in the chapter with one exception: "Remove Drop from screen." This is rather common. Even with breaking the idea down into parts and working them out one at a time, little bits can be missed. Fortunately, this piece of functionality is simple enough and with some ingenuity, we will see how we can slip it in during assembly.

One way to approach assembling the above algorithm is to start by combining all of the elements into one sketch and not worrying about how they interact. In other words, everything but having the timer trigger the drops and testing for intersection. To get this going, all we need to do is copy/paste from each part's global variables, *setup()* and *draw()*!

Here are the global variables: a Catcher object, an array of Drop objects, a Timer object, and an integer to store the total number of drops.

```
Catcher catcher;      // One catcher object
Timer timer;          // One timer object
Drop[] drops;         // An array of drop objects

int totalDrops = 0;   // totalDrops
```

In *setup()*, the variables are initialized. Note, however, we can skip initializing the individual drops in the array since they will be created one at a time. We will also need to call the timer's *start()* function.

```
void setup() {
  size(400,400);

  catcher = new Catcher(32);      // Create the catcher with a radius of 32
  drops = new Drop[1000];         // Create 1000 spots in the array
  timer = new Timer(2000);        // Create a timer that goes off every 2 seconds

  timer.start();                  // Starting the timer
}
```

In *draw()*, the objects call their methods. Again, we are just taking the code from each part we did separately earlier in this chapter and pasting in sequence.

Example 10-9: Using all the objects in one sketch

```
Catcher catcher;      // One catcher object
Timer timer;          // One timer object
Drop[] drops;         // An array of drop objects

int totalDrops = 0;   // totalDrops

void setup() {
  size(400,400);
  smooth();

  catcher = new Catcher(32);      // Create the catcher with a radius of 32
  drops = new Drop[1000];         // Create 1000 spots in the array
  timer = new Timer(2000);        // Create a timer that goes off every 2 seconds

  timer.start();                  // Starting the timer
}
```

```
void draw() {
  background(255);
```

```
catcher.setLocation(mouseX,mouseY); // Set catcher location
catcher.display();                  // Display the catcher
```

From Part 1.
The Catcher!

```
// Check the timer
if (timer.isFinished()) {
  println("2 seconds have passed!");
  timer.start();
}
```

From Part 3.
The Timer!

```
// Deal with raindrops
// Initialize one drop
drops[totalDrops] = new Drop();
//Increment totalDrops
totalDrops++;
// If we hit the end of the array
if (totalDrops >= drops.length) {
  totalDrops = 0; // Start over
}

// Move and display all drops
for (int i = 0; i < totalDrops; i++) {
  drops[i].move();
  drops[i].display();
}
```

From Part 4.
The Raindrops!

```
}
```

The next step is to take these concepts we have developed and have them work together. For example, we should only create a new raindrop whenever two seconds have passed (as indicated by the timer's *isFinished()* function).

```
// Check the timer
if (timer.isFinished()) {
  // Deal with raindrops
  // Initialize one drop
  drops[totalDrops] = new Drop();
  // Increment totalDrops
  totalDrops++;
  // If we hit the end of the array
  if (totalDrops >= drops.length) {
    totalDrops = 0; // Start over
  }
  timer.start();
}
```

Objects working together! Here when the timer "is finished," a Drop object is added (by incrementing "totalDrops").

We also need to find out when the Catcher object intersects a Drop. In Section 10.5, we tested for intersection by calling the *intersect()* function we wrote inside the Ball class.

```
boolean intersecting = ball1.intersect(ball2);
if (intersecting) {
  println("The circles are intersecting!");
}
```

We can do the same thing here, calling an *intersect()* function in the Catcher class and passing through every raindrop in the system. Instead of printing out a message, we will actually want to affect the raindrop itself, telling it to disappear, perhaps. This code assumes that the *caught()* function will do the job.

```
// Move and display all drops
for (int i = 0; i < totalDrops; i++) {
  drops[i].move();
  drops[i].display();
  if (catcher.intersect(drops[i])) {
    drops[i].caught();
  }
}
```

> Objects working together! Here, the Catcher object checks to see if it intersects any Drop object in the drops array.

Our Catcher object did not originally contain the function *intersect()*, nor did Drop include *caught()*. So these are some new functions we will need to write as part of the integration process.

intersect() is easy to incorporate since we solved the problem already in Section 10.5 and can literally copy it into the Catcher class (changing the argument from a Ball object to a Drop object).

```
// A function that returns true or false based if the catcher intersects a raindrop
boolean intersect(Drop d) {
  // Calculate distance
  float distance = dist(x,y,d.x,d.y);
  // Compare distance to sum of radii
  if (distance < r + d.r) {
    return true;
  } else {
    return false;
  }
}
```

> In addition to calling functions, we can access variables inside of an object using the dot syntax.

When the drop is caught, we will set its location to somewhere offscreen (so that it can't be seen, the equivalent of "disappearing") and stop it from moving by setting its speed equal to 0. Although we did not work out this functionality in advance of the integration process, it is simple enough to throw in right now.

```
// If the drop is caught
void caught() {
  speed = 0;      // Stop it from moving by setting speed equal to zero
  y = -1000;      // Set the location to somewhere way off-screen
}
```

And we are finished! For reference, Example 10-10 is the entire sketch. The timer is altered to execute every 300 ms, making the game ever so slightly more difficult.

Example 10-10: The raindrop catching game

```
Catcher catcher;      // One catcher object
Timer timer;          // One timer object
Drop[] drops;         // An array of drop objects

int totalDrops = 0;   // totalDrops
void setup() {
  size(400,400);
  smooth();

  catcher = new Catcher(32);   // Create the catcher with a radius of 32
  drops = new Drop[1000];      // Create 1000 spots in the array
  timer = new Timer(300);      // Create a timer that goes off every 2 seconds

  timer.start();               // Starting the timer
}

void draw() {
  background(255);
  catcher.setLocation(mouseX,mouseY);  // Set catcher location
  catcher.display();                   // Display the catcher

  // Check the timer
  if (timer.isFinished()) {
    // Deal with raindrops
    // Initialize one drop
    drops[totalDrops] = new Drop();
    // Increment totalDrops
    totalDrops++;
    // If we hit the end of the array
    if (totalDrops >= drops.length) {
      totalDrops = 0;  // Start over
    }
    timer.start();
  }

  // Move and display all drops
  for (int i = 0; i < totalDrops; i++) {
    drops[i].move();
    drops[i].display();
    if (catcher.intersect(drops[i])) {
      drops[i].caught();
    }
  }
}

class Catcher {
  float r;       // radius
  color col;     // color
  float x,y;     // location

  Catcher(float tempR) {
    r = tempR;
    col = color(50,10,10,150);
    x = 0;
    y = 0;
  }
```

fig. 10.9

```
  void setLocation(float tempX, float tempY) {
    x = tempX;
    y = tempY;
  }

  void display() {
    stroke(0);
    fill(col);
    ellipse(x,y,r*2,r*2);
  }

  // A function that returns true or false based if the catcher intersects a raindrop
  boolean intersect(Drop d) {
    float distance = dist(x,y,d.x,d.y);    // Calculate distance
    if (distance < r + d.r) {              // Compare distance to sum of radii
      return true;
    } else {
      return false;
    }
  }

}

class Drop {

  float x,y;          // Variables for location of raindrop
  float speed;        // Speed of raindrop
  color c;
  float r;            // Radius of raindrop

  Drop() {
    r = 8;                   // All raindrops are the same size
    x = random(width);       // Start with a random x location
    y = -r*4;                // Start a little above the window
    speed = random(1,5);     // Pick a random speed
    c = color(50,100,150);   // Color
  }

  // Move the raindrop down
  void move() {
    y += speed;  // Increment by speed
  }

  // Check if it hits the bottom
  boolean reachedBottom() {
    if (y > height+r*4) {  // If we go a little beyond the bottom
      return true;
    } else {
      return false;
    }
  }

  // Display the raindrop
  void display() {
    // Display the drop
    fill(c);
```

```
    noStroke();
    for (int i = 2; i < r; i++) {
      ellipse(x,y+i*4,i*2,i*2);
    }
  }

  // If the drop is caught
  void caught() {
    speed = 0;  // Stop it from moving by setting speed equal to zero
    // Set the location to somewhere way off-screen
    y = -1000;
  }
}

class Timer {

  int savedTime;  // When Timer started
  int totalTime;  // How long Timer should last

  Timer(int tempTotalTime) {
    totalTime = tempTotalTime;
  }

  // Starting the timer
  void start() {
    savedTime = millis();
  }

  boolean isFinished() {
    // Check out much time has passed
    int passedTime = millis() - savedTime;
    if (passedTime > totalTime) {
      return true;
    } else {
      return false;
    }
  }

}
```

 Exercise 10-4: Implement a scoring system for the game. Start the player off with 10 points. For every raindrop that reaches the bottom, decrease the score by 1. If all 1,000 raindrops fall without the score getting to zero, a new level begins and the raindrops appear faster. If 10 raindrops reach the bottom during any level, the player loses. Show the score onscreen as a rectangle that decreases in size. Do not try to implement all of these features at once. Do them one step at a time!

10.9 Getting Ready for Act II

The point of this chapter is not to learn how to program a game of catching falling raindrops, rather it is to develop an approach to problem solving—taking an idea, breaking it down into parts, developing pseudocode for those parts, and implementing them one very small step at a time.

It is important to remember that getting used to this process takes time and it takes practice. Everyone struggles through it when first learning to program.

Before we embark on the rest of this book, let's take a moment to consider what we have learned and where we are headed. In these 10 chapters, we have focused entirely on the fundamentals of programming.

- **Data**—in the form of variables and arrays.
- **Control Flow**—in the form of conditional statements and loops.
- **Organization**—in the form of functions and objects.

These concepts are not unique to *Processing* and will carry you through to any and all programming languages and environments, such as C++, Actionscript (as in Flash), and server-side programming languages such as PHP. The syntax may change, but the fundamental concepts will not.

Starting with Chapter 13 the book will focus on some advanced concepts available in *Processing*, such as three-dimensional translation and rotation, image processing and video capture, networking, and sound. Although these concepts are certainly not unique to *Processing*, the details of their implementation will be more specific to the environment we have chosen.

Before we move on to these advanced topics we will take a quick look at basic strategies for fixing errors in your code (Chapter 11: Debugging) as well as how to use *Processing* libraries (Chapter 12). Many of these advanced topics require importing libraries that come with *Processing* as well as libraries made for this book or by third parties. One of the strengths of *Processing* is its ability to be easily extended with libraries. We will see some hints of how to create your own libraries in the final chapter of this book.

Onward, ho!

Lesson Five Project

Step 1. Develop an idea for a project that can be created with *Processing* using simple shape drawing and the fundamentals of programming. If you feel stuck, try making a game such as Pong or Tic-Tac-Toe.

Step 2. Follow the strategy outlined in this chapter and break the idea down into smaller parts, implementing the algorithm for each one individually. Make sure to use object-oriented programming for each part.

Step 3. Bring the smaller parts together in one program. Did you forget any elements or features?

Use the space provided below to sketch designs, notes, and pseudocode for your project.

11 Debugging

"The difference between the right word and the almost right word
is the difference between lightning and a lightning bug."
—Mark Twain

"L'appétit vient en mangeant."
—The French

Bugs happen.

Five minutes ago, your code was working perfectly and you swear, all you did was change the color of some object! But now, when the spaceship hits the asteroid, it doesn't spin any more. But it was totally spinning five minutes ago! And your friend agrees: "Yeah, I saw it spin. That was cool." The **rotate()** function is there. What happened? It should work. This makes no sense at all! The computer is probably broken. Yeah. *Yeah.* It is definitely the computer's fault.

No matter how much time you spend studying computer science, reading programming books, or playing audio recordings of code while you sleep hoping it will soak in that way, there is just no way to avoid getting stuck on a bug.

It can be really frustrating.

A bug is any defect in a program. Sometimes it is obvious that you have a bug; your sketch will quit (or not run at all) and display an error in the message console. These types of bugs can be caused by simple typos, variables that were never initialized, looking for an element in an array that doesn't exist, and so on. For some additional clues on "error" bugs, take a look at the Appendix on errors at the end of this book.

Bugs can also be more sinister and mysterious. If your *Processing* sketch does not function the way you intended it to, you have a bug. In this case, your sketch might run without producing any errors in the message console. Finding this type of bug is more difficult since it will not necessarily be as obvious where to start looking in the code.

In this chapter, we will discuss a few basic strategies for fixing bugs ("debugging") with *Processing*.

11.1 Tip #1: Take a break.

Seriously. Go away from your computer. Sleep. Go jogging. Eat an orange. Play scrabble. Do something other than working on your code. I can't tell you how many times I have stared at my code for hours unable to fix it, only to wake up the next morning and solve the problem in five minutes.

11.2 Tip #2: Get another human being involved.

Talk through the problem with a friend. The process of showing your code to another programmer (or nonprogrammer, even) and walking through the logic out loud will often reveal the bug. In many cases, it is something obvious that you did not see because you know your code so well. The process of explaining it to someone else, however, forces you to go through the code more slowly. If you do not have a friend nearby, you can also do this out loud to yourself. Yes, you will look silly, but it helps.

11.3 Tip #3: Simplify

Simplify. Simplify! SIMPLIFY!

In Chapter 10, we focused on the process of incremental development. The more you develop your projects step-by-step, in small, easy to manage pieces, the fewer errors and bugs you will end up having. Of course, there is no way to avoid problems completely, so when they do occur, the philosophy of incremental development can also be applied to debugging. Instead of building the code up piece by piece, debugging involves taking the code apart piece by piece.

One way to accomplish this is to comment out large chunks of code in order to isolate a particular section. Following is the main tab of an example sketch. The sketch has an array of Snake objects, a Button object, and an Apple object. (The code for the classes is not included.) Let's assume that everything about the sketch is working properly, except that the Apple is invisible. To debug the problem, everything is commented out except for the few lines of code that deal directly with initializing and displaying the Apple object.

```
// Snake[] snakes = new Snake[100];
// Button button;
Apple apple;

void setup() {
  size(200,200);
  apple = new Apple();
  /*for (int i = 0; i < snakes.length; i++) {
    snakes[i] = new Snake();
  }
  button = new Button(10,10,100,50);
  smooth();*/
}

void draw() {
  background(0);
  apple.display();
  // apple.move();
```

> Only the code that makes the Apple object and displays the object is left uncommented. This way, we can be sure that none of the other code is the cause of the issue.

```
  /*for (int i = 0; i < snakes. length; i++) {
    snakes[i].display();
    snakes[i].slither();
    snakes[i].eat(apple);
  }

  if (button.pressed()) {
    applet.restart();
  }*/
```

> Large blocks of code can be commented out between /*and*/
>
> /*All of this is commented out */

```
}

/*void mousePressed() {
  button.click(mouseX,mouseY);
}*/
```

Once all the code is commented out, there are two possible outcomes. Either the apple still does not appear or it does. In the former, the issue is most definitely caused by the apple itself, and the next step would be to investigate the insides of the ***display()*** function and look for a mistake.

If the apple does appear, then the problem is caused by one of the other lines of code. Perhaps the ***move()*** function sends the apple offscreen so that we do not see it. Or maybe the Snake objects cover it up by accident. To figure this out, I would recommend putting back lines of code, one at a time. Each time you add back in a line of code, run the sketch and see if the apple disappears. As soon as it does, you have found the culprit and can root out the cause. Having an object-oriented sketch as above (with many classes) can really help the debugging process. Another tactic you can try is to create a new sketch and just use one of the classes, testing its basic features. In other words, do not worry about fixing your entire program just yet. First, create a new sketch that only does one thing with the relevant class (or classes) and reproduce the error. Let's say that, instead of the apple, the snakes are not behaving properly. To simplify and find the bug, we could create a sketch that just uses one snake (instead of an array) without the apple or the button. Without the bells and whistles, the code will be much easier to deal with.

```
Snake snake;

void setup() {
  size(200,200);
  snake = new Snake();
}

void draw() {
  background(0);
  snakes.display();
  snakes.slither();
  //snakes.eat(apple);
}
```

> Since this version does not include an Apple object, we cannot use this line of code. As part of the debugging process, however, we might incrementally add back in the apple and uncomment this line.

Although we have not yet looked at examples that involve external devices (we will in many of the chapters that follow), simplifying your sketch can also involve turning off connections to these devices, such as a camera, microphone, or network connection and replacing them with "dummy" information. For example, it is much easier to find an image analysis problem if you just load a JPG, rather than use a live video source. Or load a local text file instead of connecting to a URL XML feed. If the problem goes away, you can then say definitively: "Aha, the web server is probably down" or "My camera must be broken." If it does not, then you can dive into your code knowing the problem is there. If you are worried about worsening the problem by taking out sections of code, just make a copy of your sketch first before you begin removing features.

11.4 Tip #4: *println( )* is your friend.

Using the message window to display the values of variables can be really helpful. If an object is completely missing on the screen and you want to know why, you can print out the values of its location variables. It might look something like this:

```
println("x: " + thing.x + " y: " + thing.y);
```

Let's say the result is:

```
x:  9000000  y:  -900000
x:  9000116  y:  -901843
x:  9000184  y:  -902235
x:  9000299  y:  -903720
x:  9000682  y:  -904903
```

It is pretty obvious that these values are not reasonable pixel coordinates. So something would be off in the way the object is calculating its (*x,y*) location. However, if the values were perfectly reasonable, then you would move on. Maybe the color is the problem?

```
println("brightness: " + brightness(thing.col) + " alpha: " + alpha(thing.col));
```

Resulting in:

```
brightness: 150.0 alpha: 0.0
```

Well, if the alpha value of the object's color is zero, that would explain why you can't see it! We should take a moment here to remember Tip #3: Simplify. This process of printing variable values will be much more effective if we are doing it in a sketch that only deals with the Thing object. This way, we can be sure that it is not another class which is, say, drawing over the top of the Thing by accident.

You may have also noticed that the above print statements concatenate actual text with the variables. (See Chapter 17 for more on concatenation.) It is generally a good idea to do this. The following line of code only prints the value of *x*, with no explanation.

```
println(x);
```

This can be confusing to follow in the message window, especially if you are printing different values in different parts of the code. How do you know what is *x* and what is *y*? If you include your own notes in *println()*, there can't be any confusion:

```
println("The x value of the thing I'm looking for is: " + x);
```

In addition, *println()* can be used to indicate whether or not a certain part of the code has been reached. For example, what if in our "bouncing ball" example, the ball never bounces off of the right-hand side of the window? The problem could be (a) you are not properly determining when it hits the edge, or (b) you are doing the wrong thing when it hits the edge. To know if your code correctly detects when it hits the edge, you could write:

```
if (x > width) {
  println("X is greater than width. This code is happening now!");
  xspeed *= -1;
}
```

If you run the sketch and never see the message printed, then something is probably flawed with your boolean expression.

Admittedly, *println()* is not a perfect debugging tool. It can be hard to track multiple pieces of information with the message window. It can also slow your sketch down rather significantly (depending on how much printing you are doing). More advanced development environments usually offer debugging tools which allow you to track specific variables, pause the program, advance line by line in the code, and so on. This is one of the trade-offs we get using *Processing*. It is much simpler to use, but it does not have all of the advanced features. Still, in terms of debugging, some sleep, a little common sense, and *println()* can get you pretty far.

12 Libraries

"If truth is beauty, how come no one has their hair done in the library?"
—Lily Tomlin

Many of the chapters that follow require the use of *Processing* libraries. This chapter will cover how to download, install, and use these libraries. I recommend that you read the chapter for a basic sense of libraries now (we will start talking about them immediately in Chapter 14: Translation and Rotation) and, if necessary, refer back to it when you suddenly find yourself downloading one (which first occurs in Chapter 15: Video).

12.1 Libraries

Whenever we call a *Processing* function, such as ***line()***, ***background()***, ***stroke()***, and so on, we are calling a function that we learned about from the *Processing* reference page (or perhaps even from this book!). That reference page is a list of all the available functions in the core *Processing library*. In computer science, a library refers to a collection of "helper" code. A library might consist of functions, variables, and objects. The bulk of things we do are made possible by the core *Processing library*.

In most programming languages, you are required to specify which libraries you intend to use at the top of your code. This tells the compiler (see Chapter 2) where to look things up in order to translate your source code into machine code. If you were to investigate the files inside of your *Processing* application directory, you would find a file named *core.jar* inside of the folder *lib*. That jar file contains the compiled code for just about everything we do in *Processing*. Since it is used in every program, *Processing* just assumes that it should be imported and does not require that you explicitly write an import statement. However, if this were not the case, you would have the following line of code at the top of every single sketch:

```
import processing.core.*;
```

"Import" indicates we are going to make use of a library, and the library we are going to use is "processing. core." The ".*" is a wildcard, meaning we would like access to everything in the library. The naming of the library using the dot syntax (processing dot core) has to do with how collections of classes are organized into "packages" in the Java programming language. As you get more comfortable with *Processing* and programming, this is likely a topic you will want to investigate further. For now, all we need to know is that "processing.core" is the name of the library.

While the *core* library covers all the basics, for other more advanced functionality, you will have to import specific libraries that are not *assumed*. Our first encounter with this will come in Chapter 14, where in order to make use of the OpenGL renderer, the OpenGL library will be required:

```
import processing.opengl.*;
```

Many of the chapters that follow will require the explicit use of external *Processing* libraries, such as video, networking, serial, and so on. Documentation for these libraries can be found on the *Processing* web site at http://www.processing.org/reference/libraries/. There, you will find a list of libraries that come with *Processing*, as well as links to third party libraries available for download on the web.

12.2 Built-in Libraries

Using a built-in library is easy because there is no installation required. These libraries come with your *Processing* application. The list of built-in libraries (full list available at above URL) is not terribly long and all but a few are covered in this book as listed below.

- **Video**—For capturing images from a camera, playing movie files, and recording movie files. Covered in Chapters 16 and 21.
- **Serial**—For sending data between *Processing* and an external device via serial communication. Covered in Chapter 19.
- **OpenGL**—For rendering a sketch with graphics acceleration. Covered in Chapter 14.
- **Network**—For creating client and server sketches that can communicate across the internet. Covered in Chapter 19.
- **PDF**—For creating high resolution PDFs of graphics generated in *Processing*. Covered in Chapter 21.
- **XML**—For importing data from XML documents. Covered in Chapter 18.

Examples specifically tailored toward using the above libraries are found in the chapters listed. The *Processing* web site also has superb documentation for these libraries (found on the "libraries" page). The only generic knowledge you need regarding *Processing* built-in libraries is that you must include the appropriate import statement at the top of your program. This statement will automatically be added to the sketch if you select SKETCH→IMPORT LIBRARY. Or, you can simply type the code in manually (using the import library menu option does not do anything other than just add the text for the import statement).

```
import processing.video.*;
import processing.serial.*;
import processing.opengl.*;
import processing.net.*;
import processing.pdf.*;
import processing.xml.*;
```

12.3 Contributed Libraries

The world of third party (also known as "contributed") libraries for *Processing* resembles the wild west. As of the writing of this book, there are 47 contributed libraries, with capabilities ranging from sound generation and analysis, to packet sniffing, to physics simulations, to GUI controls. Several of these contributed libraries will be demonstrated over the course of the remainder of this book. Here, we will take a look at the process of downloading and installing a contributed library.

The first thing you need to do is figure out where you installed *Processing*. On a Mac, the application is most likely found in the "Applications" directory, on a PC, "Program Files." We will make this assumption, but have no fear if you installed it somewhere else (*Processing* can be installed in any directory and will work just fine), just replace the path listed below with your own file path!

Once you have determined where you installed *Processing*, take a look inside the *Processing* folder. See Figure 12.1.

/Applications/Processing 0135/

or

c:/Program Files/Processing 0135/

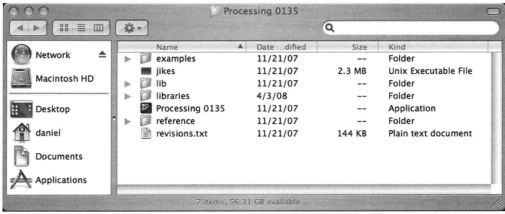

fig. 12.1

Inside the libraries directory, you will find folders for each of the built-in libraries, along with a "howto.txt" file that provides tips and instructions related to making your own library (a topic beyond the scope of this book). See Figure 12.2.

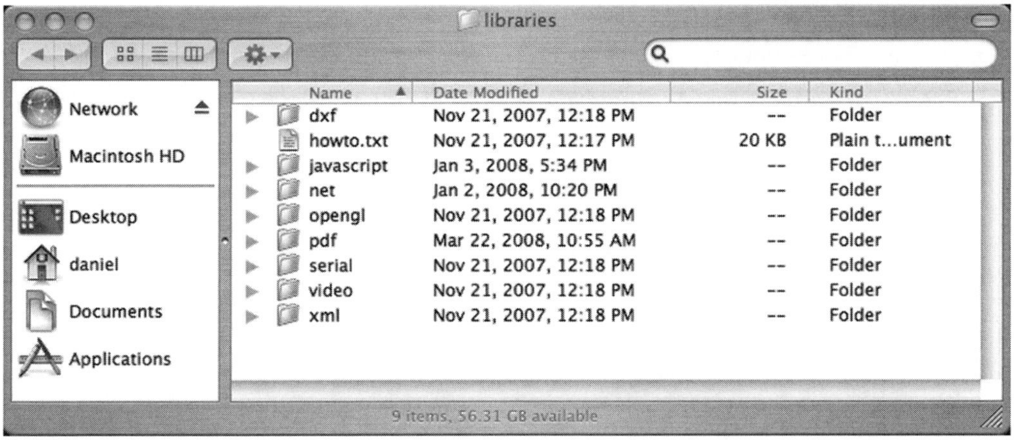

fig. 12.2

The libraries directory is where you will install contributed libraries.

The first use of a third party library can be found in Chapter 18 of this book. The "simpleML" library, designed to make HTML and XML data retrieval simple, is available for download at the book's web site, *http://www.learningprocessing.com/libraries.* If you want to get a jump start on Chapter 18, download the file simpleML.zip and follow the instructions below, and illustrated in Figure 12.3. The process for installing other contributed libraries will be identical, with the exception of filenames.

> **Step 1.** Extract the ZIP file. This can usually be accomplished by double-clicking the file or with any decompression application, such as Winzip on a PC.

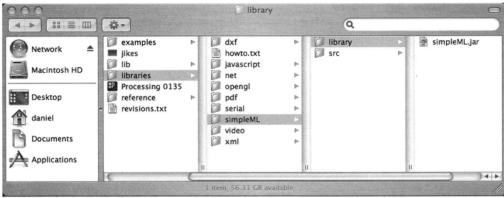

fig. 12.3

Step 2. Copy the extracted files to the *Processing* libraries folder. Most libraries you download will automatically unpack with the right directory structure. The full directory structure should look like this:

/Processing 0135/libraries/simpleML/library/simpleML.jar

More generically:

/Processing 0135/libraries/libraryName/library/libraryName.jar

Some libraries may include additional files in the "library" folder, as well as the source code (which is commonly stored one directory up, in the "libraryName" folder). If the library does not automatically unpack itself with the above directory structure, you can manually create these folders (using the finder or explorer) and place the libraryName.jar file in the appropriate location yourself.

Step 3. Restart *Processing*. If *Processing* was running while you performed Step 2, you will need to quit *Processing* and restart it in order for the library to be recognized. Once you have restarted, if everything has gone according to plan, the library will appear under the "Sketch→Import Library" option shown in Figure 12.4.

fig. 12.4

The newly installed library will now appear in the list! What to do once you have installed the library really depends on which library you have installed. Examples that make use in code of a contributed library can be found in Chapter 18 (simpleML, Yahoo API) and Chapter 20 (Sonia, Minim).

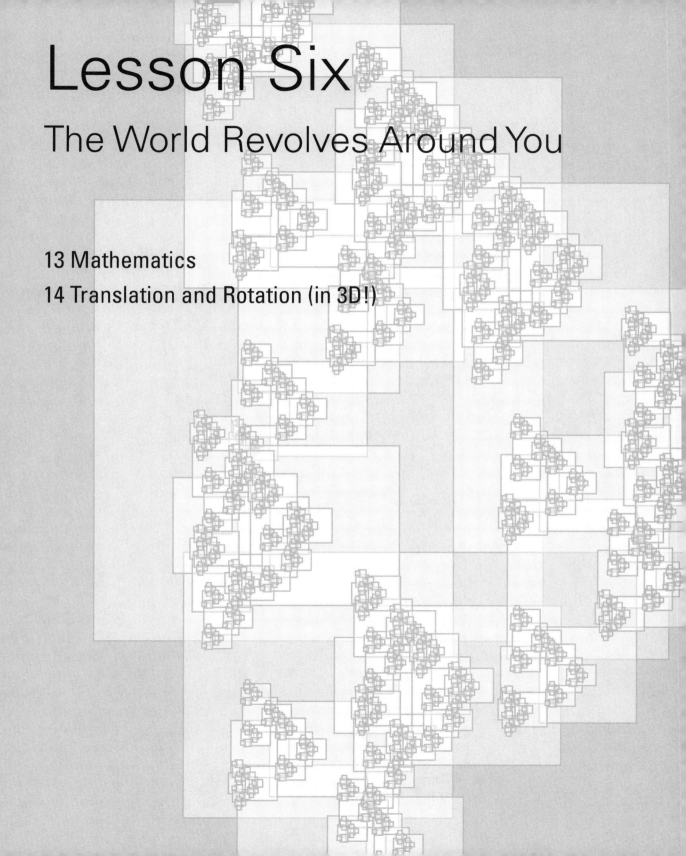

Lesson Six

The World Revolves Around You

13 Mathematics

"If people do not believe that mathematics is simple, it is only because they do not realize how complicated life is."
—John von Neumann

"If you were cosine squared, I'd be sine squared, because together we'd be one."
—Anonymous

In this chapter:
– Probability.
– Perlin noise.
– Trigonometry.
– Recursion.

Here we are. The fundamentals are finished and we are going to start looking at some more sophisticated topics in *Processing*. You may find there is less of a story to follow from chapter to chapter. Nonetheless, although the concepts do not necessarily build on each other as fluidly as they did previously, the chapters are ordered with a step-by-step learning approach in mind.

Everything we do from here on out will still employ the same flow structure of ***setup()*** and ***draw()***. We will continue to use functions from the *Processing* library and algorithms made of conditional statements and loops, and organize sketches with an object-oriented approach in mind. At this point, however, the descriptions will assume a knowledge of these essential topics and I encourage you to return to earlier chapters to review as needed.

13.1 Mathematics and Programming

Did you ever start to feel the sweat beading on your forehead the moment your teacher called you up to the board to write out the solution to the latest algebra assignment? Does the mere mention of the word "calculus" cause a trembling sensation in your extremities?

Relax, there is no need to be afraid. There is nothing to fear, but the fear of mathematics itself. Perhaps at the beginning of reading this book, you feared computer programming. I certainly hope that, by now, any terrified sensations associated with code have been replaced with feelings of serenity. This chapter aims to take a relaxed and friendly approach to a few useful topics from mathematics that will help us along the journey of developing *Processing* sketches.

You know, we have been using math all along.

For example, we have likely had an algebraic expression on almost every single page since learning variables.

```
x = x + 1;
```

And most recently, in Chapter 10, we tested intersection using the Pythagorean Theorem.

```
float d = dist(x1,x2,y1,y2);
```

These are just a few examples we have seen so far and as you get more and more advanced, you may even find yourself online, late at night, googling "Sinusoidal Spiral Inverse Curve." For now, we will start with a selection of useful mathematical topics.

13.2 Modulus

We begin with a discussion of the *modulo operator*, written as a percent sign, in *Processing*. *Modulus* is a very simple concept (one that you learned without referring to it by name when you first studied division) that is incredibly useful for keeping a number within a certain boundary (a shape on the screen, an index value within the range of an array, etc.) The modulo operator calculates the remainder when one number is divided by another. It works with both integers and floats.

> *20 divided by 6 equals 3 remainder 2. (In other words: 6*3 + 2 = 18 + 2 = 20.)*

therefore:

> *20 modulo 6 equals 2   or   20 % 6 = 2*

Here are a few more, with some blanks for you to fill in.

17 divided by 4 equals 4 remainder 1	*17 % 4 = 1*
3 divided by 5 equals 0 remainder 3	*3 % 5 = 3*
10 divided by 3.75 equals 2 remainder 2.5	*10.0 % 3.75 = 2.5*
100 divided by 50 equals _____ remainder _____	*100 % 40 = _____*
9.25 divided by 0.5 equals _____ remainder _____	*9.25 % 0.5 = _____*

You will notice that if $A = B \% C$, A can never be larger than C. The remainder can never be larger than the divisor.

0 % 3 = 0
1 % 3 = 1
2 % 3 = 2
3 % 3 = 0
4 % 3 = 1
etc.

Therefore, modulo can be used whenever you need to cycle a counter variable back to zero. The following lines of code:

```
x = x + 1;
if (x >= limit) {
  x = 0;
}
```

can be replaced by:

```
x = (x + 1) % limit;
```

This is very useful if you want to count through the elements of an array one at a time, always returning to 0 when you get to the length of the array.

Example 13-1: Modulo

```
// 4 random numbers
float[] randoms = new float[4];
int index = 0; // Which number are we using

void setup() {
  size(200,200);
  // Fill array with random values
  for (int i = 0; i < randoms.length; i++) {
    randoms[i] = random(0,256);
  }
  frameRate(1);
}

void draw() {
  // Every frame we access one element of the array
  background(randoms[index]);
  // And then go on to the next one
  index = (index + 1) % randoms.length;
}
```

> Using the modulo operator to cycle a counter back to 0.

13.3 Random Numbers

In Chapter 4, we were introduced to the ***random()*** function, which allowed us to randomly fill variables. *Processing*'s random number generator produces what is known as a "uniform" distribution of numbers. For example, if we ask for a random number between 0 and 9, 0 will come up 10% of the time, 1 will come up 10% of the time, 2 will come up 10% of the time, and so on. We could write a simple sketch using an array to prove this fact. See Example 13-2.

> *Pseudo-Random Numbers*
>
> The random numbers we get from the ***random()*** function are not truly random and are known as "pseudo-random." They are the result of a mathematical function that simulates randomness. This function would yield a pattern over time, but that time period is so long that for us, it is just as good as pure randomness!

Example 13-2: Random number distribution

```
// An array to keep track of how often random numbers are picked.
float[] randomCounts;

void setup() {
  size(200,200);
  randomCounts = new float[20];
}

void draw() {
  background(255);

  // Pick a random number and increase the count
  int index = int(random(randomCounts.length));
  randomCounts[index]++;

  // Draw a rectangle to graph results
  stroke(0);
  fill(175);
  for (int x = 0; x < randomCounts.length; x++) {
    rect(x*10,0,9,randomCounts[x]);
  }
}
```

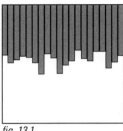

fig. 13.1

With a few tricks, we can change the way we use ***random()*** to produce a nonuniform distribution of random numbers and generate *probabilities* for certain events to occur. For example, what if we wanted to create a sketch where the background color had a 10% chance of being green and a 90% chance of being blue?

13.4 Probability Review

Let's review the basic principles of probability, first looking at single event probability, that is, the likelihood of something to occur.

Given a system with a certain number of possible outcomes, the probability of any given event occurring is the number of outcomes which qualify as that event divided by total number of possible outcomes. The simplest example is a coin toss. There are a total of two possible outcomes (heads or tails). There is only one way to flip heads, therefore the probability of heads is one divided by two, that is, 1/2 or 50%.

Consider a deck of 52 cards. The probability of drawing an ace from that deck is:

number of aces/number of cards = 4/52 = 0.077 = ~8%

The probability of drawing a diamond is:

number of diamonds/number of cards = 13/52 = 0.25 = 25%

We can also calculate the probability of multiple events occurring in sequence as the product of the individual probabilities of each event.

The probability of a coin flipping up heads three times in a row is:

(1/2) * (1/2) * (1/2) = 1/8 (or 0.125).

In other words, a coin will land heads three times in a row one out of eight times (with each "time" being three tosses).

Exercise 13-1: What is the probability of drawing two aces in a row from the deck of cards?

13.5 Event Probability in Code

There are few different techniques for using the ***random()*** function with probability in code. For example, if we fill an array with a selection of numbers (some repeated), we can randomly pick from that array and generate events based on what we select.

```
int[] stuff = new int[5];
stuff[0] = 1;
stuff[1] = 1;
stuff[2] = 2;
stuff[3] = 3;
stuff[4] = 3;
int index = int(random(stuff.length));
if (stuff[index] == 1) {
  // do something
}
```

> Picking a random element from an array.

If you run this code, there will be a 40% chance of selecting the value 1, a 20% chance of selecting the value 2, and a 40% chance of selecting the value 3.

Another strategy is to ask for a random number (for simplicity, we consider random floating point values between 0 and 1) and only allow the event to happen if the random number we pick is within a certain range. For example:

```
float prob = 0.10;      // A probability of 10%
float r = random(1);    // A random floating point value between 0 and 1
if (r < prob) {         // If our random is less than .1

   /*INSTIGATE THE EVENT HERE*/
}
```

> This code will only be executed 10% of the time.

This same technique can also be applied to multiple outcomes.

Outcome A — 60% | Outcome B — 10% | Outcome C — 30%

To implement this in code, we pick one random float and check where it falls.

- *Between 0.00 and 0.60 (10%) → outcome A.*
- *Between 0.60 and 0.70 (60%) → outcome B.*
- *Between 0.70 and 1.00 (30%) → outcome C.*

Example 13-3 draws a circle with a three different colors, each with the above probability (red: 60%, green: 10%, blue: 30%). This example is displayed in Figure 13.2.

Example 13-3: Probabilities

```
void setup() {
  size(200,200);
  background(255);
  smooth();
  noStroke();
}

void draw() {

  // Probabilities for 3 different cases
  // These need to add up to 100%!
  float red_prob = 0.60;   // 60% chance of red color
  float green_prob = 0.10; // 10% chance of green color
  float blue_prob = 0.30;  // 30% chance of blue color

  float num = random(1);   // pick a random number between 0 and 1

  // If random number is less than .6
  if (num < red_prob) {
    fill(255,53,2,150);
  // If random number is between .6 and .7
  } else if (num < green_prob + red_prob) {
    fill(156,255,28,150);
  // All other cases (i.e. between .7 and 1.0)
  } else {
    fill(10,52,178,150);
  }
  ellipse(random(width),random(height),64,64);
}
```

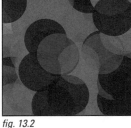
fig. 13.2

Exercise 13-2: Fill in the blanks in the following code so that the circle has a 10% chance of moving up, a 20% chance of moving down, and a 70% chance of doing nothing.

```
float y = 100;
void setup() {
  size(200,200);
  smooth();
}
```

```
        void draw() {
          background(0);
          float r = random(1);

          _____

          _____


          _____

          _____


          _____

          _____


          _____

          ellipse(width/2,y,16,16);
        }
```

13.6 Perlin Noise

One of the qualities of a good random number generator is that the numbers produced appear to have no relationship. If they exhibit no discernible pattern, they are considered *random*.

In programming behaviors that have an organic, almost lifelife quality, a little bit of randomness is a good thing. However, we do not want too much randomness. This is the approach taken by Ken Perlin, who developed a function in the early 1980's entitled "Perlin noise" that produces a naturally ordered (i.e., "smooth") sequence of pseudo-random numbers. It was originally designed to create procedural textures, for which Ken Perlin won an Academy Award for Technical Achievement. Perlin noise can be used to generate a variety of interesting effects including clouds, landscapes, marble textures, and so on.

Figure 13.3 shows two graphs,—a graph of Perlin noise over time (the *x*-axis represents time; note how the curve is smooth) compared to a graph of pure random numbers over time. (Visit this book's web site for the code that generated these graphs.)

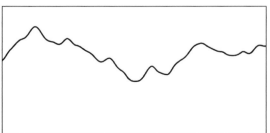

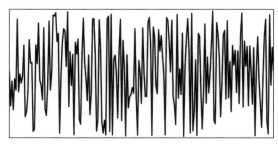

Perlin Noise   Random

fig. 13.3

Noise Detail

If you visit the *Processing.org* noise reference, you will find that noise is calculated over several "octaves." You can change the number of octaves and their relative importance by calling the *noiseDetail()* function. This, in turn, can change how the noise function behaves. See *http://processing.org/reference/noiseDetail_.html*.

You can read more about how noise works from Ken Perlin himself: *http://www.noisemachine.com/talk1/*.

Processing has a built-in implementation of the Perlin noise algorithm with the function *noise()*. The *noise()* function takes one, two, or three arguments (referring to the "space" in which noise is computed: one, two, or three dimensions). This chapter will look at one-dimensional noise only. Visit the *Processing* web site for further information about two-dimensional and three-dimensional noise.

One-dimensional Perlin noise produces as a linear sequence of values over time. For example:

0.364, 0.363, 0.363, 0.364, 0.365

Note how the numbers move up or down randomly, but stay close to the value of their predecessor. Now, in order to get these numbers out of *Processing*, we have to do two things: (1) call the function *noise()*, and (2) pass in as an argument the current "time." We would typically start at time $t = 0$ and therefore call the function like so: "noise(t);"

```
float t = 0.0;
float noisevalue = noise(t); // Noise at time 0
```

We can also take the above code and run it looping in *draw()*.

```
float t = 0.0;
void draw() {
  float noisevalue = noise(t);
  println(noisevalue);
}
```

Output:
0.28515625
0.28515625
0.28515625
0.28515625

The above code results in the same value printed over and over. This is because we are asking for the result of the *noise()* function at the same point in "time"—0.0—over and over. If we increment the "time" variable *t*, however, we will get a different result.

```
float t = 0.0;
void draw() {
  float noisevalue = noise(t);
  println(noisevalue);

  t += 0.01;
}
```

Output:
0.12609221
0.12697512
0.12972163
0.13423012
0.1403218

Time moves forward!

How quickly we increment t also affects the smoothness of the noise. Try running the code several times, incrementing t by $0.01, 0.02, 0.05, 0.1, 0.0001$, and so on.

By now, you may have noticed that ***noise()*** always returns a floating point value between 0 and 1. This detail cannot be overlooked, as it affects how we use Perlin noise in a *Processing* sketch. Example 13-4 assigns the result of the ***noise()*** function to the size of a circle. The noise value is scaled by multiplying by the width of the window. If the width is 200, and the range of ***noise()*** is between 0.0 and 1.0, the range of ***noise()*** multiplied by the width is 0.0 to 200.0. This is illustrated by the table below and by Example 13-4.

Noise Value	Multiplied by	Equals
0	200	0
0.12	200	24
0.57	200	114
0.89	200	178
1	200	200

Example 13-4: Perlin noise

```
float time = 0.0;
float increment = 0.01;


void setup() {
  size(200,200);
  smooth(); {


void draw() {
  background(255);


  float n = noise(time)*width;
```

Get a noise value at "time" and scale it according to the window's width.

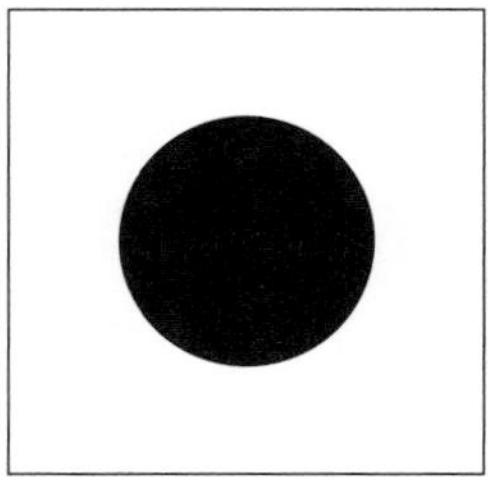

fig. 13.4

```
  // With each cycle, increment the "time"
  time += increment;


  // Draw the ellipse with size determined by Perlin noise
  fill(0);
  ellipse(width/2,height/2,n,n);
}
```

Exercise 13-3: Complete the following code which uses Perlin noise to set the location of a circle. Run the code. Does the circle appear to be moving "naturally"?

```
// Noise "time" variables
float xtime = 0.0;
float ytime = 100.0;
float increment = 0.01;

void setup() {
  size(200,200);
  smooth();
}

void draw() {
  background(0);
  float x = _____;
  float y = _____;
  _____;
  _____;
  // Draw the ellipse with size determined by Perlin noise
  fill(200);
  ellipse(_____,_____,_____,_____);
}
```

In this sketch, we want to use noise for two different values. So that the output of the noise function is not identical, we start at two different points in time.

13.7 Angles

Some of the examples in this book will require a basic understanding of how angles are defined in *Processing*. In Chapter 14, for example, we will need to know about angles in order to feel comfortable using the *rotate()* function to rotate and spin objects.

In order to get ready for these upcoming examples, we need to learn about *radians* and *degrees*. It is likely you are familiar with the concept of an angle in degrees. A full rotation goes from zero to 360°. An angle of 90° (a right angle) is one-fourth of 360°, shown in Figure 13.5 as two perpendicular lines.

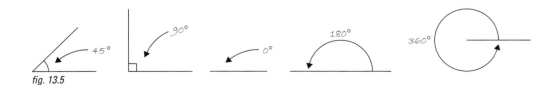

fig. 13.5

It is fairly intuitive for us to think angles in terms of degrees. For example, the rectangle in Figure 13.6 is rotated 45° around its center.

Processing, however, requires angles to be specified in *radians*. A radian is a unit of measurement for angles defined by the ratio of the length of the arc of a circle to the radius of that circle. One radian is the angle at which that ratio equals one (see Figure 13.7). An angle of 180° = PI radians. An angle of 360° = 2*PI radians, and 90° = PI/2 radians, and so on.

fig. 13.6

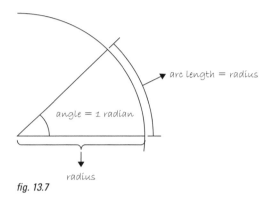

fig. 13.7

The formula to convert from degrees to radians is:

Radians = 2 * PI * (degrees/360)

Fortunately for us, if we prefer to think in degrees but code with radians, *Processing* makes this easy. The **radians()** function will automatically convert values from degrees to radians. In addition, the constants PI and TWO_PI are available for convenient access to these commonly used numbers (equivalent to 180° and 360°, respectively). The following code, for example, will rotate shapes by 60° (rotation will be fully explored in the next chapter).

```
float angle = radians(60);
rotate(angle);
```

PI, What Is It?

The mathematical constant PI (or π) is a real number defined as the ratio of a circle's circumference (the distance around the perimeter) to its diameter (a straight line that passes through the circle center). It is equal to approximately 3.14159.

Exercise 13-4: A dancer spins around two full rotations. How many degrees did the dancer rotate? How many radians?

Degrees: _____   Radians: _____

13.8 Trigonometry

Sohcahtoa. Strangely enough, this seemingly nonsense word, *sohcahtoa*, is the foundation for a lot of computer graphics work. Any time you need to calculate an angle, determine the distance between points, deal with circles, arcs, lines, and so on, you will find that a basic understanding of trigonometry is essential.

Trigonometry is the study of the relationships between the sides and angles of triangles and *sohcahtoa* is a mnemonic device for remembering the definitions of the trigonometric functions, sine, cosine, and tangent. See Figure 13.8.

- **soh**: sine   = opposite/hypotenuse
- **cah**: cosine = adjacent/hypotenuse
- **toa**: tangent = opposite/adjacent

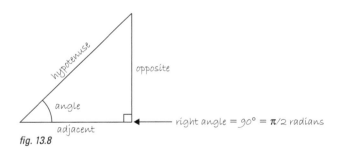

fig. 13.8

Any time we display a shape in *Processing*, we have to specify a pixel location, given as *x* and *y* coordinates. These coordinates are known as Cartesian coordinates, named for the French mathematician René Descartes who developed the ideas behind Cartesian space.

Another useful coordinate system, known as *polar coordinates*, describes a point in space as an angle of rotation around the origin and a radius from the origin. We can't use polar coordinates as arguments to a function in *Processing*. However, the trigonometric formulas allow us to convert those coordinates to Cartesian, which can then be used to draw a shape. See Figure 13.9.

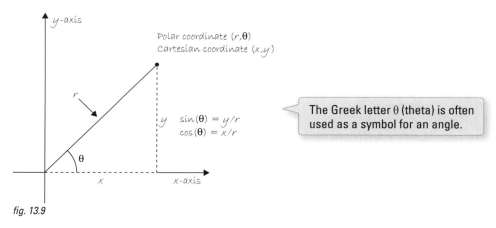

fig. 13.9

The Greek letter θ (theta) is often used as a symbol for an angle.

sine(theta) $= y/r \rightarrow y = r *$ sine(theta)
cosine(theta) $= x/r \rightarrow x = r *$ cosine(theta)

For example, if *r* is 75 and theta is 45° (or PI/4 radians), we can calculate *x* and *y* as follows. The functions for sine and cosine in *Processing* are **sin()** and **cos()**, respectively. They each take one argument, a floating point angle measured in radians.

```
float r = 75;
float theta = PI / 4; // We could also say: float theta = radians(45);
float x = r * cos(theta);
float y = r * sin(theta);
```

This type of conversion can be useful in certain applications. For example, how would you move a shape along a circular path using Cartesian coordinates? It would be tough. Using polar coordinates, however, this task is easy. Simply increment the angle!

Here is how it is done with global variables *r* and *theta*.

Example 13-5: Polar to Cartesian

```
// A Polar coordinate
float r = 75;
float theta = 0;

void setup() {
  size(200,200);
  background(255);
  smooth();
}

void draw() {
  // Polar to Cartesian conversion
  float x = r * cos(theta);
  float y = r * sin(theta);
```

Polar coordinates (*r*, theta) are converted to Cartesian (*x,y*) for use in the *ellipse()* function.

fig. 13.10

```
    // Draw an ellipse at x,y
    noStroke();
    fill(0);
    ellipse(x+width/2, y+height/2, 16, 16); // Adjust for center of window

    // Increment the angle
    theta += 0.01;
}
```

Exercise 13-5: Using Example 13-5, draw a spiral path. Start in the center and move outward. Note that this can be done by changing only one line of code and adding one line of code!

13.9 Oscillation

Trigonometric functions can be used for more than geometric calculations associated with right triangles. Let's take a look at Figure 13.11, a graph of the sine function where $y = \sin(x)$.

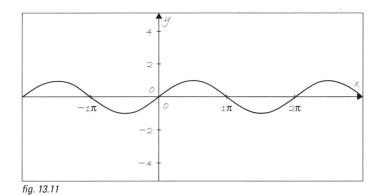

fig. 13.11

You will notice that the output of sine is a smooth curve alternating between −1 and 1. This type of behavior is known as *oscillation*, a periodic movement between two points. A swinging pendulum, for example, oscillates.

We can simulate oscillation in a *Processing* sketch by assigning the output of the sine function to an object's location. This is similar to how we used *noise()* to control the size of a circle (see Example 13-4), only with *sin()* controlling a location. Note that while *noise()* produces a number between 0 and 1.0, *sin()* outputs a range between −1 and 1. Example 13-6 shows the code for an oscillating pendulum.

Example 13-6: Oscillation

```
float theta = 0.0;

void setup() {
  size(200,200);
  smooth();
}

void draw() {
  background(255);

  // Get the result of the sine function
  // Scale so that values oscillate between 0 and width
  float x = (sin(theta) + 1) * width/2;

  // With each cycle, increment theta
  theta += 0.05;

  // Draw the ellipse at the value produced by sine
  fill(0);
  stroke(0);
  line(width/2,0,x,height/2);
  ellipse(x,height/2,16,16);
}
```

fig. 13.12

The output of the **sin()** function oscillates smoothly between −1 and 1. By adding 1 we get values between 0 and 2. By multiplying by 100, we get values between 0 and 200 which can be used as the ellipse's *x* location.

Exercise 13-6: Encapsulate the above functionality into an Oscillator object. Create an array of Oscillators, each moving at different rates along the x and y axes. Here is some code for the Oscillator class to help you get started.

```
class Oscillator {
  float xtheta;
  float ytheta;

  _____

  Oscillator() {
    xtheta = 0;
    ytheta = 0;

    _____

  }
  void oscillate() {

    _____

    _____

  }
  void display() {
    float x = _____
    float y = _____
    ellipse(x,y,16,16);
  }
}
```

Exercise 13-7: Use the sine function to create a "breathing" shape, that is, one whose size oscillates.

We can also produce some interesting results by drawing a sequence of shapes along the path of the sine function. See Example 13–7.

Example 13-7: Wave

```
// Starting angle
float theta = 0.0;

void setup() {
  size(200,200);
  smooth();
}

void draw() {
  background(255);

  // Increment theta (try different values for "angular velocity" here)
  theta += 0.02;

  noStroke();
  fill(0);

  float x = theta;
  // A simple way to draw the wave with an ellipse at each location
  for (int i = 0; i <= 20; i++) {
    // Calculate y value based off of sine function
    float y = sin(x)*height/2;
    // Draw an ellipse
    ellipse(i*10,y+height/2,16,16);
    //Move along x-axis
    x += 0.2;
  }
}
```

fig. 13.13

> A *for* loop is used to draw all the points along a sine wave (scaled to the pixel dimension of the window).

*Exercise 13-8: Rewrite the above example to use the **noise()** function instead of **sin()**.*

13.10 Recursion

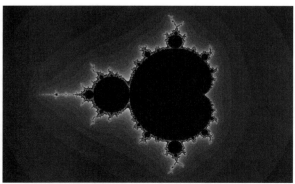

fig. 13.14 The Mandelbrot set:
http://processing.org/learning/topics/mandelbrot.html

In 1975, Benoit Mandelbrot coined the term *fractal* to describe self-similar shapes found in nature. Much of the stuff we encounter in our physical world can be described by idealized geometrical forms—a postcard has a rectangular shape, a ping-pong ball is spherical, and so on. However, many naturally occurring structures cannot be described by such simple means. Some examples are snowflakes, trees, coastlines, and mountains. Fractals provide a geometry for describing and simulating these types of self-similar shapes (by "self-similar" we mean no matter how "zoomed out" or "zoomed in," the shape ultimately appears the same). One process for generating these shapes is known as recursion.

We know that a function can call another function. We do this whenever we call any function inside of the *draw()* function. But can a function call itself? Can *draw()* call *draw()*? In fact, it can (although calling *draw()* from within *draw()* is a terrible example, since it would result in an infinite loop).

Functions that call themselves are *recursive* and are appropriate for solving different types of problems. This occurs in mathematical calculations; the most common example of this is "factorial."

The factorial of any number n, usually written as $n!$, is defined as:

$$n! = n * n - 1 * \ldots * 3 * 2 * 1$$
$$0! = 1$$

We could write a function to calculate factorial using a *for* loop in *Processing*:

```
int factorial(int n) {
  int f = 1;
  for (int i = 0; i < n; i++) {
    f = f * (i+1);
  }
  return f;
}
```

If you look closely at how factorial works, however, you will notice something interesting. Let's examine 4! and 3!

$$4! = 4 * 3 * 2 * 1$$
$$3! = 3 * 2 * 1$$
$$\text{therefore}\ldots 4! = 4 * 3!$$

We can describe this in more general terms. For any positive integer n:

$$n! = n * (n - 1)!$$
$$1! = 1$$

Written in English:

The *factorial* of N is defined as N times the *factorial* of $N - 1$.

The definition of *factorial* includes *factorial*?! It is kind of like saying "tired" is defined as "the feeling you get when you are tired." This concept of self-reference in functions is known as *recursion*. And we can use recursion to write a function for factorial that calls itself.

```
int factorial(int n) {
  if (n == 1) {
    return 1;
  } else {
    return n * factorial(n-1);
  }
}
```

Crazy, I know. But it works. Figure 13.15 walks through the steps that happen when ***factorial(4)*** is called.

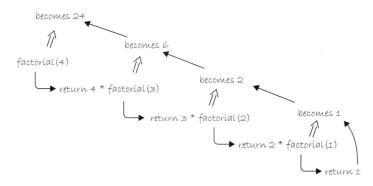

fig. 13.15

The same principle can be applied to graphics with interesting results. Take a look at the following recursive function. The results are shown in Figure 13.16.

```
void drawCircle(int x, int y, float radius) {
  ellipse(x, y, radius, radius);
  if(radius > 2) {
    radius *=  0.75f;
    drawCircle(x, y, radius);
  }
}
```

fig. 13.16

What does ***drawCircle()*** do? It draws an ellipse based on a set of parameters received as arguments, and then calls itself with the same parameters (adjusting them slightly). The result is a series of circles each drawn inside the previous circle.

Notice that the above function only recursively calls itself if the radius is greater than two. This is a crucial point. *All recursive functions must have an exit condition!* This is identical to iteration. In Chapter 6, we learned that all ***for*** and ***while*** loops must include a boolean test that eventually evaluates to false, thus exiting the loop. Without one, the program would crash, caught inside an infinite loop. The same can be said about recursion. If a recursive function calls itself forever and ever, you will most likely be treated to a nice frozen screen.

The preceding circles example is rather trivial, since it could easily be achieved through simple iteration. However, in more complex scenarios where a method calls itself more than once, recursion becomes wonderfully elegant.

Let's revise *drawCircle()* to be a bit more complex. For every circle displayed, draw a circle half its size to the left and right of that circle. See Example 13–8.

Example 13-8: Recursion

```
void setup() {
  size(200,200);
  smooth();
}

void draw() {
  background(255);
  stroke(0);
  noFill();
  drawCircle(width/2,height/2,100);
}

void drawCircle(float x, float y, float radius) {
  ellipse(x, y, radius, radius);
  if(radius > 2) {
    drawCircle(x + radius/2, y, radius/2);
    drawCircle(x - radius/2, y, radius/2);
  }
}
```

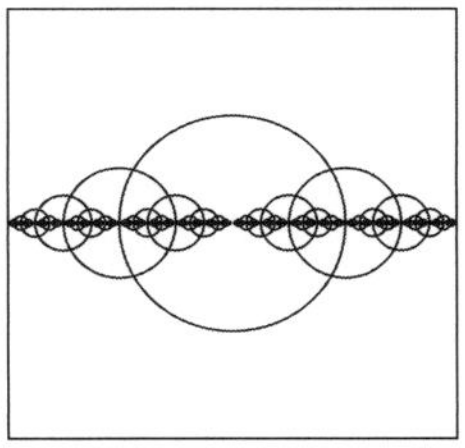

fig. 13.17

> *drawCircle()* calls itself twice, creating a branching effect. For every circle, a smaller circle is drawn to the left *and* right.

With a teeny bit more code, we could add a circle above and below. This result is shown in Figure 13.18.

```
void drawCircle(float x, float y, float radius) {
  ellipse(x, y, radius, radius);
  if(radius > 8) {
    drawCircle(x + radius/2, y, radius/2);
    drawCircle(x - radius/2, y, radius/2);
    drawCircle(x, y + radius/2, radius/2);
    drawCircle(x, y - radius/2, radius/2);
  }
}
```

fig. 13.18

Just try recreating this sketch with iteration instead of recursion! I dare you!

Exercise 13-9: Complete the code which generates the following pattern (Note: the solution uses lines, although it would also be possible to create the image using rotated rectangles, which we will learn how to do in Chapter 14).

```
void setup() {
  size(400,200);
}

void draw() {
  background(255);
  stroke(0);
  branch(width/2,height,100);
}

void branch(float x, float y, float h) {

  _____;

  _____;

  if (_____) {

  _____;

  _____;

  }
}
```

13.11 Two-Dimensional Arrays

In Chapter 9, we learned that an array keeps track of multiple pieces of information in linear order, a one-dimensional list. However, the data associated with certain systems (a digital image, a board game, etc.) lives in two dimensions. To visualize this data, we need a multi-dimensional data structure, that is, a multi-dimensional array.

A two-dimensional array is really nothing more than an array of arrays (a three-dimensional array is an array of arrays of arrays). Think of your dinner. You could have a one-dimensional list of everything you eat:

(lettuce, tomatoes, salad dressing, steak, mashed potatoes, string beans, cake, ice cream, coffee)

Or you could have a two-dimensional list of three courses, each containing three things you eat:

(lettuce, tomatoes, salad dressing) and (steak, mashed potatoes, string beans) and (cake, ice cream, coffee)

In the case of an array, our old-fashioned one-dimensional array looks like this:

```
int[] myArray = {0,1,2,3};
```

And a two-dimensional array looks like this:

```
int[][] myArray = {{0,1,2,3},{3,2,1,0},{3,5,6,1},{3,8,3,4}};
```

For our purposes, it is better to think of the two-dimensional array as a matrix. A matrix can be thought of as a grid of numbers, arranged in rows and columns, kind of like a bingo board. We might write the two-dimensional array out as follows to illustrate this point:

```
int[][] myArray = { {0, 1, 2, 3},
                    {3, 2, 1, 0},
                    {3, 5, 6, 1},
                    {3, 8, 3, 4} };
```

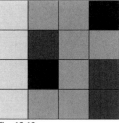

We can use this type of data structure to encode information about an image. For example, the grayscale image in Figure 13.19 could be represented by the following array:

```
int[][] myArray = { {236, 189, 189,   0},
                    {236,  80, 189, 189},
                    {236,   0, 189,  80},
                    {236, 189, 189,  80} };
```

fig. 13.19

To walk through every element of a one-dimensional array, we use a *for* loop, that is:

```
int[] myArray = new int[10];
for (int i = 0; i < myArray.length; i++) {
  myArray[i] = 0;
}
```

For a two-dimensional array, in order to reference every element, we must use two nested loops. This gives us a counter variable for every column and every row in the matrix. See Figure 13.20.

```
int cols = 10;
int rows = 10;
int[][] myArray = new int[cols][rows];
```

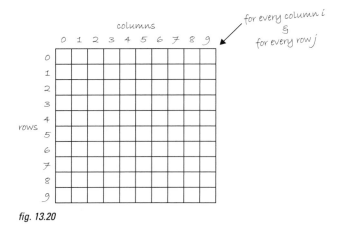

fig. 13.20

```
for (int i = 0; i < cols; i++) {
  for (int j = 0; j < rows; j++) {
    myArray[i][j] = 0;
  }
}
```

> Two nested loops allow us to visit every spot in a two-dimensional array. For every column *i*, visit every row *j*.

For example, we might write a program using a two-dimensional array to draw a grayscale image as in Example 13–9.

Example 13-9: Two-dimensional array

```
// Set up dimensions
size(200,200);
int cols = width;
int rows = height;

// Declare 2D array
int[][] myArray = new int[cols][rows];

// Initialize 2D array values
for (int i = 0; i < cols; i++) {
  for (int j = 0; j < rows; j++) {
    myArray[i][j] = int(random(255));
  }
}

// Draw points
for (int i = 0; i < cols; i++) {
  for (int j = 0; j < rows; j++) {
    stroke(myArray[i][j]);
    point(i,j);
  }
}
```

fig. 13.21

A two-dimensional array can also be used to store objects, which is especially convenient for programming sketches that involve some sort of "grid" or "board." Example 13-10 displays a grid of Cell objects stored in a two-dimensional array. Each cell is a rectangle whose brightness oscillates from 0–255 with a sine function.

Example 13-10: Two-dimensional array of objects

```
// 2D Array of objects
Cell[][] grid;

// Number of columns and rows in the grid
int cols = 10;
int rows = 10;

void setup() {
  size(200,200);
  grid = new Cell[cols][rows];
  for (int i = 0; i < cols; i++) {
    for (int j = 0; j < rows; j++) {
      // Initialize each object
      grid[i][j] = new Cell(i*20,j*20,20,20,i+j);
    }
  }
}

void draw() {
  background(0);
  for (int i = 0; i < cols; i++) {
    for (int j = 0; j < rows; j++) {
      // Oscillate and display each object
      grid[i][j].oscillate();
      grid[i][j].display();
    }
  }
}

// A Cell object
class Cell {
  float x,y;   // x,y location
  float w,h;   // width and height
  float angle; // angle for oscillating brightness

  // Cell Constructor
  Cell(float tempX, float tempY, float tempW, float tempH, float tempAngle) {
    x = tempX;
    y = tempY;
    w = tempW;
    h = tempH;
    angle = tempAngle;
  }

  // Oscillation means increase angle
  void oscillate() {
    angle += 0.02;
  }

  void display() {
    stroke(255);
    // Color calculated using sine wave
    fill(127+127*sin(angle));
    rect(x,y,w,h);
  }
}
```

> A two-dimensional array can be used to store objects.

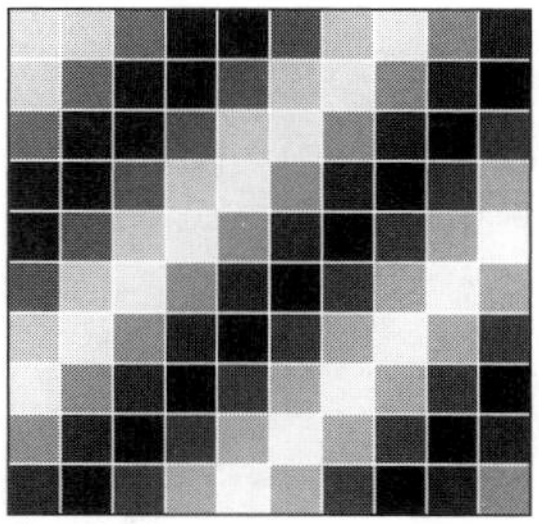

fig. 13.22

> The counter variables *i* and *j* are also the column and row numbers, and are used as arguments to the constructor for each object in the grid.

> A cell object knows about its location in the grid as well as its size with the variables *x, y, w, h.*

Exercise 13-10: Develop the beginnings of a Tic-Tac-Toe game. Create a Cell object that can exist in one of two states: O or nothing. When you click on the cell, its state changes from nothing to "O". Here is a framework to get you started.

```
Cell[][] board;

int cols = 3;
int rows = 3;

void setup() {
  // FILL IN
}

void draw() {
  background(0);
  for (int i = 0; i < cols; i++) {
    for (int j = 0; j < rows; j++) {
      board[i][j].display();
    }
  }
}

void mousePressed() {
    // FILL IN
}

// A Cell object
class Cell {
  float x,y;
  float w,h;
  int state;

  // Cell Constructor
  Cell(float tempX, float tempY, float tempW, float tempH) {
    // FILL IN
  }

  void click(int mx, int my) {
    // FILL IN
  }
```

```
    void display() {
      // FILL IN
    }
}
```

Exercise 13-11: If you are feeling saucy, go ahead and complete the Tic–Tac–Toe game adding X and alternating player turns with mouse clicks.

14 Translation and Rotation (in 3D!)

"What is the Matrix?"
—*Neo*

In this chapter:
– 2D and 3D translation.
– Using P3D and OPENGL.
– Vertex shapes.
– 2D and 3D rotation.
– Saving the transformation state in the stack: ***pushMatrix()*** and ***popMatrix().***

14.1 The *Z*-Axis

As we have seen throughout this book, pixels in a two-dimensional window are described using Cartesian coordinates: an *X* (horizontal) and a *Y* (vertical) point. This concept dates all the way back to Chapter 1, when we began thinking of the screen as a digital piece of graph paper.

In three-dimensional space (such as the actual, real-world space where you are reading this book), a third axis (commonly referred to as the *Z*-axis) refers to the depth of any given point. In a *Processing* sketch's window, a coordinate along this *Z*-axis indicates how far in front or behind the window a pixel lives. Scratching your head is a perfectly reasonable response here. After all, a computer window is only two dimensional. There are no pixels floating in the air in front of or behind your LCD monitor! In this chapter, we will examine how using the theoretical *Z*-axis will create the *illusion* of three-dimensional space in your *Processing* window.

We can, in fact, create a three-dimensional illusion with what we have learned so far. For example, if you were to draw a rectangle in the middle of the window and slowly increase its width and height, it might appear as if it is moving toward you. See Example 14-1.

Example 14-1: A growing rectangle, or a rectangle moving toward you?

```
float r = 8;

void setup() {
  size(200,200);
}

void draw() {
  background(255);

  // Display a rectangle in the middle of the screen
  stroke(0);
  fill(175);
  rectMode(CENTER);
  rect(width/2,height/2,r,r);

  // Increase the rectangle size
  r++;
}
```

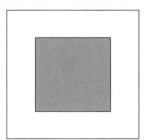
fig. 14.1

Is this rectangle flying off of the computer screen about to bump into your nose? Technically, this is of course not the case. It is simply a rectangle growing in size. But we have created the *illusion* of the rectangle moving toward you.

Fortunately for us, if we choose to use 3D coordinates, *Processing* will create the illusion for us. While the idea of a third dimension on a flat computer monitor may seem imaginary, it is quite real for *Processing*. *Processing* knows about perspective, and selects the appropriate two-dimensional pixels in order to create the three-dimensional effect. We should recognize, however, that as soon as we enter the world of 3D pixel coordinates, a certain amount of control must be relinquished to the *Processing* renderer. You can no longer control exact pixel locations as you might with 2D shapes, because *XY* locations will be adjusted to account for 3D perspective.

In order to specify points in three dimensions, the coordinates are specified in the order you would expect: *x*, *y*, *z*. Cartesian 3D systems can be described as "left-handed" or "right-handed." If you use your right hand to point your index finger in the positive *y* direction (up) and your thumb in the positive *x* direction (to the right), the rest of your fingers will point toward the positive *z* direction. It is left-handed if you use your left hand and do the same. In *Processing*, the system is left-handed, as shown in Figure 14.2.

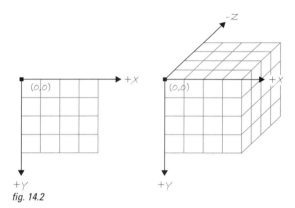

fig. 14.2

Our first goal is to rewrite Example 14-1 using the 3D capabilities of *Processing*. Assume the following variables:

```
int x = width/2;
int y = height/2;
int z = 0;
int r = 10;
```

In order to specify the location for a rectangle, the **rect()** function takes four arguments: an *x* location, a *y* location, a width, and a height.

```
rect(x,y,w,h);
```

Our first instinct might be to add another argument to the *rect()* function.

`rect(x,y,z,w,h);` ◁ Incorrect! We cannot use an (*x,y,z*) coordinate in *Processing*'s shape functions such as *rect(), ellipse(), line(),* and so on. Other functions in *Processing* can take three arguments for *x,y,z* and we will see this later in the chapter.

The *Processing* reference page for *rect()*, however, does not allow for this possibility. In order to specify 3D coordinates for shapes in the *Processing* world, we must learn to use a new function, called *translate()*.

The *translate()* function is not exclusive to 3D sketches, so let's return to two dimensions to see how it works.

The function *translate()* moves the origin point—(0,0)—relative to its previous state. We know that when a sketch first starts, the origin point lives on the top left of the window. If we were to call the function *translate()* with the arguments (50,50), the result would be as shown in Figure 14.3.

> **Where is the origin?**
>
> The "origin" in a *Processing* sketch is the point (0,0) in two dimensions or (0,0,0) in three dimensions. It is always at the top left corner of the window unless you move it using *translate()*.

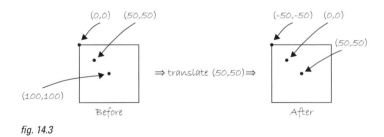

fig. 14.3

You can think of it as moving a pen around the screen, where the pen indicates the origin point.

In addition, the origin always resets itself back to the top left corner at the beginning of *draw()*. Any calls to *translate()* only apply to the current cycle through the *draw()* loop. See Example 14-2.

Example 14-2: Multiple translations

```
void setup() {
  size(200,200);
  smooth();
}

void draw() {
  background(255);
  stroke(0);
  fill(175);

  // Grab mouse coordinates, constrained to window
  int mx = constrain(mouseX,0,width);
  int my = constrain(mouseY,0,height);

  // Translate to the mouse location
  translate(mx,my);
  ellipse(0,0,8,8);

  // Translate 100 pixels to the right
  translate(100,0);
  ellipse(0,0,8,8);

  // Translate 100 pixels down
  translate(0,100);
  ellipse(0,0,8,8);

  // Translate 100 pixels left
  translate(-100,0);
  ellipse(0,0,8,8);
}
```

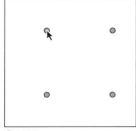

fig. 14.4

Now that we understand how *translate()* works, we can return to the original problem of specifying 3D coordinates. *translate()*, unlike *rect()*, *ellipse()*, and other shape functions, can accept a third argument for a Z coordinate.

```
// Translation along the z-axis
translate(0,0,50);
rectMode(CENTER);
rect(100,100,8,8);
```

The above code translates 50 units along the Z-axis, and then draws a rectangle at (100,100). While the above is technically correct, when using *translate()*, it is a good habit to specify the (x,y) location as part of the translation, that is:

```
// Translation along the z-axis II
translate(100,100,50);
rectMode(CENTER);
rect(0,0,8,8);
```
When using *translate()*, the rectangle's location is (0,0) since *translate()* moved us to the location for the rectangle.

Finally, we can use a variable for the Z location and animate the shape moving toward us.

Example 14-3: A rectangle moving along the *z*-axis

```
float z = 0; // a variable for the Z (depth) coordinate

void setup() {
  size(200,200,P3D);
}

void draw() {
  background(0);
  stroke(255);
  fill(100);

  // Translate to a point before displaying a shape there
  translate(width/2,height/2,z);
  rectMode(CENTER);
  rect(0,0,8,8);

  z++; // Increment Z (i.e. move the shape toward the viewer)
}
```

> When using (*x,y,z*) coordinates, we must tell *Processing* we want a 3D sketch. This is done by adding a third argument "P3D" to the **size()** function. See Section 14.2 for more details.

Although the result does not *look* different from Example 14-1, it is quite different conceptually as we have opened the door to creating a variety of three-dimensional effects on the screen with *Processing*'s 3D engine.

*Exercise 14-1: Fill in the appropriate **translate()** functions to create this pattern. Once you are finished, try adding a third argument to **translate()** to move the pattern into three dimensions.*

```
size(200,200);
background(0);
stroke(255);
fill(255,100);

translate(_____,_____);
rect(0,0,100,100);
translate(_____,_____);
rect(0,0,100,100);
translate(_____,_____);
line(0,0,-50,50);
```

The **translate()** function is particularly useful when you are drawing a collection of shapes relative to a given centerpoint. Harking back to a Zoog from the first 10 chapters of this book, we saw code like this:

```
void display() {
  // Draw Zoog's body
  fill(150);
  rect(x,y,w/6,h*2);

  // Draw Zoog's head
  fill(255);
  ellipse(x,y-h/2,w,h);
}
```

The **display()** function above draws all of Zoog's parts (body and head, etc.) relative to Zoog's *x*,*y* location. It requires that *x* and *y* be used in both **rect()** and **ellipse()**. **translate()** allows us to simply set *Processing*'s origin (0,0) at Zoog's (*x*,*y*) location and therefore draw the shapes relative to (0,0).

```
void display() {
  // Move origin (0,0) to (x,y)
  translate(x,y);

  // Draw Zoog's body
  fill(150);
  rect(0,0,w/6,h*2);

  // Draw Zoog's head
  fill(255);
  ellipse(0,-h/2,w,h);
}
```

> **translate()** can be used to draw a collection of shapes relative to a given point.

14.2 P3D vs. OPENGL

If you look closely at Example 14-3, you will notice that we have added a third argument to the **size()** function. Traditionally, **size()** has served one purpose: to specify the width and height of our *Processing* window. The **size()** function, however, also accepts a third parameter indicating a drawing mode. The mode tells *Processing* what to do behind the scenes when rendering the display window. The default mode (when none is specified) is "JAVA2D," which employs existing Java 2D libraries to draw shapes, set colors, and so on. We do not have to worry about how this works. The creators of *Processing* took care of the details.

If we want to employ 3D translation (or rotation as we will see later in this chapter), the JAVA2D mode will no longer suffice. Running the example in the default mode results in the following error:

*"**translate(x, y, z)** can only be used with OPENGL or P3D, use **translate(x, y)** instead."*

Instead of switching to **translate(x,y)**, we want to select a different mode. There are two options:

- **P3D**—P3D is a 3D renderer developed by the creators of *Processing*. It should also be noted that anti-aliasing (enabled with the **smooth()** function) is not available with P3D.
- **OPENGL**—OPENGL is a 3D renderer that employs hardware acceleration. If you have an OpenGL compatible graphics card installed on your computer (which is pretty much every computer), you can use this mode. Although at the time of the writing of this book, there are still a few, minor kinks to be worked out with this mode (you may find things look slightly different between P3D and OPENGL), it may prove exceptionally useful in terms of speed. If you are planning to display large numbers of shapes onscreen in a high-resolution window, this mode will likely have the best performance.

To specify a mode, add a third argument in all caps to the **size()** function.

```
size(200,200);          // using the default JAVA2D mode
size(200,200,P3D);      // using P3D
size(200,200,OPENGL);   // using OPENGL
```

When using the OPENGL mode, you must also import the OPENGL library.

This can be done by selecting the SKETCH → IMPORT LIBRARY menu option or by manually adding the following line of code to the top of your sketch (see Chapter 12 for a detailed explanation on libraries):

```
import processing.opengl.*;
```

Exercise 14-2: Run any Processing *sketch in P3D, then switch to OPENGL. Notice any difference?*

14.3 Vertex Shapes

Up until now, our ability to draw to the screen has been limited to a small list of primitive two-dimensional shapes: rectangles, ellipses, triangles, lines, and points. For some projects, however, creating your own custom shapes is desirable. This can be done through the use of the functions ***beginShape()***, ***endShape()***, and ***vertex()***.

Consider a rectangle. A rectangle in *Processing* is defined as a reference point, as well as a width and height.

```
rect(50,50,100,100);
```

But we could also consider a rectangle to be a polygon (a closed shape bounded by line segments) made up of four points. The points of a polygon are called vertices (plural) or vertex (singular). The following code draws exactly the same shape as the ***rect()*** function by setting the vertices of the rectangle individually. See Figure 14.5.

```
beginShape();
vertex(50,50);
vertex(150,50);
vertex(150,150);
vertex(50,150);
endShape(CLOSE);
```

fig. 14.5

beginShape() indicates that we are going to create a custom shape made up of some number of vertex points: a single *polygon.* ***vertex()*** specifies the points for each vertex in the polygon and ***endShape()*** indicates that we are finished adding vertices. The argument "CLOSE" inside of ***endShape(CLOSE)*** declares that the shape should be closed, that is, that the last vertex point should connect to the first.

The nice thing about using a custom shape over a simple rectangle is flexibility. For example, the sides are not required to be perpendicular. See Figure 14.6.

```
stroke(0);
fill(175);
beginShape();
vertex(50,50);
vertex(150,25);
vertex(150,175);
vertex(25,150);
endShape(CLOSE);
```

fig. 14.6

We also have the option of creating more than one shape, for example, in a loop, as shown in Figure 14.7.

```
stroke(0);
for (int i = 0; i < 10; i++) {
  beginShape();
  fill(175);
  vertex(i*20,10-i);
  vertex(i*20+15,10+i);
  vertex(i*20+15,180+i);
  vertex(i*20,180-i);
  endShape(CLOSE);
}
```

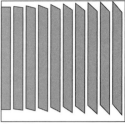

fig. 14.7

You can also add an argument to *beginShape()* specifying exactly what type of shape you want to make. This is particularly useful if you want to make more than one polygon. For example, if you create six vertex points, there is no way for *Processing* to know that you really want to draw two triangles (as opposed to one hexagon) unless you say *beginShape(TRIANGLES)*. If you do not want to make a polygon at all, but want to draw points or lines, you can by saying *beginShape(POINTS)* or *beginShape(LINES)*. See Figure 14.8.

```
stroke(0);
beginShape(LINES);
for (int i = 10; i < width; i+=20) {
  vertex(i,10);
  vertex(i,height-10);
}
endShape();
```

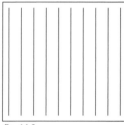

fig. 14.8

Note that LINES is meant for drawing a series of individual lines, not a continous loop. For a continuous loop, do not use any argument. Instead, simply specify all the vertex points you need and include *noFill()*. See Figure 14.9.

```
noFill();
stroke(0);
beginShape();
for (int i = 10; i < width; i+=20) {
  vertex(i,10);
  vertex(i,height-10);
}
endShape();
```

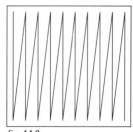

fig. 14.9

The full list of possible arguments for *beginShape()* is available in the *Processing* reference

http://processing.org/reference/beginShape_.html
POINTS, LINES, TRIANGLES, TRIANGLE_FAN, TRIANGLE_STRIP, QUADS, QUAD_STRIP

In addition, *vertex()* can be replaced with *curveVertex()* to join the points with curves instead of straight lines. With *curveVertex()*, note how the first and last points are not displayed. This is because they are required to define the curvature of the line as it begins at the second point and ends at the second to last point. See Figure 14.10.

```
noFill();
stroke(0);
beginShape();
for (int i = 10; i < width; i+=20) {
  curveVertex(i,10);
  curveVertex(i,height-10);
}
endShape();
```

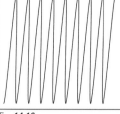

fig. 14.10

Exercise 14-3: Complete the vertices for the shape pictured.

```
size(200,200);
background(255);
stroke(0);
fill(175);

beginShape();
vertex(20, 20);
vertex(_____,_____);
vertex(_____,_____);
vertex(_____,_____);
vertex(_____,_____);
endShape(_____);
```

14.4 Custom 3D Shapes

Three-dimensional shapes can be created using *beginShape()*, *endShape()*, and *vertex()* by placing multiple polygons side by side in the proper configuration. Let's say we want to draw a four-sided pyramid made up of four triangles, all connected to one point (the apex) and a flat plane (the base). If your shape is simple enough, you might be able to get by with just writing out the code. In most cases, however, it is best to start sketching it out with pencil and paper to determine the location of all the vertices. One example for our pyramid is shown in Figure 14.11.

Example 14-4 takes the vertices from Figure 14.11 and puts them in a function that allows us to draw the pyramid with any size. (As an exercise, try making the pyramid into an object.)

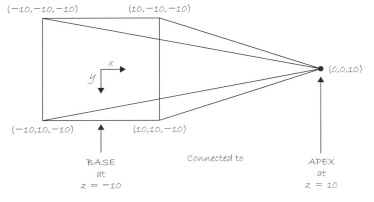

BASE
at
z = −10

Connected to

APEX
at
z = 10

```
vertex(-10,-10,-10);   vertex(10,-10,-10);   vertex( 10,10,-10);   vertex(-10, 10,-10);
vertex( 10,-10,-10);   vertex(10, 10,-10);   vertex(-10,10,-10);   vertex(-10,-10,-10);
vertex(  0,  0, 10);   vertex( 0,  0, 10);   vertex(  0, 0, 10);   vertex(  0,  0, 10);
```
fig. 14.11

Example 14-4: Pyramid using *beginShape(TRIANGLES)*

```
void setup() {
  size(200,200,P3D);
}

void draw() {
  background(255);
  translate(100,100,0);
  drawPyramid(150);
}

void drawPyramid(int t) {
  stroke(0);
```

> Since the pyramid's vertices are drawn relative to a centerpoint, we must call ***translate()*** to place the pyramid properly in the window.

> The function sets the vertices for the pyramid around the centerpoint at a flexible distance, depending on the number passed in as an argument.

```
  // this pyramid has 4 sides, each drawn as a separate triangle
  // each side has 3 vertices, making up a triangle shape
  // the parameter "t" determines the size of the pyramid

  beginShape(TRIANGLES);
  fill(255,150);
  vertex(-t,-t,-t);
  vertex( t,-t,-t);
  vertex( 0, 0, t);

  fill(150,150);
  vertex( t,-t,-t);
  vertex( t, t,-t);
  vertex( 0, 0, t);

  fill(255,150);
  vertex( t, t,-t);
  vertex(-t, t,-t);
  vertex( 0, 0, t);
```

> Note that each polygon can have its own color.

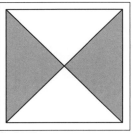

fig. 14.12

```
  fill(150,150);
  vertex(-t, t,-t);
  vertex(-t,-t,-t);
  vertex( 0, 0, t);
  endShape();
}
```

Exercise 14-4: Create a pyramid with only three sides. Include the base (for a total of four triangles). Use the space below to sketch out the vertex locations as in Figure 14.11.

*Exercise 14-5: Create a three-dimensional cube using eight quads—**beginShape(QUADS)**. (Note that a simpler way to make a cube in* Processing *is with the **box()** function.)*

14.5 Simple Rotation

There is nothing particularly three dimensional about the visual result of the pyramid example. The image looks more like a flat rectangle with two lines connected diagonally from end to end. Again, we have to remind ourselves that we are only creating a three-dimensional *illusion*, and it is not a particularly effective one without animating the pyramid structure within the virtual space. One way for us to demonstrate the difference would be to rotate the pyramid. So let's learn about rotation.

For us, in our physical world, rotation is a pretty simple and intuitive concept. Grab a baton, twirl it, and you have a sense of what it means to rotate an object.

Programming rotation, unfortunately, is not so simple. All sorts of questions come up. Around what axis should you rotate? At what angle? Around what origin point? *Processing* offers several functions related to rotation, which we will explore slowly, step by step. Our goal will be to program a solar system simulation with multiple planets rotating around a star at different rates (as well as to rotate our pyramid in order to better experience its three dimensionality).

But first, let's try something simple and attempt to rotate one rectangle around its center. We should be able to get rotation going with the following three principles:

1. Shapes are rotated in *Processing* with the ***rotate()*** function.
2. The ***rotate()*** function takes one argument, an angle measured in radians.
3. ***rotate()*** will rotate the shape in the *clockwise* direction (to the right).

OK, armed with this knowledge, we should be able to just call the **rotate()** function and pass in an angle. Say, 45° (or PI/4 radians) in *Processing*. Here is our first (albeit flawed) attempt, with the output shown in Figure 14.13.

```
rotate(radians(45));
rectMode(CENTER);
rect(width/2,height/2,100,100);
```

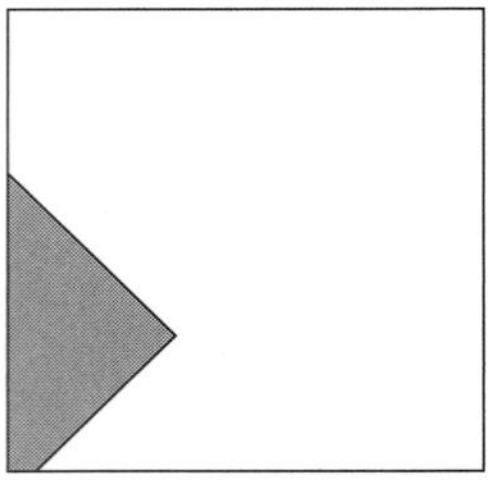

fig. 14.13

Shoot. What went wrong? The rectangle looks rotated, but it is in the wrong place!

The single most important fact to remember about rotation in *Processing* is that *shapes always rotate around the point of origin.* Where is the point of origin in this example? The top left corner! The origin has not been translated. The rectangle therefore will not spin around its own center. Instead, it rotates around the top left corner. See Figure 14.14.

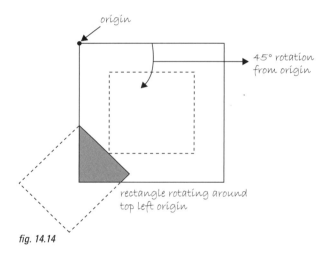

fig. 14.14

Sure, there may come a day when all you want to do is rotate shapes around the top left corner, but until that day comes, you will always need to first move the origin to the proper location before rotating, and then display the rectangle. **translate()** to the rescue!

```
translate(width/2,height/2);
rotate(radians(45));
rectMode(CENTER);
rect(0,0,100,100);
```

> Because we translated in order to rotate, the rectangle now lives at the point (0,0).

We can expand the above code using the **mouseX** location to calculate an angle of rotation and thus animate the rectangle, allowing it to spin. See Example 14-5.

Example 14-5: Rectangle rotating around center

```
void setup() {
  size(200,200);
}

void draw() {
  background(255);
  stroke(0);
  fill(175);

  // Translate origin to center
  translate(width/2,height/2);

  // theta is a common name of a variable to store an angle

  float theta = PI*mouseX / width;

  // Rotate by the angle theta
  rotate(theta);

  // Display rectangle with CENTER mode
  rectMode(CENTER);
  rect(0,0,100,100);
}
```

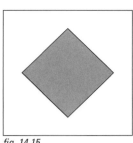

fig. 14.15

The angle ranges from 0 to PI, based on the ratio of *mouseX* location to the sketch's width.

Exercise 14-6: Create a line that spins around its center (like twirling a baton). Draw a circle at both endpoints.

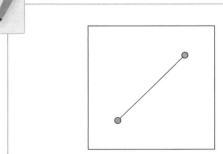

14.6 Rotation Around Different Axes

Now that we have basic rotation out of the way, we can begin to ask the next important rotation question:

Around what axis do we want to rotate?

In the previous section, our square rotated around the Z-axis. This is the default axis for two-dimensional rotation. See Figure 14.16.

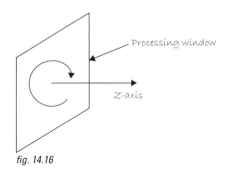

fig. 14.16

Processing will also allow for rotation around the *x* or *y*-axis with the functions **rotateX()** and **rotateY()**, which each require P3D or OPENGL mode. The function **rotateZ()** also exists and is the equivalent of **rotate()**. See Examples 14-6, 14-7 and 14-8.

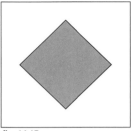

fig. 14.17

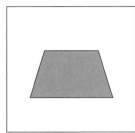

fig. 14.18

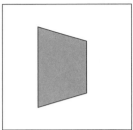

fig. 14.19

Example 14-6: *rotateZ*	**Example 14-7:** *rotateX*	**Example 14-8:** *rotateY*

```
float theta = 0.0;

void setup() {
  size(200,200,P3D);
}

void draw() {
  background(255);
  stroke(0);
  fill(175);

  translate(width/2,
    height/2);
  rotateZ(theta);
  rectMode(CENTER);
  rect(0,0,100,100);

  theta += 0.02;
}
```

```
float theta = 0.0;

void setup() {
  size(200,200,P3D);
}

void draw() {
  background(255);
  stroke(0);
  fill(175);

  translate(width/2,
    height/2);
  rotateX(theta);
  rectMode(CENTER);
  rect(0,0,100,100);

  theta += 0.02;
}
```

```
float theta = 0.0;

void setup() {
  size(200,200,P3D);
}

void draw() {
  background(255);
  stroke(0);
  fill(175);

  translate(width/2,
    height/2);
  rotateY(theta);
  rectMode(CENTER);
  rect(0,0,100,100);

  theta += 0.02;
}
```

The rotate functions can also be used in combination. The results of Example 14-9 are shown in Figure 14.20.

Example 14-9: Rotate around more than one axis

```
void setup() {
  size(200,200,P3D);
}

void draw() {
  background(255);
  stroke(0);
  fill(175);

  translate(width/2,height/2);
  rotateX(PI*mouseY/height);
  rotateY(PI*mouseX/width);
  rectMode(CENTER);
  rect(0,0,100,100);
}
```

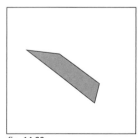

fig. 14.20

Returning to the pyramid example, we will see how rotating makes the three-dimensional quality of the shape more apparent. The example is also expanded to include a second pyramid that is offset from the first pyramid using translate. Note, however, that it rotates around the same origin point as the first pyramid (since ***rotateX()*** and ***rotateY()*** are called before the second ***translate()***).

Example 14-10: Pyramid

```
float theta = 0.0;

void setup() {
  size(200,200,P3D);
}

void draw() {
  background(144);
  theta += 0.01;

  translate(100,100,0);
  rotateX(theta);
  rotateY(theta);
  drawPyramid(50);

  // translate the scene again
  translate(50,50,20);

  // call the pyramid drawing function
  drawPyramid(10);

}

void drawPyramid(int t) {
  stroke(0);

  // this pyramid has 4 sides, each drawn as a separate triangle
  // each side has 3 vertices, making up a triangle shape
  // the parameter "t" determines the size of the pyramid

  fill(150,0,0,127);
  beginShape(TRIANGLES);
  vertex(-t,-t,-t);
  vertex( t,-t,-t);
  vertex( 0, 0, t);

  fill(0,150,0,127);
  vertex( t,-t,-t);
  vertex( t, t,-t);
  vertex( 0, 0, t);

  fill(0,0,150,127);
  vertex( t, t,-t);
  vertex(-t, t,-t);
  vertex( 0, 0, t);

  fill(150,0,150,127);
  vertex(-t, t,-t);
  vertex(-t,-t,-t);
  vertex( 0, 0, t);
  endShape();
}
```

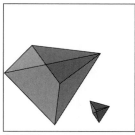

fig. 14.21

*Exercise 14-7: Rotate the 3D cube you made in Exercise 14-5. Can you rotate it around the corner or center? You can also use the Processing function **box()** to make the cube.*

Exercise 14-8: Make a Pyramid class.

14.7 Scale

In addition to ***translate()*** and ***rotate()***, there is one more function, ***scale()***, that affects the way shapes are oriented and drawn onscreen. ***scale()*** increases or decreases the size of objects onscreen. Just as with ***rotate()***, the scaling effect is performed relative to the origin's location.

scale() takes a floating point value, a percentage at which to scale: 1.0 is 100%. For example, ***scale(0.5)*** draws an object at 50% of its size and ***scale(3.0)*** increases the object's size to 300%.

Following is a re-creation of Example 14-1 (the growing square) using ***scale()***.

Example 14-11: A growing rectangle, using *scale()*

```
float r = 0.0;

void setup() {
  size(200,200);
}

void draw() {
  background(0);

  // Translate to center of window
  translate(width/2,height/2);
  // Scale any shapes according to value of r
  scale(r);

  // Display a rectangle in the middle of the screen
  stroke(255);
  fill(100);
  rectMode(CENTER);
  rect(0,0,10,10);

  // Increase the scale variable
  r += 0.02;
}
```

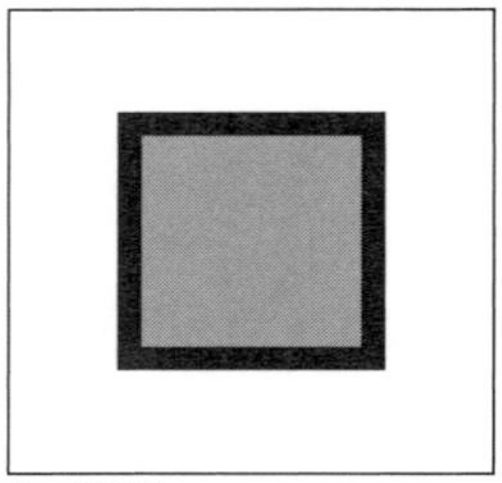

fig. 14.22

> ***scale()*** increases the dimensions of an object relative to the origin by a percentage (1.0 = 100%). Notice how in this example the scaling effect causes the outline of the shape to become thicker.

scale() can also take two arguments (for scaling along the *x* and *y*-axes with different values) or three arguments (for the *x*-, *y*-, and *z*-axes).

14.8 The Matrix: Pushing and Popping

What is the matrix?

In order to keep track of rotations and translations and how to display the shapes according to different transformations, *Processing* (and just about any computer graphics software) uses a matrix.

How matrix transformations work is beyond the scope of this book; however, it is useful to simply know that the information related to the coordinate system is stored in what is known as a *transformation matrix*. When a translation or rotation is applied, the transformation matrix changes. From time to time, it is useful to save the current state of the matrix to be restored later. This will ultimately allow us to move and rotate individual shapes without them affecting others.

What is the matrix?

A matrix is a table of numbers with rows and columns. In *Processing*, a *transformation* matrix is used to describe the window *orientation*—is it translated or rotated? You can view the current matrix at any time by calling the function ***printMatrix()***. This is what the matrix looks like in its "normal" state, with no calls to ***translate()*** or ***rotate()***.

```
1.0000  0.0000  0.0000
0.0000  1.0000  0.0000
```

This concept is best illustrated with an example. Let's give ourselves an assignment: Create a *Processing* sketch where two rectangles rotate at different speeds in different directions around their respective centerpoints.

As we start developing this example, we will see where the problems arise and how we will need to implement the functions ***pushMatrix()*** and ***popMatrix()***.

Starting with essentially the same code from Section 14.4, we can rotate a square around the *Z*-axis in the top left corner of the window. See Example 14-12.

Example 14-12: Rotating one square

```
float theta1 = 0;

void setup() {
  size(200,200,P3D);
}

void draw() {
  background (255);
  stroke(0);
  fill(175);
  rectMode(CENTER);

  translate(50,50);
  rotateZ(theta1);
  rect(0,0,60,60);

  theta1 += 0.02;
}
```

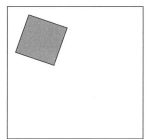

fig. 14.23

Making some minor adjustments, we now implement a rotating square in the bottom right-hand corner.

Example 14-13: Rotating another square

```
float theta2 = 0;

void setup() {
  size(200,200,P3D);
}

void draw() {
  background (255);
  stroke(0);
  fill(175);
  rectMode(CENTER);

  translate(150,150);
  rotateY(theta2);
  rect(0,0,60,60);

  theta2 += 0.02;
}
```

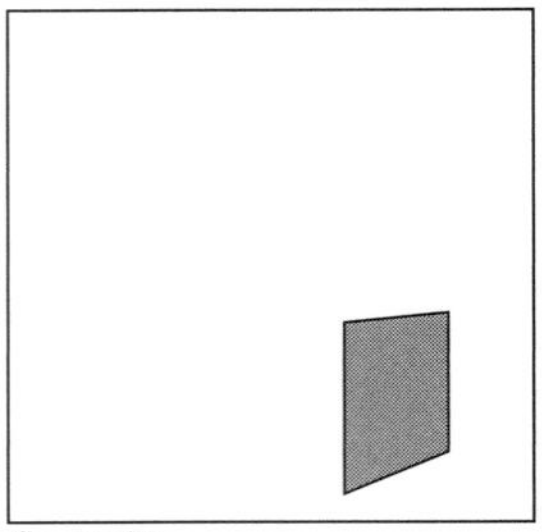

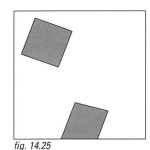

fig. 14.24

Without careful consideration, we might think to simply combine the two programs. The **setup()** function would stay the same, we would incorporate two globals, theta1 and theta2, and call the appropriate translation and rotation for each rectangle. We would also adjust translation for the second square from **translate(150,150)** to **translate(100,100),** since we have already translated to **(50,50)** with the first square.

```
float theta1 = 0;
float theta2 = 0;

void setup() {
  size(200,200,P3D);
}

void draw() {
  background(255);
  stroke(0);
  fill(175);
  rectMode(CENTER);

  translate(50,50);
  rotateZ(theta1);
  rect(0,0,60,60);

  theta1 += 0.02;

  translate(100,100);
  rotateY(theta2);
  rect(0,0,60,60);

  theta2 += 0.02;
}
```

fig. 14.25

> This first call to **rotateZ()** affects all shapes drawn afterward. Both squares rotate around the center of the first square.

Running this example will quickly reveal a problem. The first (top left) square rotates around its center. However, while the second square does rotate around its center, it also rotates around the first square! Remember, all calls to translate and rotate are relative to the coordinate system's previous state. We need a way to restore the matrix to its original state so that individual shapes can act independently.

Saving and restoring the rotation/translation state is accomplished with the functions *pushMatrix()* and *popMatrix()*. To get started, let's think of them as *saveMatrix()* and *restoreMatrix()*. (Note there are no such functions.) Push = save. Pop = restore.

For each square to rotate on its own, we can write the following algorithm (with the new parts bolded).

1. **Save the current transformation matrix.** This is where we started, with (0,0) in the top left corner of the window and no rotation.
2. Translate and rotate the first rectangle.
3. Display the first rectangle.
4. **Restore matrix from Step 1 so that it isn't affected by Steps 2 and 3!**
5. Translate and rotate the second rectangle.
6. Display the second rectangle.

Rewriting our code in Example 14-14 gives the correct result as shown in Figure 14.26.

Example 14-14: Rotating both squares

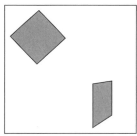

fig. 14.26

```
float theta1 = 0;
float theta2 = 0;

void setup() {
  size(200,200,P3D);
}

void draw() {
  background(255);
  stroke(0);
  fill(175);
  rectMode(CENTER);

  pushMatrix();                    1

  translate(50,50);                2
  rotateZ(theta1);
  rect(0,0,60,60);                 3

  popMatrix();                     4
  pushMatrix();
  translate(150,150);              5
  rotateY(theta2);
  rect(0,0,60,60);                 6
  popMatrix();

  theta1 += 0.02;
  theta2 += 0.02;
}
```

Although technically not required, it is a good habit to place *pushMatrix()* and *popMatrix()* around the second rectangle as well (in case we were to add more to this code). A nice rule of thumb when starting is to use *pushMatrix()* and *popMatrix()* before and after translation and rotation for all shapes so that they can be treated as individual entities. In fact, this example should really be object oriented, with every object making its own calls to *pushMatrix()*, *translate()*, *rotate()*, and *popMatrix()*. See Example 14-5.

Example 14-15: Rotating many things using objects

```
// An array of Rotater objects
Rotater[] rotaters;

void setup() {
  size(200,200);
  rotaters = new Rotater[20];
  // Rotaters are made randomly
  for (int i = 0; i < rotaters.length; i++) {
    rotaters[i] = new Rotater(random(width),random(height),random(-0.1,0.1),random(48));
  }
}

void draw() {
  background(255);
  // All Rotaters spin and are displayed
  for (int i = 0; i < rotaters.length; i++) {
    rotaters[i].spin();
    rotaters[i].display();
  }
}
```

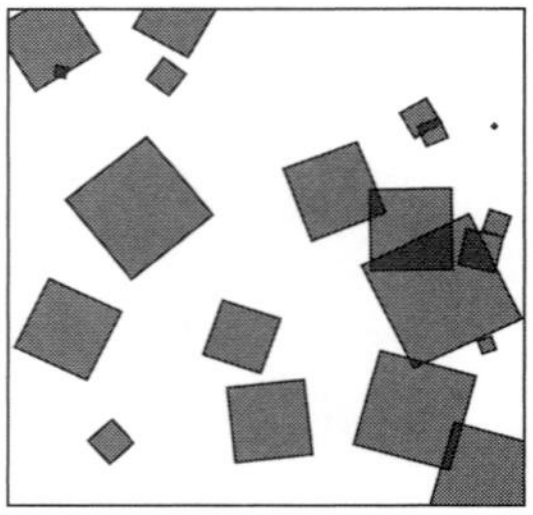

fig. 14.27

```
// A Rotater class
class Rotater {
  float x,y;   // x,y location
  float theta; // angle of rotation
  float speed; // speed of rotation
  float w;     // size of rectangle

  Rotater(float tempX, float tempY, float tempSpeed, float tempW) {
    x = tempX;
    y = tempY;
    theta = 0;          // Angle is always initialized to 0
    speed = tempSpeed;
    w = tempW;
  }

  // Increment angle
  void spin() {
    theta += speed;
  }

  // Display rectangle
  void display() {
    rectMode(CENTER);
    stroke(0);
```

```
    fill(0,100);
    // Note the use of pushMatrix()
    // and popMatrix() inside the object's
    // display method!
    pushMatrix();
    translate(x,y);
    rotate(theta);
    rect(0,0,w,w);
    popMatrix();
  }
}
```

> *pushMatrix()* and *popMatrix()* are called inside the class' *display()* method. This way, every Rotater object is rendered with its own independent translation and rotation!

Interesting results can also be produced from *nesting* multiple calls to *pushMatrix()* and *popMatrix()*. There must always be an equal amount of calls to both *pushMatrix()* and *popMatrix()*, but they do not always have to come one right after the other.

To understand how this works, let's take a closer look at the meaning of "push" and "pop." "Push" and "pop" refer to a concept in computer science known as a *stack*. Knowledge of how a stack works will help you use *pushMatrix()* and *popMatrix()* properly.

A stack is exactly that: a stack. Consider an English teacher getting settled in for a night of grading papers stored in a pile on a desk, a stack of papers. The teacher piles them up one by one and reads them in reverse order of the pile. The first paper placed on the stack is the last one read. The last paper added is the first one read. Note this is the exact opposite of a queue. If you are waiting in line to buy tickets to a movie, the first person in line is the first person to get to buy tickets, the last person is the last. See Figure 14.28.

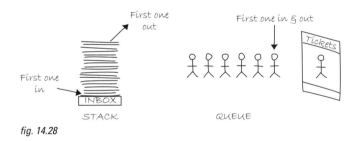

fig. 14.28

Pushing refers to the process of putting something in the stack, *popping* to taking something out. This is why you must always have an equal number of *pushMatrix()* and *popMatrix()* calls. You can't pop something if it does not exist! (If you have an incorrect number of pushes and pops, *Processing* will say: "Too many calls to popMatrix() (and not enough to pushMatrix).")

Using the rotating squares program as a foundation, we can see how nesting *pushMatrix()* and *popMatrix()* is useful. The following sketch has one circle in the center (let's call it the sun) with another circle rotating it (let's call it earth) and another two rotating around it (let's call them moon #1 and moon #2).

Example 14-16: Simple solar system

```
// Angle of rotation around sun and planets
float theta = 0;

void setup() {
  size(200,200);
  smooth();
}

void draw() {

  background(255);
  stroke(0);

  // Translate to center of window
  // to draw the sun.
  translate(width/2,height/2);
  fill(255,200,50);
  ellipse(0,0,20,20);

  // The earth rotates around the sun
  pushMatrix();
  rotate(theta);
  translate(50,0);
  fill(50,200,255);
  ellipse(0,0,10,10);

  // Moon #1 rotates around the earth
  pushMatrix();
  rotate(-theta*4);
  translate(15,0);
  fill(50,255,200);
  ellipse(0,0,6,6);
  popMatrix();

  // Moon #2 also rotates around the earth
  pushMatrix();
  rotate(theta*2);
  translate(25,0);
  fill(50,255,200);
  ellipse(0,0,6,6);
  popMatrix();

  popMatrix();

  theta += 0.01;
}
```

fig. 14.29

pushMatrix() is called to save the transformation state before drawing moon #1. This way we can pop and return to earth before drawing moon #2. Both moons rotate around the earth (which itself is rotating around the sun).

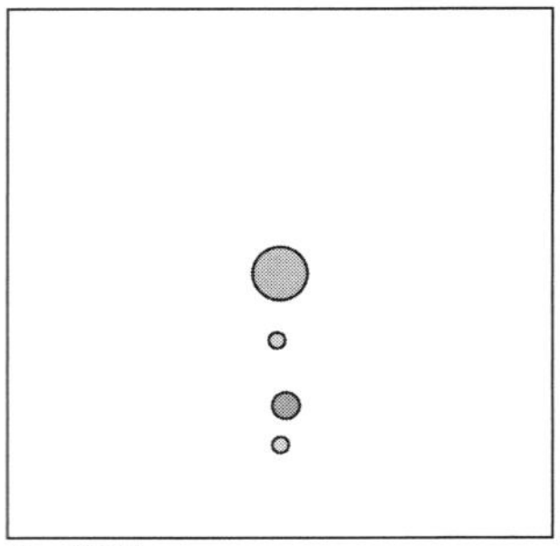

pushMatrix() and *popMatrix()* can also be nested inside *for* or *while* loops with rather unique and interesting results. The following example is a bit of a brainteaser, but I encourage you to play around with it.

Example 14-17: Nested push and pop

```
// Global angle for rotation
float theta = 0;

void setup(){
  size(200, 200);
  smooth();
}

void draw(){
  background(100);
  stroke(255);

  // Translate to center of window
  translate(width/2,height/2);

  // Loop from 0 to 360 degrees (2*PI radians)
  for(float i=0; i < TWO_PI; i+=0.2) {
    // Push, rotate and draw a line!
    pushMatrix();
    rotate(theta+i);
    line(0,0,100,0);
    // Loop from 0 to 360 degrees (2*PI radians)
    for(float j=0; j < TWO_PI; j+=0.5) {
      // Push, translate, rotate and draw a line!
      pushMatrix();
      translate(100,0);
      rotate(-theta-j);
      line(0,0,50,0);
      // We're done with the inside loop, pop!
      popMatrix();
    }
    // We're done with the outside loop, pop!
    popMatrix();
  }
  endShape();

  // Increment theta
  theta+=0.01;
}
```

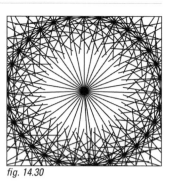
fig. 14.30

> The transformation state is saved at the beginning of each cycle through the for loop and restored at the end. Try commenting out these lines to see the difference!

*Exercise 14-9: Take either your pyramid or your cube shape and make it into a class. Have each object make its own call to **pushMatrix()** and **popMatrix()**. Can you make an array of objects all rotating independently in 3D?*

14.9 A *Processing* Solar System

Using all the translation, rotation, pushing, and popping techniques in this chapter, we are ready to build a *Processing* solar system. This example will be an updated version of Example 14-16 in the previous section (without any moons), with two major changes:

- Every planet will be an object, a member of a Planet class.
- An array of planets will orbit the sun.

Example 14-18: Object-oriented solar system

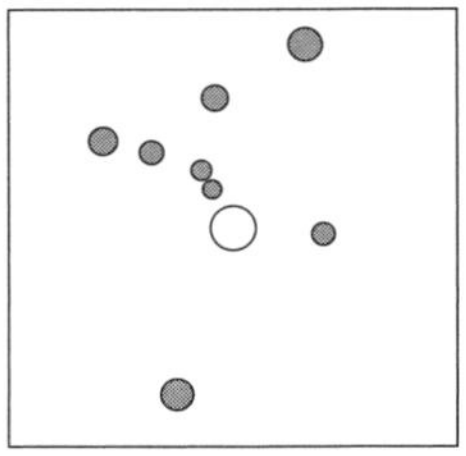

```
// An array of 8 planet objects
Planet[] planets = new Planet[8];

void setup() {
  size(200,200);
  smooth();

  // The planet objects are initialized using the counter variable
  for (int i = 0; i < planets.length; i++) {
    planets[i] = new Planet(20+i*10,i+8);
  }
}

void draw() {

  background(255);

  // Drawing the Sun
  pushMatrix();
  translate(width/2,height/2);
  stroke(0);
  fill(255);
  ellipse(0,0,20,20);

  // Drawing all Planets
  for (int i = 0; i < planets.length; i++) {
    planets[i].update();
    planets[i].display();
  }

  popMatrix();
}

class Planet {

  float theta;       // Rotation around sun
  float diameter;    // Size of planet
  float distance;    // Distance from sun
  float orbitspeed;  // Orbit speed

  Planet(float distance_, float diameter_) {
    distance = distance_;
    diameter = diameter_;
    theta = 0;
    orbitspeed = random(0.01,0.03);
  }

  void update() {
    // Increment the angle to rotate
    theta += orbitspeed;
  }

  void display() {

    pushMatrix();
    rotate(theta);          // rotate orbit
    translate(distance,0);  // translate out distance
```

fig. 14.31

> Each planet object keeps track of its own angle of rotation.

> Before rotation and translation, the state of the matrix is saved with **_pushMatrix()._**

```
    stroke(0);
    fill(175);
    ellipse(0,0,diameter,diameter);
    // Afer we are done, restore matrix!

    popMatrix();
  }
}
```

> Once the planet is drawn, the matrix is restored with **popMatrix()** so that the next planet is not affected.

Exercise 14-10: How would you add moons to the planets? Hint: Write a Moon class that is virtually identical to the Planet. Then, incorporate a Moon variable into the Planet class. (In Chapter 22, we will see how this could be made more efficient with advanced OOP techniques.)

*Exercise 14-11: Extend the solar system example into three dimensions. Try using **sphere()** or **box()** instead of **ellipse()**. Note **sphere()** takes one argument, the sphere's radius. **box()** can take one argument (size, in the case of a cube) or three arguments (width, height, and depth.)*

Lesson Six Project

Create a virtual ecosystem. Make a class for each "creature" in your world. Using the techniques from Chapters 13 and 14, attempt to infuse your creatures with personality. Some possibilities:

- Use Perlin noise to control the movements of creatures.
- Make the creatures look like they are breathing with oscillation.
- Design the creatures using recursion.
- Design the custom polygons using *beginShape()*.
- Use rotation in the creatures' behaviors.

Use the space provided below to sketch designs, notes, and pseudocode for your project.

Lesson Seven

Pixels Under a Microscope

15 Images

16 Video

15 Images

"Politics will eventually be replaced by imagery. The politician will be only too happy to abdicate in favor of his image, because the image will be much more powerful than he could ever be."
—*Marshall McLuhan*

"When it comes to pixels, I think I've had my fill. There are enough pixels in my fingers and brains that I probably need a few decades to digest all of them."
—*John Maeda*

In this chapter:
- The PImage class.
- Displaying images.
- Changing image color.
- The pixels of an image.
- Simple image processing.
- Interactive image processing.

A digital image is nothing more than data—numbers indicating variations of red, green, and blue at a particular location on a grid of pixels. Most of the time, we view these pixels as miniature rectangles sandwiched together on a computer screen. With a little creative thinking and some lower level manipulation of pixels with code, however, we can display that information in a myriad of ways. This chapter is dedicated to breaking out of simple shape drawing in *Processing* and using images (and their pixels) as the building blocks of *Processing* graphics.

15.1 Getting Started with Images

By now, we are quite comfortable with the idea of data types. We specify them often—a float variable called *speed*, an int named *x*, perhaps even a char entitled *letterGrade*. These are all *primitive* data types, bits sitting in the computer's memory ready for our use. Though perhaps a bit trickier, we are also beginning to feel at ease with objects, *complex* data types that store multiple pieces of data (along with functionality)—our Zoog class, for example, included floating point variables for location, size, and speed as well as methods to move, display itself, and so on. Zoog, of course, is a user-defined class; we brought Zoog into this programming world, defining what it means to be a Zoog, and defining the data and functions associated with a Zoog object.

In addition to user-defined objects, *Processing* has a bunch of handy classes all ready to go without us writing any code. (Later, in Chapter 23, we will find out that we also have access to a vast library of Java classes.) The first *Processing*-defined class we will examine is PImage, a class for loading and displaying an image such as the one shown in Figure 15.1.

fig. 15.1

Example 15-1: "Hello World" images

```
// Declaring a variable of type PImage
PImage img;

void setup() {
  size(320,240);
  // Make a new instance of a PImage by loading an image file
  img = loadImage("mysummervacation.jpg");
}

void draw() {
  background(0);
  image(img,0,0);
}
```

> Declaring a variable of type PImage, a class available to us from the *Processing* core library.

> The *image()* function displays the image at a location—in this case the point (0,0).

Using an instance of a PImage object is no different than using a *user-defined* class. First, a variable of type PImage, named "img," is declared. Second, a *new* instance of a PImage object is created via the *loadImage()* method. *loadImage()* takes one argument, a *String* (*Strings* are explored in greater detail in Chapter 17) indicating a file name, and loads the that file into memory. *loadImage()* looks for image files stored in your *Processing* sketch's data folder.

The Data Folder: How do I get there?

Images can be added to the data folder automatically via:

Sketch → Add File…

or manually:

Sketch → Show Sketch Folder

This will open up the sketch folder as shown in Figure 15.2. If there is no data directory, create one. Otherwise, place your image files inside. *Processing* accepts the following file formats for images: GIF, JPG, TGA, and PNG.

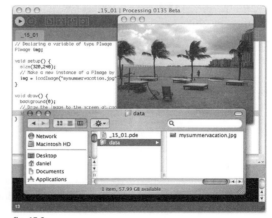

fig. 15.2

In Example 15-1, it may seem a bit peculiar that we never called a "constructor" to instantiate the PImage object, saying **"new PImage( )"**. After all, in all the object-related examples to date, a constructor is a must for producing an object instance.

```
Spaceship ss = new Spaceship();
Flower flr = new Flower(25);
```

And yet:

```
PImage img = loadImage("file.jpg");
```

In fact, the ***loadImage()*** function performs the work of a constructor, returning a brand new instance of a PImage object generated from the specified filename. We can think of it as the PImage constructor for loading images from a file. For creating a blank image, the ***createImage()*** function is used.

```
// Create a blank image, 200X200 pixels with RGB color
PImage img = createImage(200,200,RGB);
```

We should also note that the process of loading the image from the hard drive into memory is a slow one, and we should make sure our program only has to do it once, in ***setup()***. Loading images in ***draw()*** may result in slow performance, as well as "Out of Memory" errors.

Once the image is loaded, it is displayed with the ***image()*** function. The ***image()*** function must include three arguments—the image to be displayed, the *x* location, and the *y* location. Optionally, two arguments can be added to resize the image to a certain width and height.

```
image(img,10,20,90,60);
```

Exercise 15-1: Load and display an image. Control the image's width and height with the mouse.

15.2 Animation with an Image

From here, it is easy to see how you can use images to further develop examples from previous chapters.

Example 15-2: Image "sprite"

```
PImage head; // A variable for the image file
float x,y;   // Variables for image location
float rot;   // A variable for image rotation

void setup() {
  size(200,200);
  // load image, initialize variables
  head = loadImage("face.jpg");
  x = 0.0f;
  y = width/2.0f;
  rot = 0.0f;
}

void draw() {
  background(255);

  // Translate and rotate
  translate(x,y);
  rotate(rot);
  image(head,0,0); // Draw image
```

fig. 15.3

> Images can be animated just like regular shapes using variables, ***translate()***, ***rotate()***, and so on.

```
// Adjust variables to create animation
x += 1.0;
rot += 0.01;
if (x > width) {
  x = 0;
  }
}
```

Exercise 15-2: Rewrite this example in an object-oriented fashion where the data for the image, location, size, rotation, and so on is contained in a class. Can you have the class swap images when it hits the edge of the screen?

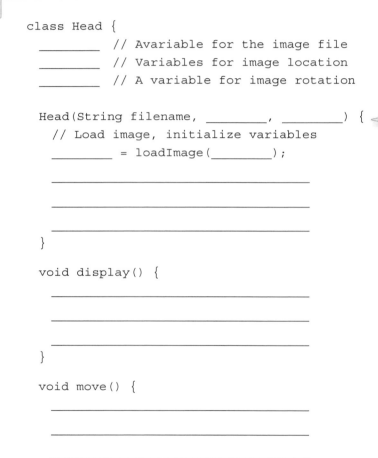

```
class Head {
  _____    // A variable for the image file
  _____    // Variables for image location
  _____    // A variable for image rotation

  Head(String filename, _____, _____) {
    // Load image, initialize variables
    _____ = loadImage(_____);

    _____

    _____

    _____
  }

  void display() {

    _____

    _____

    _____
  }

  void move() {

    _____

    _____

    _____

    _____

    _____

    _____
  }
}
```

String is also a class we get for free and will be explored further in Chapter 17.

15.3 My Very First Image Processing Filter

Every now and then, when displaying an image, we choose to alter its appearance. Perhaps we would like the image to appear darker, transparent, bluish, and so on. This type of simple image filtering is achieved with *Processing*'s **tint()** function. **tint()** is essentially the image equivalent of shape's **fill()**, setting the color and alpha transparency for displaying an image on screen. An image, nevertheless, is not usually all one color. The arguments for **tint()** simply specify how much of a given color to use for every pixel of that image, as well as how transparent those pixels should appear.

For the following examples, we will assume that two images (a sunflower and a dog) have been loaded and the dog is displayed as the background (which will allow us to demonstrate transparency). See Figure 15.4. For color versions of these images visit: *http://www.learningprocessing.com*)

```
PImage sunflower = loadImage("sunflower.jpg");
PImage dog = loadImage("dog.jpg");
background(dog);
```

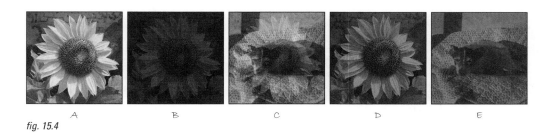

A   B   C   D   E

fig. 15.4

If **tint()** receives one argument, only the brightness of the image is affected.

```
tint(255);
image(sunflower,0,0);
```
A The image retains its original state.

```
tint(100);
image(sunflower,0,0);
```
B The image appears darker.

A second argument will change the image's alpha transparency.

```
tint(255,127);
image(sunflower,0,0);
```
C The image is at 50% opacity.

Three arguments affect the brightness of the red, green, and blue components of each color.

```
tint(0,200,255)
image(sunflower,0,0);
```
D None of it is red, most of it is green, and all of it is blue.

Finally, adding a fourth argument to the method manipulates the alpha (same as with two arguments). Incidentally, the range of values for **tint()** can be specified with **colorMode()** (see Chapter 1).

```
tint(255,0,0,100);
image(sunflower,0,0);
```
E The image is tinted red and transparent.

*Exercise 15-3: Display an image using **tint()**. Use the mouse location to control the amount of red, green, and blue tint. Also try using the distance of the mouse from the corners or center.*

 *Exercise 15-4: Using **tint()**, create a montage of blended images. What happens when you layer a large number of images, each with different alpha transparency, on top of each other? Can you make it interactive so that different images fade in and out?*

15.4 An Array of Images

One image is nice, a good place to start. It will not be long, however, until the temptation of using many images takes over. Yes, we could keep track of multiple images with multiple variables, but here is a magnificent opportunity to rediscover the power of the array. Let's assume we have five images and want to display a new background image each time the user clicks the mouse.

First, we set up an array of images, as a global variable.

```
// Image Array
PImage[] images = new PImage[5];
```

Second, we load each image file into the appropriate location in the array. This happens in *setup()*.

```
// Loading Images into an Array
images[0] = loadImage("cat.jpg");
images[1] = loadImage("mouse.jpg");
images[2] = loadImage("dog.jpg");
images[3] = loadImage("kangaroo.jpg");
images[4] = loadImage("porcupine.jpg");
```

Of course, this is somewhat awkward. Loading each image individually is not terribly elegant. With five images, sure, it is manageable, but imagine writing the above code with 100 images. One solution is to store the filenames in a *String* array and use a *for* statement to initialize all the array elements.

```
// Loading Images into an Array from an array of filenames
String[] filenames = {"cat.jpg","mouse.jpg","dog.jpg","kangaroo.jpg","porcupine.jpg"};
for (int i = 0; i < filenames.length; i++) {
  images[i] = loadImage(filenames[i]);
}
```

Concatenation: A New Kind of Addition

Usually, a plus sign (+) means, add. 2 + 2 = 4, right?

With text (as stored in a *String*, enclosed in quotes), + means *concatenate,* that is, join two *Strings* together.

"Happy" + " Trails" = "Happy Trails"

"2" + "2" = "22"

See more about *Strings* in Chapter 17.

Even better, if we just took a little time out of our hectic schedules to plan ahead, numbering the image files ("animal1.jpg", "animal2.jpg", "animal3.jpg", etc.), we can really simplify the code:

```
// Loading images with numbered files
for (int i = 0; i < images.length; i++) {
  images[i] = loadImage("animal" + i + ".jpg");
}
```

Once the images are loaded, it's on to **draw()**. There, we choose to display one particular image, picking from the array by referencing an index ("0" below).

```
image(images[0],0,0);
```

Of course, hard-coding the index value is foolish. We need a variable in order to dynamically display a different image at any given moment in time.

```
image(images[imageindex],0,0);
```

The "imageindex" variable should be declared as a global variable (of type integer). Its value can be changed throughout the course of the program. The full version is shown in Example 15-3.

Example 15-3: Swapping images

```
int maxImages = 10; // Total # of images
int imageIndex = 0; // Initial image to be displayed is the first
PImage[] images = new PImage[maxImages]; // The image array
```
> Declaring an array of images.

```
void setup() {
  size(200,200);
  // Loading the images into the array
  // Don't forget to put the JPG files in the data folder!
  for (int i = 0; i < images.length; i++) {
    images[i] = loadImage("animal" + i + ".jpg");
  }
}
```
> Loading an array of images.

```
void draw() {
  image(images[imageIndex],0,0); // Displaying one image
}
```
> Displaying one image from the array.

```
void mousePressed() {
  // A new image is picked randomly when the mouse is clicked
  // Note the index to the array must be an integer!
  imageIndex = int(random(images.length));
}
```
> Picking a new image to display by changing the index variable!

To play the images in sequence as an animation, follow Example 15-4.

Example 15-4: Image sequence

```
void draw() {
  background(0);
  image(images[imageIndex],0,0);
  // increment image index by one each cycle
  // use modulo "%" to return to 0 once the size
  //of the array is reached
  imageIndex = (imageIndex + 1) % images.length;
}
```
> Remember modulus? The % sign? It allows us to cycle a counter back to 0. See Chapter 13 for a review.

Exercise 15-5: Create multiple instances of an image sequence onscreen. Have them start at different times within the sequence so that they are out of sync. Hint: Use object-oriented programming to place the image sequence in a class.

15.5 Pixels, Pixels, and More Pixels

If you have been diligently reading this book in precisely the prescribed order, you will notice that so far, the only offered means for drawing to the screen is through a function call. "Draw a line between these points" or "Fill an ellipse with red" or "load this JPG image and place it on the screen here." But somewhere, somehow, someone had to write code that translates these function calls into setting the individual pixels on the screen to reflect the requested shape. A line does not appear because we say *line()*, it appears because we color all the pixels along a linear path between two points. Fortunately, we do not have to manage this lower-level-pixel-setting on a day-to-day basis. We have the developers of *Processing* (and Java) to thank for the many drawing functions that take care of this business.

Nevertheless, from time to time, we do want to break out of our mundane shape drawing existence and deal with the pixels on the screen directly. *Processing* provides this functionality via the *pixels* array.

We are familiar with the idea of each pixel on the screen having an *X* and *Y* position in a two-dimensional window. However, the array *pixels* has only one dimension, storing color values in linear sequence. See Figure 15.5.

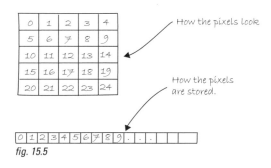

fig. 15.5

Take the following example. This sketch sets each pixel in a window to a random grayscale value. The *pixels* array is just like an other array, the only difference is that we do not have to declare it since it is a *Processing* built-in variable.

Example 15-5: Setting pixels

```
size(200,200);
// Before we deal with pixels
loadPixels();
// Loop through every pixel
for (int i = 0; i < pixels.length; i++) {
  // Pick a random number, 0 to 255
  float rand = random(255);
```

> We can get the length of the pixels array just like with any array.

fig. 15.6

```
    // Create a grayscale color based on random number
    color c = color(rand);
    // Set pixel at that location to random color
    pixels[i] = c;
}
// When we are finished dealing with pixels
updatePixels();
```

> We can access individual elements of the pixels array via an index, just like with any other array.

First, we should point out something important in the above example. Whenever you are accessing the pixels of a *Processing* window, you must alert *Processing* to this activity. This is accomplished with two functions:

- ***loadPixels()***—This function is called *before* you access the pixel array, saying "load the pixels, I would like to speak with them!"
- ***updatePixels()***—This function is called *after* you finish with the pixel array, saying "Go ahead and update the pixels, I'm all done!"

In Example 15-5, because the colors are set randomly, we did not have to worry about where the pixels are onscreen as we access them, since we are simply setting all the pixels with no regard to their relative location. However, in many image processing applications, the *XY* location of the pixels themselves is crucial information. A simple example of this might be, set every even column of pixels to white and every odd to black. How could you do this with a one-dimensional pixel array? How do you know what column or row any given pixel is in?

When programming with pixels, we need to be able to think of every pixel as living in a two-dimensional world, but continue to access the data in one dimension (since that is how it is made available to us). We can do this via the following formula:

1. Assume a window or image with a given WIDTH and HEIGHT.
2. We then know the pixel array has a total number of elements equaling WIDTH * HEIGHT.
3. For any given *X, Y* point in the window, the location in our one-dimensional pixel array is:

LOCATION = X + Y * WIDTH

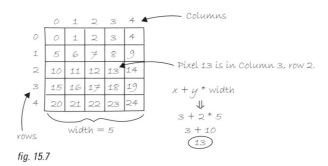

fig. 15.7

This may remind you of two-dimensional arrays in Chapter 13. In fact, we will need to use the same nested *for* loop technique. The difference is that, although we want to use *for* loops to think about the pixels in two dimensions, when we go to actually access the pixels, they live in a one-dimensional array, and we have to apply the formula from Figure 15.7.

Let's look at how it is done, completing the even/odd column problem. See Figure 15.8.

Example 15-6: Setting pixels according to their 2D location

```
size(200,200);
loadPixels();
// Loop through every pixel column
for (int x = 0; x < width; x++) {
  // Loop through every pixel row
  for (int y = 0; y < height; y++){


    // Use the formula to find the 1D location
    int loc = x + y * width;


    if (x % 2 == 0){ // If we are an even column
      pixels[loc] = color(255);
    } else {          // If we are an odd column
      pixels[loc] = color(0);
    }
  }
}
updatePixels();
```

Two loops allow us to visit every column (*x*) and every row (*y*).

fig. 15.8

The location in the pixel array is calculated via our formula: 1D pixel location = $x + y *$ width

We use the column number (*x*) to determine whether the color should be black or white.

Exercise 15-6: Complete the code to match the corresponding screenshots.

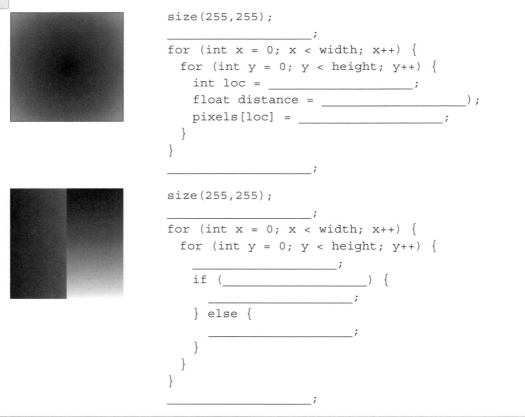

```
size(255,255);
_____;
for (int x = 0; x < width; x++) {
  for (int y = 0; y < height; y++) {
    int loc = _____;
    float distance = _____);
    pixels[loc] = _____;
  }
}
_____;
```

```
size(255,255);
_____;
for (int x = 0; x < width; x++) {
  for (int y = 0; y < height; y++) {
    _____;
    if (_____) {
      _____;
    } else {
      _____;
    }
  }
}
_____;
```

15.6 Intro to Image Processing

The previous section looked at examples that set pixel values according to an arbitrary calculation. We will now look at how we might set pixels according to those found in an existing PImage object. Here is some pseudocode.

1. Load the image file into a PImage object.
2. For each pixel in the PImage, retrieve the pixel's color and set the display pixel to that color.

The PImage class includes some useful fields that store data related to the image—width, height, and pixels. Just as with our user-defined classes, we can access these fields via the dot syntax.

```
PImage img = createImage(320,240,RGB); // Make a PImage object
println(img.width);  // Yields 320
println(img.height); // Yields 240
img.pixels[0] = color(255,0,0); // Sets the first pixel of the image to red
```

Access to these fields allows us to loop through all the pixels of an image and display them onscreen.

Example 15-7: Displaying the pixels of an image

```
PImage img;

void setup() {
  size(200,200);
  img = loadImage("sunflower.jpg");
}

void draw() {

  loadPixels();
  // Since we are going to access the image's pixels too
  img.loadPixels();
  for (int y = 0; y < height; y++) {
    for (int x = 0; x < width; x++) {
      int loc = x + y*width;

      // Image Processing Algorithm would go here
      float r = red   (img.pixels [loc]);
      float g = green(img.pixels[loc]);
      float b = blue (imq.pixels[loc];


      // Image Processing would go here

      // Set the display pixel to the image pixel
      pixels[loc] = color(r,g,b);
    }
  }
  updatePixels();
}
```

fig. 15.9

> We must also call **loadPixels()** on the PImage since we are going to read its pixels.

> The functions **red()**, **green()**, and **blue()** pull out the three color components from a pixel.

> If we were to change the RGB values, we would do it here, before setting the pixel in the display window.

Now, we could certainly come up with simplifications in order to merely display the image (e.g., the nested loop is not required, not to mention that using the **image()** function would allow us to skip all this pixel work entirely). However, Example 15-7 provides a basic framework for getting the red, green, and blue values for each pixel based on its spatial orientation (*XY* location); ultimately, this will allow us to develop more advanced image processing algorithms.

Before we move on, I should stress that this example works because the display area has the same dimensions as the source image. If this were not the case, you would simply need to have two pixel location calculations, one for the source image and one for the display area.

```
int imageLoc = x + y*img.width;
int displayLoc = x + y*width;
```

Exercise 15-7: Using Example 15-7, change the values of r, g, and b before displaying them.

15.7 Our Second Image *Processing* Filter, Making Our Own *Tint( )*

Just a few paragraphs ago, we were enjoying a relaxing coding session, colorizing images and adding alpha transparency with the friendly *tint()* method. For basic filtering, this method did the trick. The pixel by pixel method, however, will allow us to develop custom algorithms for mathematically altering the colors of an image. Consider brightness—brighter colors have higher values for their red, green, and blue components. It follows naturally that we can alter the brightness of an image by increasing or decreasing the color components of each pixel. In the next example, we dynamically increase or decrease those values based on the mouse's horizontal location. (Note that the next two examples include only the image processing loop itself, the rest of the code is assumed.)

Example 15-8: Adjusting image brightness

```
for (int x = 0; x < img.width; x++) {
  for (int y = 0; y < img.height; y++) {
    // Calculate the 1D pixel location
    int loc = x + y*img.width;
    // Get the R,G,B values from image
    float r = red (img.pixels[loc]);
    float g = green (img.pixels[loc]);
    float b = blue (img.pixels[loc]);
    // Change brightness according to the mouse here
    float adjustBrightness = ((float)mouseX / width) * 8.0;
    r *= adjustBrightness;
    g *= adjustBrightness;
    b *= adjustBrightness;
    // Constrain RGB to between 0-255
    r = constrain(r,0,255);
    g = constrain(g,0,255);
    b = constrain(b,0,255);
    // Make a new color and set pixel in the window
    color c = color(r,g,b);
    pixels[loc] = c;
  }
}
```

fig. 15.10

We calculate a multiplier ranging from 0.0 to 8.0 based on *mouseX* position. That multiplier changes the RGB value of each pixel.

The RGB values are constrained between 0 and 255 before being set as a new color.

Since we are altering the image on a per pixel basis, all pixels need not be treated equally. For example, we can alter the brightness of each pixel according to its distance from the mouse.

Example 15-9: Adjusting image brightness based on pixel location

```
for (int x = 0; x < img.width; x++) {
  for (int y = 0; y < img.height; y++) {
    // Calculate the 1D pixel location
    int loc = x + y*img.width;
    // Get the R,G,B values from image
    float r = red   (img.pixels[loc]);
    float g = green (img.pixels[loc]);
    float b = blue  (img.pixels[loc]);
    // Calculate an amount to change brightness
    // based on proximity to the mouse
    float distance = dist(x,y,mouseX,mouseY);
    float adjustBrightness = (50-distance)/50;
    r *= adjustBrightness;
    g *= adjustBrightness;
    b *= adjustBrightness;
    // Constrain RGB to between 0-255
    r = constrain(r,0,255);
    g = constrain(g,0,255);
    b = constrain(b,o,255);
    // Make a new color and set pixel in the window
    color c = color(r,g,b);
    pixels[loc] = c;
  }
}
```

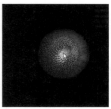

fig. 15.11

The closer the pixel is to the mouse, the lower the value of "distance" is. We want closer pixels to be brighter, however, so we invert the value with the formula:

adjustBrightness = (50-distance)/50

Pixels with a distance of 50 (or greater) have a brightness of 0.0 (or negative which is equivalent to 0 here) and pixels with a distance of 0 have a brightness of 1.0.

Exercise 15-8: Adjust the brightness of the red, green, and blue color components separately according to mouse interaction. For example, let **mouseX** *control red,* **mouseY** *green, distance blue, and so on.*

15.8 Writing to Another PImage Object's Pixels

All of our image processing examples have read every pixel from a source image and written a new pixel to the *Processing* window directly. However, it is often more convenient to write the new pixels to a destination image (that you then display using the ***image()*** function). We will demonstrate this technique while looking at another simple pixel operation: *threshold*.

A *threshold* filter displays each pixel of an image in only one of two states, black or white. That state is set according to a particular threshold value. If the pixel's brightness is greater than the threshold, we color the pixel white, less than, black. Example 15-10 uses an arbitrary threshold of 100.

fig. 15.12

Example 15-10: Brightness threshold

```
PImage source;      // Source image
PImage destination; // Destination image

void setup() {
  size(200,200);
  source = loadImage("sunflower.jpg");
  destination = createImage(source.width, source.height, RGB);
}

void draw() {
  float threshold = 127;

  // We are going to look at both image's pixels
  source.loadPixels();
  destination.loadPixels();

  for (int x = 0; x < source.width; x++) {
    for (int y = 0; y < source.height; y++) {
      int loc = x + y*source.width;
      // Test the brightness against the threshold
      if (brightness(source.pixels[loc]) > threshold) {
        destination.pixels[loc] = color(255); // White
      } else {
        destination.pixels[loc] = color(0);    // Black
      }
    }
  }

  // We changed the pixels in destination
  destination.updatePixels();
  // Display the destination
  image(destination,0,0);
}
```

> We need two images, a source (original file) and destination (to be displayed) image.

> The destination image is created as a blank image the same size as the source.

> **brightness()** returns a value between 0 and 255, the overall brightness of the pixel's color. If it is more than 100, make it white, less than 100, make it black.

> Writing to the destination image's pixels.

> We have to display the destination image!

Exercise 15-9: Tie the threshold to mouse location.

This particular functionality is available without per pixel processing as part of *Processing's* **filter()** function. Understanding the lower level code, however, is crucial if you want to implement your own image processing algorithms, not available with **filter()**.

If all you want to do is threshold, Example 15-11 is much simpler.

Example 15-11: Brightness threshold with filter

```
// Draw the image
image(img,0,0);
// Filter the window with a threshold effect
// 0.5 means threshold is 50% brightness
filter(THRESHOLD,0.5);
```

More on filter():

filter(mode);
filter(mode,level);

The *filter()* function offers a set of prepackaged filters for the display window. It is not necessary to use a PImage, the filter will alter the look of whatever is drawn in the window at the time it is executed. Other available modes besides THRESHOLD are GRAY, INVERT, POSTERIZE, BLUR, OPAQUE, ERODE, and DILATE. See the *Processing* reference (*http://processing.org/reference/filter_.html*) for examples of each.

15.9 Level II: Pixel Group Processing

In previous examples, we have seen a one-to-one relationship between source pixels and destination pixels. To increase an image's brightness, we take one pixel from the source image, increase the RGB values, and display one pixel in the output window. In order to perform more advanced image processing functions, however, we must move beyond the one-to-one pixel paradigm into *pixel group processing*.

Let's start by creating a new pixel out of two pixels from a source image—a pixel and its neighbor to the left.

If we know the pixel is located at (x,y):

```
int loc = x + y*img.width;
color pix = img.pixels[loc];
```

Then its left neighbor is located at $(x - 1,y)$:

```
int leftLoc = (x-1) + y*img.width;
color leftPix = img.pixels[leftLoc];
```

We could then make a new color out of the difference between the pixel and its neighbor to the left.

```
float diff = abs(brightness(pix) - brightness(leftPix));
pixels[loc] = color(diff);
```

Example 15-12 shows the full algorithm, with the results shown in Figure 15.13.

Example 15-12: Pixel neighbor differences (edges)

```
// Since we are looking at left neighbors
// We skip the first column
for (int x = 1; x < width; x++) {
  for (int y = 0; y < height; y++) {
    // Pixel location and color
    int loc = x + y*img.width;
    color pix = img.pixels[loc];           Reading the pixel to the left.

    // Pixel to the left location and color
    int leftLoc = (x-1) + y*img.width;
    color leftPix = img.pixels[leftLoc];
```

fig. 15.13

```
    // New color is difference between pixel and left neighbor
    float diff = abs(brightness(pix) - brightness(leftPix));
    pixels[loc] = color(diff);
  }
}
```

Example 15-12 is a simple vertical edge detection algorithm. When pixels differ greatly from their neighbors, they are most likely "edge" pixels. For example, think of a picture of a white piece of paper on a black tabletop. The edges of that paper are where the colors are most different, where white meets black.

In Example 15-12, we look at two pixels to find edges. More sophisticated algorithms, however, usually involve looking at many more neighboring pixels. After all, each pixel has eight immediate neighbors: top left, top, top right, right, bottom right, bottom, bottom left, and left. See Figure 15.14.

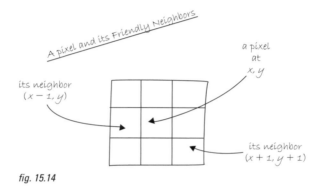

fig. 15.14

These image processing algorithms are often referred to as a "spatial convolution." The process uses a *weighted average* of an input pixel and its neighbors to calculate an output pixel. In other words, that new pixel is a function of an area of pixels. Neighboring areas of different sizes can be employed, such as a 3×3 matrix, 5×5, and so on.

Different combinations of weights for each pixel result in various effects. For example, we "sharpen" an image by subtracting the neighboring pixel values and increasing the centerpoint pixel. A blur is achieved by taking the average of all neighboring pixels. (Note that the values in the convolution matrix add up to 1.)

For example,

```
Sharpen:
 -1    -1    -1
 -1     9    -1
 -1    -1    -1

Blur:
 1/9  1/9  1/9
 1/9  1/9  1/9
 1/9  1/9  1/9
```

Example 15-13 performs a convolution using a 2D array (see Chapter 13 for a review of 2D arrays) to store the pixel weights of a 3 × 3 matrix. This example is probably the most advanced example we have encountered in this book so far, since it involves so many elements (nested loops, 2D arrays, PImage pixels, etc.).

Example 15-13: Sharpen with convolution

```
PImage img;
int w = 80;

// It's possible to perform a convolution
// the image with different matrices

float[][] matrix = { {  -1, -1, -1 },
                     {  -1,  9, -1 },
                     {  -1, -1, -1 } };
void setup() {
  size(200,200);
  img = loadImage("sunflower.jpg");
}

void draw() {
  // We're only going to process a portion of the image
  // so let's set the whole image as the background first
  image(img,0,0);
  // Where is the small rectangle we will process
  int xstart = constrain(mouseX-w/2,0,img.width);
  int ystart = constrain(mouseY-w/2,0,img.height);
  int xend = constrain(mouseX+w/2,0,img.width);
  int yend = constrain(mouseY+w/2,0,img.height);
  int matrixsize = 3;
  loadPixels();
  // Begin our loop for every pixel
  for (int x = xstart; x < xend; x++) {
    for (int y = ystart; y < yend; y++) {
      color c = convolution(x,y,matrix,matrixsize,img);
      int loc = x + y*img.width;
      pixels[loc] = c;
    }
  }
  updatePixels();

  stroke(0);
  noFill();
  rect(xstart,ystart,w,w);
}
color convolution(int x, int y, float[][] matrix, int matrixsize, PImage img) {
  float rtotal = 0.0;
  float gtotal = 0.0;
  float btotal = 0.0;
  int offset = matrixsize / 2;
  // Loop through convolution matrix
  for (int i = 0; i < matrixsize; i++) {
    for (int j= 0; j < matrixsize; j++) {
      // What pixel are we testing
```

The convolution matrix for a "sharpen" effect stored as a 3 × 3 two-dimensional array.

fig. 15.15

In this example we are only processing a section of the image—an 80 × 80 rectangle around the mouse location.

Each pixel location (x,y) gets passed into a function called *convolution()* which returns a new color value to be displayed.

```
        int xloc = x+i-offset;
        int yloc = y+j-offset;
        int loc = xloc + img.width*yloc;
        // Make sure we haven't walked off the edge of the pixel array
        loc = constrain(loc,0,img.pixels.length-1);
        // Calculate the convolution
        rtotal += (red(img.pixels[loc]) * matrix[i][j]);
        gtotal += (green(img.pixels[loc]) * matrix[i][j]);
        btotal += (blue(img.pixels[loc]) * matrix[i][j]);
      }
    }
    // Make sure RGB is within range
    rtotal = constrain(rtotal,0,255);
    gtotal = constrain(gtotal,0,255);
    btotal = constrain(btotal,0,255);
    // Return the resulting color
    return color(rtotal,gtotal,btotal);
  }
}
```

> It is often good when looking at neighboring pixels to make sure we have not gone off the edge of the pixel array by accident.

> We sum all the neighboring pixels multiplied by the values in the convolution matrix.

> After the sums are constrained within a range of 0–255, a new color is made and returned.

Exercise 15-10: Try different values for the convolution matrix.

*Exercise 15-11: Using the framework established by our image processing examples, create a filter that takes two images as input and generates one output image. In other words, each pixel displayed should be a function of the color values from two pixels, one from one image and one from another. For example, can you write the code to blend two images together (without using **tint()**)?*

15.10 Creative Visualization

You may be thinking: "Gosh, this is all very interesting, but seriously, when I want to blur an image or change its brightness, do I really need to write code? I mean, can't I use *Photoshop*?" Indeed, what we have achieved here is merely an introductory understanding of what highly skilled programmers at Adobe do. The power of *Processing*, however, is the potential for real-time, interactive graphics applications. There is no need for us to live within the confines of "pixel point" and "pixel group" processing.

Following are two examples of algorithms for drawing *Processing* shapes. Instead of coloring the shapes randomly or with hard-coded values as we have in the past, we select colors from the pixels of a PImage object. The image itself is never displayed; rather, it serves as a database of information that we can exploit for our own creative pursuits.

In this first example, for every cycle through *draw()*, we fill one ellipse at a random location onscreen with a color taken from its corresponding location in the source image. The result is a "pointillist-like" effect. See Figure 15.16.

Example 15-14: "Pointillism"

```
PImage img;
int pointillize = 16;

void setup() {
  size(200,200);
  img = loadImage("sunflower.jpg");
  background(0);
  smooth();
}

void draw() {
  // Pick a random point
  int x = int(random(img.width));
  int y = int(random(img.height));
  int loc = x + y*img.width;

  // Look up the RGB color in the source image
  loadPixels();
  float r = red(img.pixels[loc]);
  float g = green(img.pixels[loc]);
  float b = blue(img.pixels[loc]);
  noStroke();

  // Draw an ellipse at that location with that color
  fill(r,g,b,100);
  ellipse(x,y,pointillize,pointillize);
}
```

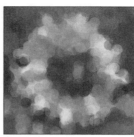

fig. 15.16

> Back to shapes! Instead of setting a pixel, we use the color from a pixel to draw a circle.

In this next example, we take the data from a two-dimensional image and, using the 3D translation techniques described in Chapter 14, render a rectangle for each pixel in three-dimensional space. The z location is determined by the brightness of the color. Brighter colors appear closer to the viewer and darker ones further away.

  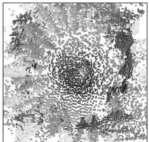

fig. 15.17

Example 15-15: 2D image mapped to 3D

```
PImage img;         // The source image
int cellsize = 2; // Dimensions of each cell in the grid
int cols, rows;   // Number of columns and rows in our system

void setup() {
  size(200,200,P3D);
```

```
    img = loadImage("sunflower.jpg"); // Load the image
    cols = width/cellsize;            // Calculate # of columns
    rows = height/cellsize;           // Calculate # of rows
}

void draw() {
  background(0);
  loadPixels();
  // Begin loop for columns
  for (int i = 0; i < cols; i++) {
  // Begin loop for rows
  for (int j = 0; j < rows; j++) {
  int x = i*cellsize + cellsize/2; // x position
  int y = j*cellsize + cellsize/2; // y position
  int loc = x + y*width;           // Pixel array location
  color c = img.pixels[loc];       // Grab the color
  // Calculate a z position as a function of mouseX and pixel brightness
  float z = (mouseX/(float)width) * brightness(img.pixels[loc])- 100.0;
  // Translate to the location, set fill and stroke, and draw the rect
  pushMatrix();
    translate(x,y,z);
    fill(c);
    noStroke();
    rectMode(CENTER);
    rect(0,0,cellsize,cellsize);
    popMatrix();
    }
  }
}
```

> A *z* value for 3D translation is calculated as a function of the pixel's brightness as well as mouse location.

Exercise 15-12: Create a sketch that uses shapes to display a pattern that covers an entire window. Load an image and color the shapes according to the pixels of that image. The following image, for example, uses triangles.

16 Video

"I have no memory. It's like looking in a mirror and seeing nothing but mirror."
—Alfred Hitchcock

In this chapter:
- Displaying live video.
- Displaying recorded video.
- Creating a software mirror.
- How to use a video camera as a sensor.

16.1 Before Processing

Now that we have explored static images in *Processing*, we are ready to move on to moving images, specifically from a live camera (and later, from a recorded movie). Using a digital video camera connected to a PC or Mac requires a few simple steps before any code can be written.

On a Mac:

- Attach a camera to your computer.
- Make sure any necessary software and drivers for the camera are installed.
- Test the camera in another program, such as iChat, to make sure it is working.

On a PC:

- Attach a camera to your computer.
- Make sure any necessary software and drivers for the camera are installed.
- Test the camera. (Use whatever software that came with your camera that allows you to view the video stream.)
- Install QuickTime (version 7 or higher). If you are using a previous version of QuickTime, you must make sure you choose "custom" installation and select "QuickTime for Java."
- You will also need to install a vdig (video digitizer) that allows QuickTime applications (what we are creating) to capture video in Windows. The vdig situation is in flux so I recommend you check this book's web site for updates. Although no longer being developed, a free vdig is available at this site: *http://eden.net.nz/7/20071008/*. You can also consider using Abstract Plane's vdig (*http://www.abstractplane.com.au/products/vdig.jsp*), which costs a small fee, but has more advanced features.

Admittedly, the process is a bit less complicated on a Mac. This is because *Processing* uses the QuickTime libraries in Java to handle video. On Apple computers, QuickTime comes preinstalled (although sometimes software updates can cause issues), whereas on Windows, we have to make sure we have taken the steps to install and properly configure QuickTime. At the end of this chapter, we will see that there are few third party libraries available in *Processing* that do not require QuickTime for video capture on Windows.

Exercise 16-1: Hook a camera up to your computer. Does it work in another program (not Processing)? If you are on a PC, install a vdig and test.

16.2 Live Video 101

Once you have made sure you have a working camera connected to your machine, you can start writing *Processing* code to capture and display the image. We begin by walking through the basic steps of importing the video library and using the Capture class to display live video.

Step 1. Import the *Processing* video library.

If you skipped Chapter 12 on *Processing* libraries, you might want to go back and review the details. There is not much to it here, however, since the video library comes with the *Processing* application. All you need to do is import the library. This is done by selecting the menu option Sketch→Import Library→video, or by typing the following line of code (which should go at the very top of your sketch):

```
import processing.video.*;
```

Using the "Import Library" menu option does nothing other than automatically insert that line into your code, so manual typing is entirely equivalent.

Step 2. Declare a Capture object

We learned in Chapter 12 how to create objects from classes built into the *Processing* language. For example, we made PImage objects from the *Processing* PImage class. PImage, it should be noted, is part of the *processing.core* library and, therefore, no import statement was required. The *processing.video* library has two useful classes inside of it—Capture, for live video, and Movie, for recorded video. We will start with declaring a Capture object.

```
Capture video;
```

Step 3. Initialize the Capture object.

The Capture object "video" is just like any other object. As we learned in Chapter 8, to construct an object, we use the **new** operator followed by the constructor. With a Capture object, this code typically appears in **setup()**, assuming you want to start capturing video when the sketch begins.

```
video = new Capture();
```

The above line of code is missing the appropriate arguments for the constructor. Remember, this is not a class we wrote ourselves so there is no way for us to know what is required between the parentheses without consulting the reference. The online reference for the Capture constructor can be found on the *Processing* web site at:

http://www.processing.org/reference/libraries/video/Capture.html

The reference will show there are several ways to call the constructor (see *overloading* in Chapter 23 about multiple constructors). A typical way to call the Capture constructor is with four arguments:

```
void setup() {
  video = new Capture(this,320,240,30);
}
```

Let's walk through the arguments used in the Capture constructor.

- **this**—If you are confused by what *this* means, you are not alone. We have never seen a reference to *this* in any of the examples in this book so far. Technically speaking, *this* refers to the instance of a class in which the word *this* appears. Unfortunately, such a definition is likely to induce head spinning. A nicer way to think of it is as a self-referential statement. After all, what if you needed to refer to your *Processing* program within your own code? You might try to say "me" or "I." Well, these words are not available in Java, so instead we say "this." The reason we pass "this" into the Capture object is we are telling it: "Hey listen, I want to do video capture and when the camera has a new image I want you to alert *this* applet."
- **320**—Fortunately for us, the first argument, *this*, is the only confusing one. 320 refers to the width of the video captured by the camera.
- **240**—The height of the video.
- **30**—The desired framerate captured, in frames per second (fps). What framerate you choose really depends on what you are doing. If you only intend to capture an image from the camera every so often when the user clicks the mouse, for example, you would not need a high framerate and could bring that number down. However, if you want to display full motion video onscreen, then 30 is a good bet. This, of course, is simply your desired framerate. If your computer is too slow or you request a very high resolution image from the camera, the result might be a slower framerate.

    Step 4. Read the image from the camera.

There are two strategies for reading frames from the camera. We will briefly look at both and somewhat arbitrarily choose one for the remainder of the examples in this chapter. Both strategies, however, operate under the same fundamental principle: *we only want to read an image from the camera when a new frame is available to be read.*

In order to check if an image is available, we use the function ***available()***, which returns true or false depending on whether something is there. If it is there, the function ***read()*** is called and the frame from the camera is read into memory. We do this over and over again in the ***draw()*** loop, always checking to see if a new image is free for us to read.

```
void draw() {
  if (video.available()) {
    video.read();
  }
}
```

The second strategy, the "event" approach, requires a function that executes any time a certain event, in this case a camera event, occurs. If you recall from Chapter 3, the function *mousePressed()* is executed whenever the mouse is pressed. With video, we have the option to implement the function *captureEvent()*, which is invoked any time a capture event occurs, that is, a new frame is available from the camera. These event functions (*mousePressed()*, *keyPressed()*, *captureEvent()*, etc.) are sometimes referred to as a "callback." And as a brief aside, if you are following closely, this is where *this* fits in. The Capture object, "video," knows to notify *this* applet by invoking *captureEvent()* because we passed it a reference to ourselves when creating "video."

captureEvent() is a function and therefore needs to live in its own block, outside of *setup()* and *draw()*.

```
void captureEvent(Capture video) {
  video.read();
}
```

To summarize, we want to call the function *read()* whenever there is something for us to read and we can do so by either checking manually using *available()* within *draw()* or allowing a callback to handle it for us—*captureEvent()*. Many other libraries that we will explore in later chapters (such as network and serial) will work exactly the same way.

Step 5. Display the video image.

This is, without a doubt, the easiest part. We can think of a Capture object as a PImage that changes over time and, in fact, a Capture object can be utilized in an identical manner as a PImage object.

```
image(video,0,0);
```

All of this is put together in Example 16-1.

Example 16-1: Display video

```
// Step 1. Import the video library
import processing.video.*;          Step 1. Import the video library!

// Step 2. Declare a Capture object
Capture video;                      Step 2. Declare a Capture object!

void setup() {
  size(320,240);
  // Step 3. Initialize Capture object via Constructor
  // video is 320x240, @15 fps
  video = new Capture(this,320,240,15);
}
```

fig. 16.1

Step 3. Initialize Capture object! This starts the capturing process.

```
void draw() {
  // Check to see if a new frame is available
  if (video.available()) {
    // If so, read it.
    video.read();
  }
  // Display the video image
  image(video,0,0);
}
```

> Step 4. Read the image from the camera.

> Step 5. Display the image.

Again, anything we can do with a PImage (resize, tint, move, etc.) we can do with a Capture object. As long as we *read()* from that object, the video image will update as we manipulate it. See Example 16-2.

Example 16-2: Manipulate video image

```
// Step 1. Import the video library
import processing.video.*;

Capture video;

void setup() {
  size(320,240);
  video = new Capture(this,320,240,15);
}

void draw() {
  if (video.available()) {
    video.read();
  }

  // Tinting using mouse location
  tint(mouseX,mouseY,255);
  // Width and height according to mouse
  image(video,0,0,mouseX,mouseY);
}
```

fig. 16.2

> A video image can also be tinted and resized just as with a PImage.

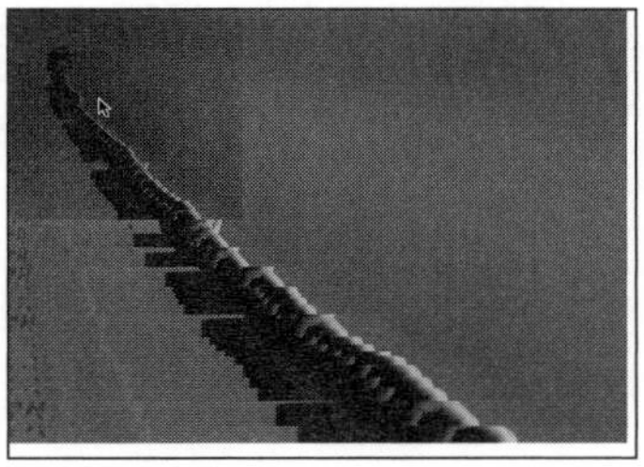

Every single image example from Chapter 15 can be recreated with video. Following is the "adjusting brightness" example (15-19) with a video image.

Example 16-3: Adjust video brightness

```
// Step 1. Import the video library
import processing.video.*;

// Step 2. Declare a Capture object
Capture video;

void setup() {
  size(320,240);
  // Step 3. Initialize Capture object via Constructor
  video = new Capture(this,320,240,15); // video is 320x240, @15 fps
  background(0);
}
```

```
void draw() {
  // Check to see if a new frame is available
  if (video.available()) {
    // If so, read it.
    video.read();
  }

  loadPixels();
  video.loadPixels();
  for (int x = 0; x < video.width; x++) {
    for (int y = 0; y < video.height; y++) {
      // calculate the 1D location from a 2D grid
      int loc = x + y*video.width;
      // get the R,G,B values from image
      float r,g,b;
      r = red   (video.pixels[loc]);
      g = green (video.pixels[loc]);
      b = blue  (video.pixels[loc]);

      // calculate an amount to change brightness based on proximity to the mouse
      float maxdist = 100;// dist(0,0,width,height);
      float d = dist(x,y,mouseX,mouseY);
      float adjustbrightness = (maxdist-d)/maxdist;
      r *= adjustbrightness;
      g *= adjustbrightness;
      b *= adjustbrightness;
      // constrain RGB to make sure they are within 0-255 color range
      r = constrain(r,0,255);
      g = constrain(g,0,255);
      b = constrain(b,0,255);
      // make a new color and set pixel in the window
      color c = color(r,g,b);
      pixels[loc] = c;
    }
  }
  updatePixels();
}
```

fig. 16.3

 Exercise 16-2: Recreate Example 15-14 (pointillism) to work with live video.

16.3 Recorded Video

Displaying recorded video follows much of the same structure as live video. *Processing*'s video library only accepts movies in QuickTime format. If your video file is a different format, you will either have to convert it or investigate using a third party library. Note that playing a recorded movie on Windows does *not* require a vdig.

Step 1. Instead of a Capture object, declare a Movie object.

```
Movie movie;
```

Step 2. Initialize Movie object.

```
movie = new Movie(this, "testmovie.mov");
```

The only necessary arguments are *this* and the movie's filename enclosed in quotes. The movie file should be stored in the sketch's data directory.

Step 3. Start movie playing.

Here, there are two options, *play()*, which plays the movie once, or *loop()*, which loops it continuously.

```
movie.loop();
```

Step 4. Read frame from movie.

Again, this is identical to capture. We can either check to see if a new frame is available, or use a callback function.

```
void draw() {
  if (movie.available()) {
    movie.read();
  }
}
```

Or:

```
void movieEvent(Movie movie) {
  movie.read();
}
```

Step 5. Display the movie.

```
image(movie,0,0);
```

Example 16-4 shows the program all put together.

Example 16-4: Display QuickTime movie

```
import processing.video.*;

Movie movie; // Step 1. Declare Movie object

void setup() {
  size(200,200);
  // Step 2. Initialize Movie object
  movie = new Movie(this, "testmovie.mov"); // Movie file should be in data folder
  // Step 3. Start movie playing
  movie.loop();
}

// Step 4. Read new frames from movie
void movieEvent(Movie movie) {
  movie.read();
}

void draw() {
  // Step 5. Display movie.
  image(movie,0,0);
}
```

Although *Processing* is by no means the most sophisticated environment for dealing with displaying and manipulating recorded video (and it should be noted that performance with large video files will tend to be fairly sluggish), there are some more advanced features available in the video library. There are functions for obtaining the duration (length measured in seconds) of a video, for speeding it up and slowing it down, and for jumping to a specific point in the video (among others).

Following is an example that makes use of *the jump()* (jump to a specific point in the video) and *duration()* (returns the length of movie) functions.

Example 16-5: Scrubbing forward and backward in movie

```
// If mouseX is 0, go to beginning
// If mouseX is width, go to end
// And everything else scrub in between

import processing.video.*;

Movie movie;

void setup() {
  size(200,200);
  background(0);
  movie = new Movie(this, "testmovie.mov");
}

void draw() {
  // Ratio of mouse X over width
  float ratio = mouseX / (float) width;
  // Jump to place in movie based on duration
  movie.jump(ratio*movie.duration());
  movie.read();          // read frame
  image(movie,0,0);  // display frame
}
```

The *jump()* function allows you to jump immediately to a point of time within the video. *duration()* returns the total length of the movie in seconds.

*Exercise 16-3: Using the **speed()** method in the Movie class, write a program where the user can control the playback speed of a movie with the mouse. Note **speed()** takes one argument and multiplies the movie playback rate by that value. Multiplying by 0.5 will cause the movie to play half as fast, by 2, twice as fast, by −2, twice as fast in reverse, and so on.*

16.4 Software Mirrors

With small video cameras attached to more and more personal computers, developing software that manipulates an image in real-time is becoming increasingly popular. These types of applications are sometimes referred to as "mirrors," as they provide a digital reflection of a viewer's image. *Processing*'s extensive library of functions for graphics and its ability to capture from a camera in real-time make it an excellent environment for prototyping and experimenting with software mirrors.

As we saw earlier in this chapter, we can apply basic image processing techniques to video images, reading and replacing the pixels one by one. Taking this idea one step further, we can read the pixels and apply the colors to shapes drawn onscreen.

We will begin with an example that captures a video at 80 × 60 pixels and renders it on a 640 × 480 window. For each pixel in the video, we will draw a rectangle 8 pixels wide and 8 pixels tall.

Let's first just write the program that displays the grid of rectangles. See Figure 16.4.

fig. 16.4

Example 16-6: Drawing a grid of 8 × 8 squares

```
// Size of each cell in the grid, ratio of window size to video size
int videoScale = 8;
// Number of columns and rows in our system
int cols, rows;

void setup(){
  size(640,480);
  // Initialize columns and rows
  cols = width/videoScale;
  rows = height/videoScale;
}

void draw(){
  // Begin loop for columns
  for (int i = 0; i < cols; i++) {
    // Begin loop for rows
    for (int j = 0; j < rows; j++) {
      // Scaling up to draw a rectangle at (x,y)
      int x = i*videoScale;
      int y = j*videoScale;
      fill(255);
      stroke(0);
      rect(x,y,videoScale,videoScale);
    }
  }
}
```

> The videoScale variable tells us the ratio of the window's pixel size to the grid's size.
>
> 80 * 8 = 640
> 60 * 8 = 480

> For every column and row, a rectangle is drawn at an (*x,y*) location scaled and sized by videoScale.

Knowing that we want to have squares 8 pixels wide by 8 pixels high, we can calculate the number of columns as the width divided by eight and the number of rows as the height divided by eight.

- 640/8 = 80 columns
- 480/8 = 60 rows

We can now capture a video image that is 80 × 60. This is useful because capturing a 640 × 480 video from a camera can be slow compared to 80 × 60. We will only want to capture the color information at the resolution required for our sketch.

fig. 16.5

For every square at column *i* and row *j*, we look up the color at pixel (*i,j*) in the video image and color it accordingly. See Example 16-7 (new parts in bold).

Example 16-7: Video pixelation

```
// Size of each cell in the grid, ratio of window size to video size
int videoScale = 8;
// Number of columns and rows in our system
int cols, rows;
// Variable to hold onto Capture object
Capture video;

void setup() {
  size(640,480);
  // Initialize columns and rows
  cols = width/videoScale;
  rows = height/videoScale;
  background(0);
  video = new Capture(this,cols,rows,30);
}

void draw() {
  // Read image from the camera
  if (video.available()) {
    video.read();
  }

  video.loadPixels();
  // Begin loop for columns
  for (int i = 0; i < cols; i++) {
    // Begin loop for rows
    for (int j = 0; j < rows; j++) {
      // Where are we, pixel-wise?
      int x = i*videoScale;
      int y = j*videoScale;

      // Looking up the appropriate color in the pixel array
      color c = video.pixels[i+j*video.width];

      fill(c);
      stroke(0);
      rect(x,y,videoScale,videoScale);
    }
  }
}
```

> The color for each square is pulled from the Capture object's pixel array.

As you can see, expanding the simple grid system to include colors from video only requires a few additions. We have to declare and initialize the Capture object, read from it, and pull colors from the pixel array.

Less literal mappings of pixel colors to shapes in the grid can also be applied. In the following example, only the colors black and white are used. Squares are larger where brighter pixels in the video appear, and smaller for darker pixels. See Figure 16.6.

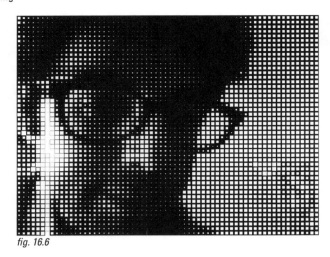

fig. 16.6

Example 16-8: Brightness mirror

```
// Each pixel from the video source is drawn as a
// rectangle with size based on brightness.

import processing.video.*;

// Size of each cell in the grid
int videoScale = 10;
// Number of columns and rows in our system
int cols, rows;
// Variable for capture device
Capture video;

void setup() {
  size(640,480);
  // Initialize columns and rows
  cols = width/videoScale;
  rows = height/videoScale;
  smooth();
  // Construct the Capture object
  video = new Capture(this,cols,rows,15);
}

void draw() {
  if (video.available()) {
    video.read();
  }
  background(0);

video.loadPixels();
  // Begin loop for columns
  for (int i = 0; i < cols; i++) {
  // Begin loop for rows
    for (int j = 0; j < rows; j++) {
      // Where are we, pixel-wise?
      int x = i*videoScale;
      int y = j*videoScale;
      // Reversing x to mirror the image
      int loc = (video.width - i -1) + j*video.width;
```

> In order to mirror the image, the column is reversed with the following formula:
>
> mirrored column = width − column − 1

```
// Each rect is colored white with a size determined by brightness
color c = video.pixels[loc];
float sz = (brightness(c)/255.0)*videoScale;
rectMode(CENTER);
fill(255);
noStroke();
rect(x + videoScale/2,y+videoScale/2,sz,sz);
}
}
}
```

> A rectangle size is calculated as a function of the pixel's brightness. A bright pixel is a large rectangle, and a dark pixel is a small one.

It is often useful to think of developing software mirrors in two steps. This will also help you think beyond the more obvious mapping of pixels to shapes on a grid.

Step 1. Develop an interesting pattern that covers an entire window.
Step 2. Use a video's pixels as a look-up table for coloring that pattern.

For example, say for Step 1, we write a program that scribbles a random line around the window. Here is our algorithm, written in pseudocode.

- Start with *x* and *y* as coordinates at the center of the screen.
- Repeat forever the following:
  —Pick a new *x* and *y* (staying within the edges).
  —Draw a line from the old (*x,y*) to the new (*x,y*).
  —Save the new (*x,y*).

Example 16-9: The scribbler

```
// Two global variables
float x;
float y;

void setup() {
  size(320,240);
  smooth();
  background(255);
  // Start x and y in the center
  x = width/2;
  y = height/2;
}

void draw() {

  // Pick a new x and y
  float newx = constrain(x + random(-20,20),0,width);
  float newy = constrain(y + random(-20,20),0,height);

  // Draw a line from x,y to the newx,newy
  stroke(0);
  strokeWeight(4);
  line(x,y,newx,newy);

  // Save newx, newy in x,y
  x = newx;
  y = newy;
}
```

fig. 16.7

> A new *x,y* location is picked as the current (*x,y*) plus or minus a random value. The new location is constrained within the window's pixels.

> We save the new location in (*x,y*) in order to start the process over again.

Now that we have finished our pattern generating sketch, we can change *stroke()* to set a color according to the video image. Note again the new lines of code added in bold in Example 16-10.

Example 16-10: The scribbler mirror

```
import processing.video.*;

// Two global variables
float x;
float y;

// Variable to hold onto Capture object
Capture video;

void setup() {
  size(320,240);
  smooth();
  // framerate(30);
  background(0);
  // Start x and y in the center
  x = width/2;
  y = height/2;
  // Start the capture process
  video = new Capture(this,width,height,15);
}

void draw() {

  // Read image from the camera
  if (video.available()) {
    video.read();
  }
  video.loadPixels();

  // Pick a new x and y
  float newx = constrain(x + random(-20,20),0,width-1);
  float newy = constrain(y + random(-20,20),0,height-1);

  // Find the midpoint of the line
  int midx = int((newx + x) / 2);
  int midy = int((newy + y) / 2);
  // Pick the color from the video, reversing x
  color c =  video.pixels[(width-1-midx) + midy*video.width];

  // Draw a line from x,y to the newx,newy
  stroke(c);
  strokeWeight(4);
  line(x,y,newx,newy);

  // Save newx, newy in x,y
  x = newx;
  y = newy;
}
```

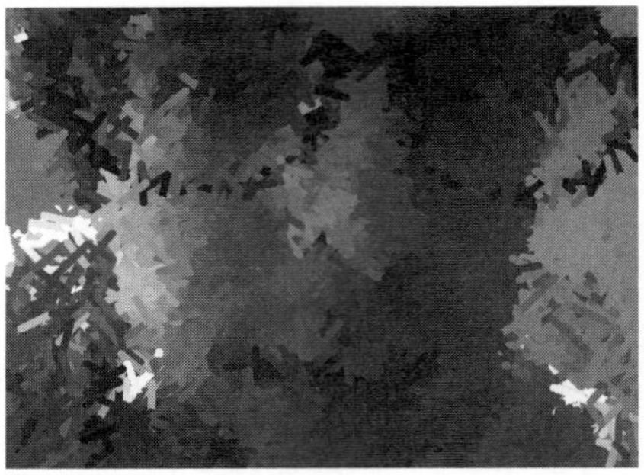

fig. 16.8

> If the window were larger (say 800 × 600), we might want to introduce a videoScale variable so that we do not have to capture such a large image.

> The color for the scribbler is pulled from a pixel in the video image.

Exercise 16-4: Create your own software mirror using the methodology from Examples 16-9 and 16-10. Create your system without the video first and then incorporate using the video to determine colors, behaviors, and so on.

16.5 Video as Sensor, Computer Vision

Every example in this chapter has treated the video camera as a data source data for digital imagery displayed onscreen. This section will provide a simple introduction to things you can do with a video camera when you do not display the image, that is, "computer vision." Computer vision is a scientific field of research dedicated to machines that *see*, using the camera as a sensor.

In order to better understand the inner workings of computer vision algorithms, we will write all of the code ourselves on a pixel by pixel level. However, to explore these topics further, you might consider downloading some of the third party computer vision libraries that are available for *Processing*. Many of these libraries have advanced features beyond what will be covered in this chapter. A brief overview of the libraries will be offered at the end of this section.

Let's begin with a simple example.

The video camera is our friend because it provides a ton of information. A 320 × 240 image is 76,800 pixels! What if we were to boil down all of those pixels into one number: the overall brightness of a room? This could be accomplished with a one dollar light sensor (or "photocell"), but as an exercise we will make our webcam do it.

We have seen in other examples that the brightness value of an individual pixel can be retrieved with the **brightness()** function, which returns a floating point number between 0 and 255. The following line of code retrieves the brightness for the first pixel in the video image.

```
float brightness = brightness(video.pixels[0]);
```

We can then compute the overall (i.e., average) brightness by adding up all the brightness values and dividing by the total number of pixels.

```
video.loadPixels();
// Start with a total of 0
float totalBrightness = 0;
// Sum the brightness of each pixel
for (int i = 0; i < video.pixels.length; i++) {
  color c = video.pixels[i];
  totalBrightness += brightness(c);      ◁── Sum all brightness values.
}


// Compute the average
float averageBrightness = totalBrightness / video.pixels.length;
// Display the background as average brightness
background(averageBrightness);
```

Average brightness = total brightness / total pixels

Before you start to cheer too vigorously from this accomplishment, while this example is an excellent demonstration of an algorithm that analyzes data provided by a video source, it does not begin to harness the power of what one can "see" with a video camera. After all, a video image is not just a collection of colors, but it is a collection of spatially oriented colors. By developing algorithms that search through the pixels and recognize patterns, we can start to develop more advanced computer vision applications.

Tracking the brightest color is a good first step. Imagine a dark room with a single moving light source. With the techniques we will learn, that light source could replace the mouse as a form of interaction. Yes, you are on your way to playing Pong with a flashlight.

First, we will examine how to search through an image and find the x,y location of the brightest pixel. The strategy we will employ is to loop through all the pixels, looking for the "world record" brightest pixel (using the *brightness()* function). Initially, the world record will be held by the first pixel. As other pixels beat that record, they will become the world record holder. At the end of the loop, whichever pixel is the current record holder gets the "Brightest Pixel of the Image" award.

Here is the code:

```
// The record is 0 when we first start
float worldRecord = 0.0;
// Which pixel will win the prize?
int xRecordHolder = 0;
int yRecordHolder = 0;

for (int x = 0; x < video.width; x++) {
  for (int y = 0; y < video.height; y++) {
    // What is current brightness
    int loc = x+y*video.width;
    float currentBrightness = brightness(video.pixels[loc]);
    if (currentBrightness > worldRecord) {
      // Set a new record
      worldRecord = currentBrightness;
      // This pixel holds the record!
      xRecordHolder = x;
      yRecordHolder = y;
    }
  }
}
```

> When we find the new brightest pixel, we must save the (x,y) location of that pixel in the array so that we can access it later.

A natural extension of this example would be to track a specific color, rather than simply the brightest. For example, we could look for the most "red" or the most "blue" in a video image. In order to perform this type of analysis, we will need to develop a methodology for comparing colors. Let's create two colors, $c1$ and $c2$.

```
color c1 = color(255,100,50);
color c2 = color(150,255,0);
```

Colors can only be compared in terms of their red, green, and blue components, so we must first separate out these values.

```
float r1 = red(c1);
float g1 = green(c1);
float b1 = blue(c1);
float r2 = red(c2);
float g2 = green(c2);
float b2 = blue(c2);
```

Now, we are ready to compare the colors. One strategy is to take the sum of the absolute value of the differences. That is a mouthful, but it is really fairly simple. Take $r1$ minus $r2$. Since we only care about the magnitude of the difference, not whether it is positive or negative, take the absolute value (the positive version of the number). Do this for green and blue and add them all together.

```
float diff = abs(r1-r2) + abs(g1-g2) + abs(b1-b2);
```

While this is perfectly adequate (and a fast calculation at that), a more accurate way to compute the difference between colors is to take the "distance" between colors. OK, so you may be thinking: "Um, seriously? How can a color be far away or close to another color?" Well, we know the distance between *two points* is calculated via the Pythagorean Theorem. We can think of color as a point in three-dimensional space, only instead of *x*, *y*, and *z*, we have *r*, *g*, and *b*. If two colors are near each other in this color space, they are similar; if they are far, they are different.

```
float diff = dist(r1,g1,b1,r2,g2,b2);
```

> Although more accurate, because the **dist()** function involves a square root in its calculation, it is slower than the absolute value of the difference method. One way around this is to write your own color distance function without the square root.
> colorDistance = $(r1 - r2)*(r1 - r2) + (g1 - g2)*(g1 - g2) + (b1 - b2)*(b1 - b2)$

Looking for the "most red" pixel in an image, for example, is therefore looking for the color "closest" to red—(255,0,0).

By adjusting the brightness tracking code to look for the closest pixel to any given color (rather than the brightest), we can put together a color tracking sketch. In the following example, the user can click the mouse on a color in the image to be tracked. A black circle will appear at the location that most closely matches that color. See Figure 16.9.

Example 16-11: Simple color tracking

```
import processing.video.*;

// Variable for capture device
Capture video;
color trackColor;

void setup() {
  size(320,240);
  video = new Capture(this,width,height,15);
  // Start off tracking for red
  trackColor = color(255,0,0);
  smooth();
}
```

> A variable for the color we are searching for.

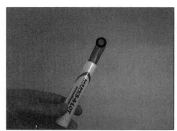

fig. 16.9

```
void draw() {
  // Capture and display the video
  if (video.available()) {
    video.read();
  }
  video.loadPixels();
  image(video,0,0);


  // Closest record, we start with a high number

  float worldRecord = 500;
  // XY coordinate of closest color
  int closestX = 0;
  int closestY = 0;
  // Begin loop to walk through every pixel
  for (int x = 0; x < video.width; x++) {
    for (int y = 0; y < video.height; y++) {
      int loc = x + y*video.width;
      // What is current color
      color currentColor = video.pixels[loc];
      float r1 = red(currentColor);
      float g1 = green(currentColor);
      float b1 = blue(currentColor);
      float r2 = red(trackColor);
      float g2 = green(trackColor);
      float b2 = blue(trackColor);
      // Using euclidean distance to compare colors
      float d = dist(r1,g1,b1,r2,g2,b2);

      // If current color is more similar to tracked color than
      // closest color, save current location and current difference
      if (d < worldRecord) {
        worldRecord = d;
        closestX = x;
        closestY = y;
      }
    }
  }

  if (worldRecord < 10) {
    // Draw a circle at the tracked pixel
    fill(trackColor);
    strokeWeight(4.0);
    stroke(0);
    ellipse(closestX,closestY,16,16);
  }
}


void mousePressed() {
  // Save color where the mouse is clicked in trackColor variable
  int loc = mouseX + mouseY*video.width;
  trackColor = video.pixels[loc];
}
```

> Before we begin searching, the "world record" for closest color is set to a high number that is easy for the first pixel to beat.

> We are using the *dist( )* function to compare the current color with the color we are tracking.

> We only consider the color found if its color distance is less than 10. This threshold of 10 is arbitrary and you can adjust this number depending on how accurate you require the tracking to be.

Exercise 16-5: Take any Processing *sketch you previously created that involves mouse interaction and replace the mouse with color tracking. Create an environment for the camera that is simple and high contrast. For example, point the camera at a black tabletop with a small white object. Control your sketch with the object's, location. The picture shown illustrates the example that controls the "snake" (Example 9-9) with a tracked bottlecap.*

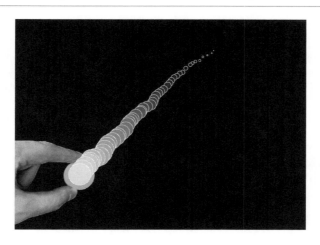

16.6 Background Removal

The distance comparison for color proves useful in other computer vision algorithms as well, such as background removal. Let's say you wanted to show a video of you dancing the hula, only you did not want to be dancing in your office where you happen to be, but at the beach with waves crashing behind you. Background removal is a technique that allows you to remove the background of an image (your office) and replace it with any pixels you like (the beach), while leaving the foreground (you dancing) intact.

Here is our algorithm.

- Memorize a background image.
- Check every pixel in the current video frame. If it is very different from the corresponding pixel in the background image, it is a foreground pixel. If not, it is a background pixel. Display only foreground pixels.

To demonstrate the above algorithm, we will perform a reverse green screen. The sketch will remove the background from an image and replace it with green pixels.

Step one is "memorizing" the background. The background is essentially a snapshot from the video. Since the video image changes over time, we must save a copy of a frame of video in a separate PImage object.

```
PImage backgroundImage;

void setup() {
  backgroundImage = createImage(video.width,video.height,RGB);
}
```

When backgroundImage is created, it is a blank image, with the same dimensions as the video. It is not particularly useful in this form, so we need to copy an image from the camera into the background image when we want to memorize the background. Let's do this when the mouse is pressed.

```
void mousePressed() {
  // Copying the current frame of video into the backgroundImage object
  // Note copy takes 5 arguments:
  // The source image
  // x,y,width, and height of region to be copied from the source
  // x,y,width, and height of copy destination
  backgroundImage.copy(video,0,0,video.width,video.height,0,0,video.width,video.height);
  backgroundImage.updatePixels();
}
```

> *copy( )* allows you to copy pixels from one image to another. Note that *updatePixels( )* should be called after new pixels are copied!

Once we have the background image saved, we can loop through all the pixels in the current frame and compare them to the background using the distance calculation. For any given pixel (x,y), we use the following code:

```
int loc = x + y*video.width;              // Step 1, what is the 1D pixel location
color fgColor = video.pixels[loc];        // Step 2, what is the foreground color
color bgColor = backgroundImage.pixels[loc];// Step 3, what is the background color

// Step 4, compare the foreground and background color
float r1 = red(fgColor); float g1 = green(fgColor); float b1 = blue(fgColor);
float r2 = red(bgColor); float g2 = green(bgColor); float b2 = blue(bgColor);
float diff = dist(r1,g1,b1,r2,g2,b2);

// Step 5, Is the foreground color different from the background color
if (diff > threshold) {
  // If so, display the foreground color
  pixels[loc] = fgColor;
} else {
  // If not, display green
  pixels[loc] = color(0,255,0);
}
```

The above code assumes a variable named "threshold." The lower the threshold, the *easier* it is for a pixel to be in the foreground. It does not have to be very different from the background pixel. Here is the full example with threshold as a global variable.

Example 16-12: Simple background removal

```
// Click the mouse to memorize a current background image

import processing.video.*;

// Variable for capture device
Capture video;
// Saved background
PImage backgroundImage;
// How different must a pixel be to be a foreground pixel
float threshold = 20;
```

fig. 16.10

```
void setup() {
  size(320,240);
  video = new Capture(this, width, height, 30);
  // Create an empty image the same size as the video
  backgroundImage = createImage(video.width,video.height,RGB);
}


void draw() {
  // Capture video
  if (video.available()) {
    video.read();
  }

  loadPixels();
  video.loadPixels();
  backgroundImage.loadPixels();
```

> We are looking at the video's pixels, the memorized backgroundImage's pixels, as well as accessing the display pixels. So we must *loadPixels()* for all!

```
// Draw the video image on the background
image(video,0,0);
// Begin loop to walk through every pixel
for (int x = 0; x < video.width; x++) {
  for (int y = 0; y < video.height; y++) {
    int loc = x + y*video.width; // Step 1, what is the 1D pixel location
    color fgColor = video.pixels[loc]; // Step 2, what is the foreground color
    // Step 3, what is the background color
    color bgColor = backgroundImage.pixels[loc];
    // Step 4, compare the foreground and background color
    float r1 = red(fgColor);
    float g1 = green(fgColor);
    float b1 = blue(fgColor);
    float r2 = red(bgColor);
    float g2 = green(bgColor);
    float b2 = blue(bgColor);
    float diff = dist(r1,g1,b1,r2,g2,b2);
    // Step 5, Is the foreground color different from the background color
    if (diff > threshold) {
      // If so, display the foreground color
      pixels[loc] = fgColor;
      } else {
      // If not, display green
      pixels[loc] = color(0,255,0);
    }
  }
}
 updatePixels();
}
```

> We could choose to replace the background pixels with something other than the color green!

```
void mousePressed() {
  // Copying the current frame of video into the backgroundImage object
  // Note copy takes 5 arguments:
  // The source image
  // x,y,width, and height of region to be copied from the source
  // x,y,width, and height of copy destination
  backgroundImage.copy(video,0,0,video.width,video.height,0,0,video.width,video.
  height);
  backgroundImage.updatePixels();
}
```

When you ultimately get to running this example, step out of the frame, click the mouse to memorize the background without you in it, and then step back into the frame; you will see the result as seen in Figure 16.10.

If this sketch does not seem to work for you at all, check and see what "automatic" features are enabled on your camera. For example, if your camera is set to automatically adjust brightness or white balance, you have a problem. Even though the background image is memorized, once the entire image becomes brighter or changes hue, this sketch will think all the pixels have changed and are therefore part of the foreground! For best results, disable all automatic features on your camera.

 Exercise 16-6: Instead of replacing the background with green pixels, replace it with another image. What values work well for threshold and what values do not work at all? Try controlling the threshold variable with the mouse.

16.7 Motion Detection

Today is a happy day. Why? Because all of the work we did to learn how to remove the background from a video gets us motion detection for free. In the background removal example, we examined each pixel's relationship to a stored background image. Motion in a video image occurs when a pixel color differs greatly from what it used to be one frame earlier. In other words, motion detection is exactly the same algorithm, only instead of saving a background image once, we save the previous frame of video constantly!

The following example is identical to the background removal example with only one important change—*the previous frame of video is always saved whenever a new frame is available.*

```
// Capture video
if (video.available()) {
  // Save previous frame for motion detection!!
  prevFrame.copy(video,0,0,video.width,video.height,0,0,video.width,video.height);
  video.read();
}
```

(The colors displayed are also changed to black and white and some of the variable names are different, but these are trivial changes.)

Example 16-13: Simple motion detection

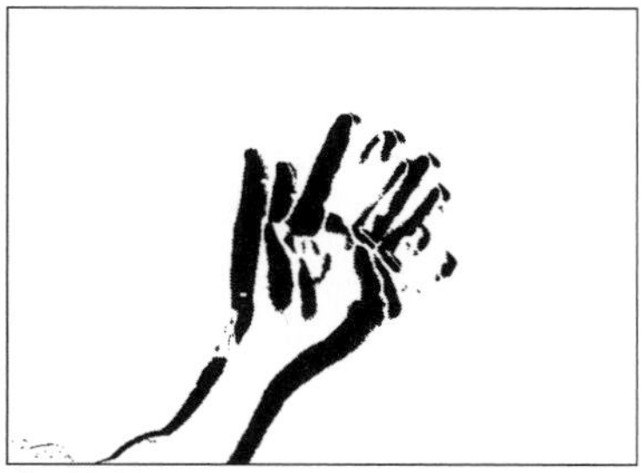

```
import processing.video.*;

// Variable for capture device
Capture video;
// Previous Frame
PImage prevFrame;
// How different must a pixel be to be a "motion" pixel
float threshold = 50;

void setup() {
  size(320,240);
  video = new Capture(this, width, height, 30);
  // Create an empty image the same size as the video
  prevFrame = createImage(video.width,video.height,RGB);
}

void draw() {
  // Capture video
  if (video.available()) {
    // Save previous frame for motion detection!!
    prevFrame.copy(video,0,0,video.width,video.height,0,0,video.width,video.height);
    prevFrame.updatePixels();
    video.read();
  }

  loadPixels();
  video.loadPixels();
  prevFrame.loadPixels();

  // Begin loop to walk through every pixel
  for (int x = 0; x < video.width; x++) {
    for (int y = 0; y < video.height; y++) {
      int loc = x + y*video.width; // Step 1, what is the 1D pixel location
      color current = video.pixels[loc]; // Step 2, what is the current color
      color previous = prevFrame.pixels[loc]; // Step 3, what is the previous color
      // Step 4, compare colors (previous vs. current)
      float r1 = red(current); float g1 = green(current); float b1 = blue(current);
      float r2 = red(previous); float g2 = green(previous); float b2 = blue(previous);
      float diff = dist(r1,g1,b1,r2,g2,b2);
      // Step 5, How different are the colors?
      if (diff > threshold) {
        // If motion, display black
        pixels[loc] = color(0);
      } else {
        // If not, display white
        pixels[loc] = color(255);
      }
    }
  }
  updatePixels();
}
```

fig. 16.11

> Before we read the new frame, we always save the previous frame for comparison!

> If the color at that pixel has changed, then there is "motion" at that pixel.

What if we want to just know the "overall" motion in a room? At the start of section 16.5, we calculated the average brightness of an image by taking the sum of each pixel's brightness and dividing it by the total number of pixels.

Average Brightness = Total Brightness / Total Number of Pixels

We can calculate the average motion the same way:

Average Motion = Total Motion / Total Number of Pixels

The following example displays a circle that changes color and size based on the average amount of motion. Note again that you do not need to *display* the video in order to analyze it!

Example 16-14: Overall motion

```
import processing.video.*;

// Variable for capture device
Capture video;
// Previous Frame
PImage prevFrame;
// How different must a pixel be to be a "motion" pixel
float threshold = 50;

void setup() {
  size(320,240);
  // Using the default capture device
  video = new Capture(this, width, height, 15);
  // Create an empty image the same size as the video
  prevFrame = createImage(video.width,video.height,RGB);
}

void draw() {
  background(0);

  // If you want to display the videoY
  // You don't need to display it to analyze it!
  image(video,0,0);

  // Capture video
  if (video.available()) {
    // Save previous frame for motion detection!!
    prevFrame.copy(video,0,0,video.width,video.height,0,0,video.width,video.height);
    prevFrame.updatePixels();
    video.read();
  }

  loadPixels();
  video.loadPixels();
  prevFrame.loadPixels();

  // Begin loop to walk through every pixel
  // Start with a total of 0
  float totalMotion = 0;
  // Sum the brightness of each pixel
  for (int i = 0; i < video.pixels.length; i++) {
    color current = video.pixels[i];
    // Step 2, what is the current color
    color previous = prevFrame.pixels[i];
    // Step 3, what is the previous color
```

```
// Step 4, compare colors (previous vs. current)
float r1 = red(current); float g1 = green(current);
float b1 = blue(current);
float r2 = red(previous); float g2 = green(previous);
float b2 = blue(previous);

float diff = dist(r1,g1,b1,r2,g2,b2);

totalMotion += diff;
}

float avgMotion = totalMotion / video.pixels.length;

// Draw a circle based on average motion
smooth();
noStroke();
fill(100+avgMotion*3,100,100);
float r = avgMotion*2;
ellipse(width/2,height/2,r,r);
}
```

> Motion for an individual pixel is the difference between the previous color and current color.

> totalMotion is the sum of all color differences.

> averageMotion is total motion divided by the number of pixels analyzed.

Exercise 16-7: Create a sketch that looks for the average location of motion. Can you have an ellipse follow your waving hand?

16.8 Computer Vision Libraries

There are several computer vision libraries already available for *Processing* (and there will inevitably be more). The nice thing about writing your own computer vision code is that you can control the vision algorithm at the lowest level, performing an analysis that conforms precisely to your needs. The benefit to using a third party library is that since there has been a great deal of research in solving common computer vision problems (detecting edges, blobs, motion, tracking color, etc.), you do not need to do all of the hard work yourself! Here is a brief overview of three libraries currently available.

JMyron (WebCamXtra) by Josh Nimoy et al.
http://webcamxtra.sourceforge.net/

One advantage of using JMyron is its freedom from needing a vdig on Windows. It also includes many built-in functions to perform some of the tasks explained in this chapter: motion detection and color tracking. It will also search for groups of similar pixels (known as blobs or globs).

LibCV by Karsten Schmidt
http://toxi.co.uk/p5/libcv/

Much like JMyron, LibCV does not require QuickTime or WinVDIG for Windows machines. Instead of using native code, however, it uses the Java Media Framework (JMF) to connect to and capture images from a digital video camera. LibCV also includes functions not available in some of the other computer vision libraries, such as "background learning, background subtraction, difference images, and keystoning (perspective correction)."

BlobDetection by Julien "v3ga" Gachadoat
http://www.v3ga.net/processing/BlobDetection/

This library, as made obvious by its name, is specifically designed for detecting blobs in an image. Blobs are defined as areas of pixels whose brightness is above or below a certain threshold. The library takes any image as input and returns an array of Blob objects, each of which can tell you about its edge points and bounding box.

16.9 The Sandbox

Up until now, every single sketch we have created in this book could be published online. Perhaps you have already got a web site full of your *Processing* work. Once we start working with a video camera, however, we run into a problem. There are certain security restrictions with web applets and this is something we will see here and there throughout the rest of the book. A web applet, for example, cannot connect to a video camera on a user's computer. For the most part, applets are not allowed to connect to any local devices.

It makes sense that there are security requirements. If there weren't, a programmer could make an applet that connects to your hard drive and deletes all your files, send an e-mail out to all of his or her friends and say: "Check out this really cool link!" Applications do not have security requirements. After all, you can go and download applications that erase and reformat hard drives. But downloading and installing an application is different from just popping on a URL and loading an applet. There is an assumed level of trust with applications.

Incidentally, whether or not a feature of *Processing* will work in a web applet is listed on every single reference page under "Usage." If it says "Web" it can be used in a web applet.

If you must publish a camera connecting a *Processing* sketch online, there are ways around this and I will offer some tips and suggestions on this book's website: *http://www.learningprocssing.com/sandbox/*.

Lesson Seven Project

Develop a software mirror that incorporates computer vision techniques. Follow these steps.

Step 1. Design a pattern with no color. This could be a static pattern (such as a mosaic) or a moving one (such as the "scribbler" example) or a combination.

Step 2. Color that pattern according to a JPG image.

Step 3. Replace the JPG with images from a live camera (or recorded QuickTime).

Step 4. Using computer vision techniques, alter the behavior of the patterns' elements according to the properties of the image. For example, perhaps brighter pixels cause shapes to spin or pixels that change a lot cause shapes to fly off the screen, and so on.

Use the space provided below to sketch designs, notes, and pseudocode for your project.

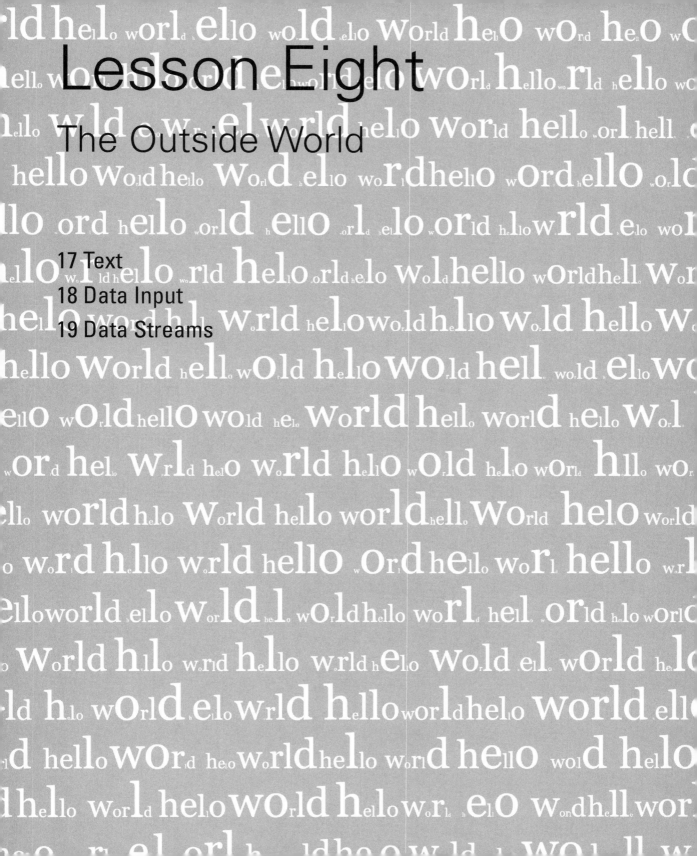

Lesson Eight

The Outside World

17 Text

"I could entertain future historians by saying I think all this superstring stuff is crazy."
—*Richard Feynman*

In this chapter:
- Storing text in a *String* object.
- Basic *String* functionality.
- Creating and loading fonts.
- Displaying text.

17.1 Where do *Strings* come from?

In Chapter 15, we explored a new object data type built into the *Processing* environment for dealing with images—PImage. In this chapter, we will introduce another new data type, another class we get for free with *Processing*, called *String*.

The *String* class is not a completely new concept. We have dealt with *Strings* before whenever we have printed some text to the message window or loaded an image from a file.

```
println("printing some text to the message window!");  // Printing a String
PImage img = loadImage("filename.jpg");                // Using a String for a file name
```

Nevertheless, although we have used a *String* here and there, we have yet to explore them fully and unleash their potential. In order to understand the origins of the *String*, let's remind ourselves where classes come from. We know we can create our own classes (Zoog, Car, etc.). We can use classes built into the *Processing* environment, such as PImage. And finally, in the last chapter we learned that we could import additional *Processing* libraries to use certain classes such as Capture or Movie.

Nevertheless, these classes come from our lives in the *Processing* bubble. We have yet to venture out into the great unknown, the world of thousands upon thousands of available Java classes. Before we leap over the Java API cliff (which we will do in Chapter 23), it is useful to just peek over the edge and explore one of the most basic and fundamental Java classes out there, the *String* class, which we will use to store and manipulate text.

Where do we find documentation for the* String *class?
In order to learn the details about built-in variables, functions, and classes, the *Processing* reference has always been our guide. Although technically a Java class, because the *String* class is so commonly used, *Processing* includes documentation in its reference. In addition, no import statement is required.

http://www.processing.org/reference/String.html

This page only covers a few of the available methods of the *String* class. The full documentation can be found at Sun's Java site:

http://java.sun.com/j2se/1.4.2/docs/api/java/lang/String.html
(Also note the URL for the entire Java API: *http://java.sun.com/j2se/1.4.2/docs/api*).

We are not going to cover how to use the Java documentation just yet (see Chapter 23 for more), but you can whet your appetite by just visiting and perusing the above links.

17.2 What is a *String*?

A *String*, at its core, is really just a fancy way of storing an array of characters—if we did not have the *String* class, we would probably have to write some code like this:

```
char[] sometext = {'H', 'e', 'l', 'l', 'o', ' ', 'W', 'o', 'r', 'l', 'd'};
```

Clearly, this would be a royal pain in the *Processing* behind. It is much simpler to do the following and make a *String* object:

```
String sometext = "How do I make a String? Type characters between quotes!";
```

It appears from the above that a *String* is nothing more than a list of characters in between quotes. Nevertheless, this is only the data of a *String*. We must remember that a *String* is an object with methods (which you can find on the reference page). This is the same as how a PImage object stored the data associated with an image as well as had functionality in the form of methods: *copy()*, *loadPixels()*, and so on. We will look more closely at *String* methods in Chapter 18. However, here are a few examples.

The method *charAt()* returns the individual character in the *String* at a given index. Strings are just like arrays in that the first character is index #0!

Exercise 17-1: What is the result of the following code?

```
String message = "a bunch of text here.";
char c = message.charAt(3);
println(c);

_____
```

Another useful method is *length()*. This is easy to confuse with the *length* property of an array. However, when we ask for the length of a *String* object, we must use the parentheses since we are calling a function called *length()* rather than accessing a property called length.

```
String message = "This String is 34 characters long.";
println(message.length());
```

Exercise 17-2: Loop through and print every character of a String one at a time.

```
String message = "a bunch of text here.";
for (int i = 0; i < _____ ); i++) {
  char c = _____ ;
  println(c);
}
```

We can also change a String to all uppercase (or lowercase) using the ***toUpperCase()*** method.

```
String uppercase = message.toUpperCase();
println(uppercase);
```

You might notice something a bit odd here. Why didn't we simply say *"message.toUpperCase()"* and then print the "message" variable? Instead, we assigned the result of *"message.toUpperCase()"* to a new variable with a different name—"uppercase".

This is because a *String* is a special kind of object. It is *immutable*. An immutable object is one whose data can never be changed. Once we create a *String*, it stays the same for life. Any time we want to change the *String*, we have to create a new one. So in the case of converting to uppercase, the method ***toUpperCase()*** returns a copy of the *String* object with all caps.

The last method we will cover in this chapter is ***equals()***. You might first think to compare *Strings* using the "==" operator.

```
String one = "hello";
String two = "hello";
println(one == two);
```

Technically speaking, when "==" is used with objects, it compares the memory addresses for each object. Even though each string contains the same data—"hello"—if they are different object instances, then "==" could result in a false comparison. The ***equals()*** function ensures that we are checking to see if two *String* objects contain the exact same sequence of characters, regardless of where that data is stored in the computer's memory.

```
String one = "hello";
String two = "hello";
println(one.equals(two));
```

Although both of the above methods return the correct result, it is safer to use ***equals()***. Depending on how *String* objects are created in a sketch, "==" will not always work.

Exercise 17-3: Find the duplicates in the following array of Strings.

```
String words = {"I","love","coffee","I","love","tea"};

for (int i = 0; i < _____; i++) {

  for (int j = __; j < _____; j++) {

    if (_____) {

      println(_____ + "is a duplicate.");
    }
  }
}
```

One other feature of *String* objects is concatenation, joining two *Strings* together. *Strings* are joined with the " + " operator. The plus operator (+), of course, usually means *add* in the case of numbers. When used with *Strings*, it means *join*.

```
String helloworld = "Hello" + "World";
```

Variables can also be brought into a *String* using concatenation.

```
int x = 10;
String message = "The value of x is: " + x;
```

We saw a good example of this in Chapter 15 when loading an array of images with numbered filenames.

Exercise 17-4: Concatenate a String from the variables given that outputs the following message.

That rectangle is 10 pixels wide, 12 pixels tall and sitting right at (100,100).

```
float w = 10;
float h = 12;
float x = 100;
float y = 100;
String message = _____;
println(message);
```

17.3 Displaying Text

We will continue to explore the functions available as part of the *String* class in Chapter 18, which focuses on analyzing and manipulating *Strings*. What we have learned so far about *Strings* is enough to get us to the focus of this chapter: *rendering text.*

The easiest way to display a *String* is to print it in the message window. This is likely something you have been doing here and there while debugging. For example, if you needed to know the horizontal mouse location, you would write:

```
println(mouseX);
```

Or if you needed to determine that a certain part of the code was executed, you might print out a descriptive message.

```
println("We got here and we're printing out the mouse location!!!");
```

While this is valuable for debugging, it is not going to help our goal of displaying text for a user. To place text on screen, we have to follow a series of simple steps.

1. **Choose a font by selecting "Tools" → "Create Font."** This will create and place the font file in your data directory. Make note of the font filename for Step 3. *Processing* uses a special font format, "vlw," that uses images to display each letter. Because of this, you should create the font at the size you intend to display. See Figure 17.1.

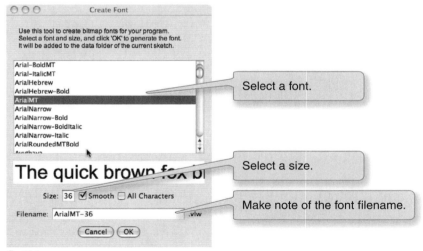

fig. 17.1

2. **Declare an object of type PFont.**

```
PFont f;
```

3. **Load the font by referencing the font file name in the function** *loadFont()*. This should be done only once, usually in *setup()*. Just as with loading an image, the process of loading a font into memory is slow and would seriously affect the sketch's performance if placed inside *draw()*.

```
f = loadFont("ArialMT-16.vlw");
```

4. **Specify the font using** *textFont()*. *textFont()* takes one or two arguments, the font variable and the font size, which is optional. If you do not include the font size, the font will be displayed at the size originally loaded. Specifying a font size that is different from the font size loaded can result in pixelated or poor quality text.

```
textFont(f,36);
```

5. **Specify a color using** *fill()*.

```
fill(0);
```

6. **Call the** *text()* **function to display text.** (This function is just like shape or image drawing, it takes three arguments—the text to be displayed, and the *x* and *y* coordinate to display that text.)

```
text("Mmmmm... Strings... ",10,100);
```

All the steps together are shown in Example 17-1.

Example 17-1: Simple displaying text

```
PFont f;    // STEP 2 Declare PFont variable

void setup() {
  size(200,200);
  f = loadFont("ArialMT-16.vlw"); // STEP 3 Load Font
}

void draw() {
  background(255);
  textFont(f,16);      // STEP 4 Specify font to be used
  fill(0);             // STEP 5 Specify font color
  text ("Mmmmm... Strings... ",10,100); // STEP 6 Display Text
}
```

Mmmmm... Strings...

fig. 17.2

Fonts can also be created using the function *createFont()*.

```
myFont = createFont("Georgia", 24, true);
```

The arguments to *createFont()* are font name, font size, and a boolean that enables smoothing (anti-aliasing).

createFont() allows you to use a font that may be installed on your local machine, but not available as part of *Processing*'s font options. In addition, *createFont()* allows the font to be scaled to any size without it looking pixelated or smushed. For more about *createFont()*, visit the *Processing* reference: *http://processing.org/reference/createFont_.html*. You can see all the available fonts with "*PFont.list()*."

```
println(PFont.list());
```
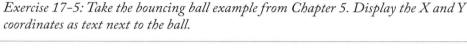
Print all fonts available to **createFont()** to the message window.

For demonstration purposes, **createFont()** will be used for all examples, rather than **loadFont()**.

Exercise 17-5: Take the bouncing ball example from Chapter 5. Display the X and Y coordinates as text next to the ball.

17.4 Text Animation

Now that we understand the steps required to display text, we can apply other concepts from this book to animate text in real-time.

To get started, let's look at two more useful *Processing* functions related to displaying text:

textAlign()—specifies RIGHT, LEFT, or CENTER alignment for text.

Example 17-2: Text align

```
PFont f;

void setup() {
  size(400,200);
  f = createFont("Arial",16,true);
}

void draw() {
  background(255);

  stroke(175);
  line(width/2,0,width/2,height);

  textFont(f);
  fill(0);
```

This text is centered.

This text is left aligned.

This text is right aligned.

fig. 17.3

```
    textAlign(CENTER);
    text("This text is centered.",width/2,60);

    textAlign(LEFT);
    text("This text is left aligned.",width/2,100);

    textAlign(RIGHT);
    text("This text is right aligned.",width/2,140);
}
```

> **textAlign()** sets the alignment for displaying text. It takes one argument: CENTER, LEFT, or RIGHT.

textWidth()—Calculates and returns the width of any character or text string.

Let's say we want to create a news ticker, where text scrolls across the bottom of the screen from left to right. When the news headline leaves the window, it reappears on the right-hand side and scrolls again. If we know the *x* location of the beginning of the text and we know the width of that text, we can determine when it is no longer in view (see Figure 17.4). **textWidth()** gives us that width.

To start, we declare headline, font, and *x* location variables, initializing them in **setup()**.

```
// A headline
String headline = "New study shows computer programming lowers cholesterol.";
PFont f; // Global font variable
float x; // Horizontal location of headline


void setup() {
    f = createFont("Arial",16,true); // Loading font
    x = width; // Initializing headline off-screen to the right
}
```

The **draw()** function is similar to our bouncing ball example in Chapter 5. First, we display the text at the appropriate location.

```
// Display headline at x location
textFont(f,16);
textAlign(LEFT);
text(headline,x,180);
```

We change *x* by a speed value (in this case a negative number so that the text moves to the left.)

```
// Decrement x
x = x - 3;
```

Now comes the more difficult part. It was easy to test when a circle reached the left side of the screen. We would simply ask: is *x* less than 0? With the text, however, since it is left-aligned, when *x* equals zero, it is still viewable on screen. Instead, the text will be invisible when *x* is less than 0 minus the width of the text (see Figure 17.4). When that is the case, we reset *x* back to the right-hand side of the window, that is, *width*.

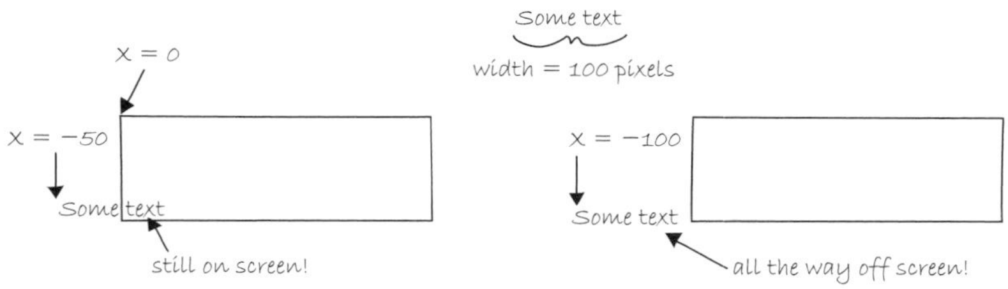

fig. 17.4

```
float w = textWidth(headline);
if (x < -w) {
    x = width;
}
```

> If *x* is less than the negative width, then it is completely off the screen

Example 17-3 is a full example that displays a different headline each time the previous headline leaves the screen. The headlines are stored in a *String* array.

Example 17-3: Scrolling headlines

```
// An array of news headlines
String[] headlines = {
  "Processing downloads break downloading record.",
  "New study shows computer programming lowers cholesterol.",
  };

PFont f;  // Global font variable
float x;   // Horizontal location
int index = 0;

void setup() {
  size(400,200);
  f = createFont("Arial",16,true);
  // Initialize headline offscreen
  x = width;
}

void draw() {
  background(255);
  fill(0);

  // Display headline at x location
  textFont(f,16);
  textAlign(LEFT);
  text(headlines[index],x,180);

  // Decrement x
  x = x - 3;

  // If x is less than the negative width,
  // then it is off the screen
  float w = textWidth(headlines[index]);
  if (x < -w) {
    x = width;
    index = (index + 1) % headlines.length;
  }
}
```

> Multiple *Strings* are stored in an array.

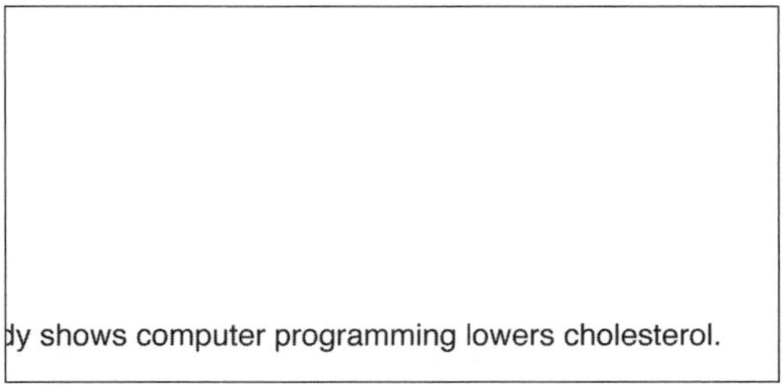

fig. 17.5

> A specific *String* from the array is displayed according to the value of the "index" variable.

> *textWidth()* is used to calculate the width of the current *String*.

> "index" is incremented when the current *String* has left the screen in order to display a new *String*.

In addition to ***textAlign()*** and ***textWidth()***, *Processing* also offers the functions ***textLeading()***, ***textMode()***, and ***textSize()*** for additional display functionality. These functions are not necessary for the examples covered in this chapter, but you can explore them on your own in the *Processing* reference.

Exercise 17-6: Create a stock ticker that loops over and over. As the last stock enters the window, the first stock appears immediately to its right.

02 ZOOG 903 AAPL 60 XDSL 10 CMG 5

17.5 Text Mosaic

Combining what we learned in Chapters 15 and 16 about the pixel array, we can use the pixels of an image to create a mosaic of characters. This is an extension of the video mirror code in Chapter 16. (Note that in Example 17-4, new text-related code is in bold.) See Figure 17.6.

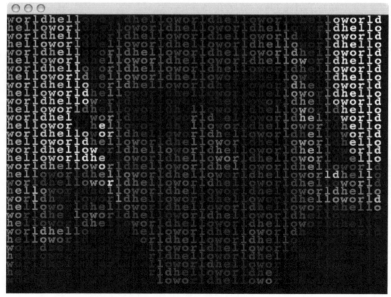

fig. 17.6

Example 17-4: Text mirror

```
import processing.video.*;

// Size of each cell in the grid, ratio of window size to video size
int videoScale = 14;
// Number of columns and rows in our system
int cols, rows;
// Variable to hold onto capture object
capture video;

//A String and Font
String chars = "helloworld";
PFont f;

void setup() {
  size(640,480);
  //set up columns and rows
  cols = width/videoScale;
  rows = height/videoScale;
  video = new Capture(this,cols,rows,15);

  // Load the font
  f = loadFont("Courier-Bold-20.vlw");
}

void draw() {
  background(0);
  // Read image from the camera
  if (video.available()) {
    video.read();
  }
  video.loadPixels();

  // Use a variable to count through chars in String
  int charcount = 0;

  // Begin loop for rows
  for (int j = 0; j < rows; j++) {
  // Begin loop for columns
    for (int i = 0; i < cols; i++) {
      // Where are we, pixel-wise?
      int x = i*videoScale;
      int y = j*videoScale;

      // Looking up the appropriate color in the pixel array
      color c = video.pixels[i+j*video.width];

      // Displaying an individual character from the String
      // Instead of a rectangle
      textFont(f);
      fill(c);
      text(chars.charAt(charcount),x,y);
      // Go on to the next character
      charcount = (charcount + 1) % chars.length();
    }
  }
}
```

> The source text used in the mosaic pattern. A longer *String* might produce more interesting results.

> Using a "fixed-width" font. In most fonts, individual characters have different widths. In a fixed-width font, all characters have the same width. This is useful here since we intend to display the letters one at a time spaced out evenly. See Section 17.7 for how to display text character by character with a nonfixed width font.

> One character from the source text is displayed colored accordingly to the pixel location. A counter variable—"charcount"—is used to walk through the source *String* one character at a time.

Exercise 17-7: Create a video text mosaic where each letter is colored white, but the size of each letter is determined by a pixel's brightness. The brighter the pixel, the bigger it is. Here is a little bit of code from the inside of the pixel loop (with some blank spots) to get you started.

```
float b = brightness(video.pixels[i+j*video.width]);
float fontSize = _____ * (_____ / _____);
textSize(fontSize);
```

17.6 Rotating Text

Translation and rotation (as seen in Chapter 14) can also be applied to text. For example, to rotate text around its center, translate to an origin point and use ***textAlign(CENTER)*** before displaying the text.

Example 17-5: Rotating text

```
PFont f;
String message = "this text is spinning";
float theta;

void setup() {
  size(200,200);
  f = createFont("Arial",20,true);
}

void draw() {
  background(255);
  fill(0);
```

fig. 17.7

```
textFont(f);                        // Set the font
translate(width/2,height/2);        // Translate to the center
rotate(theta);                      // Rotate by theta
textAlign(CENTER);
text(message,0,0);
theta += 0.05;                      // Increase rotation
}
```

> The text is center aligned and displayed at (0,0) after translating and rotating. See Chapter 14 or a review of translation and rotation.

Exercise 17-8: Display text that is centered and rotated to appear flat. Have the text scroll off into the distance.

> *A long* long time ago
> *In a* galaxy far far away

```
String info = "A long long time ago\nIn a galaxy far far away";
PFont f;
float y = 0;

void setup() {
  size(400,200,P3D);
  f = createFont("Arial",20*4,true);
}

void draw() {
  background(255);
  fill(0);
  translate(_____,_____);
  _____ (_____);
  textFont(f);
  textAlign(CENTER);
  text(info, _____,_____);
  y--;
}
```

> "\" means "new line." In Java, invisible characters can be incorporated into a *String* with an "escape sequence"—a backward slash "\" followed by a character. Here are a few more.
> \n—new line
> \r—carriage return
> \t—tab
> \'—single quote
> \"—double quote
> \\—backward slash

17.7 Display text character by character.

In certain graphics applications, displaying text with each character rendered individually is required. For example, if each character needs to move independently, then simply saying *text("a bunch of letters",0,0)* will not do.

The solution is to loop through a *String*, displaying each character one at a time.

Let's start by looking at an example that displays the text all at once. See Figure 17.8.

```
PFont f;
String message = "Each character is not
                  written individually.";

void setup() {
  size(400,200);
  f = createFont("Arial",20,true);
}

void draw() {
  background(255);
  fill(0);
  textFont(f);
  text(message,10,height/2);
}
```

> Each character is not written individually.

fig. 17.8

> Displaying a block of text all at once using *text()*.

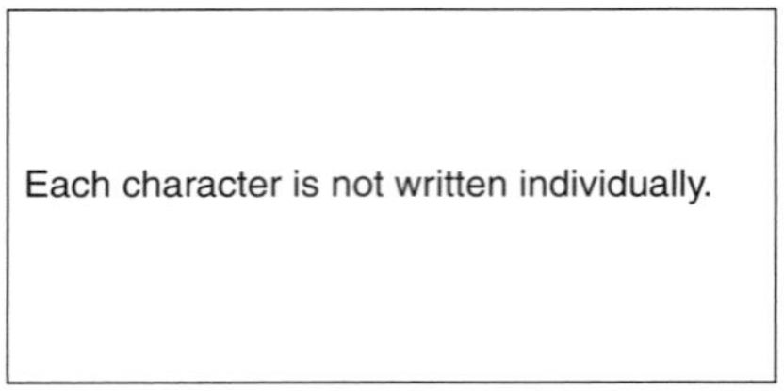

We rewrite the code to display each character in a loop, using the *charAt()* function. See Figure 17.9.

```
int x = 10;

for (int i = 0; i < message.length(); i++) {
  text(message.charAt(i),x,height/2);
  x += 10;
}
```

> The first character is at pixel 10.

> All characters are spaced 10 pixels apart.

> Each character is displayed one at a time with the *charAt()* function.

> Each char act er is writt en indi vi dual ly.

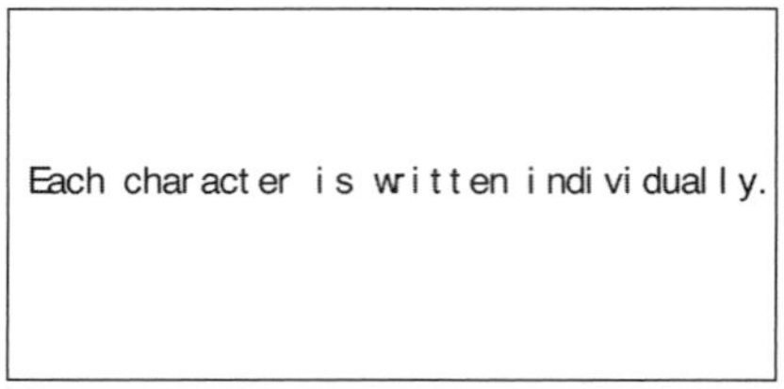

fig. 17.9 (Note how the spacing is incorrect.)

Calling the *text()* function for each character will allow us more flexibility in future examples (for coloring, sizing, and placing characters within one *String* individually). This example has a pretty major flaw, however. Here, the *x* location is increased by 10 pixels for each character. Although this is approximately correct, because each character is not exactly 10 pixels wide, the spacing is off. The proper spacing can be achieved using the *textWidth()* function as demonstrated in the following code. Note how this example achieves the proper spacing even with each character being a random size! See Figure 17.10.

```
int x = 10;
for (int i = 0; i < message.length(); i++) {
  textSize(random(12,36));
  text(message.charAt(i),x,height/2);
  x += textWidth(message.charAt(i));
}
```

> *textWidth()* spaces the characters out properly.

> EaCh chara₍c₎te₍r₎ is writ₍t₎en in₍d₎i₍vi₎d₍ually₎.

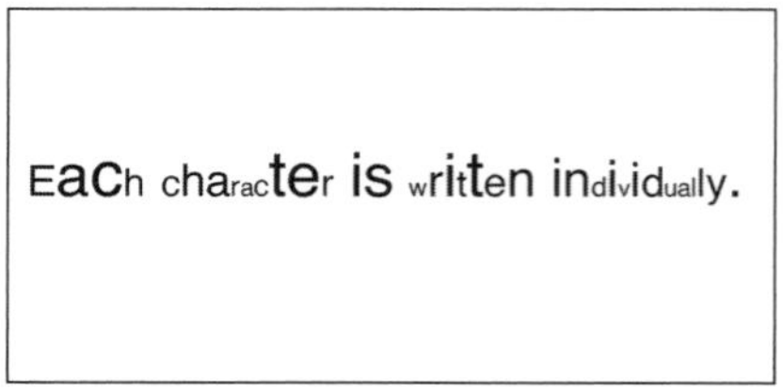

fig. 17.10 (Note how the spacing is correct even with differently sized characters!)

*Exercise 17-9: Using **textWidth()**, redo Example 17-4 (the text "mirror") to use a non-fixed-width font with proper character spacing. The following image uses Arial.*

This "letter by letter" methodology can also be applied to a sketch where characters from a *String* move independently of one another. The following example uses object-oriented design to make each character from the original *String* a *Letter* object, allowing it to both be displayed in its proper location as well as move about the screen individually.

Example 17-6: Text breaking up

```
PFont f;
String message = "click mouse to shake it up";
// An array of Letter objects
Letter[] letters;

void setup() {
  size(260,200);
  // Load the font
  f = createFont("Arial",20,true);
  textFont(f);

  // Create the array the same size as the String
  letters = new Letter[message.length()];
  // Initialize Letters at the correct x location
  int x = 16;
  for (int i = 0; i < message.length(); i++) {
    letters[i] = new Letter(x,100,message.charAt(i));
    x += textwidth(message.charAt(i));
  }
}
```

fig. 17.11

Letter objects are initialized with their location within the *String* as well as what character they should display.

```
void draw() {
  background(255);
  for (int i = 0; i < letters.length; i++) {
    // Display all letters
    letters[i].display();

    // If the mouse is pressed the letters shake
    // If not, they return to their original location
    if (mousePressed) {
      letters[i].shake();
    } else {
      letters[i].home();
    }
  }
}


// A class to describe a single Letter
class Letter {
  char letter;
  // The object knows its original "home" location
  float homex,homey;
  // As well as its current location
  float x,y;

  Letter (float x_, float y_, char letter_) {
    homex = x = x_;
    homey = y = y_;
    letter = letter_;
  }

  // Display the letter
  void display() {
    fill(0);
    textAlign(LEFT);
    text(letter,x,y);
  }

  // Move the letter randomly
  void shake() {
    x += random(-2,2);
    y += random(-2,2);
  }

  // Return the letter home
  void home() {
    x = homex;
    y = homey;
  }
}
```

> The object knows about its original "home" location within the *String* of text, as well as its current (*x,y*) location should it move around the screen.

> At any point, the current location can be set back to the home location by calling the ***home()*** function.

The character by character method also allows us to display text along a curve. Before we move on to letters, let's first look at how we would draw a series of boxes along a curve. This example makes heavy use of the trigonometric functions covered in Chapter 13.

Example 17-7: Boxes along a curve

```
PFont f;
// The radius of a circle
float r = 100;
// The width and height of the boxes
float w = 40;
float h = 40;

void setup() {
  size(320,320);
  smooth();
}

void draw() {
  background(255);

  // Start in the center and draw the circle
  translate(width/2,height/2);
  noFill();
  stroke(0);
  ellipse(0, 0, r*2, r*2);

  // 10 boxes along the curve
  int totalBoxes = 10;
  // We must keep track of our position along the curve
  float arclength = 0;

  // For every box
  for (int i = 0; i < totalBoxes; i++) {
    // Each box is centered so we move half the width
    arclength += w/2;
    // Angle in radians is the arclength divided by the radius
    float theta = arclength/r;

    pushMatrix();
    // Polar to cartesian coordinate conversion
    translate(r*cos(theta), r*sin(theta));
    // Rotate the box
    rotate(theta);
    // Display the box
    fill(0,100);
    rectMode(CENTER);
    rect(0,0,w,h);
    popMatrix();
    // Move halfway again
    arclength += w/2;
  }
}
```

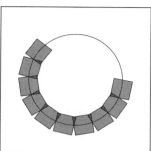

fig. 17.12

> Our curve is a circle with radius *r* in the center of the window.

> We move along the curve according to the width of the box.

Even if you find the mathematics of this example to be difficult, Figure 17.12 should reveal the next step. What we need to do is replace each box with a character from a *String* that fits inside the box. And since characters do not all have the same width, instead of using a variable "w" that stays constant, each box will have a variable width along the curve according to the ***textWidth()*** function.

Example 17-8: Characters along a curve

```
// The message to be displayed
String message = "text along a curve";


PFont f;
// The radius of a circle
float r = 100;

void setup() {
  size(320,320);
  f = createFont("Georgia",40,true);
  textFont(f);
  textAlign(CENTER);        <──  The text must be centered!
  smooth();
}


void draw() {
  background(255);

  // Start in the center and draw the circle
  translate(width/2, height/2);
  noFill();
  stroke(0);
  ellipse(0, 0, r*2, r*2);


  // We must keep track of our position along the curve
  float arclength = 0;

  // For every box
  for (int i = 0; i < message.length(); i++) {
    // The character and its width
    char currentChar = message.charAt(i);
    float w = textWidth(currentChar);     Instead of a constant width, we
                                          check the width of each character.

    // Each box is centered so we move half the width
    arclength += w/2;
    // Angle in radians is the arclength divided by the radius
    // Starting on the left side of the circle by adding PI
    float theta = PI + arclength/r;
                                       Polar to Cartesian conversion
                                       allows us to find the point along
    pushMatrix();                      the curve. See Chapter 13 for a
    // Polar to cartesian coordinate conversion   review of this concept.
    translate(r*cos(theta), r*sin(theta));
    // Rotate the box
    rotate(theta+PI/2); // rotation is offset by 90 degrees
    // Display the character
    fill(0);
    text(currentChar,0,0);
    popMatrix();
    // Move halfway again
    arclength += w/2;
  }
}
```

fig. 17.13

Exercise 17-10: Create a sketch that starts with characters randomly scattered (and rotated). Have them slowly move back toward their "home" location. Use an object-oriented approach as seen in Example 17-6.[1]

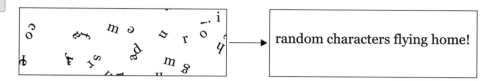

One way to solve this is to use interpolation. Interpolation refers to the process of calculating values in between two given pieces of data. In this exercise, we want to know the in-between *x* locations (and *y* locations) from the random starting point to the target location in the *String*. One interpolation method is to simply take the average. Think of it as walking to a wall by always taking a step halfway.

```
x = (x + targetX) / 2;
y = (y + targetY) / 2;
```

Another possibility is to simply go 10% of the way there.

```
x = 0.9*x + 0.1*targetX;
y = 0.9*y + 0.1*targetY;
```

Processing's **lerp()** function will do interpolation for you. Visit the reference page for more information: *http://processing.org/reference/lerp_.html*.

Consider making your sketch interactive. Can you push the letters around using the mouse?

---

[1]The origins of this exercise can be traced back to John Maeda's 1995 work: *Flying Letters.*

18 Data Input

"A million monkeys were given a million typewriters. It's called the Internet."
—Simon Munnery

In this chapter:
- Manipulating *Strings*.
- Reading and writing text files.
- HTTP requests, parsing HTML.
- XML, RSS feeds.
- The Yahoo search API.
- The applet sandbox.

This chapter will move beyond displaying text and examine how to use *String* objects as the basis for reading and writing data. We will start by learning more sophisticated methods for manipulating *Strings*, searching in them, chopping them up, and joining them together. Afterward, we will see how these skills allow us to use input from data sources, such as text files, web pages, XML feeds, and third party APIs, and take a step into the world of data visualization.

18.1 Manipulating Strings

In Chapter 17, we touched on a few of the basic functions available in the Java *String* class, such as ***charAt()***, ***toUpperCase()***, ***equals()***, and ***length()***. These functions are documented on the *Processing* reference page for *Strings*. Nevertheless, in order to perform some more advanced data parsing techniques, we will need to explore some additional *String* manipulation functions documented in the Java API (more about the Java API to come in Chapter 23).

http://java.sun.com/j2se/1.4.2/docs/api/java/lang/String.html

Let's take a closer look at the following two *String* functions: ***indexOf()*** and ***substring()***.

indexOf() locates a sequence of characters within a *String*. It takes one argument, a search *String*, and returns a numeric value that corresponds to the first occurrence of the search *String* inside of the *String* being searched.

```
String search = "def";
String toBeSearched = "abcdefghi";
int index = toBeSearched.indexOf(search);
```

> The value of index in this example is 3.

Strings are just like arrays, in that the first character is index number zero and the last character is the length of the *String* minus one.

Exercise 18-1: Predict the result of the code below.

```
String sentence = "The quick brown fox jumps over the lazy dog.";

println(sentence.indexOf("quick"));    _____

println(sentence.indexOf("fo"));    _____

println(sentence.indexOf("The"));    _____

println(sentence.indexOf("blah blah"));    _____
```

If you are stuck on the last line of Exercise 18-1, it is because there is no way for you to know the answer without consulting the Java reference (or making an educated guess). If the search *String* cannot be found, ***indexOf()*** returns −1. This is a good choice because " −1" is not a legitimate index value in the *String* itself, and therefore can indicate "not found." There are no *negative* indices in a *String* of characters or in an array.

After finding a search phrase within a *String*, we might want to separate out part of the *String*, saving it in a different variable. A part of a *String* is known as *substring* and *substrings* are made with the ***substring()*** function which takes two arguments, a start index and an end index. ***substring()*** returns the *substring* in between the two indices.

```
String alphabet = "abcdefghi";
String sub = alphabet.substring(3,6);
```
> The *String* sub is now "def".

Note that the *substring* begins at the specified *start index* (the first argument) and extends to the character at *end index* (the second argument) *minus one*. I know. I know. Wouldn't it have been easier to just take the *substring* from the start index all the way to the end index? While this might initially seem true, it is actually quite convenient to stop at end index minus one. For example, if you ever want to make a *substring* that extends to the end of a *String*, you can simply go all the way to ***thestring.length()***. In addition, with end index minus one marking the end, the length of the *substring* is easily calculated as *end index minus begin index*.

Exercise 18-2: Fill in the blanks to get the substring "fox jumps over the lazy dog" (without the period).

```
String sentence = "The quick brown fox jumps over the lazy dog.";

int foxIndex = sentence.indexOf(_____);

int periodIndex = sentence.indexOf(".");

String sub = _____ . _____ (_____ , _____);
```

18.2 Splitting and Joining

In Chapter 17, we saw how *Strings* can be joined together (referred to as "concatenation") using the "+" operator. Let's review with an example that uses concatenation to get user input from a keyboard .

Example 18-1: User input

```
PFont f;

// Variable to store text currently being typed
String typing = "";
// Variable to store saved text when return is hit
String saved = "";

void setup() {
  size(300,200);
  f = createFont("Arial",16,true);
}

void draw() {
  background(255);
  int indent = 25;

  // Set the font and fill for text
  textFont(f);
  fill(0);

  // Display everything
  text("Click in this applet and type. \nHit return to save what you typed.",indent,40);
  text(typing,indent,90);
  text(saved,indent,130);
}

void keyPressed() {
  // If the return key is pressed, save the String and clear it
  if (key == '\n') {
    saved = typing;
    typing = "";
  // Otherwise, concatenate the String
  } else {
    typing = typing + key;
  }
}
```

> For keyboard input, we use two variables. One will store the text as it is being typed. Another will keep a copy of the typed text once the Enter key is pressed.

> A *String* can be cleared by setting it equal to "".

> Each character typed by the user is added to the end of the *String* variable.

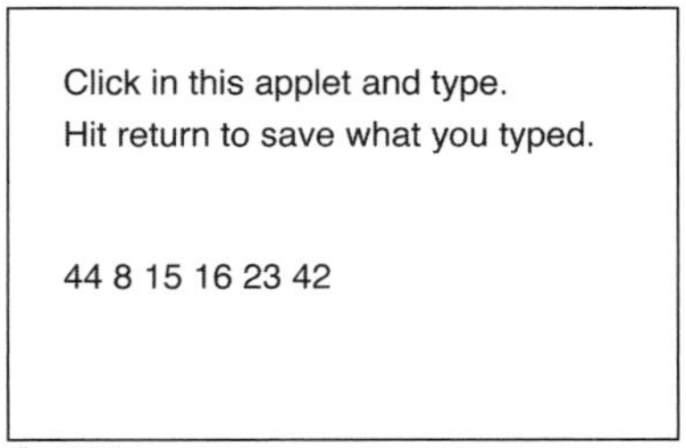

Click in this applet and type.
Hit return to save what you typed.

44 8 15 16 23 42

fig. 18.1

Exercise 18-3: Create a sketch that chats with the user. For example, if a user enters "cats" the sketch might reply "How do cats make you feel?"

Processing has two additional functions that make joining *Strings* (or the reverse, splitting them up) easy. In sketches that involve parsing data from a file or the web, we will often get that data in the form of an array of *Strings* or as one long *String*. Depending on what we want to accomplish, it is useful to know how to switch between these two modes of storage. This is where these two new functions, ***split()*** and ***join()***, will come in handy.

"one long string or array of strings" ⟵⟶ {"one", "long", "string", "or", "array", "of", "strings"}

Let's take a look at the ***split()*** function. ***split()*** separates a longer *String* into an array of *Strings*, based on a split character known as the *delimiter*. It takes two arguments, the *String* to be split and the delimiter. (The delimiter can be a single character or a *String*.)

```
// Splitting a String based on spaces
String spaceswords = "The quick brown fox jumps over the lazy dog.";
String[] list = split(spaceswords, " ");
for (int i = 0; i < list.length; i++) {
println(list[i] + " " + i);
}
```

> This period is not set as a delimeter and therefore will be included in the last *String* in the array: "dog."

Here is an example using a comma as the delimiter.

```
// Splitting a String based on commas
String commaswords = "The,quick,brown,fox,jumps,over,the,lazy,dog.";
String[] list = split(commaswords, ',');
for (int i = 0; i < list.length; i++) {
    println(list[i] + " " + i);
}
```

If you want to use more than one delimiter to split up a text, you must use the *Processing* function *splitTokens(). splitTokens()* works identically is *split()* with one exception: any character that appears in the *String* qualifies as a delimiter.

```
// Splitting a String based on multiple delimiters
String stuff = "hats & apples, cars + phones % elephants dog.";
String[] list = splitTokens(stuff, " &,+.");
for (int i = 0; i < list.length; i++) {
    println(list[i] + " " + i);
}
```

> The period is set as a delimiter and therefore will not be included in the last *String* in the array: "dog".

Exercise 18-4: Fill in what the above code will print in the Processing *message window:*

hats_____

_____

_____

_____

_____

If we are splitting numbers in a *String*, the resulting array can be converted into an integer array with *Processing*'s *int()* function.

```
// Calculate sum of a list of numbers in a String
String numbers = "8,67,5,309";
// Converting the String array to an int array
int[] list = int(split(numbers, ','));
int sum = 0;
for (int i = 0; i < list.length; i++) {
  sum = sum + list[i];
}
println(sum);
```

> Numbers in a *String* are not numbers and cannot be used in mathematical operations unless we convert them first.

The reverse *of split()* is *join()*. *join()* takes an array of *Strings* and joins them together into one long String. *The join()* function also takes two arguments, the array to be joined and a *separator*. The separator can either be a single character or a *String* of characters.

Consider the following array:

```
String[] lines = {"It", "was", "a", "dark", "and", "stormy", "night."};
```

Using the + operator along with a *for* loop, we can join a *String* together as follows:

```
// Manual Concatenation
String onelongstring = "";
for (int i = 0; i < lines.length; i++) {
    onelongstring = onelongstring + lines[i] + " ";
}
```

The join() function, however, allows us to bypass this process, achieving the same result in only one line of code.

```
// Using Processing's join()
String onelongstring = join(lines," ");
```

Exercise 18-5: Split the following String into an array of floating point numbers and calculate the average.

```
String floats = "5023.23:52.3:10.4:5.9, 901.3---2.3";

float[] numbers = _____(_____(_____,"_____"));
float total = 0;
for (int i = 0; i < numbers.length; i++) {

    _____ += _____;
}

float avg = _____;
```

18.3 Reading and Writing Text Files

Data can come from many different places: web sites, news feeds, databases, and so on. When developing an application that involves a data source, such as a data visualization, it is important to separate out the logic for what the program will ultimately do with the data from the retrieval of the data itself.

In fact, while working out the visuals, it is especially useful to develop with "dummy" or "fake" data. In keeping with our *one-step-at-a-time* mantra, once the meat of the program is completed with dummy data, you can then focus solely on how to retrieve the actual data from the real source.

We are going to follow this model in this section, working with the simplest means of data retrieval: reading from a text file. Text files can be used as a very simple database (we could store settings for a program, a list of high scores, numbers for a graph, etc.) or to simulate a more complex data source.

In order to create a text file, you can use any simple text editor. Windows Notepad or Mac OS X TextEdit will do, just make sure you format the file as "plain text." It is also advisable to name the text files with the ".txt" extension, just to avoid any confusion. And just as with image files in Chapter 15, these text files should be placed in the sketch's "data" directory in order for them to be recognized by the *Processing* sketch.

Once the text file is in place, *Processing's* **loadStrings()** function is used to read the content of the file into a *String* array. The individual lines of text in the file (see Figure 18.2) each become an individual element in the array.

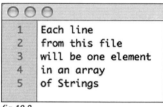

fig 18.2

```
String[] lines = loadStrings("file.txt");
println("there are " + lines.length + " lines");
for (int i=0; i < lines.length; i++) {
println(lines[i]);
}
```

> This code will print all the lines from the source text file. Shown in Figure 18.2.

To run the code, create a text file called "file.txt", type a bunch of lines in that file, and place it in your sketch's data directory.

Exercise 18-6: Rewrite Example 17-3 so that it loads the headlines from a text file.

Text from a data file can be used to generate a simple visualization. In Example 18-2, loads data file shown in Figure 18.3. The results of visualizing this data are shown in Figure 18.4.

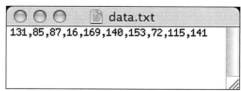

fig. 18.3 Contents of "Data.txt"

Example 18-2: Graphing comma separated numbers from a text file

```
int[] data;

void setup() {
  size(200,200);
  // Load text file as a String
  String[] stuff = loadStrings("data.txt");
  // Convert string into an array of integers
  // using ',' as a delimiter
  data = int(split(stuff[0],','));
}

void draw() {
  background(255);
  stroke(0);
  for (int i = 0; i < data.length; i++) {
    fill(data[i]);
    rect(i*20,0,20,data[i]);
  }
  noLoop();
}
```

> The text from the file is loaded into an array. This array has one element because the file only has one line. That element is then split into an array of ints.

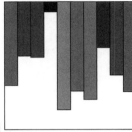
fig. 18.4

> The array of ints is used to set the color and height of each rectangle.

We can also use the contents of a text file to initialize objects by passing the data from the text file into an object constructor. In Example 18-3, the text file has 10 lines, each line representing one instance of an object with the values for that object's variables separated by commas. See Figure 18.5.

Example 18-3: Creating objects from a text file

```
Bubble[] bubbles;

void setup() {
  size(200,200);
  smooth();
  // Load text file as an array of String
  String[] data = loadStrings("data.txt");
  bubbles = new Bubble[data.length];

  for (int i = 0; i < bubbles.length; i++) {

    float[] values = float(split(data[i],","));
    bubbles[i] = new Bubble(values[0],values[1],values[2]);
  }
}

void draw() {
  background(100);
  // Display and move all bubbles
  for (int i = 0; i < bubbles.length; i++) {
    bubbles[i].display();
    bubbles[i].drift();
  }
}
// A Class to describe a "Bubble"
class Bubble {
  float x,y;
  float diameter;
```

> The size of the array of Bubble objects is determined by the total number of lines in the text file.

> Each line is split into an array of floating point numbers.

> The values in the array are passed into the Bubble class constructor.

```
float speed;
float r,g;

// The constructor initializes color and size
// Location is filled randomly
Bubble(float r_, float g_, float diameter_) {
  x = random(width);
  y = height;
  r = r_;
  g = g_;
  diameter = diameter_;
}

// Display the Bubble
void display() {
  stroke(255);
  fill(r,g,255,150);
  ellipse(x,y,diameter,diameter);
}

// Move the bubble
void drift() {
  y += random(-3,-0.1);
  x += random(-1,1);
  if (y < -diameter*2) {
    y = height + diameter*2;
  }
}
}
```

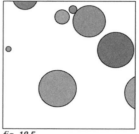 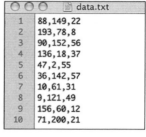

fig. 18.5

Now that we are comfortable with the idea of loading information from a text file to initialize *Processing* sketches, we are ready to ask the following question: What if we want to save information so that it can be loaded the next time a program is run? For example, let's say we want to revise Example 18-3 so that the bubbles change on a mouse rollover. (We have worked on rollovers with a rectangle before in Exercise 5-5, and Example 9-11 but this rollover example will use a circle.) See Figure 18.6.

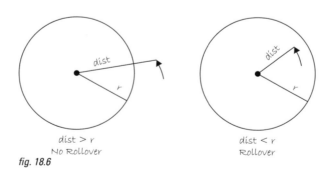

fig. 18.6

```
boolean rollover(int mx, int my) {
  if (dist(mx,my,x,y) < diameter/2) {
    return true;
  } else {
    return false;
  }
}
```

The **rollover()** function in the Bubble class returns a boolean value (true or false) depending on whether the arguments (*mx,my*) are inside the circle.

The *rollover()* function checks to see if the distance between a given point (*mx,my*) and the bubble's location (*x,y*) is less than the radius of the circle; the radius is defined as the diameter divided by two (see Figure 18.6). If this is true, then that point (*mx,my*) must be inside the circle. Calling this function using the mouse location as the arguments allows us to test whether the mouse is, in fact, rolling over any of the bubbles.

```
for (int i = 0; i < bubbles.length; i++) {
  bubbles[i].display();
  bubbles[i].drift();
  if (bubbles[i].rollover(mouseX,mouseY)) {
    bubbles[i].change();
  }
}
```

Once we implement the *change()* function to adjust the Bubble's variables, we can save the new information in a text file with *Processing's* *saveStrings()* function. *saveStrings()* is essentially the opposite of *loadStrings()*, receiving a filename and a *String* array and saving that array to the file.

```
String[] stuff = {"Each String", "will be saved", "on a", "separate line"};
saveStrings("data.txt", stuff);
```

This code will create the text file in Figure 18.7.

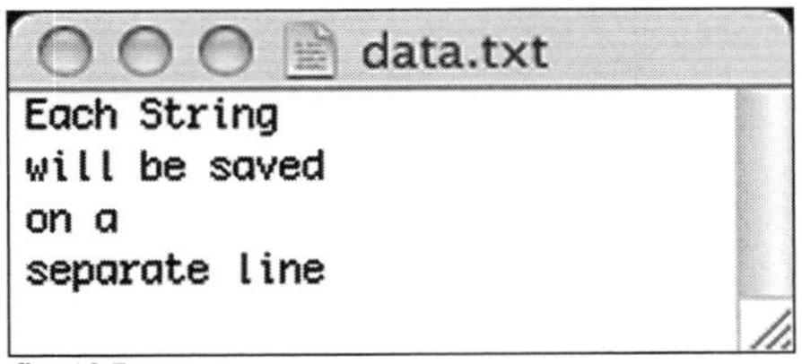

```
○ ○ ○  📄 data.txt
Each String
will be saved
on a
separate line
```

fig. 18.7

saveStrings(), however, does not store the text file in the data folder, but rather places it in the local sketch directory. If we want the file to be written to the data directory, we must specify the path. Also, if the file already exists, it will be overwritten.

Knowing this, we can concoct a *saveData()* function for the Bubbles sketch that rewrites "data.txt" with the properties from the objects in their current state. In this example, we will save the new data whenever the mouse is pressed.

We first create an array of *Strings* with a size equal to the total number of Bubble objects.

```
void saveData() {
  String[] data = new String[bubbles.length];
  for (int i = 0; i < bubbles.length; i++) {
    data[i] = bubbles[i].r + "," + bubbles[i].g + "," + bubbles[i].diameter;
  }
  saveStrings("data/data.txt",data);
}
void mousePressed() {
  saveData();
}
```

Each element of the *String* array is made by concatenating the values of each Bubble object's variables.

Since the original data file is overwritten, whenever you run the sketch again, the new values are loaded. Here is the entire example for reference. Figure 18-18 shows the new data file after *saveStrings()*:

Example 18-4: Loading and saving data to text file

```
// An array of Bubble objects
Bubble[] bubbles;

void setup() {
  size(200,200);
  smooth();
  // Load text file as a string
  String[] data = loadStrings("data.txt");          Bubble data is loaded in setup().
  // Make as many objects as lines in the text file
  bubbles = new Bubble[data.length];
  // Convert values to floats and pass into Bubble constructor
  for (int i = 0; i < bubbles.length; i++) {
    float[] values = float(split(data[i],","));
    bubbles[i] = new Bubble(values[0],values[1],values[2]);
  }
}

void draw() {
  background(255);
  // Display and move all bubbles
  for (int i = 0; i < bubbles.length; i++) {
    bubbles[i].display();
    bubbles[i].drift();
    // Change bubbles if mouse rolls over
    if (bubbles[i].rollover(mouseX,mouseY)) {
      bubbles[i].change();
    }
  }
}

// Save new Bubble data when mouse is Pressed
void mousePressed() {
  saveData();                                        Bubble data is saved in
}                                                    mousePressed().

void saveData() {
  // For each Bubble make one String to be saved
  String[] data = new String[bubbles.length];
  for (int i = 0; i < bubbles.length; i++) {
    // Concatenate bubble variables
    data[i] = bubbles[i].r + "," + bubbles[i].g + "," + bubbles[i].diameter;
  }
  // Save to File
  saveStrings("data/data.txt",data);
}

// A Bubble class        The same file is overwritten by
class Bubble {           adding the "data" folder path
  float x,y;             to saveStrings() as shown in
  float diameter;        Figure 18.8.
  float speed;
  float r,g;

  Bubble(float r_,float g_, float diameter_) {
    x = random(width);
    y = height;
    r = r_;
    g = g_;
```

```
data.txt
117.74119,162.56252,31.550926
193.0,78.0,8.0
82.645065,155.95206,71.16294
93.12722,22.832039,72.0
53.581787,12.430585,69.64311
32.257603,107.33057,72.0
6.539798,112.43094,52.02985
45.104065,100.08362,70.185394
159.73688,84.82494,17.886131
71.0,200.0,21.0
```

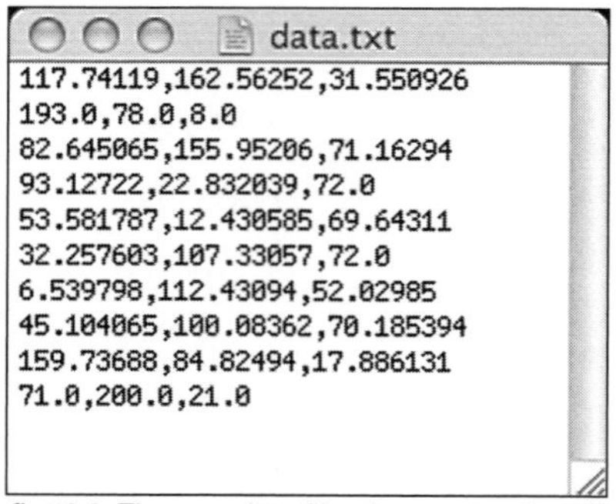

fig 18.8 The new data file after save strings ()

```
      diameter = diameter_;
    }

    // True or False if point is inside circle
    boolean rollover(int mx, int my) {
      if (dist(mx,my,x,y) < diameter/2) {
        return true;
      } else {
        return false;
      }
    }
  // Change Bubble variables
  void change() {
    r = constrain(r + random(-10,10),0,255);
    g = constrain(g + random(-10,10),0,255);
    diameter = constrain(diameter + random(-2,4),4,72);
  }
  // Display Bubble
  void display() {
    stroke(0);
    fill(r,g,255,150);
    ellipse(x,y,diameter,diameter);
  }
  // Bubble drifts upwards
  void drift() {
    y += random(-3,-0.1);
    x += random(-1,1);
    if (y < -diameter*2) {
      y = height + diameter*2;
    }
  }
}
```

Exercise 18-7: Create a sketch that visualizes the following data. Feel free to add to and change the text.

```
○ ○ ○    📄 people.txt
bob,4,10,1,900,200,150,122.5
penelope,7,2,4,90,23,255,135.2
jane,6,150,9,812,67,10,9.9
```

18.4 Text Parsing

Now that we are comfortable with how *loadStrings()* works for text files stored locally, we can start to examine what we might do with textual data we retrieve from other sources such as a URL.

```
String[] lines = loadStrings("http://www.yahoo.com");
```

When you send a URL path into *loadStrings()*, you get back the raw HTML ("Hypertext Markup Language") source of the requested web page. It is the same stuff that appears upon selecting "View Source" from a browser's menu options. You do not need to be an HTML expert to follow this section, but if you are not familiar at all with HTML, you might read *http://en.wikipedia.org/wiki/HTML*.

Unlike with the comma-delimited data from a text file that was specially formatted for use in a *Processing* sketch, it is not practical to have the resulting raw HTML stored in an array of *Strings* (each element representing one line from the source). Converting the array into one long *String* can make things a bit simpler. As we saw earlier in the chapter, this can be achieved using *join()*.

```
String onelongstring = join(lines," ");
```

When pulling raw HTML from a web page, it is likely you do not want all of the source, but just a small piece of it. Perhaps you are looking for weather information, a stock quote, or a news headline. We can take advantage of the *String* manipulation functions we learned—*indexOf()*, *substring()*, and *length()*—to find pieces of data within a large block of text. We saw an early example of this in Exercise 18-2. Take, for example, the following *String*:

```
String stuff = "Number of apples:62. Boy, do I like apples or what!";
```

Let's say we want to pull out the number of apples from the above text. Our algorithm would be as follows:

1. Find the *end of the substring* "apples:". Call it start.
2. Find the *first period* after "apples:". Call it end.
3. Make a *substring* of the characters between start and end.
4. Convert the *String* to a number (if we want to use it as such).

In code, this look's like:

```
int start    = stuff.indexOf("apples: ") + 8;    // STEP 1
int end      = stuff.indexOf(".",start);          // STEP 2
String apples = stuff.Substring(start,end);       // STEP 3
int apple_no = int(apples);                        // STEP 4
```

> The "end" of a *String* can be found by searching for the index of that *String* and adding the length to that index (in this case 8).

The above code will do the trick, but we should be a bit more careful to make sure we do not run into any errors if we do not find the *substrings*. We can add some error checking and generalize the code into a function:

```
// A function that returns a substring between two substrings
String giveMeTextBetween(String s, String startTag, String endTag) {
    String found = "";
    // Find the index of the beginning tag
    int startIndex = s.indexOf(startTag);
    // If we don't find anything
    if (startIndex == -1) return "";
    // Move to the end of the beginning tag
    startIndex += startTag.length();
```

> A function to return a *String* found between two *Strings*. If beginning or end "tag" is not found, the function returns an empty *String*.

```
     // Find the index of the end tag
     int endIndex = s.indexOf(endTag, startIndex);
     // If we don't find the end tag,
     if (endIndex == -1) return "";
     // Return the text in between
     return s.substring(startIndex,endIndex);
}
```

> **IndexOf()** can also take a second argument, an integer. That second argument means: Find the first occurrence of the search *String* after this specified index. We use it here to ensure that end index follows start index.

With this technique, we are ready to connect to a web site from within *Processing* and grab data to use in our sketches. For example, we could read the HTML source from *http://www.nytimes.com* and look for today's headlines, search *http://finance.yahoo.com* for stock quotes, count how many times the word "Flickr" appears on your favorite blog, and so on. HTML, however, is an ugly, scary place with inconsistently formatted pages that are difficult to reverse engineer and parse effectively. Not to mention the fact that companies change the source code of web pages rather often, so any example that I might make while I am writing this paragraph might break by the time you read this paragrap.

For grabbing data from the web, an XML (Extensible Markup Language) feed will prove to be more reliable and easier to parse. Unlike HTML (which is designed to make content viewable by a human's eyes) XML is designed to make content viewable by a computer and facilitate the sharing of data across different systems. We will get into how XML works more in Section 18.17. For now, let's examine how we might grab the weather for any given zip code from Yahoo's XML weather feed. Information about all of Yahoo's XML feeds can be found here: *http://developer.yahoo.com/rss/*. The weather XML feed is here:

> *http://xml.weather.yahoo.com/forecastrss?p=10025*

One way to grab the data from a weather feed is to use the *Processing* XML library (which facilitates reading from an XML document). However, in order to demonstrate *String* parsing on a lower level, as an exercise, we will use our **loadStrings()** scraping techniques and search for bits of information embedded in the XML source manually. Admittedly, this is somewhat of a silly pursuit since XML is designed to be parsed without having to resort to this methodology. For comparison, we will look at this sample example using two different XML libraries in Sections 18.7 and 18.8.

Looking in the XML source from the above URL, we can see that the temperature today (which happens to be August 1, 2007 at the time of this writing) is 88°F—*temp = "88"*.

```
     <yweather:condition text="Fair" code="34" temp="88" date="Wed, 01 Aug 2007
     3:51 pm EDT"/>
```

The temperature is variable but the XML format is not, and therefore we can deduce that the start tag for our search should be:

> **temp**="
> and the end tag:
> "
> (i.e., the first quote after the start tag).

Knowing the start and end tags, we can use **giveMeTextBetween()** to pull out the temperature.

```
String url = "http://xml.weather.yahoo.com/forecastrss?p=10003";
String[] lines = loadStrings(url);
// Get rid of the array in order to search
// the whole page
String xml = join(lines, " ");

// Searching for temperature
String tag1 = "temp=\"";
String tag2 = "\"";
temp = int(giveMeTextBetween
(xml,tag1,tag2));
println(temp);
```

> A quote in Java marks the beginning or end of a *String*. So how do we include an actual quote in a *String*?
>
> The answer is via an "escape" sequence. (We encountered this in Exercise 17-8.) A quote can be included in a *String* using a backward slash, followed by a quote. For example:
> ```
> String q = "This String has a quote \"in it";
> ```

Example 18-5 retrieves the temperature from Yahoo's weather XML feed and displays it onscreen. The example also uses object-oriented programming, putting all of the *String* parsing functionality into a WeatherGrabber class.

Example 18-5: Parsing Yahoo's XML weather feed manually

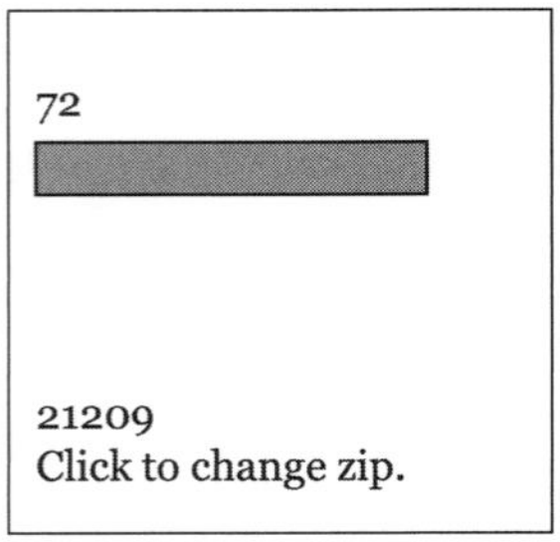

```
PFont f;

String[] zips = {"10003","21209","90210"};
int counter = 0;

// The WeatherGrabber object does the work for us!
WeatherGrabber wg;

void setup() {
  size(200,200);
  // Make a WeatherGrabber object
  wg = new WeatherGrabber(zips[counter]);
  // Tell it to request the weather
  wg.requestWeather();
  f = createFont("Georgia",16,true);
}

void draw() {
  background(255);
  textFont(f);
  fill(0);

  // Get the values to display
  String weather = wg.getWeather();
  int temp = wg.getTemp();

  // Display all the stuff we want to display
  text(zips[counter],10,160);
  text(weather,10,90);
  text(temp,10,40);
  text("Click to change zip.",10,180);

  // Draw a little thermometer based on the temperature
  stroke(0);
  fill(175);
  rect(10,50,temp*2,20);
}
```

fig. 18.9

> The WeatherGrabber object is initialized with a zip code. The XML data is loaded and parsed upon calling the **requestWeather()** function.

> The weather and temperature information is pulled from the WeatherGrabber object.

```
void mousePressed() {
  // Increment the counter and get the weather at the next zip code
  counter = (counter + 1) % zips.length;
  wg.setZip(zips[counter]);
  wg.requestWeather();
}
```

> The data is requested again with a new zip code every time the mouse is pressed.

```
// A WeatherGrabber class
class WeatherGrabber {
  int temperature = 0;
  String weather = "";
  String zip;

  WeatherGrabber(String tempZip) {
    zip = tempZip;
  }

  // Set a new Zip code
  void setZip(String tempZip) {
    zip = tempZip;
  }

  // Get the temperature
  int getTemp() {
    return temperature;
  }

  // Get the weather
  String getWeather() {
    return weather;
  }

  // Make the actual XML request
  void requestWeather() {
    // Get all the HTML/XML source code into an array of strings
    // (each line is one element in the array)
    String url = "http://xml.weather.yahoo.com/forecastrss?p=" + zip;
    String[] lines = loadStrings(url);

    String xml = join(lines, ""); // Turn array into one long String

    // Searching for weather condition
    String lookfor = " <yweather:condition text=\"";
    String end = "\"";
    weather = giveMeTextBetween (xml,lookfor,end);

    // Searching for temperature
    lookfor = "temp=\"";
    temperature = int(giveMeTextBetween (xml,lookfor,end));
  }

  // A function that returns a substring between two substrings
  String giveMeTextBetween(String s, String before, String after) {
    String found = "";
    int start = s.indexOf(before); // Find the index of the beginning tag
    if (start == -1) return ""; // If we don't find anything, send back a blank
                                // String
    start += before.length(); // Move to the end of the beginning tag
    int end = s.indexOf(after,start); // Find the index of the end tag
    if (end == -1) return ""; // If we don't find the end tag, send back a blank String
    return s.substring(start,end); // Return the text in between
  }
}
```

Exercise 18-8: Expand Example 18-5 to also search for the next day's high and low temperature.

 Exercise 18-9: Take a look at Yahoo's "Word of the Day" XML feed available at this URL: http://xml.education.yahoo.com/rss/wotd/. Use the manual parsing techniques to pull out the Word of the Day from the feed.

18.5 Text Analysis

Loading text from a URL need not only be an exercise in parsing out small bits of information. It is possible with *Processing* to analyze large amounts of text found on the web from news feeds, articles, and speeches, to entire books. A nice source is *Project Gutenberg (http://www.gutenberg.org/)*—which makes available thousands of public domain texts. Algorithms for analyzing text merits an entire book itself, but we will look at one simple beginner example here.

Example 18-6 retrieves the entire text of Shakespeare's play *King Lear*, and uses **split Tokens ()** to make an array of all the words in the play. The sketch then displays the words one by one, along with a count of how many times the word appears in the text.

Example 18-6: Analyzing King Lear

```
PFont f; // A variable to hold onto a font

String[] kinglear; // The array to hold all of the text
int counter = 0;   // Where are we in the text

// We will use spaces and punctuation as delimiters
String delimiters = " ,.?!;:";

void setup() {
  size(200,200);
  // Load the font
  f = loadFont("Georgia-Bold-16.vlw");

  // Load King Lear into an array of strings
  String url = "http://www.gutenberg.org/dirs/etext97/1ws3310.txt";
  String[] rawtext = loadStrings(url);
  // Join the big array together as one long string
  String everything = join(rawtext," ");
  // Split the array into words using any delimiter
  kinglear = splitTokens(everything,delimiters);
  frameRate(5);
}

void draw() {
  background(255);

  // Pick one word from King Lear
  String theword = kinglear[counter];

  // Count how many times that word appears in King Lear
  int total = 0;
```

> Any punctuation is used as a delimiter.

> All the lines in *King Lear* are first joined as one big *String* and then split up into an array of individual words. Note the use of **splitTokens()** since we are using spaces and punctuation marks all as delimiters.

> This loop counts the number of occurrences of the current word being displayed.

```
for (int i = 0; i < kinglear.length; i++) {
  if (theword.equals(kinglear[i])) {
    total++;
  }
}
// Display the text and total times the word appears
textFont(f);
fill(0);
text(theword,10,90);
text(total,10,110);

stroke(0);
fill(175);
rect(10,50,total/4,20);

// Move onto the next word
counter = (counter + 1) % kinglear.length;
}
```

> The word "Lear" appears 226 times in the text of *King Lear.*

Lear
226

fig. 18.10

*Exercise 18-10: Count the number of times each letter of the alphabet appears in King Lear Visualize those counts. Here is one possibility (you should be more creative). Note this sketch will require the use of the **charAt()** function.*

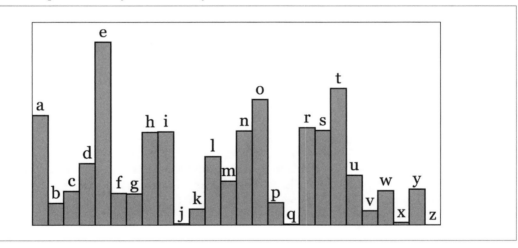

18.6 Asynchronous Requests

As we have seen, the **loadStrings()** function can be used for retrieving raw data from web pages. Nonetheless, unless your sketch only needs to load the data once during **setup()**, you may have a problem. For example, consider a sketch that grabs the price of AAPL stock from an XML feed every 5 min. Each time **loadStrings()** is called, the sketch will pause while waiting to receive the data. Any animation will stutter. This is because **loadStrings()** is a "blocking" function, in other words, the sketch will sit and wait at that line of code until **loadStrings()** completes its task. With a local text file, this is extremely fast. Nonetheless, a request for a web page (known as an "HTTP request") is *asynchronous*, meaning the web server can take its time getting back to you with the data requested. Who knows how long **loadStrings()** will take? No one, you are at the mercy of the server!

The simpleML library (available for download at this book's web site: *http://www.learningprocessing. com/simpleML/*) gets around this problem by executing these HTTP requests to web servers in parallel without pausing your *Processing* sketch, allowing the sketch to multitask and continue animating while the data retrieval is in process.

The library functions in a similar manner to the *Processing* video library, which we became familiar with in Chapter 16. To retrieve a web page, you must create an instance of an HTMLRequest object, passing in a reference to the the sketch itself (*this*) and the URL you want to request.

```
HTMLRequest req = new HTMLRequest(this,"http://www.yahoo.com");
```

The request will not begin, however, until you call makeRequest().

```
req.makeRequest();
```

Finally, to receive the data, you must write a function called ***netEvent()***. This function will be invoked the instant the request is finished and data is available.

This function is another example of a *callback* function, the same as ***captureEvent()*** (see Chapter 16)or ***mousePressed()***. In this case, instead of an event being triggered when the user clicks the mouse or an image from the camera is available, the event is triggered when the HTML request finishes (or XML as we will see in a moment).

The HTML source of the web page is returned as a *String* via the function ***readRawSource()***.

```
void netEvent(HTMLRequest ml) {
    String html = ml.readRawSource();
    println(html);
}
```

Example 18-7 retrieves Yahoo's homepage every ten seconds using the simpleML library. The visualization here is arbitrary (lines are colored according to the characters in Yahoo's HTML source); however, what is important is to notice how the animation never pauses while waiting for the data to arrive.

Example 18-7: Loading a URL with simpleML

```
import simpleML.*;

// A Request object, from the library
HTMLRequest htmlRequest;

Timer timer = new Timer(5000);

String html = "";   // String to hold data from request
int counter = 0;    // Counter to animate rectangle across window
int back = 255;     // Background brightness

void setup() {
  size(200,200);
```

```
  // Create and make an asynchronous request
  htmlRequest = new HTMLRequest(this,"http://www.yahoo.com");
  htmlRequest.makeRequest();
  timer.start();
  background(0);
}
```

> An HTML Request object to request the source from a URL.

```
void draw() {
  background(back);

  // Every 5 seconds, make a new request
  if (timer.isFinished()) {
    htmlRequest.makeRequest();
    println("Making request!");
    timer.start();
  }
```

> A request is made every 5 s. The data is not received here, however, this is only the request.

```
  // Draw some lines with colors based on characters from data retrieved
  for (int i = 0; i < width; i++) {
    if (i < html.length()) {
      int c = html.charAt(i);
      stroke(c,150);
      line(i,0,i,height);
    }
  }

  // Animate rectangle and dim rectangle
  fill(255);
  noStroke();
  rect(counter,0,10,height);
  counter = (counter + 1) % width;
  back = constrain(back - 1,0,255);
}
```

> The data is received in the ***netEvent()*** function which is automatically called whenever data is ready.

```
// When a request is finished
void netEvent(HTMLRequest ml) {
  html = ml.readRawSource();  // Read the raw data
  back = 255;                 // Reset background
  println("Request completed!");// Print message
}

// Timer Class from Chapter 10
class Timer {
  int savedTime;
  boolean running = false;
  int totalTime;

  Timer(int tempTotalTime) {
    totalTime = tempTotalTime;
  }

  void start() {
    running = true;
    savedTime = millis();
  }

  boolean isFinished() {
    int passedTime = millis() - savedTime;
    if (running && passedTime > totalTime) {
      running = false;
```

fig. 18.11

```
      return true;
    } else {
      return false;
    }
  }
}
```

18.7 Beginner XML

The examples in Section 18.4 demonstrated the process of manually searching through text for individual pieces of data. Admittedly, manually parsing the raw XML data from *http://xml.weather.yahoo.com/ forecastrss?p=10003* was not the most efficient strategy. Yes, if you need information from an oddly formed HTML page, these manual techniques are required. However, because XML is designed to facilitate the sharing of data across different systems, it can be parsed without manual searching, using an XML parsing library.

XML organizes information in a tree structure. Let's imagine a list of students. Each student has an id number, name, address, e-mail, and telephone number. Each student's address has a city, state, and zip code. An XML tree for this dataset might look like Figure 18.12.

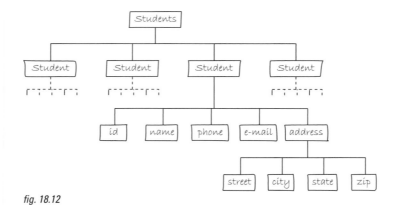

fig. 18.12

The XML source itself (with two students listed) is:

```
<?xml version="1.0" encoding="UTF-8"?>
<students>
    <student>
        <id>001</id>
        <name>Daniel Shiffman</name>
        <phone>555-555-5555</phone>
        <email>daniel@shiffman.net</email>
        <address>
            <street>123 Processing Way</street>
            <city>Loops</city>
            <state>New York</state>
            <zip>01234</zip>
        </address>
    </student>
```

```
<student>
        <id>002</id>
        <name>Zoog</name>
        <phone>555-555-5555</phone>
        <email>zoog@planetzoron.uni</email>
        <address>
                <street>45.3 Nebula 5</street>
                <city>Boolean City</city>
                <state>Booles</state>
                <zip>12358</zip>
        </address>
    </student>
</students>
```

Note the similarities to object-oriented programming. We could think of the XML tree in the following terms. The XML document represents an array of student objects. Each student object has multiple pieces of information, an id, a name, a phone number, an e-mail address, and a mailing address. The mailing address is also an object that also has multiple pieces of data, such as street, city, state, and zip.

Exercise 18-11: Revisit the "Bubble" Example 18-3. Design an XML tree structure for Bubble objects. Diagram the tree and write out the XML source. (Use the empty diagram and fill in the blanks below.)

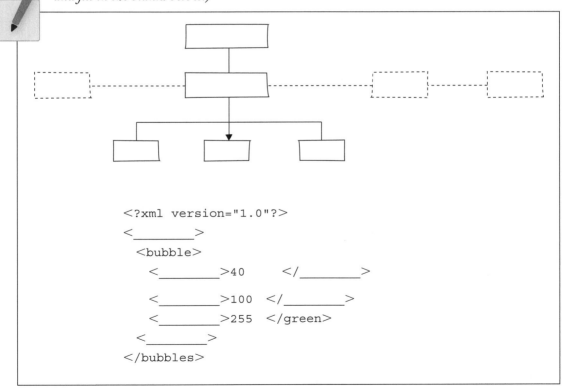

Returning to the weather example, we can now make some sense of Yahoo's XML data with the tree structure terms of a tree. Here is the raw XML source. (Note I have edited it for simplification purposes.)

```
<?xml version="1.0" encoding="UTF-8" standalone="yes" ?>
<rss version="2.0" xmlns:yweather="http://xml.weather.yahoo.com/ns/rss/1.0">
      <channel>
   <item>
      <title>Conditions for New York, NY at 3:51 pm EST</title>
      <geo:lat>40.67</geo:lat>
      <geo:long>-73.94</geo:long>
      <link>http://xml.weather.yahoo.com/forecast/USNY0996_f.html</link>
      <pubDate>Mon, 20 Feb 2006 3:51 pm EST</pubDate>
      <yweather:condition text="Fair" code="34" temp="35" date="Mon, 20 Feb 2006
         3:51 pm EST"/>
      <yweather:forecast day="Mon" date="20 Feb 2006" low="25" high="37"
         text="Clear" code="31"/>
   </item>
      </channel>
</rss>
```

The data is mapped in the tree stucture shown in Figure 18.13.

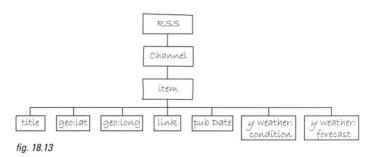

fig. 18.13

You may be wondering what the top level "RSS" is all about. Yahoo's XML weather data is provided in RSS format. RSS stands for "Really Simple Syndication" and is a standardized XML format for syndicating web content (such as news articles, etc.). You can read more about RSS on wikipedia: *http://en.wikipedia.org/wiki/RSS.*

Now that we have a handle on the tree structure, we should look at the specifics inside that structure. With the exception of the first line (which simply indicates that this page is XML formatted), this XML document contains a nested list of *elements*, each with a start tag, that is, <channel> , and an end tag, that is, </channel> . Some of these elements have content between the tags:

```
<title>Conditions for New York, NY at 3:51 pm EST</title>
```

and some have attributes (formatted by *Attribute Name* equals *Attribute Value in quotes*):

```
<yweather:forecast day ="Mon" date="20 Feb 2006" low="25" high="37" text="Clear"
   code="31"/>
```

There are several XML Parsing libraries available for *Processing* and we will explore two in this chapter. The first, designed for this book, is the simplest (but has the fewest features): the simpleML library. simpleML can perform the following three tasks:

- Retrieve the text from one XML element as a *String*.
- Retrieve the text from one attribute of an XML element as a *String*.
- Retrieve the text from many XML elements (with the same tag) as an array of *Strings*.

Requests for XML data are made via an XMLRequest object.

```
XMLRequest req = new XMLRequest(this,"http://xml.weather.yahoo.
com/forecastrss?p=10003");
```

Again, the request will not begin until you call *makeRequest()*.

```
req.makeRequest();
```

Just as with the HTML request, to receive the data from the XML request, you must implement *netEvent()*, this time with an *XMLRequest* object as its argument.

The function *getElementText()* returns the content from a single XML element (the name of that element must be passed into the function). For an attribute, use *getElementAttributeText()* with the name of the element, followed by the name of the attribute.

For example, with the following XML data:

```
<geo:lat>40.67</geo:lat>
<yweather:forecast day="Mon" date="20 Feb 2006" low="25" high="37"
  text="Clear" code="31"/>
```

The code to grab data is:

```
void netEvent(XMLRequest ml) {
    // Getting the text of one Element
    String lat = ml.getElementText("geo:lat");

    // Getting the text of one Attribute from one Element
    String temperature = ml.getElementAttributeText("yweather:forecast","high");

    println("Latitude is: " + lat);
    println("The high temperature is:
      " + temperature);
}
```

> The content of an XML element is retrieved by passing in the element name (in this case "geo:lat") to the *getElementText()* function.

> The content of an XML element's attribute is retrieved by passing in the element name (in this case "yweather:forecast") as well as the attribute name (in this case "high") to the *getElementAttrributeText()* function.

The method *getElementArray()* can also be called to retrieve XML elements that appear multiple times. It returns an array of *Strings*, one *String* for every element in the XML document. The following example grabs all of the headlines from Yahoo's Top Stories XML Feed.

Example 18-8: Loading XML with simpleML

```
import simpleML.*;

XMLRequest xmlRequest;

void setup() {
  size(200,200);
```

```
  // Creating and starting the request
  xmlRequest = new XMLRequest(this,"http://rss.news.yahoo.com/rss/topstories");
  xmlRequest.makeRequest();
}

void draw() {
  noLoop();// Nothing to see here
}

// When the request is complete
void netEvent(XMLRequest ml) {
  // Retrieving an array of all XML elements inside "<title*>" tags
  String[] headlines = ml.getElementArray("title");
  for (int i = 0; i < headlines.length; i++) {
    println(headlines[i]);
  }
}
```

> An array of XML elements can be retrieved using **getElementArray**. This only works for elements with the same name that appear multiple times in the XML document.

Exercise 18-12: Visualize the Yahoo weather data using simpleML. Following is part of the code to get you started. This is the XML in case you forgot: `<yweather:condition text="Fair" code="34" temp="35" date="Mon, 20 Feb 2006 3:51 pm EST"/`

```
import simpleML.*;

// Variables for temperature and weather
int temperature = 0;
String weather = "";

void setup() {
  // FILL THIS IN HOWEVER YOU LIKE!
}

void draw() {
  // FILL THIS IN HOWEVER YOU LIKE!
}

// Function that makes the weather request with a Zip Code
void getWeather(String zip) {
  String url = "http://xml.weather.yahoo.com/
forecastrss?p="+zip;
  XMLRequest req = new XMLRequest(this,url);
  req.makeRequest();
}

void netEvent(XMLRequest ml) {
  // Get the specific XML content we want

  temperature = int(ml._____("_____","_____"));

  weather = ml._____("_____","_____");
}
```

18.8 Using the *Processing* XML Library

The functionality of the simpleML library, though easy to use, is quite limited. If you want to create your own XML documents, or parse multiple elements of a document with a custom algorithm, you are out of luck. For more sophisticated XML functionality, there are two options. The first, more advanced option is *proXML* (*http://www.texone.org/proxml/*) created by Christian Riekoff. While the learning curve is a bit steeper, you have direct access to the XML tree structure and can read *and write* XML documents.

The second option, which we will explore in this chapter, is *Processing's* built-in XML library.

```
import processing.xml.*;
```

Once the library is imported, the first step is to create an XMLElement object. This object will load the data from XML documents (stored locally or on the web). The constructor requires two arguments, "*this*" and the filename or URL path for the XML document.

```
String url = "xmldocument.xml";
XMLElement xml = new XMLElement(this,url);
```

Unlike simpleML, this XML library pauses the sketch and waits for the document to load. For an asynchronous approach to XML parsing, you will need to use proXML.

An XMLElement object represents one element of an XML tree. When a document is first loaded, that element object is always the root element. simpleML did the work of traversing the tree and finding the right information for us. With the *Processing* XML library, we have to do this work ourselves. Although this is more complex, we have more control over how we search and what we search for.

Referring back to Figure 18.13, we can find the temperature via the following path:

1. **The root element of the tree is "RSS."**
2. **"RSS" has a child element named "Channel."**
3. **The 13th child of "Channel" is "item."** (The diagram is simplified to show only one child of channel.)
4. **The sixth child of "item" is "yweather:condition."**
5. **The temperature is stored in "yweather:condition" as the attribute "temp."**

The children of an element are accessed with an index (starting at zero, same as an array) passed into the *getChild()* function. The content of an element is retrieved with *getContent()* and attributes are read as either numbers—*getIntAttribute()*, *getFloatAttribute()*—or text—*getStringAttribute()*.

```
// Accessing the first child element of the root element
XMLElement channel = xml.getChild(0);
```

Following steps 1 through 5 outlined above through the XML tree, we have:

```
XMLElement xml = new XMLElement(this, url);
XMLElement channel = xml.getChild(0);
XMLElement item = channel.getChild(12);        The 13th child of an element is index #12.
XMLElement condition = item.getChild(5);
temp = condition.getIntAttribute("temp");
```

Other useful functions that can call XMLElement objects are:

- *getChildCount()*—returns the total number of children of an XMLElement.
- *getChildren()*—returns all of the children as an array of XMLElements.

In Example 18-3, we used a series of comma separated values in a text file to store information related to Bubble objects. An XML document can also be used in the same manner. Here is a possible solution to Exercise 18-11, an XML tree of Bubble objects. (Note that this solution uses element *attributes* for red and green colors; this was not the format provided in Exercise 18-11 since we had not yet learned about attributes.)

```
<?xml version = "1.0"?>
<bubbles>
   <bubble>
    <diameter>40</diameter>
    <color red="75" green="255"/>
   </bubble>
   <bubble>
    <diameter>20</diameter>
    <color red="255" green="75"/>
   </bubble>
   <bubble>
    <diameter>80</diameter>
    <color red="100" green="150"/>
   </bubble>
</bubbles>
```

> The root element is "bubbles", which has three children.

> Each child "bubble" has two children, "diameter" and "color." The "color" element has two attributes, "red" and "green".

We can use *getChildren()* to receive the array of "Bubble" elements and make a Bubble object from each one. Here is the example (which uses the identical Bubble class from earlier). The new elements are in bold.

Example 18-9: Using *Processing*'s XML library

```
import processing.xml.*;

// An array of Bubble objects
Bubble[] bubbles;

void setup() {
  size(200,200);
  smooth();

  // Load an XML document
  XMLElement xml = new XMLElement(this,"bubbles.xml");
  // Get the total number of bubbles
  int totalBubbles = xml.getChildCount();
  // Make an array the same size
  bubbles = new Bubble[totalBubbles];
  // Get all the child elements
  XMLElement[] children = xml.getChildren();

  for (int i = 0; i < children.length; i++) {
    // The diameter is child 0
```

> Getting the total number of Bubble objects with *getChildCount()*.

```
      XMLElement diameterElement = children[i].getChild(0);
      int diameter = int(diameterElement.getContent());

      // Color is child 1
      XMLElement colorElement = children[i].getChild(1);
      int r = colorElement.getIntAttribute("red");
      int g = colorElement.getIntAttribute("green");
      // Make a new Bubble object with values from XML document
      bubbles[i] = new Bubble(r,g,diameter);
   }
}

void draw() {
  background(100);
  // Display and move all bubbles
  for (int i = 0; i < bubbles.length; i++) {
    bubbles[i].display();
    bubbles[i].drift();
  }
}
```

> The diameter is the *content* of the first element while red and green are *attributes* of the second.

Exercise 18-13: Use the following XML document to initialize an array of objects. Design the objects to use all of the values in each XML element. (Feel free to rewrite the XML document to include more or less data.) If you do not want to retype the XML, it is available at this book's web site.

```xml
<?xml version="1.0"?>
<blobs>
  <blob>
    <location x="99" y="192"/>
    <speed x="-0.88238335" y="2.2704291"/>
    <size w="38" h="10"/>
  </blob>
  <blob>
    <location x="97" y="14"/>
    <speed x="2.8775783" y="2.9483867"/>
    <size w="81" h="43"/>
  </blob>
  <blob>
    <location x="159" y="193"/>
    <speed x="-1.2341062" y="0.44016743"/>
    <size w="19" h="95"/>
  </blob>
  <blob>
```

```
                  <location x="102" y="53"/>
                  <speed x="0.8000488" y="-2.2791147"/>
                  <size w="25" h="95"/>
               </blob>
               <blob>
                  <location x="152" y="181"/>
                  <speed x="1.9928784" y="-2.9540048"/>
                  <size w="74" h="19"/>
               </blob>
            </blobs>
```

18.9 The Yahoo API

Loading HTML and XML documents is convenient for pulling information from the web, however, for more sophisticated applications, many sites offer an API. An API (Application Programming Interface) is an interface through which one application can access the services of another. There are many APIs that can be used with *Processing* and you might look through the "Data / Protocols" section of the *Processing* libraries web page (*http:/processing.org/reference/libraries/index.html*) for some ideas.

In this section, we will look at an example that performs a web search, using the Yahoo API. Although you can access the Yahoo API directly, I have created a *Processing* library that makes it a bit simpler (as well as allowing the search to be performed asynchronously and not cause the sketch to pause). You will need to download both my *Processing* library, as well as the Yahoo API files (these are known as an SDK: "Software Development Kit"). Instructions for this can be found at the library page:

   http://www.learningprocessing.com/libraries/yahoo/

Once you have downloaded the files, you must first get a Yahoo API key. In many cases, companies will require that you register and get a key before having access to their API. That way, they can track your usage and make sure you are not up to anything nefarious. It is a small price to pay for free programmatic access to Yahoo's features. You can register for the ID here:

   https://developer.yahoo.com/wsregapp/index.php

Once you have the key, you are ready to go. The library works in a similar fashion to simpleML. You make a YahooSearch object and call the **search()** function. When the search is completed, it will arrive in an event callback: **searchEvent()**. There, you can ask for information about the search results, such as URLs, titles, or summaries (all available as *String* arrays).

Example 18-10: A Yahoo search

```
import pyahoo.*;

YahooSearch yahoo;

void setup() {
  size(400,400);
  // Make a search object, pass in your key
  yahoo = new YahooSearch(this,"YOUR API KEY HERE");
}

void mousePressed() {
  yahoo.search("processing.org");
}

void draw() {
  noLoop();
}

// When the search is complete
void searchEvent(YahooSearch yahoo) {
  // Get Titles and URLs
  String[] titles = yahoo.getTitles();
  String[] urls = yahoo.getUrls();
  for (int i = 0; i < titles.length; i++) {
    println("_____");
    println(titles[i]);
    println(urls[i]);
  }
}
```

> Create a *YahooSearch* object. You have to pass in the API key given to you by Yahoo.

> Search for a *String*. By default you will get back 10 results. If you want more (or less), you can request a specific number by saying:
> ```
> yahoo.search("processing.
> org", 30);
> ```

> Search results arrive as an array of *Strings*. You can also get the summaries with ***getSummaries()***.

The library can be used to perform a simple visualization. The following example searches for five names and draws a circle for each one (with a size tied to the total number of results available).

Example 18-11: Yahoo search visualization

```
import pyahoo.*;

YahooSearch yahoo;
PFont f;

// The names to search, an array of "Bubble" objects
String[] names = {"Aliki","Cleopatra","Penelope","Daniel","Peter"};
Bubble[] bubbles = new Bubble[names.length];
int searchCount = 0;

void setup() {
  size(500,300);
  yahoo = new YahooSearch(this,"YOUR APPI HERE");
  f = loadFont("Georgia-20.vlw");
  textFont(f);
  smooth();
  // Search for all names
  for (int i = 0; i < names.length; i++) {
    yahoo.search(names[i]);
  }
}
```

> The ***search()*** function is called for each name in the array.

```
void draw() {
  background(255);
  // Show all bubbles
  for (int i = 0; i < searchCount; i++) {
    bubbles[i].display();
  }
}

// Searches come in one at a time
void searchEvent(YahooSearch yahoo) {
  // Total # of results for each search
  int total = yahoo.getTotalResultsAvailable();
  // Scale down the number so that it can be viewable
  float r = sqrt(total)/75;
  // Make a new bubble object
  Bubble b = new Bubble(yahoo.getSearchString(), r,50+searchCount*100,height/2);
  bubbles[searchCount] = b;
  searchCount++;
}

// Simple "Bubble" class to represent each search
class Bubble {
  String search;
  float x,y,r;

  Bubble(String search_, float r_, float x_, float y_) {
    search = search_;
    r = r_;
    x = x_;
    y = y_;
  }

  void display() {
    stroke(0);
    fill(0,50);
    ellipse(x, y, r, r);
    textAlign(CENTER);
    fill(0);
    text(search,x,y);
  }
}
```

> **getTotalResultsAvailable()** returns the total number of web pages that Yahoo found containing the search phrase. These numbers can be quite large so they are scaled down before being used as an ellipse size.

> The search data is used to make a Bubble object for the visualization.

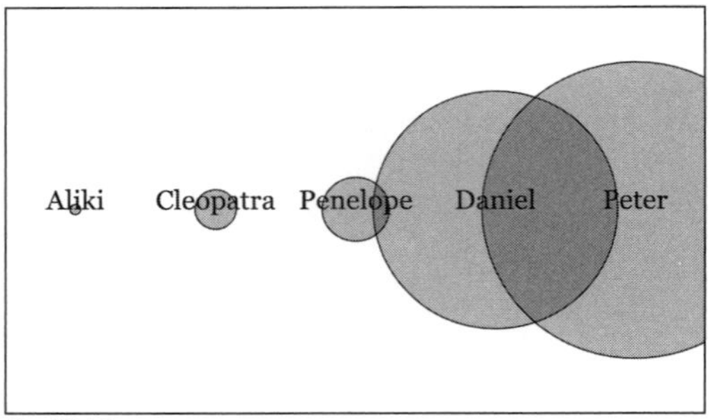

fig. 18.14

18.10 Sandbox

When running your program locally from within the *Processing* development environment, you are free to reach out across ports and networks. However, when running your program as an applet within a web browser, there are certain security requirements, just as we noticed with connecting to a video camera in Chapter 16.

Requesting a URL on the same domain is allowed. For example, if your applet is stored on your web site: *http://www.myrockindomain.com* you are in the clear with:

```
// Will work in the browser
String[] lines = loadStrings("http://www.myrockindomain.com/data.html");
```

However, if you request a URL on a different domain, you are out of luck.

```
// Will not work in the browser
String[] lines = loadStrings("http://www.yourkookoodomain.com");
```

A solution for this problem is to create a proxy script that lives on the server with your applet, connects to an external URL and passes that information back to the applet—in essence, you are tricking your applet into thinking it is retrieving only local information.

Another solution is to "sign" your applet. Signing an applet is the process of saying "Hello, my name is Daniel Shiffman and I made this applet. If you trust me say 'yes' to let this applet access resources it might not normally be allowed to access."

Again, if you are just developing sketches locally on your computer in the *Processing* development environment you will not have an issue. If you need to get your applet working on a web server and need to make requests to pages not on that server, please visit this book's web site (*http://www.learningprocessing.com/sandbox/*) for an example PHP proxy script as well as tips on how to sign your applets.

19 Data Streams

"I'm mad as hell and I'm not going to take this anymore!"
—Howard Beale, Network

In this chapter:
- Sockets.
- Servers.
- Clients.
- Multi-user processing.
- Serial input.

19.1 Synchronous vs. Asynchronous

In Chapter 18, we looked at how we can request the raw source of a URL using ***loadStrings()***, the simpleML library, or the XML library. You make the request, sit back, and await the results. You may have noticed that this process does not happen instantaneously. Sometimes the program may pause for seconds (or even minutes) while a web page or XML document loads. This is due to the length of time required for what *Processing* performs behind the scenes—an HTTP request. HTTP stands for "Hypertext Transfer Protocol," a request/response protocol for the transfer of information on the world wide web.

Let's consider, for a moment, what we mean by "request/response." Perhaps you wake up one morning and think to yourself that a vacation, say in Tuscany, is in order. You turn on your computer, launch a web browser, type *www.google.com* in the address bar, and enter "romantic getaway Tuscany villa". You, the *client*, made a request, and it is the job of google, the *server*, to provide a response.

```
                          The Client:
Just to introduce myself, I'm Firefox, the web browser, and I have a request. I was
wondering if you might be so kind as to send me your web page about vacation villas in
Tuscany?


                        [Dramatic Pause]

                          The Server:
Sure, no problem, here is my response. It's really just a whole lot of bytes, but if you
read it as html you'll see it's a nicely formatted page about Tuscany vacation rentals.
Enjoy! Oh, can you let me know that you received it ok?

                          The Client:
Got it, thanks!
                [The Client and the Server shake hands.]
```

The above process is known as an *asynchronous* request and response, bi-directional communication between a server and a client where the server responds at its leisure. The connection is established temporarily in order to transfer the web page after which it is promptly closed.

In terms of sending information along the world wide web, this methodology is perfectly adequate. Nevertheless, imagine if you were to use asynchronous communication in a multiplayer game. It would be a disaster. Having to open and close the connection every time one player sends a message to another would result in huge delays and lag between movements. For multiuser applications in *Processing* where we need near real-time communication, a different type of connection is used, a *synchronous* one known as a *socket* connection. Synchronous communication is also necessary for live performance applications that need real-time interaction between elements. See Figure 19.1.

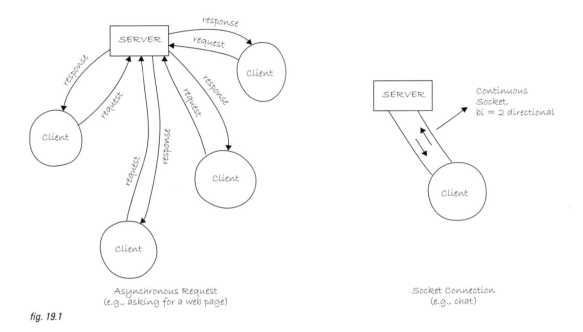

Asynchronous Request
(e.g., asking for a web page)

Socket Connection
(e.g., chat)

fig. 19.1

A network *socket* connection is a continuous connection between two programs across a network. Sockets are used for multi-user applications, such as games, instant messenger, and chat (among other things). They consist of an IP address—the numeric address of a machine on the network—and a port number—a number used to route information from one program to another.

We can use sockets in *Processing* to write programs that can communicate with each other in real-time. To do this, we will use the built-in *net* library (*processing.net*) to create servers and clients connecting via sockets.

19.2 Creating a Server

In order to create a server, we need to choose a port number. Any client that wants to connect to the server will need to know this number. Port numbers range from 0 to 65,536 and any number is fair game, however, ports 0 through 1,024 are usually reserved for common services, so it is best to avoid those. If you are unsure, a google search will turn up information on whether the port is likely used by another application. For our purposes, we will use the port 5,204 (this is the same port used in the *Processing* net library reference that you would find at *processing.org*).

To create a server, we must first import the library and create an instance of a ***Server*** object.

```
import processing.net.*;

Server server;
```

The server is initialized via the constructor, which takes two arguments: "this" (a reference to *this* applet as explained in Chapter 16) and an integer value for a port number.

```
server = new Server(this, 5204);
```

The ***Server*** starts and waits for connections as soon as it is created. It can be closed at any time by calling the ***stop()*** function.

```
server.stop();
```

You may recall from our discussion of video capturing in Chapter 16 that we used a ***callback*** function (***captureEvent()***) to handle a new frame of video available from the camera. We can find out if a new client has connected to our server with the same technique, using the callback function ***serverEvent()***. ***serverEvent()*** requires two arguments, a server (the one generating the event) and a client (that has connected). We might use this function, for example, to retrieve the IP address of the connected client.

```
// The serverEvent function is called whenever
// A new client connects
void serverEvent(Server server, Client client) {
  println("A new client has connected: " + client.ip());
}
```

> Server events occur *only* when a new client connects.

When a client sends a message (after having connected), a ***serverEvent()*** is *not* generated. Instead, we must use the ***available()*** function to determine if there is a new message from any client available to be read. If there is, a reference to the client broadcasting the method is returned and we can read the content using the ***readString()*** method. If nothing is available, the function will return the value *null,* meaning no value (or no client object exists).

```
void draw() {
  // If a client is available, we will find out
  // If there is no client, it will be "null"
  Client someClient = server.available();
  // We should only proceed if the client is not null
  if (someClient! = null) {
    println("Client says: " + SomeClient.readString());
  }
}
```

The function ***readString()*** is useful in applications where text information is sent across the network. If the data should be treated differently, for instance, as a number (as we will see in future examples), other ***read()*** methods can be called.

A server can also send messages out to clients, and this is done with the ***write()*** method.

```
server.write("Great, thanks for the message!\n");
```

Depending on what you are doing, it is often a good idea to send a **newline** character at the end of your messages. The escape sequence for adding a **newline** character to a *String* is '**\n**' (for a reminder about escape characters see Chapter 18).

Putting all of the above together, we can write a simple chat server. This server replies to any message it receives with the phrase "How does 'that' make you feel?" See Example 19-1, Figure 19.2.

Example 19-1: Simple therapy server

```
// Import the net libraries
import processing.net.*;

// Declare a server
Server server;

// Used to indicate a new message has arrived
float newMessageColor = 255;

PFont f;
String incomingMessage = "";

void setup() {
  size(400,200);
  // Create the Server on port 5204
  server = new Server(this, 5204);          This sketch runs a Server on port 5204.
  f = createFont("Arial",16,true);
}

void draw() {
  background(newMessageColor);

  // newMessageColor fades to white over time
  newMessageColor = constrain(newMessageColor+0.3,0,255);
  textFont(f);
  textAlign(CENTER);                          The most recent incoming message
  fill(255);                                  is displayed in the window.
  text(incomingMessage,width/2,height/2);

  // If a client is available, we will find out
  // If there is no client, it will be "null"
  Client client = server.available();
  // We should only proceed if the client is not null
  if (client!=null) {                                 The message is read using
    // Receive the message                            readString(). The trim()
    incomingMessage = client.readString();            function is used to remove
    incomingMessage = incomingMessage.trim();         the extra line break that
    // Print to Processing message window             comes in with the message.
    println("Client says: " + incomingMessage);
    // Write message back out (note this goes to ALL clients)
    server.write("How does " + incomingMessage + " make you feel?\n");
    // Reset newMessageColor to black
    newMessageColor = 0;                        A reply is sent using write().
  }
}

// The serverEvent function is called whenever a new client connects.
void serverEvent(Server server, Client client) {
  incomingMessage = "A new client has connected: " + client.ip();
  println(incomingMessage);
  // Reset newMessageColor to black
  newMessageColor = 0;
}
```

Once the server is running, we can create a client that connects to the server. Ultimately, we will look at an example where we write both the server and client in *Processing.* However, just to demonstrate that the server is in fact working, we can connect to it using any ***telnet*** client application. Telnet is a standard protocol for remote connections and all machines generally come with built-in telnet abilities. On a Mac, launch terminal, on Windows, go to the command prompt. I also recommend using PuTTY, a free telnet client: *http://www.chiark.greenend.org.uk/~sgtatham/putty/.*

Since we are connecting to the server from the same machine that the server is running on, the address we telnet to is *localhost,* meaning the local computer, port 5,204. We could also use the address 127.0.0.1. This is a special address reserved for programs on a computer to speak to each other locally (i.e., on the same machine) and is the equivalent of *localhost.* If we were connecting from a different computer, we would have to know the network IP address of the machine running the server.

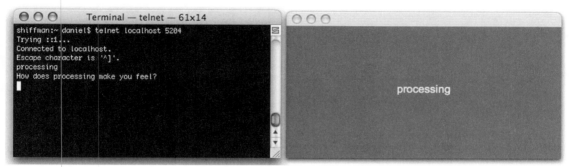

fig. 19.2

Telnet clients traditionally send messages to the server when the user types enter. The carriage return and line feed are included in the message and therefore when the server sends back the reply, you will notice that "How does processing" and "make you feel" appear on separate lines.

Exercise 19-1: Using String manipulation techniques from Chapter 15, fix Example 19-1 so that if the client sends newline characters, the server removes them before replying back to the client. You will want to alter the "incomingMessage" variable.

```
incomingMessage = client.readString();
incomingMessage = incomingMessage. _____ (_____, _____);
```

19.3 Creating a Client

Once we have written a server and tested it with telnet, we can then develop our own ***client*** in *Processing.* We start off the same way we did with a server, importing the net library and declaring an instance of a Client object.

```
import processing.net.*;

Client client;
```

The client constructor requires three arguments—"this", referring again to *this PApplet*, the IP address we want to connect to (as a *String)*, and the port number (as an integer).

```
client = new Client(this, "127.0.0.1", 5204);
```

If the server is running on a different computer than the client, you will need to know the IP address of that server computer. In addition, if there is no server running at the specified IP and port, the *Processing* sketch will give the error message: *"java.net.ConnectException: Connection refused"* meaning either the server rejected the client or that there is no server.

Sending to the server is easy using the **write()** function.

```
client.write("Hello!");
```

Reading messages from the server is done with the **read()** function. The **read()** method, however, reads from the server one byte at a time. To read the entire message as a *String*, **readString()** is used.

Before we can even contemplate reading from the server, we must be sure there is something to read. This check happens with **available()**. **available()** returns the number of bytes that are waiting to be read. We can determine if there is anything waiting to be read by asking if the number of bytes is greater than zero.

```
if (client.available() > 0) {
    String message = client.readString();
}
```

Using the code from Example 18-1, (keyboard input), we can create a *Processing* client that connects and communicates with our server, sending messages entered by the user. See Example 19-2.

Example 19-2: Simple therapy client

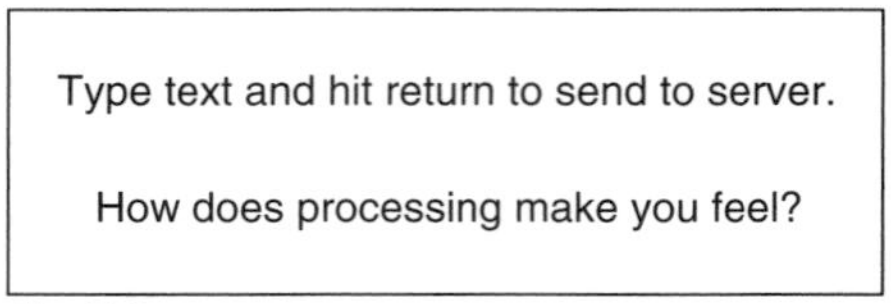

```
// Import the net libraries
import processing.net.*;

// Declare a client
Client client;

// Used to indicate a new message
float newMessageColor = 0;
// A String to hold whatever the server says
String messageFromServer = "";

// A String to hold what the user types
String typing = "";
PFont f;

void setup() {
  size(400,200);
  // Create the Client
  client = new Client(this, "127.0.0.1", 5204);
  f = createFont("Arial",16,true);
}
```

Type text and hit return to send to server.

How does processing make you feel?

fig. 19.3

Connect to server at 127.0.0.1 (localhost), port 5204

```
void draw() {
  background(255);

  // Display message from server
  fill(newMessageColor);
  textFont(f);
  textAlign(CENTER);
  text(messageFromServer,width/2,140);
  // Fade message from server to white
  newMessageColor = constrain(newMessageColor+1,0,255);

  // Display Instructions
  fill(0);
  text("Type text and hit return to send to server.",width/2,60);
  // Display text typed by user
  fill(0);
  text(typing,width/2,80);

  // If there is information available to read
    if (client.available() > 0) {
    // Read it as a String
    messageFromServer = client.readString();
    // Set brightness to 0
    newMessageColor = 0;
  }
}


// Simple user keyboard input
void keyPressed() {
  // If the return key is pressed, save the String and clear it
  if (key == '\n') {
    // When the user hits enter, write the sentence out to the Server

    client.write(typing);
    typing = "";
  } else {
    typing = typing + key;
  }
}
```

> The new message fades to white by increasing the brightness.

> We know there is a message from the Server when there are greater than zero bytes available.

> When the user hits enter, the String typed is sent to the Server.

 Exercise 19-2: Create a client and server that talk to each other. Have the client send messages typed by the user and the server respond autonomously. For example, you could use String parsing techniques to reverse the words sent by the client. Client: "How are you?" Server: "You are how?"

19.4 Broadcasting

Now that we understand the basics of how clients and servers work, we can examine more practical uses of networked communication. In the therapist client/server examples, we treated the data sent across the network as a *String*, but this may not always be the case. In this section, we will look at writing a server that broadcasts numeric data to clients.

How is this useful? What if you wanted to continuously broadcast the temperature outside your house or a stock quote or the amount of motion seen by a camera? You could set up a single computer running a

Processing server to process and broadcast that information. Client sketches from anywhere in the world could connect to this machine to receive the information.

To demonstrate the framework for such a program, we will write a server that broadcasts a number between 0 and 255 (we can only send one byte at time). We will then look at clients that retrieve the data and interpret it in their own way.

Here is the server, which increments a number randomly and broadcasts it.

Example 19-3: Server broadcasting a number (0–255)

```
// Import the net libraries
import processing.net.*;

// Declare a server
Server server;

PFont f;
int data = 0;

void setup() {
  size(200,200);
  // Create the Server on port 5204
  server = new Server(this, 5204);
  f = createFont("Arial",20,true);
}

void draw() {
  background(255);

  // Display data
  textFont(f);
  textAlign(CENTER);
  fill(0);
  text(data,width/2,height/2);

  // Broadcast data
  server.write(data);

  // Arbitrarily changing the value of data randomly
  data = (data + int(random(-2,4))) % 256;
}
// The serverEvent function is called whenever a new client connects.
void serverEvent(Server server, Client client) {
  println("A new client has connected: " + client.ip());
}
```

178

fig. 19.4

> The number is continuously sent to all clients because *write()* is called every cycle through *draw()*.

Next, we will write a client that receives the number from the server and uses it to fill a variable. The example is written with the assumption that the server and the client are running on the same computer (you can open both examples and run them together in *Processing*), but in a real world scenario this would likely not be the case. If you choose to run the server and clients on different computers, the machines must be networked locally (via a router or hub, ethernet or wifi) or on the internet. The IP address can be found in the network settings of your machine.

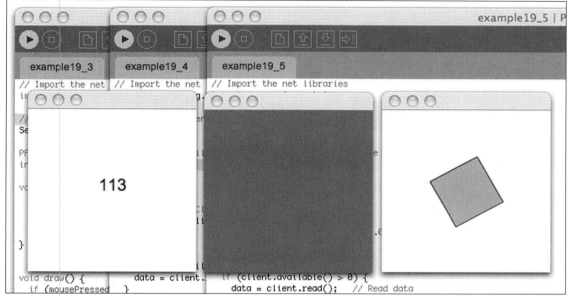

fig. 19.5 Examples 19-3, 19-4, and 19-5 all running together

Example 19-4: Client reading values as background color

```
// Import the net libraries
import processing.net.*;

// Declare a client
Client client;

// The data we will read from the server
int data;

void setup() {
  size(200,200);
  // Create the Client
  client = new Client(this, "127.0.0.1", 5204);
}

void draw() {
  if (client.available() > 0) {
    data = client.read(); // Read data
  }
  background(data);
}
```

The incoming data is used to color the background.

Example 19-5: Client reading values as rotation value

```
// Import the net libraries
import processing.net.*;

// Declare a client
Client client;

// The data we will read from the server
int data;

void setup() {
  size(200,200);
  smooth();
  // Create the Client
  client = new Client(this, "127.0.0.1", 5204);
}

void draw() {
  if (client.available() > 0) {
    data = client.read(); // Read data
  }
  background(255);
  stroke(0);
  fill(175);
  translate(width/2,height/2);
  float theta = (data/255.0) * TWO_PI;
  rotate(theta);
  rectMode(CENTER);
  rect(0,0,64,64);
}
```

> The incoming data is used to rotate a square.

Exercise 19-3: Write a client that uses the number broadcast from the server to control the location of a shape.

19.5 Multi-User Communication, Part 1: The Server

The broadcast example demonstrates one-way communication where a server broadcasts a message and many clients receive that message. The broadcast model, however, does not allow a client to turn around and send a reply back to the server. In this section, we will cover how to create a sketch that involves communication between multiple clients facilitated by a server.

Let's explore how a chat room works. Five clients (you and four friends) connect to a server. One client types a message: "Hey everyone!" That message is sent to the server, which relays it back to all five clients. Most multi-user applications function in a similar fashion. A multiplayer online game, for example, would likely have clients sending information related to their whereabouts and actions to a server that broadcasts that data back to all other clients playing the game.

A multi-user application can be developed in *Processing* using the network library. To demonstrate, we will create a networked, shared whiteboard. As a client drags its mouse around the screen, the sketch will send *X,Y* coordinates to the server that passes them back to any other connected clients. Everyone connected will be able to see the drawing actions of everyone else.

In addition to learning how to communicate between multiple clients, this example will explore how to send multiple values. How can a client send two values (an *X* and a *Y* coordinate) and have the server know which one is which?

The first step toward a solution involves developing a protocol for communication between the clients. In what format is the information sent and how is that information received and interpreted? Luckily for us, the time we spent learning how to create, manage, and parse *String* objects in Chapters 17 and 18 will provide all the tools we need.

Assume a client wants to send the mouse location: ***mouseX*** = 150 and ***mouseY*** = 125. We need to format that information as a *String* in a way that is convenient to decipher. One possibility is as follows:

> *"The first number before the comma is the X location, the second number after the comma is 125. Our data ends where an asterisk (*) appears."*

In code, it would appear as follows:

```
String dataToSend = "100,125*";
```

or, more generally:

```
String dataToSend = mouseX + "," + mouseY + "*";
```

Here, we have developed a protocol for sending and receiving data. The integer values for ***mouseX*** and ***mouseY*** are encoded as a *String* during sending (number, followed by comma, followed by number, followed by asterisk). They will have to be decoded upon receipt and we will get to that later. I should also point out that most examples will typically use a *newline* or *carriage return* to mark the end of a message (as we saw in the first section of this chapter). We use an asterisk here for two reasons: (1) an asterisk is plainly visible when displayed whereas newline is not (especially in the context of a book) and (2) using an asterisk demonstrates that you can design and implement any messaging protocol you so choose as long as it matches up in the client and server code.

What is really sent?

Data sent across a network is sent as a sequential list of individual bytes. Recalling the discussion of data types in Chapter 4, a byte is an 8-bit number, that is, a number made up of eight 0's and 1's or a value between 0 and 255.

Let's assume we want to send the number 42. We have two options:

```
client.write(42); // sending the byte 42
```

In the line above, we are really sending the actual byte 42.

```
client.write("42"); // sending the String "42"
```

In the line above, we are sending a *String*. That *String* is made up of two characters, a '4' and a '2'. We are sending two bytes! Those bytes are determined via the ASCII (American Standard Code for Information Interchange) code, a standardized means for encoding characters. The character 'A' is byte 65, the character 'B' 66, and so on. The character '4' is byte 52 and '2' is 50.

When we read the data, it is up to us to know whether we want to interpret the bytes coming in as literal numeric values or as ASCII codes for characters. We accomplish this by choosing the appropriate **read()** function.

```
int val = client.read(); // matches up with client.write(42);

String s = client.readString(); // matches up with client.write("42");
int num = int(s); // convert the String that is read into a number
```

We are now ready to create a server to receive the messages from the client. It will be the client's job to format those messages with our protocol. The job of the server remains simple: (1) receive the data and (2) relay the data. This is similar to the approach we took in Section 19.2.

Step 1. Receiving data.

```
Client client = server.available();
if (client != null) {
  incomingMessage = client.readStringUntil('*');
}
```

> Because we designed our own protocol and are not using newline/carriage return to mark the end of our message, we must use *readStringUntil()* instead of *readString()*.

What is new in this example is the function *readStringUntil()*. The *readStringUntil()* function takes one argument, a character. That character is used to mark the end of the incoming data. We are simply following the protocol established during sending. We are able to do this because we are designing both the server *and* the client.

Once that data is read, we are ready to add:

Step 2. Relaying data back out to clients.

```
Client client = server.available();
if (client != null) {
  incomingMessage = client.readStringUntil('*');
  server.write(incomingMessage);
}
```

> Writing the message back out to all clients.

Here is the full Server with some bells and whistles. A message is displayed onscreen when new clients connect as well as when the server receives data.

Example 19-6: Multi-user server

```
// Import the net libraries
import processing.net.*;

// Declare a server
Server server;

PFont f;
String incomingMessage = "";

void setup() {
  size(400,200);
  // Create the Server on port 5204
  server = new Server(this, 5204);
  f = createFont("Arial",20,true);
}

void draw() {
  background(255);

  // Display rectangle with new message color
  fill(0);
  textFont(f);
  textAlign(CENTER);
  text(incomingMessage,width/2,height/2);

  // If a client is available, we will find out
  // If there is no client, it will be "null"
  Client client = server.available();
  // We should only proceed if the client is not null
  if (client != null) {
    // Receive the message
    incomingMessage = client.readStringUntil('*');
    // Print to Processing message window
    println("Client says: " + incomingMessage);
    // Write message back out (note this goes to ALL clients)
    server.write(incomingMessage);
  }
}

// The serverEvent function is called whenever a new client connects.
void serverEvent(Server server, Client client) {
  incomingMessage = "A new client has connected: " + client.ip();
  println(incomingMessage);
}
```

> All messages received from one client are immediately relayed back out to all clients with **write()**.

19.6 Multi-User Communication, Part 2: The Client

The client's job is three-fold:

1. *Send mouseX and mouseY coordinates to server.*
2. *Retrieve messages from server.*
3. *Display ellipses in the window based on server messages.*

For Step 1, we need to adhere to the protocol we established for sending:

mouseX comma mouseY asterisk

```
String out = mouseX + "," + mouseY + "*";
client.write(out);
```

The question remains: when is the appropriate time to send that information? We could choose to insert those two lines of code into the main **draw()** loop, sending mouse coordinates every frame. In the case of a whiteboard client, however, we only need to send the coordinates when the user drags the mouse around the window.

The **mouseDragged()** function is an event handling function similar to **mousePressed()**. Instead of being called when a user clicks the mouse, it is called whenever a dragging event occurs, that is, the mouse button is pressed and the mouse is moving. Note the function is called continuously as a user drags the mouse. This is where we choose to do our sending.

```
void mouseDragged() {
  String out = mouseX + "," + mouseY + "*";
  // Send the String to the server
  client.write(out);
  // Print a message indicating we have sent data
  println("Sending: " + out);
}
```

> Put the *String* together with our protocol:
> ***mouseX*** comma ***mouseY*** asterisk.

Step 2, retrieving messages from the server, works much like the therapy client and broadcast client examples. The only difference is the use of **readStringUntil()**, which follows the "number-comma-number-asterisk" protocol.

```
if (client.available() > 0) {
  // Read message as a String, all messages end with an asterisk
  String in = client.readStringUntil('*');
  // Print message received
  println("Receiving: " + in);
}
```

Once the data is placed into a *String* object, it can be interpreted with parsing techniques from Chapter 18.

First, the *String* is split into an array of *Strings* using the comma (or asterisk) as the delimiter.

```
String[] splitUp = split(in,",*");
```

The *String* array is then converted into an array of integers (length: 2).

```
int[] vals = int(splitUp);
```

And those integers are used to display an ellipse.

```
fill(255,100);
noStroke();
ellipse(vals[0],vals[1],16,16);
```

Here is the entire client sketch:

Example 19-7: Client for multi-user whiteboard

```
// Import the net libraries
import processing.net.*;

// Declare a client
Client client;

void setup() {
  size(200,200);
  // Create the Client
  client = new Client(this, "127.0.0.1", 5204);
  background(255);
  smooth();
}

void draw() {
  // If there is information available to read from the Server
  if (client.available() > 0) {
    // Read message as a String, all messages end with an asterisk
    String in = client.readStringUntil('*');
    // Print message received
    println("Receiving: " + in);
    // Split up the String into an array of integers
    int[] vals = int(splitTokens(in,",*"));
    // Render an ellipse based on those values
    fill(0,100);
    noStroke();
    ellipse(vals[0],vals[1],16,16);
  }
}

// Send data whenever the user drags the mouse
void mouseDragged() {
    // Put the String together with our protocol: mouseX comma mouseY asterisk
    String out = mouseX + "," + mouseY + "*";
    // Send the String to the server
    client.write(out);
    // Print a message indicating we have sent data
    println("Sending: " + out);
}
```

> The client reads messages from the Server and parses them with *splitTokens()* according to our protocol.

> A message is sent whenever the mouse is dragged. Note that a client will receive its own messages! Nothing is drawn here!

19.7 Multi-User Communication, Part 3: All Together Now

When running a multi-user application, the order in which the elements are launched is important. The client sketches will fail unless the server sketch is already running.

You should first (a) identify the IP address of the server, (b) choose a port and add it to the server's code, and (c) run the server.

Afterward, you can launch the clients with the correct IP address and port.

If you are working on a multi-user project, you most likely want to run the servers and clients on separate computers. After all, this is the point of creating multi-user applications in the first place. However, for testing and development purposes, it is often convenient to run all the elements from one computer. In this case, the server IP address will be "localhost" or 127.0.0.1 (note this is the IP address used in this chapter's examples).

As will be covered in Section 21.3, *Processing*'s "export to application" feature will allow you to export a stand-alone application for your server, which you can then run in the background while you develop your client in *Processing*. Details as to how "export to application" works can be found in Chapter 18. You can also run multiple copies of a stand-alone application to simulate an environment with more than one client. Figure 19.6 shows the server running with two client instances.

fig. 19.6 *Examples 19-6 and 19-7 running together*

 Exercise 19-4: Expand the whiteboard to allow for color. Each client should send a red, green, and blue value in addition to the XY location. You will not need to make any changes to the server for this to work.

 Exercise 19-5: Create a two-player game of Pong played over the network. This is a complex assignment, so build it up slowly. For instance, you should get Pong to work first without networking (if you are stuck, an example is provided at the book's web site). You will also need to make changes to the server; specifically, the server will need to assign the players a paddle as they connect (left or right).

19.8 Serial Communication

A nice reward for learning the ins and outs of networked communication is that it makes serial communication in *Processing* a breeze. Serial communication involves reading bytes from the computer's serial port. These bytes might come from a piece of hardware you purchase (a serial joystick, for example) or one that you design yourself by building a circuit and programming a microcontroller.

This book does not cover the external hardware side of serial communication. However, if you are interested in learning more about physical computing, I recommend the book *Physical Computing: Sensing and Controlling the Physical World with Computers* (Course Technology PTR) by Dan O'Sullivan and Tom Igoe as well as *Making Things Talk: Practical Methods for Connecting Physical Objects* (Make Books) by Tom Igoe. The **Arduino** (*http://www.arduino.cc/*) and **Wiring** (*http://wiring.org.co/*) web sites are also excellent resources. Wiring and Arduino are two open-source physical computing platforms developed at the Interaction Design Institute Ivrea with a programming language modeled after *Processing*. I will provide some accompanying Arduino code for your reference, but the material in this book will only cover what to do once the data has already arrived in *Processing*.

Serial communication refers to the process of sending data in sequence, one byte at a time. This is how data was sent over the network in our client/server examples. The *Processing* serial library is designed for serial communication into the computer from a local device, most likely via a USB (Universal Serial Bus) port. The term "serial" refers to the serial port, designed to interface with modems, that is rarely found on newer computers.

The process of reading data from a serial port is virtually identical to that found in the networked client/ server examples, with a few exceptions. First, instead of importing the network library, we import the serial library and create a Serial object.

```
import processing.serial.*;
Serial port = new Serial(this, "COM1", 9600);
```

The Serial constructor takes three arguments. The first one is always "this," referring to *this* applet (see Chapter 16). Argument 2 is a *String* representing the communications port being used. Computers label ports with a name. On a PC, these will likely be "COM1," "COM2," "COM3," and so on. On UNIX-based computers (such as MAC OS X), they will be labeled "*/dev/tty.something*" where "something" represents a terminal device. If you are using a USB device, you will probably need to install USB drivers before a working port will be available. Instructions for how to get this working with Arduino can be found at the Arduino guide: *http://www.arduino.cc/en/Guide/HomePage*.

You can also print out a list of available ports using the Serial library's *list()* function, which returns an array of *String* objects.

```
String[] portList = Serial.list();
println(portList);
```

If the port you want to use is the first one in the list, for example, your call to the constructor would look like:

```
String[] portList = Serial.list();
Serial port = new Serial(this, portList[0], 9600);
```

The third argument is the rate at which the data is transmitted serially, typically 9,600 baud.

Bytes are sent out via the serial port using the *write()* function. The following data types can be sent: byte, char, int, byte array, and *String*. Remember, if you are sending a *String*, the actual data sent are raw ASCII byte values of each character.

```
port.write(65); // Sending the byte 65
```

Data can be read with the same functions found in clients and servers: *read()*, *readString()*, and *readStringUntil()*. A callback function, *serialEvent()*, is triggered whenever a serial event occurs, that is, whenever there is data available to be read.

```
void serialEvent(Serial port) {
    int input = port.read();
    println("Raw Input: " + input);
}
```

The *read()* function will return a −1 if there is nothing available to read, however, assuming you are writing the code inside *serialEvent()*, there will always be available data.

Following is an example that reads data from the serial port and uses it to color the sketch's background.

Example 19-8: Reading from serial port

```
import processing.serial.*;

int val = 0; // To store data from serial port, used to color background
Serial port; // The serial port object

void setup() {
  size(200,200);

  // In case you want to see the list of available ports
  // println(Serial.list());

  // Using the first available port (might be different on your computer)
  port = new Serial(this, Serial.list()[0], 9600);
}

void draw() {
  // Set the background
  background(val);
}

// Called whenever there is something available to read
void serialEvent(Serial port) {
  // Read the data
  val = port.read();
  // For debugging
  // println("Raw Input: " + input);
}
```

> Initializing the Serial object with the first port in the list.

> The serial data is used to color the background.

> Data from the Serial port is read in *serialEvent()* using the *read()* function and assigned to the global variable "val."

For reference, if you are using Arduino, here is some corresponding code:

```
int val;

void setup() {
  beginSerial(9600);
  pinMode(3, INPUT);
}

void loop() {
  val = analogRead(0);
  Serial.print(val,BYTE);
}
```

> This is not *Processing* code! It is Arduino code. For more about Arduino, visit: http://www.arduino.cc/.

19.9 Serial communication with handshaking

It is often advantageous to add a *handshaking* component to serial communication code. If a hardware device sends bytes faster than a *Processing* sketch can read, for example, there can sometimes be a logjam of information, causing the sketch to lag. The sensor values may arrive late, making the interaction confusing or misleading to the user. The process of sending information only when requested, known as "handshaking," alleviates this lag.

When the sketch starts up, it will send a byte to the hardware device asking for data.

Example 19-9: Handshaking

```
void setup() {
  size(200,200);

  // In case you want to see the list of available ports
  // println(Serial.list());

  // Using the first available port (might be different on your computer)
  port = new Serial(this, Serial.list()[0], 9600);
  // Request values from the hardware device

  port.write(65);
}
```

> The byte 65 tells the serial device that we want to receive data.

After the sketch finishes processing a byte inside of *serialEvent()*, it asks again for a new value.

```
// Called whenever there is something available to read
void serialEvent(Serial port) {
  // Read the data
  val = port.read();
  // For debugging
  // println("Raw Input: " + input);

  // Request a new value
  port.write(65);
}
```

> After we receive a byte, we reply asking for the next one.

As long as the hardware device is designed to only send the sensor values when requested, any possible lag will be eliminated. Here is the revised Arduino code. This example does not care what the request byte is, only that there is a byte request. A more advanced version might have different replies for different requests.

```
int val;

void setup() {
  beginSerial(9600);
  pinMode(3, INPUT);
}

void loop() {
  // Only send out if something has come in
  if (Serial.available() > 0){
  Serial.read();
    val = analogRead(0);
  Serial.print(val,BYTE);
  }
}
```

> This is not *Processing* code! It is Arduino code. For more about Arduino, visit: http://www.arduino.cc/.

19.10 Serial Communication with *Strings*

In cases where you need to retrieve multiple values from the serial port (or numbers greater than 255), the *readStringUntil()* function is handy. For example, let's assume you want to read from three sensors, using the values for the red, green, and blue components of your sketch's background color. Here, we will use the same protocol designed in the multi-user whiteboard example. We will ask the hardware device (where the sensors live) to send the data as follows:

> *Sensor Value 1 COMMA Sensor Value 2 COMMA Sensor Value 3 ASTERISK*

For example:

> 104,5,76*

Example 19-10: Serial communication with *Strings*

```
import processing.serial.*;

int r,g,b;     // Used to color background
Serial port;   // The serial port object

void setup() {
  size(200,200);

  // In case you want to see the list of available ports
  // println(Serial.list());
  // Using the first available port (might be different on your computer)
  port = new Serial(this, Serial.list()[0], 9600);

  // Request values right off the bat
  port.write(65);
}

void draw() {
  // Set the background
  background(r,g,b);
}

// Called whenever there is something available to read
void serialEvent(Serial port) {
  // Read the data
  String input = port.readStringUntil('*');
  if (input != null) {
    // Print message received
    println("Receiving: " + input);
    // Split up the String into an array of integers
    int[] vals = int(splitTokens(input,",*"));
    // Fill r,g,b variables
    r = vals[0];
    g = vals[1];
    b = vals[2];
  }

  // When finished ask for values again
  port.write(65);
}
```

> Data from the Serial port is read in *serialEvent()* using the *readStringUntil()* function with '*' as the end character.

> The data is split into an array of *Strings* with a comma or asterisk as a delimiter and converted into an array of integers.

> Three global variables are filled using the input data.

Corresponding Arduino code:

```
int sensor1 = 0;
int sensor2 = 0;
int sensor3 = 0;

void setup()
{
  beginSerial(9600);
  pinMode(3, INPUT);
}

void loop()
{
  if (Serial.available() > 0){ //only send if you have hear back
    Serial.read();
    sensor1 = analogRead(0);
    sensor2 = analogRead(1);
    sensor3 = analogRead(2);

    // Send the integer out as a String using "DEC"
    Serial.print(sensor1,DEC);
    // Send a comma -- ASCII code 44
    Serial.print(",", BYTE);
    Serial.print(sensor2,DEC);
    Serial.print(",", BYTE);
    Serial.print(sensor3,DEC);
    // Send an asterisk -- ASCII code 42
    Serial.print("*", BYTE);
  }
}
```

> This is not *Processing* code! It
> is Arduino code. For more about
> Arduino, visit: http://www.arduino.cc/.

Exercise 19-6: If you have an Arduino board, build your own interface to control a
Processing *sketch you have already made. (Before you attempt this, you should make sure you can successfully run the simple examples provided in this chapter.)*

Lesson Eight Project

Create a data visualization by loading external information (a local file, web page, XML feed, server or serial connection) into *Processing*.

Make sure you build up the project incrementally. For example, try designing the visualization first without any real data (use random numbers or hard-coded values). If you are loading data from the web, consider using a local file while you are developing the project. Do not be afraid to *fake* the data, waiting until you are finished with aspects of the design before connecting the real data.

Experiment with levels of abstraction. Try displaying information literally onscreen by writing text. Build an abstract system where the input data affects the behaviors of objects (you might even use your "ecosystem" from the Lesson Six Project).

Use the space provided below to sketch designs, notes, and pseudocode for your project.

Lesson Nine

Making Noise

20 Sound

"Check. Check. Check 1. Sibilance. Sibilance. Check. Check. Check 2. Sibilance. Sibilance."
—Barry the Roadie

In this chapter:
– Libraries for Sound.
– Simple sound playback.
– Playback with adjusting volume, pitch, and pan.
– Microphone as sound sensor.

Processing does not have built-in support for sound. Not that there is anything wrong with sound. Not that *Processing* has a personal grudge against sound. There is just no built-in sound. As we discussed in the introduction to this book, *Processing* is a programming language and development environment, rooted in Java, designed for learning to program ***in a visual context***. So, if you want to develop large-scale interactive applications primarily focused on sound, you should really ask yourself: "Is *Processing* the right programming environment for me?" This chapter will help answer that question as we explore the possibilities and limitations of working with sound in *Processing*.

Incorporating sound into *Processing* sketches can be accomplished a number of different ways. Because *Processing* does not support sound in its core library, many *Processing* developers choose to incorporate sound via a third party application geared toward sound, such as *PureData* (*http://www.puredata.org/*) or *Max/MSP* (*http://www.cycling74.com/*). *Processing* can communicate with these applications via OSC ("open sound control") a protocol for network communication between computers and multimedia devices. This can be accomplished in *Processing* by using the network library (see the previous chapter) or with the *oscP5* library, by Andreas Schlegel (*http://www.sojamo.de/libraries/oscP5*)

Visiting the *Processing* web site will also reveal a list of contributed libraries for using sound directly in *Processing*: playing sound samples, analyzing sound input from a microphone, synthesizing sound, and sending and receiving midi information. This chapter will focus on two of these elements: *sound playback* and *sound input.* For playback of sound effects we will look at the **Sonia** library (by Amit Pitaru) and the **Minim** library (by Damien Di Fede). Sound input will be demonstrated with **Sonia**.

These sound libraries are available at the following URLs:

Sonia: *http://sonia.pitaru.com/*
Minim: *http://code.compartmental.net/tools/minim/*

For a review on how to install third party libraries, visit Chapter 12. You will also want to visit *http://www.learning processing.com* to download the sample sound files used in these examples.

20.1 Really Simple Sound

Before we look at the libraries, however, there is one simple (but extremely limited) way to play a sound file in a *Processing* sketch without installing a third party library. This is through the use of the ***Movie*** class which we learned in Chapter 16. The ***Movie*** class is designed to play QuickTime movies, but can also be used to play a *WAV* or *AIFF* file. *WAV* is an audio file format that stands for "Waveform audio format" and is the standard format for **PCs**. *AIFF* stands for "Audio Interchange File Format" and is commonly used on Macintosh computers.

All of the functions we looked at in Chapter 16 are available for a sound file. The main difference, of course, is that we cannot use *image()* to display the Movie object since there is no image.

Example 20-1: Simple sound with video library

```
import processing.video.*;

Movie movie;

void setup(){
  size(200, 200);
  movie = new Movie (this, "dingdong.wav");
}

void draw(){
  background(0);
  noLoop();
}

void mousePressed() {
  movie.stop();
  movie.play();
}
```

> Construct a Movie object with a WAV (or AIFF) file.

> The sound is played whenever the mouse is pressed. Including the function *stop()* before *play()* ensures that the sound file will play from the beginning.

Exercise 20-1: Using the bouncing ball sketch from Example 5–6, play a sound effect every time the ball bounces off a window's edge.

20.2 Getting Started with Sonia and Minim

The *Movie* class will do for playing simple sound effects, but for more sophisticated playback functionality, we will need to look at libraries designed for use with sound. We will start with *Sonia* (*http://sonia.pitaru.com/*). First things first, as with any contributed library, you first need the import statement at the top of your code.

```
import pitaru.sonia_v2_9.*;
```

Sonia is an interface to a Java sound library, entitled *Jsyn* by Phil Burk. In order for it to work, *Sonia* has to communicate with the audio playback and input hardware on your computer. This communication is achieved via *Jsyn*. Before any sounds can be played, therefore, that link needs to be established, that is, the sound engine needs to be started. This is done with the following line of code, which you would place in *setup()*.

```
void setup() {
   Sonia.start(this);
}
```

Now, it would be rather irresponsible of us to make this connection to the sound hardware, but never bother to close it down when we are finished. By now, the flow of a *Processing* sketch is all too familiar, start with *setup()*, loop with *draw()*, and stop whenever you quit the sketch. The thing is, we want to terminate the sound engine during that last step, when the sketch quits. Fortunately, there is an extra hidden function we can implement entitled *stop()* that does precisely that. When a sketch quits, any last minute instructions can be executed inside the *stop()* function. This is where we will shut down the *Sonia* engine.

```
void stop(){
  Sonia.stop();
  super.stop();
}
```

Sonia.stop() is the call to stop *Sonia*. There is also, however, the line *super.stop()*. The meaning of "super" will be explored further in Chapter 22. For now, we can understand that line of code as saying "Oh, whatever else you would normally do in *stop()*, do that stuff, too."

All of the above applies to **Minim** as well. Here is the corresponding code:

```
import ddf.minim.*;

void setup() {
  size(200, 200);
  Minim.start(this);          ⟵  Start the Minim sound engine!
}

void stop() {                 ⟵  With Minim, sounds will be closed
                                  individually here. We will see this
  super.stop();                   in a moment.
}
```

20.3 Basic Sound Playback

Once this call to the library has been made, you have the whole world (of sound) in your hands. We will start by demonstrating how to play sound files. Before a sound can be played, it must be loaded into memory, much in the same way we loaded image files before displaying them. With *Sonia* , a *Sample* object is used to store a reference to a sound sample.

```
Sample dingdong;
```

The object is initialized by passing the sound filename to the constructor.

```
dingdong = new Sample("dingdong.wav");     ⟵  The file "dingdong.wav" should be placed in
                                               the data directory.
```

Just as with images, loading the sound file from the hard drive is a slow process so the previous line of code should be placed in *setup()* so as to not hamper the speed of *draw()*.

The type of sound file compatible with Sonia is somewhat limited. Only sounds that are formatted as *WAV* or *AIFF* files (16-bit mono or stereo) are allowed. If you want to use a sound file that is not stored in a compatible format, you could download a free audio editor, such as *Audacity* (*http://audacity.sourceforge.net/*) and convert the file. Most audio files can be saved raw or with compression. *Sonia* only works with raw files. However, in the next section, we will demonstrate how compressed (MP3) files can be played with the *ESS* library.

Once the sound is loaded, playing is easy.

```
dingdong.play();
```
◁─── The *play()* function plays the sound sample once.

The following example plays a doorbell sound whenever the mouse is clicked on the graphical doorbell. This Doorbell class implements simple button functionality (rollover and click) and just happens to be a solution for Exercise 9–8. The code for the new concepts (related to sound playback) is shown in bold type.

Example 20-2: Doorbell with Sonia

```
// Import the Sonia library
import pitaru.sonia_v2_9.*;

// A sample object (for a sound)
Sample dingdong;
// A doorbell object (that will trigger the sound)
Doorbell doorbell;

void setup(){
  size(200,200);
  Sonia.start(this); // Start Sonia engine.
  // Create a new sample object.
  dingdong = new Sample("dingdong.wav");
  // Create a new doorbell
  doorbell = new Doorbell(150,100,32);
  smooth();
}

void draw() {
  background(255);
  // Show the doorbell
  doorbell.display(mouseX,mouseY);
}
```

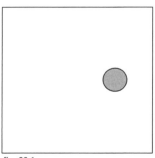

fig. 20.1

```
void mousePressed(){
  // If the user clicks on the doorbell, play the sound!
  if (doorbell.contains(mouseX,mouseY)) {
    dingdong.play();
  }
}


// Close the sound engine
public void stop(){
  Sonia.stop();
  super.stop();
}


// A Class to describe a "doorbell" (really a button)
class Doorbell {
  // Location and size
  float x;
  float y;
  float r;


// Create the doorbell
Doorbell (float x_, float y_, float r_) {
  x = x_;
  y = y_;
  r = r_;
}


// Is a point inside the doorbell (used for mouse rollover, etc.)
boolean contains(float mx, float my) {
  if (dist(mx,my,x,y) < r) {
    return true;
  } else {
    return false;
  }
}


// Show the doorbell (hardcoded colors, could be improved)
void display(float mx, float my) {
  if (contains(mx,my)) {
    fill(100);
  } else {
    fill(175);
  }
  stroke(0);
  ellipse(x,y,r,r);
  }
}
```

Exercise 20-2: Rewrite the Doorbell class to include a reference to the Sonia sample. This will allow you to easily make multiple Doorbell objects that each play a different sound. Here is some code to get you started.

```
// A Class to describe a "doorbell" (really a button)

class Doorbell {
  // Location and size
  float x;
  float y;
  float r;
    // A sample object (for a sound)

    _____ _____;

// Create the doorbell
Doorbell (float x_, float y_, float r_, _____ filename) {
    x = x_;
    y = y_;
    r = r_;

    _____ = new _____(_____);
  }

  void ring() {

    _____;
  }

  boolean contains(float mx, float my) {
    // same as original
  }

  void display(float mx, float my) {
    // same as original
  }
}
```

If you run the Doorbell example and click on the doorbell many times in rapid succession, you will notice that the sound restarts every time you click. It is not given a chance to first finish playing. While this is not much of an issue for this straightforward example, stopping a sound from restarting can be very important in other, more complex, sound sketches. The simplest way to achieve such a result is to always check and see if a sound *is playing* before you call the **play()** function. Sonia has a nice function called **isPlaying()** which does exactly this, returning true or false. We want to play the sound if it is *not already playing*, that is,

```
if (!dingdong.isPlaying()) {
  dingdong.play();
}
```

> Remember, "!" means not!

Exercise 20-3: Expand the Doorbell class to animate (perhaps moving its location and changing its size randomly) only while its sound is playing. Create an array of five Doorbell objects. Here is part of a function to add to the Doorbell class:

```
void jiggle() {
  if (_____)) {

    x += _____;

    y += _____;

    _____;

  }
}
```

With Minim instead of Sonia, very little changes. Instead of a **Sample** object, we have an **AudioPlayer** object. The following example includes the solutions for Exercises 20-2 and 20-3 (but uses the Minim code, rather than Sonia). It does not implement an array, however.

Example 20-3: Doorbell with Minim

```
import ddf.minim.*;

// A doorbell object (that will trigger the sound)
Doorbell doorbell;

void setup(){
  size(200,200);
  // start up Minim
  Minim.start(this);
  // Create a new doorbell
  doorbell = new Doorbell(150,100,32,"dingdong.wav");
  smooth();
}
```

```
void draw() {
  background(100,100,126);
  // Show the doorbell
  doorbell.display(mouseX,mouseY);
  doorbell.jiggle();
}

void mousePressed(){
  // If the user clicks on the doorbell, play the sound!
  if (doorbell.contains(mouseX,mouseY)) {
    doorbell.ring();
  }
}

// Close the sound files
public void stop(){
  doorbell.close();
  super.stop();
}
```

The doorbell object must close its sound.

```
class Doorbell {
  // Location and size
  float x;
  float y;
  float r;
  // An AudioPlayer object
  AudioPlayer dingdong;
```

An *AudioPlayer* object is used to store the sound.

```
  // Create the doorbell
  Doorbell (float x_, float y_, float r_, String filename) {
    x = x_;
    y = y_;
    r = r_;
    // load "dingdong.wav" into a new AudioPlayer
    dingdong= Minim.loadFile(filename);
  }

  // If the "doorbell" is ringing, the shape jiggles
  void jiggle() {
    if (dingdong.isPlaying()) {
      x += random(-1,1);
      y += random(-1,1);
      r = constrain(r + random(-2,2),10,100);
    }
  }
```

The doorbell only jiggles if the sound is playing.

```
  // The doorbell rings!
  void ring() {
    if (!dingdong.isPlaying()) {
      dingdong.rewind();
      dingdong.play();
    }
  }
```

The *ring()* function plays the sound, as long as it is not already playing. *rewind()* ensures the sound starts from the beginning.

```
// Is a point inside the doorbell (used for mouse rollover, etc.)
boolean contains(float mx, float my) {
  if (dist(mx,my,x,y) < r) {
    return true;
  } else {
    return false;
  }
}


// Show the doorbell (hardcoded colors, could be improved)
void display(float mx, float my) {
  if (contains(mx,my)) {
    fill( 126,114,100);
  } else {
    fill(119,152,202);
  }
  stroke(202,175,142);
  ellipse(x,y,r,r);
}

void close() {
  dingdong.close();
}
}
```

> The doorbell has a **close()** function to close the AudioPlayer object.

One of the advantages of using **Minim** over **Sonia** is that **Minim** supports MP3 files. **MP3** (or "MPEG-1 Audio Layer 3") files are compressed and therefore take up much less hard drive space than raw WAV or AIFF sound files.

```
AudioPlayer dingdong = Minim.loadFile("dingdong.mp3");
```

20.4 A Bit Fancier Sound Playback

During playback, a sound sample can be manipulated in real time. Volume, pitch, and pan can all be controlled using **Sonia** and **Minim**.

Let's start with volume in **Sonia**. A Sample object's volume can be set with the **setVolume()** function, which takes a floating point value between 0.0 and 1.0 (0.0 being silent, 1.0 being the loudest). The following snippet assumes a sample named "tone" and sets the volume based on **mouseX** position (by normalizing it to a range between 0 and 1).

```
float ratio = (float) mouseX/width;
tone.setVolume(ratio);
```

> Volume ranges from 0.0 to 1.0.

Pan works the same way, only the range is between −1.0 (for left) and 1.0 (for right).

```
float ratio = (float) mouseX/width;
tone.setPan(ratio*2 - 1);
```

> Pan ranges from −1.0 to 1.0.

The pitch is altered by changing the rate of playback (i.e., faster playback is higher pitch, slower playback is lower pitch) using **setRate()**. You can set the sample playback rate to anything you like, a fairly comprehensive range is from 0 (where you would not hear it at all) to 88,200 (a relatively fast playback rate).

```
float ratio = (float) mouseX/width;
tone.setRate(ratio*88200);
```

> A reasonable range for rate (i.e., pitch) is between 0 and 88,200.

The following example adjusts the volume and pitch of a sound according to mouse movements. Note the use of *repeat()* instead of *play()*, which loops the sound over and over rather than playing it one time.

Example 20-4: Manipulating sound (with Sonia)

```
// Import the Sonia library
import pitaru.sonia_v2_9.*;

// A Sample object (for a sound)
Sample tone;

void setup(){
  size(200,200);
  Sonia.start(this); // Start Sonia engine.
  // Create a new sample object.
  tone = new Sample("tone.wav");
  // Loop the sound forever
  // (well, at least until stop() is called)
  tone.repeat();
  smooth();
}

void draw() {
  if (tone.isPlaying()) {
    background(255);
  } else {
    background(100);
  }

  // Set the volume to a range between 0 and 1.0
  float ratio = (float) mouseX/width;
  tone.setVolume(ratio);

  // Set the rate to a range between 0 and 88,200
  // Changing the rate alters the pitch
  ratio = (float) mouseY/height;
  tone.setRate(ratio*88200);

  // Draw some rectangles to show what is going on
  stroke(0);
  fill(175);
  rect(0,160,mouseX,20);
  stroke(0);
  fill(175);
  rect(160,0,20,mouseY);
}
```

fig. 20.2

> The volume is set according to the *mouseX* position.

> The rate is set according to the *mouseY* position.

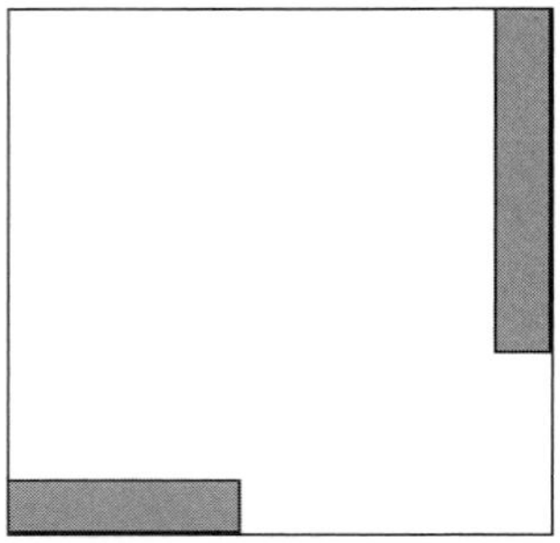

```
// Pressing the mouse stops and starts the sound
void mousePressed() {
  if (tone.isPlaying()) {
    tone.stop();
  } else {
    tone.repeat();
  }
}

// Close the sound engine
public void stop(){
  Sonia.stop();
  super.stop();
}
```

> The sound can be stopped
> with the function *stop()*.

 Exercise 20-4: In Example 20-4, flip the Y-axis so that the lower sound plays when the mouse is down rather than up.

An **AudioPlayer** object can also be manipulated with *Minim* using the functions: *setVolume()*, *setPan()*, and *addEffect()*, among others documented on the *Minim* site (*http://code.compartmental. net/tools/minim/*).

20.5 Live input

In Chapter 16, we looked at how serial communication allows a *Processing* sketch to respond to input from an external hardware device connected to a sensor. Reading input from a microphone is a similar pursuit. In essence, the microphone acts as a sensor. Not only can a microphone record sound, but it can determine if the sound is loud, quiet, high-pitched, low-pitched, and so on. For example, a *Processing* sketch could determine if it is living in a crowded room based on sound levels, or whether it is listening to a soprano or bass singer based on pitch levels. This section will cover how to retrieve and use *sound volume* data using the *Sonia* library. For analyzing sound pitch levels from a microphone, visit the *Sonia* web site (*http://sonia.pitaru.com*) for further examples.

The previous sections used a *Sample* object to play a sound. Sound input from a microphone is retrieved with a *LiveInput* object. There is a somewhat odd distinction here in the way we will use these two classes that we have yet to encounter over the course of this book.

Consider a scenario where we have three sound files. We would create three *Sample* objects.

```
Sample sample1 = new Sample("file1.wav");
Sample sample2 = new Sample("file2.wav");
Sample sample3 = new Sample("file3.wav");
```

Technically speaking, we have made three *instances* of *Sample* objects, born via the *Sample* class. If we want to play a sound, we have to refer to a specific *Sample* object.

```
sample1.play();
```

With *LiveInput*, however, we are not going to make any object *instances*. Since the *Sonia* library only allows one input source,[1] there is no reason to refer to a specific *LiveInput* object. Instead, when listening to the microphone, we refer to the *LiveInput* class as a whole:

```
LiveInput.start(); // Start LiveInput
```

Functions that we call from the class name itself (rather than from a specific object instance) are known as *static* functions. We can't create *static* functions ourselves in *Processing* so it is not something we need to worry about too much. However, since they are part of Java, we will encounter them from time to time when using contributed libraries. *LiveInput* is an example of a class with *static* functions for retrieving the sound and pitch levels from a microphone.

Let's begin by building a very simple example that ties the size of a circle to the sound level of the microphone.

Step #1 is exactly what we just did, *start the process of listening to the computer's microphone.*

```
LiveInput.start(); // Start LiveInput
```

Step #2 is *reading the volume level from the microphone itself.* We can do this two ways. Because the microphone listens in stereo, we can read the volume level from the right or left channel with *getLevel()*:

```
float rightLevel = LiveInput.getLevel(Sonia.RIGHT);
float leftLevel  = LiveInput.getLevel(Sonia.LEFT);
```

> We can specify whether we want to listen to the RIGHT or LEFT channel's volume.

We can also simply listen to both channels.

```
float level = LiveInput.getLevel();
```

> With no argument, *getLevel()* returns the volume of both RIGHT and LEFT combined.

The level returned will always range between 0.0 and 1.0.

Putting it all together, and tying the sound level to the size of an ellipse, we have:

Example 20-5: Live Input with Sonia

```
// Import the Sonia library
import pitaru.sonia_v2_9.*;

void setup(){
  size(200,200);
  Sonia.start(this);
  // Start listening to the microphone
  LiveInput.start();
  smooth();
}
```

> All functions for sound input are *static*, meaning they are called from the class name itself, *LiveInput*, rather than an object instance.

---

[1]Sonia's Live Input will listen to whatever audio source is set up as the "sound input" device on your computer. You could use a built-in microphone, a line-in from another audio source, or even potentially the CD player on your computer. A Sample object can also be treated as live input by using the function: *connectLiveInput()*.

```
void draw() {
  background(255,120,0);
  // Get the overall volume (between 0 and 1.0)
  float level = LiveInput.getLevel();
  fill(200);
  stroke(50);
  // Draw an ellipse with size based on volume
  ellipse(width/2,height/2,level*200,level*200);
}

// Close the sound engine
public void stop(){
  Sonia.stop();
  super.stop();
}
```

> The variable that stores the volume ("level") is used as the size of an ellipse.

 Exercise 20-5: Rewrite Example 20-5 with left and right volume levels mapped to different circles.

20.6 Sound Thresholding

A common sound interaction is triggering an event when a sound is made. Consider "the clapper." Clap, the lights go on. Clap again, the lights go off. A clap can be thought of as a very loud and short sound. To program "the clapper" in *Processing*, we will need to listen for volume and instigate an event when the volume is high.

In the case of clapping, we might decide that when the overall volume is greater than 0.5, the user is clapping (this is not a scientific measurement, but is good enough for this example). This value of 0.5 is known as the *threshold*. Above the threshold, events are triggered, below, they are not.

```
float vol = LiveInput.getLevel();
if (vol > 0.5) {
  // DO SOMETHING WHEN THE VOLUME IS GREATER THAN ONE!
}
```

Example 20-6 draws rectangles in the window whenever the overall volume level is greater than 0.5. The volume level is also displayed on the left-hand side as a bar.

Example 20-6: Sound threshold with Sonia

```
// Import the Sonia library
import pitaru.sonia_v2_9.*;

void setup(){
  size(200,200);
  Sonia.start(this); // Start Sonia engine.
  LiveInput.start(); // Start listening to the microphone
  smooth();
  background(255);
}
```

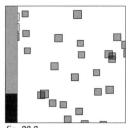

fig. 20.3

```
void draw() {
  // Get the overall volume (between 0 and 1.0)
  float vol = LiveInput.getLevel();

  // If the volume is greater than 0.5, draw a rectangle
  if (vol > 0.5) {
    stroke(0);
    fill(0,100);
    rect(random(width),random(height),vol*20,vol*20);
  }

  // Graph the overall volume
  // First draw a background strip
  fill(175);
  rect(0,0,20,height);
  // Then draw a rectangle size according to volume
  fill(0);
  rect(0,height-vol*height/2,20,vol*height/2);
}

// Close the sound engine
public void stop(){
  Sonia.stop();
  super.stop();
}
```

> If the volume is greater than 0.5 a rectangle is drawn at a random location in the window. The louder the volume, the larger the rectangle.

This application works fairly well, but does not truly emulate the *clapper*. Notice how each clap results in several rectangles drawn to the window. This is because the sound, although seemingly instantaneous to our human ears, occurs over a period of time. It may be a very short period of time, but it is enough to sustain a volume level over 0.5 for several cycles through **draw()**.

In order to have a clap trigger an event one and only one time, we need to rethink the logic of our program. In plain English, this is what we are trying to achieve:

- *If the sound level is above 0.5, then you are clapping and trigger the event. However, do not trigger the event if you just did a moment ago!*

The key here is how we define "a moment ago." One solution would be to implement a timer, that is, only trigger the event once and then wait one second before you are allowed to trigger the event again. This is a perfectly OK solution. Nonetheless, with sound, a timer is totally unnecessary since the sound itself will tell us when we are finished clapping!

- *If the sound level is less than 0.25, then it is quiet and we have finished clapping.*

OK, with these two pieces of logic, we are ready to program this "double-thresholded" algorithm. There are two thresholds, one to determine if we have started clapping, and one to determine if we have finished. We will need a boolean variable to tell us whether we are currently clapping or not.

Assume *clapping = false* to start.

- *If the sound level is above 0.5 and we are not already clapping, trigger the event and set clapping = true.*
- *If we are clapping and the sound level is less than 0.25, then it is quiet and set clapping = false.*

In code, this translates to:

```
// If the volume is greater than one and we are not clapping, draw a rectangle
if (vol > 0.5 && !clapping) {
  // Trigger event!
  clapping = true; // We are now clapping!
} else if (clapping && vol < 0.25) { // If we are finished clapping
  clapping = false;
}
```

Here is the full example where one and only one rectangle appears per clap.

Example 20-7: Sound events (double threshold) with Sonia

```
// Import the Sonia library
import pitaru.sonia_v2_9.*;

float clapLevel = 0.5;  // How loud is a clap
float threshold = 0.25; // How quiet is silence
boolean clapping = false;

void setup(){
  size(200,200);
  Sonia.start(this); // Start Sonia engine.
  LiveInput.start(); // Start listening to the microphone
  smooth();
  background(255);
}

void draw() {
  // Get the overall volume (between 0 and 2.0)
  float vol = LiveInput.getLevel();

  // If the volume is greater than 0.5 and
  // we are not clapping, draw a rectangle
  if (vol > clapLevel && !clapping) {
    stroke(0);
    fill(0,100);
    rect(random(width),random(height),vol*20,vol*20);
    clapping = true; // We are now clapping!
  // If we are finished clapping
  } else if (clapping && vol < threshold) {
    clapping = false;
  }

  // Graph the overall volume
  // First draw a background strip
  noStroke();
  fill(200);
  rect(0,0,20,height);
  // Then draw a rectangle size according to volume
  fill(100);
  rect(0,height-vol*height/2,20,vol*height/2);
```

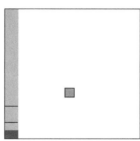

fig. 20.4

> If the volume is greater than 1.0, and we were not previously clapping, then we are clapping!

> Otherwise, if we were just clapping and the volume level has gone down below 0.25, then we are no longer clapping!

```
    // Draw lines at the threshold levels
    stroke(0);
    line(0,height-clapLevel*height/2,19,height-clapLevel*height/2 );
    line(0,height-threshold*height/2,19,height-threshold*height/2 );
}

// Close the sound engine
public void stop(){
  Sonia.stop();
  super.stop();
}
```

Exercise 20-6: Trigger the event from Example 20-7 after a sequence of two claps. Here is some code to get you started that assumes the existence of a variable named "clapCount".

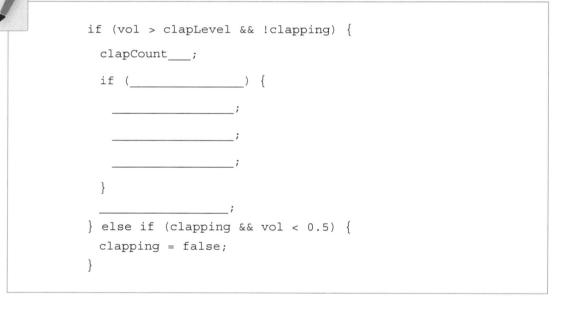

```
    if (vol > clapLevel && !clapping) {

      clapCount___;

      if (_____) {

        _____;

        _____;

        _____;

      }

      _____;

    } else if (clapping && vol < 0.5) {
      clapping = false;
    }
```

Exercise 20-7: Create a simple game that is controlled with volume. Suggestion: First make the game work with the mouse, then replace the mouse with live input. Some examples are Pong, where the paddle's position is tied to volume, or Duck Hunt, where a bullet is shot whenever the user claps.

21 Exporting

"Wait a minute. I thought that Art wanted to give up the exporting."
—Seinfeld

In this chapter:
- Web applets.
- Stand-alone applications.
- High resolution PDFs.
- Images and image sequences.
- QuickTime movies.

We have focused our energy in this book on learning to program. Nevertheless, eventually our code babies will grow up and want to find their way out in the world. This chapter is dedicated to a discussion of the various publishing options available to *Processing* sketches.

21.1 Web Applets

Processing sketches can be exported as Java applets to run on the web. How this works is covered in Chapter 2. We have seen, however, that because of security restrictions, applets cannot perform certain tasks, such as connect to a remote server or access a serial port, web camera, or other hardware device. If you have a sketch that you must publish online, but uses a feature that is restricted, there are some solutions. One possibility (as mentioned in Chapter 16) is to *sign* your applet. Some tips on how to do this are available at this book's web site (*http://www.learningprocessing.com/sandbox*).

21.2 Stand-Alone Applications

A great feature of *Processing* is that sketches can be published as stand-alone applications, meaning double-clickable programs that can run without the *Processing* development environment being installed.

If you are creating a program for an installation or kiosk environment, this feature will allow you to create applications that easily can be launched when a machine boots up. *Export Application* is also useful if you need to run multiple copies of a sketch at the same time (such as in the case of the client/server examples in Chapter 19). None of the applet security restrictions apply to applications.

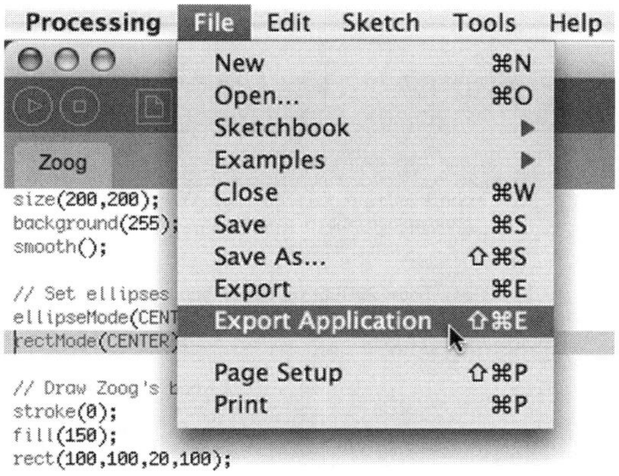

fig. 21.1

To export as an application, go to:

FILE → EXPORT APPLICATION (see Figure 21.1)

You will then notice that three new folders appear as shown in Figure 21.2.

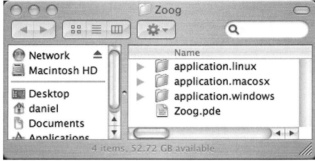

fig. 21.2

Processing auto-creates applications for three operating systems, Mac OS X, Windows, and Linux. If you ***Export Application*** from a Windows computer, the Mac application will not work properly (instructions for fixing this issue are included in a readme.txt file that appears). To avoid this, simply ***Export Application*** on a Mac.

The folder will contain all the files you need:

- *sketchName.exe* (or named simply *sketchName* on Mac and Linux). This file is the double-clickable application.
- *"source" directory*. The application folder will include a directory containing the source files for your program. This folder is not required to run the application.
- *"lib"*. This folder only appears for Windows and Linux and contains required library files. It will always contain *core.jar*, the core processing library, as well as any others you import. On Mac OS X, the library files are visible by control-clicking the application file and selecting "Show Package Contents."

The user of your application will need Java installed on his or her computer in order for the application to run properly. On a Mac, Java comes preinstalled with the operating system, so you should not have any issues as long as the end user has not messed with their Java installation. On Windows, if this is a concern, you can include Java with the application by copying the "Java" folder from the *Processing* directory to the application folder (and you must be on a PC to do this).

There are a few tricks related to the ***Export Application*** feature. For example, if you want to have your own text in the title bar, you can add the following code to *setup()*.

```
frame.setTitle("My super-awesome application!");
```

In addition, although exported applications run in windowed mode (as opposed to "present" mode), you can set applications to run full screen by adding some code. Understanding the code requires some advanced knowledge of Java and the inner workings of *Processing* sketches.

Some clues to this will be revealed in Chapter 23, but for now this code is offered simply to be copied:

```
static public void main(String args[]) {
    PApplet.main(new String[] {"--present","SketchName"});
}
```

This code can be inserted anywhere as its own block (above *setup()* is a good place for it). The "SketchName" must match the name of your *Processing* sketch.

Exercise 21-1: Export a stand-alone application for any Processing sketch you have made or any example in this book.

21.3 High-Resolution PDFs

We have been using *Processing* primarily as a means for creating graphics programs that run on a computer screen. In fact, if you recall Chapter 3, we spent a great deal of time learning about how the flow of a program works over time. Nevertheless, now is a good time to return to the idea of a static program, one whose sole purpose is to create a static image. The *Processing* PDF library allows us to take these static sketches and create high-resolution images for print. (In fact, almost all of the images in this book were produced with this method.)

Following are the required steps for using the PDF library.

Step 1. Import the library.

```
import processing.pdf.*;
```

Step 2. In *setup()*, use the *size()* function with "PDF" mode and a *String* filename argument.

```
size(400, 400, PDF, "filename.pdf");
```

Step 3. In *draw()*, do your magic!

```
background(255);
fill(175);
stroke(0);
ellipse(width/2,height/2,160,160);
```

Step 4. Call the function "*exit()*". This is very important. Calling *exit()* causes the PDF to finish rendering. Without it, the file will not open properly.

```
exit(); // Required!
```

Here is how the program looks all together:

Example 21-1: Basic PDF

```
// Import the library
import processing.pdf.*;

// Using "PDF" mode, 4th argument is the name of the file
size(400, 400, PDF, "filename.pdf");
```

```
// Draw some stuff!
background(255);
fill(175);
stroke(0);
ellipse(width/2,height/2,160,160);

// Very important, required for the PDF to render properly
exit();
```

If you run this example, you will notice that no window appears. Once you have set the *Processing* rendering mode to PDF, the sketch window will no longer appear. This is because one often uses PDF mode to create extremely high-resolution, complex images that cannot easily be displayed onscreen.

However, it is possible to see the *Processing* sketch window while rendering a PDF using the functions *beginRecord()* and *endRecord()*. This runs slower than the first example, but allows you to see what is being saved.

Example 21-2: PDF using *beginRecord()*

```
import processing.pdf.*;

void setup() {
  size(400, 400);
  beginRecord(PDF, "filename.pdf");
}
```
> *beginRecord()* starts the process. The first argument should read **PDF** and the second is the filename.

```
void draw() {
  // Draw some stuff!
  smooth();
  background(100);
  fill(0);
  stroke(255);
  ellipse(width/2,height/2,160,160);

  endRecord();
```
> *endRecord()* is called to finish the PDF.

```
  noLoop();
}
```
> There's no reason to loop any more since the PDF is finished.

endRecord() does not have to be called on the first frame rendered, and therefore this mode can be used to generate a PDF compiled from multiple cycles through *draw()*. The following example takes the "Scribbler" program from Chapter 16 and renders the result to a PDF. Here the colors are not taken from a video stream, but are picked based on a counter variable. See Figure 21.3 for a sample output.

Example 21-3: Multiple frames into one PDF

```
import processing.pdf.*;

float x = 0;
float y = 0;
```

```
void setup() {
  size(400, 400);
  beginRecord(PDF, "scribbler.pdf");
  background(255);
}

void draw() {

  // Pick a new x and y
  float newx = constrain(x + random(-20,20),0,width);
  float newy = constrain(y + random(-20,20),0,height);

  // Draw a line from x,y to the newx,newy
  stroke(frameCount%255,frameCount*3%255,
    frameCount*11%255,100);
  strokeWeight(4);
  line(x,y,newx,newy);

  // Save newx, newy in x,y
  x = newx;
  y = newy;

}

// When the mouse is pressed, we finish the PDF

void mousePressed() {
  endRecord();

  // We can tell Processing to open the PDF
  open(sketchPath("scribbler.pdf"));
  noLoop();
}
```

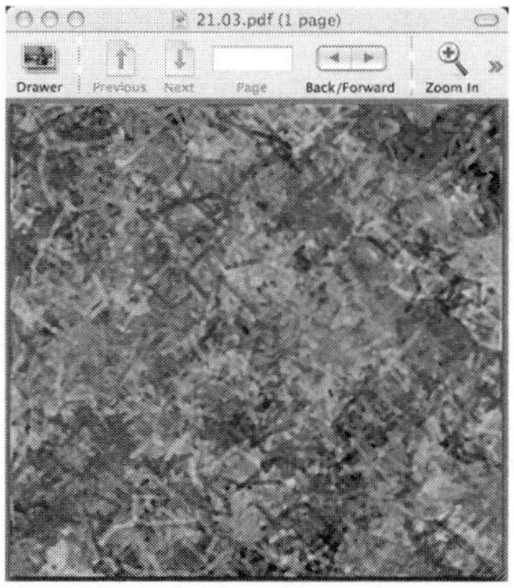

> *background( )* should be in *setup( )*. If *background( )* is placed in *draw( )* the PDF would accumulate a lot of graphics elements only to erase them over and over again.

fig. 21.3

> In this example, the user chooses when to finish rendering the PDF by clicking the mouse.

If you are rendering 3D shapes (in P3D mode or OPENGL), you will want to use *beginRaw( )* and *endRaw( )* instead of *beginRecord( )* and *endRecord( )*. This example also uses a boolean variable ("recordPDF").

Example 21-4: PDF and openGL

```
// Using OPENGL
import processing.opengl.*;
import processing.pdf.*;

// Cube rotation
float yTheta = 0.0;
float xTheta = 0.0;

// To trigger recording the PDF
boolean recordPDF = false;

void setup() {
  size(400, 400, OPENGL);
  smooth();
}
```

> A boolean variable that when set to true causes a PDF to be made.

> OPENGL or P3D mode requires the use of *beginRaw( )* and *endRaw( )* instead of *beginRecord( )* and *endRecord( )*.

```
void draw() {
  // Begin making the PDF
  if (recordPDF) {
    beginRaw(PDF, "3D.pdf");
  }
  background(255);
  stroke(0);
  noFill();
  translate(width/2,height/2);
  rotateX(xTheta);
  rotateY(yTheta);
  box(100);
  xTheta += 0.02;
  yTheta += 0.03;

  // End making the PDF
  if (recordPDF) {
    endRaw();
    recordPDF = false;
  }
}

// Make the PDF when the mouse is pressed
void mousePressed() {
  recordPDF = true;
}
```

> If you include "####" in the filename— "3D-####.pdf"—separate, numbered PDFs will be made for each frame that is rendered.

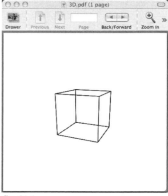

fig. 21.4

Two important notes about the **PDF** library.

- **Images**—If you are displaying images in the PDF, these will not necessarily look good after export. A 320 × 240 pixel image is still a 320 × 240 pixel image whether rendered into a high-resolution PDF or not.
- **Text**—If you are displaying text in the PDF, you will have to have the font installed in order to view the PDF properly. One way around this is to include "*textMode(SHAPE);*" after *size()*. This will render the text as a shape to the PDF and not require the font installed.

For full documentation of the **PDF** library, visit the *Processing* reference page at *http://processing.org/ reference/libraries/pdf/index.html*. While the PDF library will take care of many of your needs related to high-resolution generation, there are two other contributed libraries that might be of interest. One is **proSVG** by Christian Riekoff for exporting files in the SVG ("Scalable Vector Graphics") format: *http://www.texone.org/prosvg/*. Another is **SimplePostScript** by Marius Watz for writing vector files in the PostScript format: *http://processing.unlekker.net/SimplePostscript/*.

Exercise 21-2: Create a PDF from any Processing *sketch you have made or any example in this book.*

21.4 Images/*saveFrame( )*

High-resolution PDFs are useful for printing; however, you can also save the contents of the *Processing* window as an image file (with the same resolution as the pixel size of the window itself). This is accomplished with *save()* or *saveFrame()*.

save() takes one argument, the filename for the image you want to save. *save()* will generate image files with the following formats: JPG, TIF, TGA, or PNG, indicated by the file extension you include in the filename. If no extension is included, *Processing* will default to the TIF format.

```
background(255,0,0);
save("file.jpg");
```

If you call *save()* multiple times with the same filename, it will overwrite the previous image. However, if you want to save a sequence of images, the *saveFrame()* function will auto-number the files. *Processing* will look for the *String "####"* in the filename and replace it with a numbered sequence of images. See Figure 21.5.

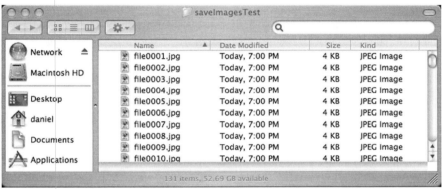

fig. 21.5

```
void draw() {
    background(random(255));
    saveFrame("file####.jpg");
}
```

This technique is commonly used to import a numbered sequence of images into video or animation software.

21.5 MovieMaker

The image sequence that resulted from *saveFrame()* can be made into a movie file, using *QuickTime Pro, iMovie,* or any number of video software packages.

For longer movies, however, having a directory full of thousands of images can prove to be a bit unwieldy. Using the *MovieMaker* class makes this process easier by writing the frames directly to a movie file. I originally developed *MovieMaker* as a contributed library, but it is now available in *Processing*'s video library itself.

```
import processing.video.*;
```

A MovieMaker object requires the following arguments (in order):

- **this**—Refers to the sketch that the movie will be associated with.
- **width**—An integer, typically the same width as the sketch.

- **height**—An integer, typically the same height as the sketch.
- **filename**—A String for the movie's file name.
- **framerate**—A frame rate for the movie, typically 30.
- **type**—What compression format should the movie use.
- **quality**—The compression quality for the movie.

An example of the constructor is as follows:

```
mm = new MovieMaker(this, width, height, "test.mov", 30, MovieMaker.H263,
    MovieMaker.HIGH);
```

The library offers many options for compression codecs. The term codec originally comes from the term "coder-decoder," referring to a hardware device that converts analog video to digital. Here, however, codec refers to a "compressor-decompressor," software that coverts video between its raw, uncompressed form (for viewing) and its compressed form (for storage). The following are the codecs available with the MovieMaker library (check the reference page for any updates to this list: *http://processing.org/reference/libraries/video/MovieMaker.html*).

> ANIMATION, BASE, BMP, CINEPAK, COMPONENT, CMYK, GIF, GRAPHICS, JPEG, MS_VIDEO, MOTION_JPEG_A, MOTION_JPEG_B, RAW, SORENSON, VIDEO, H261, H263, H264

Selecting a codec will affect the size of the movie file as well as the quality. *RAW*, for example, will store the video in its raw uncompressed (and therefore highest quality) form, but will result in an enormous video file. You can read more about the various codecs at Apple's QuickTime site.

- QuickTime: *http://www.apple.com/quicktime/*.
- QuickTime Developer: *http://developer.apple.com/quicktime/*.

Once you have selected a codec, you must then specify a codec quality, ranging from worst to lossless.

> WORST, LOW, MEDIUM, HIGH, BEST, LOSSLESS

After the MovieMaker object is constructed, frames can be added one at a time to the movie by calling the ***addFrame()*** function.

```
void draw() {

    // Some cool stuff that you are drawing!

    mm.addFrame();
}
```

Finally, in order for the movie file to play properly it has to be "finished" with the ***finishMovie()*** function. If you quit the *Processing* sketch before this function is called, the movie file will not be recognized by QuickTime! One solution is to finish the movie on a mouse click. However, if you are using mouse presses already in your applet, you might want to consider other options, such as finishing on a key press or after a timer has run out.

```
public void mousePressed() {
    mm.finishMovie();
}
```

Example 21-5 records a movie of a mouse drawing on the screen. The movie is finished when the space bar is pressed.

fig. 21.6 *Output of Example 21-5*

Example 21-5: Making a QuickTime movie

```
import processing.video.*;

MovieMaker mm; // Declare MovieMaker object

void setup() {
  size(320, 240);
  // Create MovieMaker object with size, filename,
  // framerate, compression codec and quality
  mm = new MovieMaker(this, width, height, "drawing.mov", 30, MovieMaker.H263,
    MovieMaker.HIGH);
  background(255);
}

void draw() {
  stroke(0);
  strokeWeight(4);
  if (mousePressed) {
    line(pmouseX, pmouseY, mouseX, mouseY);
  }
  mm.addFrame(); // Add window's pixels to movie
}

void keyPressed() {
  if (key == ' ') {
    println("finishing movie");
    mm.finish(); // Finish the movie if space bar is pressed!
  }
}
```

> The MovieMaker class is part of *Processing*'s video library.

> A new frame is added to the movie every cycle through ***draw()***.

> Do not forget to finish the movie! Otherwise, it will not play properly.

Exercise 21-3: Create a movie from any Processing *sketch you have made or any example in this book.*

Lesson Nine Project

Choose one or both!

1. Incorporate sound into a *Processing* sketch, either by adding sound effects or by controlling the sketch with live input.

2. Use *Processing* to generate an output other than real-time graphics. Make a print (using PDF). Make a video (using MovieMaker), and so on.

Use the space provided below to sketch designs, notes, and pseudocode for your project.

Lesson Ten

Beyond Processing

22 Advanced Object-Oriented Programming

"Do you ever think about things that you do think about?"
—*Henry Drummond,* Inherit the Wind

In this chapter:
– Encapsulation.
– Inheritance.
– Polymorphism.
– Overloading.

In Chapter 8, we introduced *object-oriented programming* ("OOP"). The driving principle of the chapter was the pairing of data and functionality into one single idea, a *class*. A *class* is a template and from that template we made *instances* of *objects* and stored them in variables and arrays. Although we learned how to write classes and make objects, we did not delve very deeply into the core principles of OOP and explore its advanced features. Now that we are nearing the end of the book (and about to leap into the world of Java in the next chapter), it is a good time to reflect on the past and take steps toward the future.

Object-oriented programming in *Processing* and Java is defined by three fundamental concepts: *encapsulation*, *inheritance*, and *polymorphism*. We are familiar with *encapsulation* already; we just have not formalized our understanding of the concept and used the terminology. *Inheritance* and *polymorphism* are completely new concepts we will cover in this chapter. (At the end of this chapter, we will also take a quick look at method *overloading*, which allows objects to have more than one way of calling the constructor.)

22.1 Encapsulation

To understand *encapsulation*, let's return to the example of a *Car* class. And let's take that example out into the world and think about a real-life Car object, operated by a real-life driver: *you*. It is a nice summer day and you are tired of programming and opt to head to the beach for the weekend. Traffic permitting, you are hoping for a nice drive where you will turn the steering wheel a bunch of times, press on the gas and brakes, and fiddle with dial on the radio.

This car that you are driving is *encapsulated*. All you have to do to drive is operate the functions: **steer()**, **gas()**, **brake()**, and **radio()**. Do you know what is under the hood? How the catalytic converter connects to the engine or how the engine connects to the intercooler? What valves and wires and gears and belts do what? Sure, if you are an experienced auto mechanic you might be able to answer these questions, but the point is you *don't have to* in order to drive the car. This is *encapsulation*.

Encapsulation is defined as hiding the inner workings of an object from the user of that object.

In terms of object-oriented programming, the "inner workings" of an object are the data (variables of that object) and functions. The "user" of the object is you, the programmer, who is making object instances and using them throughout your code.

Now, why is this a good idea? Chapter 8 (and all of the OOP examples throughout the book) emphasized the principles of modularity and reusability. Meaning, if you already figured out how to program a Car, why do it over and over again each time you have to make a Car? Just organize it all into the Car class, and you have saved yourself a lot of headaches.

Encapsulation goes a step further. OOP does not just help you organize your code, it *protects you from making mistakes*. If you do not mess with the wiring of the car while you are driving it, you are less likely to break the car. Of course, sometimes a car breaks down and you need to fix it, but this requires opening the hood and looking at the code inside the class itself.

Take the following example. Let's say you are writing a *BankAccount* class which has a floating point variable for the bank account *balance*.

```
BankAccount account = new BankAccount(1000);
```

> A bank account object with a starting balance of $1,000.

You will want to encapsulate that balance and keep it hidden. Why? Let's say you need to withdraw money from that account. So you subtract $100 from that account.

```
account.balance = account.balance - 100.
```

> Withdrawing $100 by accessing the balance variable directly.

But what if there is a fee to withdraw money? Say, $1.25? We are going to get fired from our bank programming job pretty quickly, having left this detail out. With encapsulation, we would keep our job, having written the following code instead.

```
account.withdraw(100);
```

> Withdrawing $100 by calling a method!

If the *withdraw()* function is written correctly, we will never forget the fee, since it will happen every single time the method is called.

```
void withdraw(float amount) {
  float fee = 1.25;
  account -= (amount + fee);
}
```

> This function ensures that a fee is also deducted whenever the money is withdrawn.

Another benefit of this strategy is that if the bank decides to raise the fee to $1.50, it can simply adjust the fee variable inside the BankAccount class and everything will keep working!

Technically speaking, in order to follow the principles of encapsulation, variables inside of a class should *never* be accessed directly and can only be retrieved with a method. This is why you will often see programmers use a lot of functions known as *getters* and *setters*, functions that retrieve or change the value of variables. Here is an example of a Point class with two variables (*x* and *y*) that are accessed with getters and setters.

```
class Point {
  float x,y;

  Point(float tempX, float tempY) {
    x = tempX;
    y = tempY;
  }

  // Getters
  float getX() {
    return x;
  }

  float getY() {
    return y;
  }

  // Setters
  float setX(float val) {
    x = val;
  }

  float setY(float val) {
    if (val > height) val = height;
    y = val;
  }
}
```

> The variables *x* and *y* are accessed with getter and setter functions.

> Getters and setters allow us to protect the value of variables. For example, here the value of *y* can never be set to greater than the sketch's height.

If we wanted to make a point and increment the *y* value, we would have to do it this way:

```
p.setY(p.getY() + 1);
```

> Instead of:
> ```
> p.y = p.y + 1;
> ```

Java actually allows us to mark a variable as "private" to make it illegal to access it directly (in other words, if you try to, the program will not even run).

> Although rarely seen in *Processing* examples, variables can be set as private, meaning only accessible inside the class itself. By default all variables and functions in *Processing* are "public."

```
class Point {
  private float x;
  private float y;
}
```

While encapsulation is a core principle of object-oriented programming and is very important when designing large-scale applications programmed by a team of developers, sticking to the letter of the law (as with incrementing the *y* value of the Point object above) is often rather inconvenient and almost silly for a simple *Processing* sketch. So, it is not the end of the world if you make a Point class and access the *x* and *y* variables directly. We have done this several times in the examples found in this book.

However, understanding the principle of *encapsulation* should be a driving force in how you design your objects and manage your code. Any time you start to expose the inner workings of an object outside of the class itself, you should ask yourself: Is this necessary? Could this code go inside a function inside the class? In the end, you will be a happier programmer and keep that job at the bank.

22.2 Inheritance

Inheritance, the second in our list of three fundamental object-oriented programming concepts, allows us to create new classes that are based on existing classes.

Let's take a look at the world of animals: dogs, cats, monkeys, pandas, wombats, and sea nettles. Arbitrarily, let's begin by programming a *Dog* class. A Dog object will have an age variable (an integer), as well as *eat()*, *sleep()*, and *bark()* functions.

```
class Dog {
  int age;

  Dog() {
    age = 0;
  }

  void eat() {
    // eating code goes here
  }

  void sleep() {
    // sleeping code goes here
  }

  void bark() {
    println("WOOF!");
  }
}
```

Finished with dogs, we can now move on to cats.

```
class Cat {
  int age;

  Cat() {
    age = 0;
  }

  void eat() {
    // eating code goes here
  }

  void sleep() {
    // sleeping code goes here
  }

  void meow() {
    println("MEOW!");
  }
}
```

Notice how dogs and cats have the same variables (age) and functions (eat, sleep). However, they also have a unique function for barking or meowing.

Sadly, as we move onto fish, horses, koala bears, and lemurs, this process will become rather tedious as we rewrite the same code over and over again. What if, instead, we could develop a generic *Animal* class to describe any type of animal? After all, all animals eat and sleep. We could then say the following:

- A dog is an animal and has all the properties of animals and can do all the things animals can do. In addition, a dog can bark.
- A cat is an animal and has all the properties of animals and can do all the things animals can do. In addition, a cat can meow.

Inheritance allows us to program just this. With *inheritance*, classes can inherit properties (variables) and functionality (methods) from other classes. The Dog class is a child (AKA a *subclass*) of the Animal class. Children inherit all variables and functions automatically from their parent (AKA *superclass*). Children can also include additional variables and functions not found in the parent. Inheritance follows a tree-structure (much like a phylogenetic "tree of life"). Dogs can inherit from Canines which inherit from Mammals which inherit from Animals, and so on. See Figure 22.1.

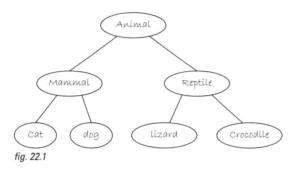

fig. 22.1

Here is how the syntax works with inheritance.

```
class Animal {
  int age;

  Animal() {
    age = 0;
  }

  void eat() {
    // eating code goes here
  }

  void sleep() {
    // sleeping code goes here
  }
}

class Dog extends Animal{
  Dog() {
    super();
  }
  void bark() {

    println("WOOF!");
  }
}
```

The Animal class is the parent (or super) class.

The variable age and the functions *eat()* and *sleep()* are inherited by Dog and Cat.

The Dog class is the child (or sub) class. This is indicated with the code "*extends Animal*"

```
class Cat extends Animal{
  Cat() {
    super();
  }
  void bark() {
    println("MEOW!");
  }
}
```

> **super()** means execute code found in the parent class.

> Since **bark()** is not part of the parent class, we have to define it in the child class.

The following new terms have been introduced:

- **extends**—This keyword is used to indicate a parent class for the class being defined. Note that classes can only extend *one* class. However, classes can extend classes that extend other classes, that is, Dog extends Animal, Terrier extends Dog. Everything is inherited all the way down the line.
- **super()**—Super calls the constructor in the parent class. In other words, whatever you do in the parent constructor, do so in the child constructor as well. This is not required, but is fairly common (assuming you want child objects to be created in the same manner as their parents). Other code can be written into the constructor in addition to **super()**.

A subclass can be expanded to include additional functions and properties beyond what is contained in the superclass. For example, let's assume that a Dog object has a hair color variable in addition to age, which is set randomly in the constructor. The class would now look like so:

```
class Dog extends Animal {
  color haircolor;

  Dog() {
    super();
    haircolor = color(random(255));
  }

  void bark() {
    println("WOOF!");
  }
}
```

> A child class can introduce new variables not included in the parent.

Note how the parent constructor is called via **super()**, setting the age to 0, but the haircolor is set inside the Dog constructor itself. Suppose a Dog object eats differently than a generic Animal. Parent functions can be *overridden* by rewriting the function inside the subclass.

```
class Dog extends Animal {
  color haircolor;

  Dog() {
    super();
    haircolor = color(random(255));
  }

  void eat() {
    // Code for how a dog specifically eats
  }
  void bark() {
    println("WOOF!");
  }
}
```

> A child can **override** a parent function if necessary.

But what if a Dog should eat the same way an Animal does, but with some additional functionality? A subclass can both run the code from a parent class and incorporate some custom code.

```
class Dog extends Animal {
  color haircolor;
  Dog() {
    super();
    haircolor = color(random(255));
  }

  void eat() {
    // Call eat() from Animal
    super.eat();
    // Add some additional code
    // for how a dog specifically eats
    println("Yum!!!");
  }

  void bark() {
    println("WOOF!");
  }
}
```

> A child can execute a function from the parent while adding its own code as well.

Exercise 22-1: Continuing with the Car example from our discussion of encapsulation, how would you design a system of classes for vehicles (that is, cars, trucks, buses, and motorcycles)? What variables and functions would you include in a parent class? And what would be added or overridden in the child classes? What if you wanted to include planes, trains, and boats in this example as well? Diagram it, modeled after Figure 22.1.

22.3 An Inheritance Example: SHAPES

Now that we have had an introduction to the theory of inheritance and its syntax, we can develop a working example in *Processing*.

A typical example of inheritance involves shapes. Although a bit of a cliche, it is useful because of its simplicity. We will create a generic "Shape" class where all Shape objects have an *x, y* location as well as a size, and a function for display. Shapes move around the screen by "jiggling" randomly.

```
class Shape {
  float x;
  float y;
  float r;

  Shape(float x_, float y_, float r_) {
    x = x_;
    y = y_;
    r = r_;
  }

  void jiggle() {
    x += random(-1,1);
    y += random(-1,1);
  }

  void display() {
    point(x,y);
  }
}
```

> A generic shape does not really know how to be displayed. This will be overridden in the child classes.

Next, we create a subclass from Shape (let's call it "Square"). It will inherit all the instance variables and methods from Shape. We write a new constructor with the name "Square" and execute the code from the parent class by calling *super()*.

> Variables are inherited from the parent.

```
class Square extends Shape {
  // we could add variables for only Square here if we so desire

  Square(float x_, float y_, float r_) {
    super(x_,y_,r_);
  }
  // Inherits jiggle() from parent

  // Add a display method
  void display() {
    rectMode(CENTER);
    fill(175);
    stroke(0);
    rect(x,y,r,r);
  }
}
```

> If the parent constructor takes arguments then *super()* needs to pass in those arguments.

> Aha, the square overrides its parent for display.

Notice that if we call the parent constructor with *super()*, we must have to include the required arguments. Also, because we want to display the square onscreen, we override *display()*. Even though we want the square to jiggle, we do not need to write the *jiggle()* function since it is inherited.

What if we want a subclass of Shape to include additional functionality? Following is an example of a Circle class that, in addition to extending Shape, contains an instance variable to keep track of color. (Note this is purely to demonstrate this feature of inheritance, it would be more logical to place a color variable in the parent Shape class.) It also expands the *jiggle()* function to adjust size and incorporates a new function to change color.

```
class Circle extends Shape {

  // inherits all instance variables from parent + adding one
  color c;

  Circle(float x_, float y_, float r_, color c_) {
    super(x_,y_,r_);  // call the parent constructor
    c = c_;           // also deal with this new instance variable
  }

  // call the parent jiggle, but do some more stuff too
  void jiggle() {
    super.jiggle();
    r += random(-1,1);
    r = constrain(r,0,100);
  }

  void changeColor() {
    c = color(random(255));
  }

  void display() {
    ellipseMode(CENTER);
    fill(c);
    stroke(0);
    ellipse(x,y,r,r);
  }
}
```

> The Circle jiggles its size as well as its *x,y* location.

> The ***changeColor()*** function is unique to circles.

To demonstrate that inheritance is working, here is a program that makes one Square object and one Circle object. The Shape, Square, and Circle classes are not included again, but are identical to the ones above. See Example 22-1.

Example 22-1: Inheritance

```
// Object oriented programming allows us to define classes in terms of other classes.
// A class can be a subclass (aka "child") of a super class (aka "parent").
// This is a simple example demonstrating this concept, known as "inheritance."

Square s;
Circle c;

void setup() {
  size(200,200);
  smooth();

  // A square and circle
  s = new Square(75,75,10);
  c = new Circle(125,125,20,color(175));
}

void draw() {
  background(255);

  c.jiggle();
  s.jiggle();

  c.display();
  s.display();
}
```

> This sketch includes one Circle object and one Square object. No Shape object is made. The Shape class just functions as part of our inheritance tree!

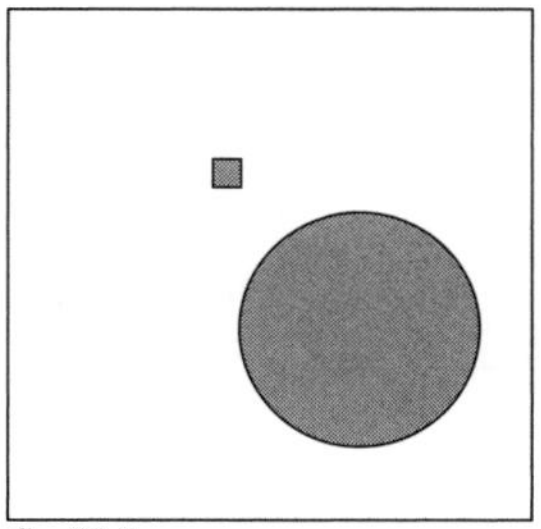

fig. 22.2

Exercise 22-2: Write a Line class that extends Shape and has variables for the two points of the line. When the line jiggles, move both points. You will not need "r" for anything in the line class (but what could you use it for?).

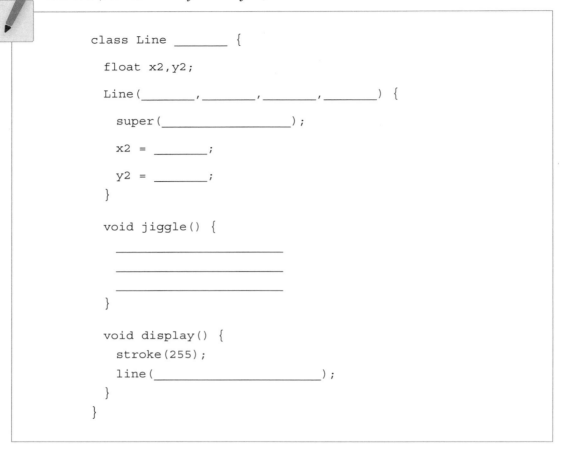

```
class Line _____ {

  float x2,y2;

  Line(_____,_____,_____,_____) {

    super(_____);

    x2 = _____;

    y2 = _____;
  }

  void jiggle() {

    _____

    _____

    _____

  }

  void display() {
    stroke(255);
    line(_____);
  }
}
```

Exercise 22-3: Do any of the sketches you have created merit the use of inheritance? Try to find one and revise it.

22.4 Polymorphism

Armed with the concepts of inheritance, we can program a diverse animal kingdom with arrays of dogs, cats, turtles, and kiwis frolicking about.

```
Dog[] dogs = new Dog[100];
Cat[] cats = new Cat[101];
Turtle[] turtles = new Turtle[23];
Kiwi[] kiwis = new Kiwi[6];
```

100 dogs. 101 cats. 23 turtles. 6 kiwis.

```
for (int i = 0; i < dogs.length; i++) {
  dogs[i] = new Dog();
}
for (int i = 0; i < cats.length; i++) {
  cats[i] = new Cat();
}
for (int i = 0; i < turtles.length; i++) {
  turtle[i] = new Turtle();
}
for (int i = 0; i < kiwis.length; i++) {
  kiwis[i] = new Kiwi();
}
```

> Because the arrays are different sizes, we need a separate loop for each array.

As the day begins, the animals are all pretty hungry and are looking to eat. So it is off to looping time.

```
for (int i = 0; i < dogs.length; i++) {
  dogs[i].eat();
}
for (int i = 0; i < cats.length; i++) {
  cats[i].eat();
}
for (int i = 0; i < turtles.length; i++) {
  turtles[i].eat();
}
for (int i = 0; i < kiwis.length; i++) {
  kiwis[i].eat();
}
```

This works great, but as our world expands to include many more animal species, we are going to get stuck writing a lot of individual loops. Isn't this unnecessary? After all, the creatures are all animals, and they all like to eat. Why not just have one array of Animal objects and fill it with all different kinds of Animals?

```
Animal[] kingdom = new Animal[1000];

for (int i = 0; i < kingdom.length; i++) {
  if (i < 100) kingdom[i] = new Dog();
  else if (i < 400) kingdom[i] = new Cat();
  else if (i < 900) kingdom[i] = new Turtle();
  else kingdom[i] = new Kiwi();
}
for (int i = 0; i < kingdom.length; i++) {
  kingdom[i].eat();
}
```

> The array is of type *Animal*, but the elements we put in the array are Dogs, Cats, Turtles, and Kiwis.

> When it is time for all the Animals to eat, we can just loop through that one big array.

The ability to treat a Dog object as either a member of the Dog class or the Animal class (its parent) is known as *Polymorphism*, the third tenet of object-oriented programming.

Polymorphism (from the Greek, *polymorphos*, meaning many forms) refers to the treatment of a single object instance in multiple forms. A Dog is certainly a Dog, but since Dog *extends* Animal, it can also be considered an Animal. In code, we can refer to it both ways.

```
Dog rover = new Dog();
Animal spot = new Dog();
```

> Normally, the type on the left must match the type on the right. With polymorphism, it is OK as long as the type on the right is a child of the type on the left.

Although the second line of code might initially seem to violate syntax rules, both ways of declaring a Dog object are legal. Even though we declare spot as an Animal, we are really making a Dog object and storing it in the spot variable. And we can safely call all of the Animal methods on spot because the rules of inheritance dictate that a Dog can do anything an Animal can.

What if the Dog class, however, overrides the *eat()* function in the Animal class? Even if spot is declared as an Animal, Java will determine that its true identity is that of a Dog and run the appropriate version of the *eat()* function.

This is particularly useful when we have an array.

Let's rewrite the Shape example from the previous section to include many Circle objects and many Square objects.

```
// Many Squares and many Circles          The old "non-polymorphism"
Square[] s = new Square[10];              way with multiple arrays.
Circle[] c = new Circle[20];

void setup() {
  size(200,200);
  smooth();

  // Initialize the arrays
  for (int i = 0; i < s.length; i++) {
    s[i] = new Square(100,100,10);
  }
  for (int i = 0; i < c.length; i++) {
    c[i] = new Circle(100,100,10,color(random(255),100));
  }
}

void draw() {
  background(100);

  // Jiggle and display all squares
  for (int i = 0; i < s.length; i++) {
    s[i].jiggle();
    s[i].display();
  }

  // Jiggle and display all circles
  for (int i = 0; i < c.length; i++) {
    c[i].jiggle();
    c[i].display();
  }
}
```

Polymorphism allows us to simplify the above by just making one array of Shape objects that contains both Circle objects and Square objects. We do not have to worry about which are which, this will all be taken care of for us! (Also, note that the code for the classes has not changed, so we are not including it here.) See Example 22.2.

Example 22-2: Polymorphism

```
// One array of Shapes
Shape[] shapes = new Shape[30];

void setup() {
  size(200,200);
  smooth();
  for (int i = 0; i < shapes.length; i++) {
    int r = int(random(2));
    // randomly put either circles or squares in our array
    if (r == 0) {
      shapes[i] = new Circle(100,100,10,color(random(255),100));
    } else {
      shapes[i] = new Square(100,100,10);
    }
  }
}

void draw() {
  background(100);
  // Jiggle and display all shapes
  for (int i = 0; i < shapes.length; i++) {
    shapes[i].jiggle();
    shapes[i].display();
  }
}
```

> The new polymorphism way with one array that has different types of objects that extend Shape.

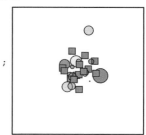

fig. 22.3

*Exercise 22-4: Add the Line class you created in Exercise 22-2 to Example 22-2. Randomly put circles, squares, and lines in the array. Notice how you barely have to change any code (you should only have to edit **setup()** above).*

Exercise 22-5: Implement polymorphism in the sketch you made for Exercise 22-3.

22.5 Overloading

In Chapter 16, we learned how to create a Capture object in order to read live images from a video camera. If you looked at the *Processing* reference page (*http://www.processing.org/reference/libraries/video/ Capture.html*), you may have noticed that the Capture constructor can be called with three, four, or five arguments:

```
Capture(parent, width, height)
Capture(parent, width, height, fps)
Capture(parent, width, height, name)
Capture(parent, width, height, name, fps)
```

Functions that can take varying numbers of arguments are actually something we saw all the way back in Chapter 1! *fill()*, for example, can be called with one number (for grayscale), three (for RGB color), or four (to include alpha transparency).

```
fill(255);
fill(255,0,255);
fill(0,0,255,150);
```

The ability to define functions with the same name (but different arguments) is known as *overloading*. With *fill()*, for example, *Processing* does not get confused about which definition of *fill()* to look up, it simply finds the one where the arguments match. A function's name in combination with its arguments is known as the function's **signature**—it is what makes that function definition unique. Let's look at an example that demonstrates how overloading can be useful.

Let's say you have a **Fish** class. Each **Fish** object has a location: *x* and *y*.

```
class Fish {
  float x;
  float y;
```

What if, when you make a Fish object, you sometimes want to make one with a random location and sometimes with a specific location. To make this possible, we could write two different constructors:

```
Fish() {
  x = random(0,width);
  y = random(0,height);
}

Fish(float tempX, float tempY) {
  x = tempX;
  y = tempY;
}
}
```

> Overloading allows us to define two constructors for the same object (as long as these constructors take different arguments).

When you create a Fish object in the main program, you can do so with either constructor:

```
Fish fish1 = new Fish();
Fish fish2 = new Fish(100,200);
```

> If two constructors are defined, an object can be initialized using either one.

23 Java

"I love coffee, I love tea, I love the Java Jive and it loves me."
—Ben Oakland and Milton Drake

In this chapter:
– *Processing* is really Java.
– If we did not have *Processing* what would our code look like?
– Exploring the Java API.
– Some useful examples: ArrayList, and Rectangle.
– Exception (error) handling—try and catch.
– Beyond *Processing*?

23.1 Revealing the Wizard

Perhaps, all along while reading this book, you have been thinking: "Gosh, this is so awesome. I love programming. I am so glad I am learning *Processing*. I can't wait to go on and learn Java!" The funny thing is, you do not really need to *learn* Java. Pulling back the curtain of *Processing*, what we will discover is that we have been learning Java all along. For example, in Java, you:

- Declare, initialize, and use variables the same way.
- Declare, initialize, and use arrays the same way.
- Employ conditional and loop statements the same way.
- Define and call functions the same way.
- Create classes the same way.
- Instantiate objects the same way.

Processing, of course, gives us some extra stuff for free (and simplifies some stuff here and there) and this is why it is a great tool for learning and for developing interactive graphics projects. Here is a list of some of what *Processing* offers that is not as easily available with just plain Java.

- A set of functions for drawing shapes.
- A set of functions for loading and displaying text, images, and video.
- A set of functions for 3D transformations.
- A set of functions for mouse and keyboard interaction.
- A simple development environment to write your code.
- A friendly online community of artists, designers, and programmers!

23.2 If we did not have *Processing*, what would our code look like?

In Chapter 2, we discussed the compilation and execution process—this is what happens when you press the play button and turn your code into a window with graphics. Step 1 of this process involves "translating" your *Processing* code into Java. In fact, when you export to applet, this same process occurs and you will notice that along with the file "Sketchname.pde," a new file will appear named

"SketchName.java." This is your "translated" code, only *translation* is somewhat of a misnomer since very little changes. Let's look at an example:

```
// Randomly Growing Square
float w = 30.0; // Variable to keep track of size of rect

void setup() {
  size(200, 200);
}

void draw() {
  background(100);
  rectMode(CENTER);
  fill(255);
  noStroke();
  rect(mouseX,mouseY,w,w);   // Draw a rect at mouse location
  w += random(-1,1);         // Randomly adjust size variable
}
```

> What we are used to seeing, our regular old *Processing* code.

Exporting the sketch, we can open up the Java file and look at the Java source.

```
// Randomly Growing Square with Java Stuff
import processing.core.*;
import java.applet.*;
import java.awt.*;
import java.awt.image.*;
import java.awt.event.*;
import java.io.*;
import java.net.*;
import java.text.*;
import java.util.*;
import java.util.zip.*;

public class JavaExample extends PApplet {
  float w = 30.0f; // Variable to keep track of size of rect

  public void setup() {
    size(200, 200);
  }

  public void draw() {
    background(100);
    rectMode(CENTER);
    fill(255);
    noStroke();
    rect(mouseX,mouseY,w,w);   // draw a rect at mouse location
    w += random(-1,1);         // randomly adjust size variable
  }
}
```

> The translated Java code has some new stuff at the top, but everything else stays the same.

It is clear that little has changed, rather, some code has been added before and after the usual *setup()* and *draw()* stuff.

- **Import Statements**—At the top, there are a set of import statements allowing access to certain libraries. We have seen this before when using *Processing* libraries. If we were using regular Java instead of *Processing*, specifying all libraries would always be required. *Processing*, however, assumes a base set of libraries from Java (e.g., *java.applet.**) and from *Processing* (e.g., *processing.core.**) which is why we do not see these in every sketch.

- **public**—In Java, variables, functions, and classes can be "public" or "private." This designation indicates what level of access should be granted to a particular piece of code. It is not something we have to worry much about in the simpler *Processing* environment, but it becomes an important consideration when moving on to larger Java programs. As an individual programmer, you are most often granting or denying access to yourself, as a means for protecting against errors. We encountered some examples of this in Chapter 22's discussion about encapsulation.
- **class JavaExample**—Sound somewhat familiar? Java, it turns out, is a true object-oriented language. There is nothing written in Java that is not part of a class! We are used to the idea of the *Zoog* class, *Car* class, *PImage* class, and so on, but it is important to note that the sketch as a whole is a class, too! *Processing* fills this stuff in for us so we do not have to worry about classes when we are first learning to program.
- **extends PApplet**—Well, after reading Chapter 22, we should be quite comfortable with what this means. This is just another example of inheritance. Here, the class JavaExample is a *child* of the class PApplet (or, equivalently, PApplet is the *parent* of JavaExample). PApplet is a class developed by the creators of *Processing* and by *extending* it, our sketch has access to all of the *Processing* goodies— ***setup()***, ***draw()***, ***mouseX***, ***mouseY***, and so on. This little bit of code is the secret behind how almost everything works in a *Processing* sketch.

Processing has served us so well because it eliminates the need to worry about the above four elements, all the while providing access to the benefits of the Java programming language. The rest of this chapter will show how we can begin to make use of access to the full Java API. (We briefly began this journey when we worked with String parsing in Chapters 17 and 18.)

23.3 Exploring the Java API

The *Processing* reference quickly became our best friend forever while learning to program. The Java API will start off more as an acquaintance we bump into from time to time. That acquaintance might turn into a really excellent friend someday, but for now, small doses will be just fine.

We can explore the full Java documentation by visiting:

http://java.sun.com/

There, we can click over to API specifications:

http://java.sun.com/reference/api/index.html

and find a selection of versions of Java. On a Mac, *Processing* will run with the selected version of Java (run Java Preferences, found, e.g., in: /Applications/Utilities/Java/J2SE 5.0/). On a PC, the *Processing* "standard" download comes with Java version 1.4.2 (the Windows expert version allows you to install your own version of Java). Versions of Java will change in the future with updated info at processing.org.

In any case, while there are differences between the version of Java, for what we are doing, they will not be terribly relevant, and we can look at the API for J2SE 1.4.2 for pretty much whatever we want to do. See Figure 23.1.

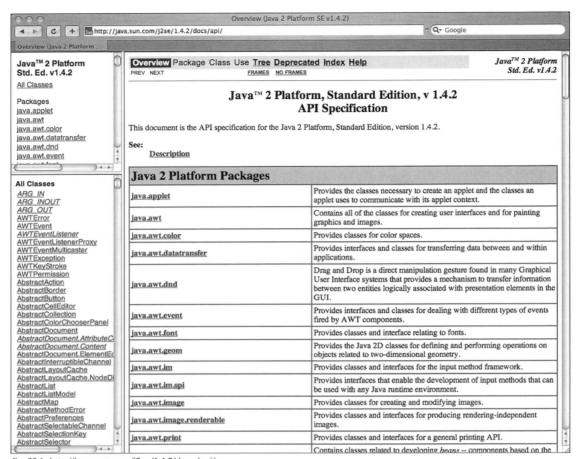

fig. 23.1 http://java.sun.com/j2se/1.4.2/docs/api/

And so, very quickly, you will find yourself completely lost. And that is OK. The Java API is huge. Humongous. It is not really meant to be read or even *perused*. It is really pure reference, for looking up specific classes that you know you need to look up.

For example, you might be working on a program that requires sophisticated random number generation beyond what **random()** can do, and you overheard a conversation about the class "Random" and thought "Hey, maybe I should check that out!" The reference page for a specific class can be found by scrolling down the "All Classes" list or else by selecting the right *package* (in this case the package **java.util**). A package, much like a library, is a collection of classes (the API organizes them by topic). The easiest way to find a class, though, is to just type the name of the class and Java (i.e., "Java Random") into google. The documentation page is just about always the first result. See Figure 23.2.

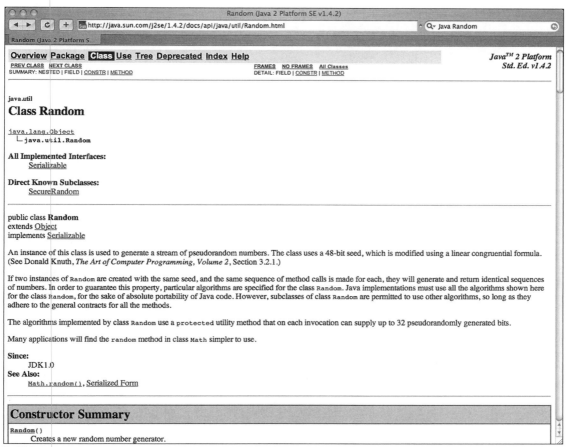

fig. 23.2

Just as with the *Processing* reference, the Java page includes an explanation of what the class does, the **Constructors** for creating an object instance, and available fields (variables) and methods (functions). Since Random is part of the java.util package (which *Processing* imports by assumption), we do not need to explicitly write an import statement to use it.

Here is some code that makes a **Random** object and calls the function **nextBoolean()** on it to get a random *true* or *false.*

Example 23-1: Using java.util.Random instead of *random()*

```
Random r;

void setup() {
  size(200,200);
  r = new Random();
}
```

> Declaring a Random object and calling the constructor as found at http://java.sun.com/j2se/1.4.2/docs/api/java/util/Random.html

```
void draw() {
  boolean trueorfalse = r.nextBoolean();
  if (trueorfalse) {
    background(0);
  } else {
    background(255);
  }
}
```

> Calling a function found at http://java.sun.com/
> j2se/1.4.2/docs/api/java/util/Random.html

Exercise 23-1: Visit the Java reference page for Random and use it to get a random integer between 0 and 9. http://java.sun.com/j2se/1.4.2/docs/api/java/util/Random.html.

23.4 Other Useful Java Classes: *ArrayList*

In Chapter 6, we learned how to use an array to keep track of ordered lists of information. We created an array of *N* objects and used a *"for"* loop to access each element in the array. The size of that array was fixed—we were limited to having *N* and only *N* elements.

There are alternatives. One option is to use a very large array and use a variable to track how much of the array to use at any given time (see Chapter 10's rain catcher example). *Processing* also offers **expand()**, **contract()**, **subset()**, **splice()** and other methods for resizing arrays. It would be great, however, to have a class that implements a flexibly sized array, allowing items to be added or removed from the beginning, middle, and end of that array.

This is exactly what the Java class ArrayList, found in the java.util package, does.

The reference page is here: http://java.sun.com/j2se/1.4.2/docs/api/java/util/ArrayList.html.

Using an ArrayList is conceptually similar to a standard array, but the syntax is different. Here is some code (that assumes the existence of a class "Particle") demonstrating identical results, first with an array, and second with an ArrayList. All of the methods used in this example are documented on the JavaDoc reference page.

```
// THE STANDARD ARRAY WAY
int MAX = 10;
//declaring the array
Particle[] parray = new Particle[MAX];

// Initialize the array in setup
void setup() {
  for (int i = 0; i < parray.length; i++) {
    parray[i] = new Particle();
  }
}
// Loop through the array to call methods in draw
void draw() {
  for (int i = 0; i < parray.length; i++) {
```

> **The Standard Array Way**
> This is what we have been doing all along, accessing elements of the array via an index and brackets—[].

```
      Particle p = parray[i];
      p.run();
      p.display();
    }
  }


// THE NEWFANGLED ARRAYLIST WAY
int MAX = 10;
// Declaring and creating the ArrayList instance
ArrayList plist = new ArrayList();

void setup() {
  for (int i = 0; i < MAX; i++) {
    plist.add(new Particle());
  }
}

void draw() {
  for (int i = 0; i < plist.size(); i++) {
    Particle p = (Particle) plist.get(i);
    p.run();
    p.display();
  }
}
```

> **The New ArrayList Way**
> Elements of an ArrayList are added and accessed with functions (rather than brackets)—***add()*** and ***get()***. All of these functions are documented in the Java reference: http://java.sun.com/j2se/1.4.2/docs/api/java/util/ArrayList.html.

> An object is added to an ArrayList with ***add()***.

> The size of the ArrayList is returned by ***size()***.

> An object is accessed from the ArrayList with ***get()***. You must "cast" whatever comes out of the ArrayList with a type, that is (Particle). Casting is discussed in Chapter 4.

In this last "for" loop, we have to cast the object as we *get* it out of the ArrayList. An ArrayList does not keep track of the type of objects stored inside—even though it may seem redundant, it is our job to remind the program by placing the class type (i.e., Particle) in parentheses. This process is known as *casting*.

Of course, the above example is somewhat silly, because it does not take advantage of the ArrayList's resizability, using a fixed size of 10. Following is a better example that adds one new Particle to the ArrayList with each cycle through ***draw()***. We also make sure the ArrayList never gets larger than 100 particles. See Figure 23.3.

> The term "particle system" was coined in 1983 by William T. Reeves as he developed the "Genesis" effect for the end of the movie, *Star Trek II: The Wrath of Khan*.
>
> A particle system is typically a collection of independent objects, usually represented by a simple shape or dot. It can be used to model types of natural phenomena, such as explosions, fire, smoke, sparks, waterfalls, clouds, fog, petals, grass, bubbles, and so on.

Example 23-2: Simple particle system with ArrayList

```
ArrayList particles;

void setup() {
  size(200,200);
  particles = new ArrayList();
  smooth();
}
```

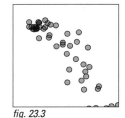

fig. 23.3

```
void draw() {

  particles.add(new Particle());
```

A new Particle object is added to the ArrayList every cycle through **draw()**.

```
  background(255);

  // Iterate through our ArrayList and get each Particle

  for (int i = 0; i < particles.size(); i++) {
    Particle p = (Particle) particles.get(i);
    p.run();
    p.gravity();
    p.display();
  }
```

The ArrayList keeps track of how many elements it is storing and we iterate through them all.

```
  // Remove the first particle when the list gets over 100.
  if (particles.size() > 100) {
    particles.remove(0);
  }
}
```

If the ArrayList has more than 100 elements in it, we delete the first element, using **remove()**.

```
// A simple Particle class
class Particle {
  float x;
  float y;
  float xspeed;
  float yspeed;

  Particle() {
    x = mouseX;
    y = mouseY;
    xspeed = random(-1,1);
    yspeed = random(-2,0);  }

  void run() {
    x = x + xspeed;
    y = y + yspeed;
  }

  void gravity() {
    yspeed += 0.1;
  }

  void display() {
    stroke(0);
    fill(0,75);
    ellipse(x,y,10,10);
  }
}
```

Exercise 23-2: Rewrite Example 23-2 so that particles are removed from the list whenever they leave the window (i.e., their y location is greater than height).

Hint: Add a function that returns a boolean in the Particle class.

```
_____ finished() {

  if (_____) {

    return _____;
  } else {
    return false;
  }
}
```

Hint: In order for this to work properly, you must iterate through elements of the ArrayList backward! Why? Because when an element is removed, all subsequent elements are shifted to the left (see Figure 23.4).

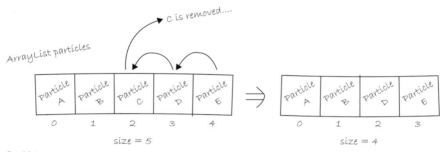

fig. 23.4

```
for (int i = _____; i _____; i_____) {
  Particle p = (Particle) particles.get(i);
  p.run();
  p.gravity();
  p.render();

  if (_____) {

    _____;
  }
}
```

23.5 Other Useful Java Classes: *Rectangle*

The second helpful Java class we will examine is the Rectangle class:

  http://java.sun.com/j2se/1.4.2/docs/api/java/awt/Rectangle.html.

A Java Rectangle specifies an area in a coordinate space that is enclosed by the Rectangle object's top-left point (*x, y*), its width, and its height. Sound familiar? Of course, the *Processing* function *rect()* draws a rectangle with precisely the same parameters. The ***Rectangle*** class encapsulates the idea of a rectangle into an object.

A Java Rectangle has useful methods, for instance, ***contains()***. *contains()* offers a simple way of checking if a point or rectangle is located inside that rectangle, by receiving an *x* and *y* coordinate and returning true or false, based on whether the point is inside the rectangle or not.

Here is a simple rollover implemented with a Rectangle object and ***contains()***. See Example 23.3.

Example 23-3: Using a java.awt.Rectangle object

```
Rectangle rect1, rect2;

void setup() {
  size(200,200);
  rect1 = new Rectangle(25,25,50,50);
  rect2 = new Rectangle(125,75,50,75);
}

void draw() {
  background(255);
  stroke(0);

  if (rect1.contains(mouseX,mouseY)) {
    fill(200);
  } else {
    fill(100);
  }

  rect(rect1.x, rect1.y, rect1.width,rect1.height);

  // Repeat for the second Rectangle
  // (of course, we could use an array or ArrayList here!)
  if (rect2.contains(mouseX,mouseY)) {
    fill(200);
  } else {
    fill(100);
  }
  rect(rect2.x, rect2.y, rect2.width,rect2.height);
}
```

fig. 23.5

> This sketch uses two Rectangle objects. The arguments for the constructor (*x,y*,width,height) are documented in the Java reference: http://java.sun.com/j2se/1.4.2/docs/api/java/awt/Rectangle.html.

> The ***contains()*** function is used to determine if the mouse is located inside the rectangle.

> A Rectangle object only knows about the variables associated with a rectangle. It cannot display one. So we use *Processing*'s ***rect()*** function in combination with the Rectangle's data.

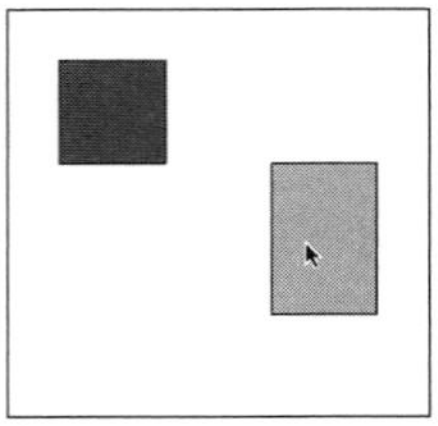

Let's have some fun and combine the ArrayList "particle" example with the Rectangle "rollover." In Example 23-4, particles are made every frame and pulled down by gravity toward the bottom of the window. If they run into a rectangle, however, they are caught. The particles are stored in an ArrayList and a Rectangle object determines if they have been caught or not. (This example contains answers to Exercise 23-2.)

Example 23-4: Super fancy ArrayList and rectangle particle system

```
// Declaring a global variable of type ArrayList
ArrayList particles;
// A "Rectangle" will suck up particles
Rectangle blackhole;

void setup() {
  size(200,200);
  blackhole = new Rectangle(50,150,100,25);
  particles = new ArrayList();
  smooth();
}

void draw() {
  background(255);

  // Displaying the Rectangle
  stroke(0);
  fill(175);
  rect(blackhole.x, blackhole.y, blackhole.width,blackhole.height);

  // Add a new particle at mouse location
  particles.add(new Particle(mouseX,mouseY));

  // Loop through all Particles
  for (int i = particles.size()-1; i >= 0; i--) {
    Particle p = (Particle) particles.get(i);
    p.run();
    p.gravity();
    p.display();
    if (blackhole.contains(p.x,p.y)) {
      p.stop();
    }
    if (p.finished()) {
      particles.remove(i);
    }
  }
}

// A simple Particle Class
class Particle {
  float x;
  float y;
  float xspeed;
  float yspeed;
  float life;

  // Make the Particle
  Particle(float tempX, float tempY) {
    x = tempX;
    y = tempY;
    xspeed = random(-1,1);
    yspeed = random(-2,0);
    life = 255;
  }
```

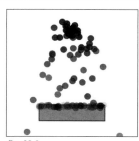

fig. 23.6

> If the Rectangle contains the location of the Particle, stop the Particle from moving.

```
// Move
void run() {
  x = x + xspeed;
  y = y + yspeed;
}

// Fall down
void gravity() {
  yspeed += 0.1;
}

// Stop moving
void stop() {
  xspeed = 0;
  yspeed = 0;
}

// Ready for deletion
boolean finished() {
  life -= 2.0;
  if (life < 0) return true;
  else return false;
}

// Show
void display() {
  stroke(0);
  fill(0,life);
  ellipse(x,y,10,10);
}
}
```

> The Particle has a "life" variable which decreases. When it reaches 0 the Particle can be removed from the ArrayList.

 Exercise 23-3: Write a Button class that includes a Rectangle object to determine if the mouse has clicked inside the button's area. (This is an extension of Exercise 9-8.)

23.6 Exception (Error) Handling

In addition to a very large library of useful classes, the Java programming language includes some features beyond what we have covered while learning *Processing*. We will explore one of those features now: *exception handling*.

Programming mistakes happen. We have all seen them.

```
java.lang.ArrayIndexOutOfBoundsException

java.io.IOException: openStream() could not open file.jpg

java.lang.NullPointerException
```

It is sad when these errors occur. Really, it is. The error message prints out and the program sputters to a halt, never to continue running again. Perhaps you have developed some techniques for protecting against these error messages. For example:

```
if (index < somearray.length) {
  somearray[index] = random(0,100);
}
```

The above is a form of "error checking." The code uses a conditional to check that the index is valid before an element at that index is accessed. The above code is quite conscientious and we should all aspire to be so careful.

Not all situations are as simple to avoid, however, and this is where *exception handling* comes into play. Exception handling refers to the process of handling *exceptions*, out of the ordinary events (i.e., errors) that occur during the execution of a program.

The code structure for exception handling in Java is known as *try catch*. In other words, "*Try* to run some code. If you run into a problem, however, *catch* the error and run some other code." If an error is caught using try catch, the program is allowed to continue. Let's look at how we might rewrite the array index error checking code *try catch* style.

```
try {
    somearray[index] = 200;
} catch (Exception e) {
    println("Hey, that's not a valid index!");
}
```

> The code that might produce an error goes within the "try" section. The code that should happen if an error occurs goes in the "catch" section.

The above code catches any possible exception that might occur. The type of error caught is the generic *Exception*. However, if you want to execute certain code based on a specific exception, you can, as the following code demonstrates.

```
try {
    somearray[index] = 200;
} catch (ArrayIndexOutOfBoundsException e) {
    println ("Hey, that's not a valid index!");
} catch (NullPointerException e) {
    println("I think you forgot to create the array!");
} catch (Exception e) {
    println("Hmmm, I dunno, something weird happened!");
    e.printStackTrace();
}
```

> Different "catch" sections catch different types of exceptions. In addition, each exception is an object and can therefore have methods called on it. For example:
>
> *e.printStackTrace();*
>
> displays more detailed information about the exception.

The above code, nevertheless, does nothing more than print out custom error messages. There are situations where we want more than just an explanation. For example, take the examples from Chapter 18 where we loaded data from a URL path. What if our sketch had failed to connect to the URL? It would have crashed and quit. With exception handling, we can catch that error and fill the array with *Strings* manually so that the sketch can continue running.

```
String[] lines;
String url = "http://wwww.rockinurl.com";
try {
  lines = loadStrings(url);
} catch (Exception e) {
  lines = new String[3];
  lines[0] = "I could not connect to " + url + "!!!";
  lines[1] = "But here is some stuff to work with";
  lines[2] = "anyway.";
}

println(lines);
```

> If a problem occurs connecting to the URL, we will just fill the array with dummy text so that the sketch can still run.

23.7 Java Outside of *Processing*

Here we are, the very last section of this book. You can can take a break now if you want. Maybe go outside and have a walk. A little jog around the block even. It will be good for you.

OK, back now? Great, let's go on.

As we close out this chapter and the book, we will cover one final topic: what to do if and when you decide you want to start coding outside of *Processing*.

But why would I ever want to do this?

One instance that would merit another programming environment is in the case of making an application that does not involve any graphics! Perhaps you need to write a program that takes all of your financial info from spreadsheets and logs it in a database. Or a chat server that runs in the background on your computer. While both of these could be written in the *Processing* environment, they do not necessarily need any of the features of *Processing* to run.

In the case of developing larger and larger projects that involve many classes, the *Processing* environment can become a bit difficult to use. For example, what if your project involves, say, 20 classes. Creating a *Processing* sketch with 20 tabs (and what if it were 40? or 100?) can be hard to manage, let alone fit on the screen. In this case, a development environment designed for large-scale Java projects would be better. Since *Processing* is Java, you can still use all of the functions available in *Processing* in other development environments by importing the core libraries.

So, what do you do? First, I would say do not rush. Enjoy *Processing* and take the time to feel comfortable with your own coding process and style before getting yourself wrapped up in the myriad of issues and questions that come along with programming in Java.

If you feel ready, a good first step is to just take some time browsing the Java web site:

http://java.sun.com/

Start with one of the tutorials:

http://java.sun.com/docs/books/tutorial/

The tutorials will cover the same material found in this book, but from a pure Java perspective.

The next step would be to just try compiling and running a "Hello World" Java program.

```java
public class HelloWorld {

  public static void main(String[] args) {
    System.out.println("Hello World. I miss you Processing.");
  }

}
```

The Java site has tutorials which explain all the elements in a Hello World program, as well as provide instructions on how to compile and run it on the "command line."

http://java.sun.com/docs/books/tutorial/getStarted/index.html

Finally, if you are feeling ambitious, go and download Eclipse:

http://www.eclipse.org/

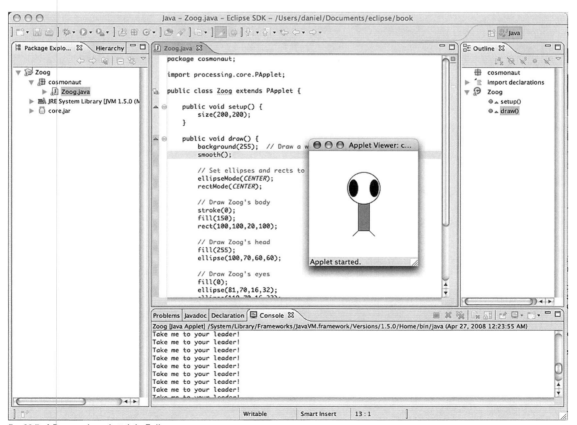

fig. 23.7 A Processing *sketch in Eclipse*

Eclipse is a development environment for Java with many advanced features. Some of those features will give you a headache and some will make you wonder how you ever programmed without Eclipse. Just remember, when you started with *Processing* in Chapter 2, you were probably up and running with your first sketch in less than five minutes. With something like *Eclipse*, you could need a much longer time to get started. See Figure 23.7.

Visit this book's web site for links and tutorials about how to run a *Processing* sketch within the Eclipse environment.

Thanks for reading. Feedback is encouraged and appreciated, so come on down to *http://www.learningprocessing.com* and sound off!

Appendix: Common Errors

This appendix offers a brief overview of common errors that occur in *Processing*, what those errors mean and why they occur. The language of error messages can often be cryptic and confusing, mostly due to their origins in the Java programming language.

For these error messages, we will use the following conventions:

Variables in the error messages will be named "myVar".
Arrays in the error messages will be named "myArray".
If the error is specifically related to an object variable, the variable will be named "myObject".
If the error is related to a class, the class will be named "Thing".
If the error is related to a function, the function will be named "function".

ERROR	PAGE NO.
unexpected token: _____	440
Found one too many { characters without a } to match it.	440
No accessible field named "myVar" was found in type "Temporary_####_####"	441
The variable "myVar" may be accessed here before having been definitely assigned a value.	442
java.lang.NullPointerException	442
Type "Thing" was not found.	444
Perhaps you wanted the overloaded version "type function (type $1, type $2, …);" instead?	445
No method named "fnction" was found in type "Temporary_####_####". However, there is an accessible method "function" whose name closely matches the name "fnction".	445
No accessible method with signature "function (type, type, …)" was found in type "Temporary_3018_2848".	445
java.lang.ArrayIndexOutOfBoundsException	446

Error:

unexpected token: something

Translation:

I'm expecting a piece of code here that you forgot, most likely some punctuation, like a semicolon, parenthesis, curly bracket, and so on.

This error is pretty much always caused by a typo. Unfortunately, the line of code that the error points to can be misleading. The "something" is sometimes correct and the actual error is caused by line before or after. Any time you forget or include an improper comma, semicolon, quote, parenthesis, bracket, and so on, you will get this error. Here are some examples:

ERROR		CORRECTED
`int val = 5`	Missing semicolon.	`int val = 5;`

`if (x < 5 {`
`  ellipse(0,0,10,10);`
`}`
	Missing close parenthesis.	`if (x < 5) {`
		`  ellipse(0,0,10,10);`
		`}`

`for (int i = 0, i < 5, i++) {`
`  println(i);`
`}`
	For loop should be separated by semicolons, not commans.	`for (int i = 0; i < 5; i++)`
		`  println(i);{`

Error:

Found one too many { characters without a } to match it.

Translation:

You forgot to close a block of code, such as an if statement, a loop, a function, a class, and so on.

Any time you have an open curly bracket in your code ("{"), you must have a matching close curly bracket ("}"). And since blocks of code are often nested inside each other, it is easy to forget one by accident, resulting in this error.

ERROR	CORRECTED

`void setup() {`
`  for (int i = 0; i < 10; i++) {`
`    if (i > 5) {`
`      line(0,i,i,0);`
`      println("i is greater than 5");`
`  }`
`}`   Missing a close curly bracket!
	`void setup() {`
	`  for (int i = 0; i < 10; i++) {`
	`    if (i > 5) {`
	`      line(0,i,i,0);`
	`      println("i is greater than 5");`
	`    }`
	`  }`
	`}`

Error:

No accessible field named "myVar" was found in type "Temporary_7665_1082"

Translation:

I do not know about the variable "myVar." It is not declared anywhere I can see.

This error will happen if you do not declare a variable. Remember, you can't use a variable until you have said what type it should be. You will get the error if you write:

```
myVar = 10;
```

instead of:

```
int myVar = 10;
```

Of course, you should only declare the variable once, otherwise you can run into trouble. So this is perfectly OK:

```
int myVar = 10;
myVar = 20;
```
> OK! The variable was declared.

This error can also occur if you try to use a local variable outside of the block of code where it was declared. For example:

```
if (mousePressed) {
  int myVar = 10;
}
ellipse(myVar,10,10,10);
```
> ERROR! myVar is local to the if statement so it cannot be accessed here.

Here is a corrected version:

```
int myVar = 0;
if (mousePressed) {
  myVar = 10;
}
ellipse(myVar,10,10,10);
```
> OK! The variable is declared outside of the if statement.

Or if you have declared a variable in *setup()*, but try to use it in *draw()*.

```
void setup() {
  int myVar = 10;
}

void draw() {
  ellipse(myVar,10,10,10);
}
```
> ERROR! myVar is local to the *setup()* so it cannot be accessed here.

Corrected:

```
int myVar = 0;

void setup() {
  myVar = 10;
}
```

```
void draw() {
  ellipse(myVar,10,10,10);          OK! The variable is global.
}
```

The same error will occur if you use an array in any of the above scenarios.

```
myArray[0] = 10;                    ERROR! No array was declared.
```

___

Error:

The variable "myVar" may be accessed here before having been definitely assigned a value.

Translation:

You declared the variable "myVar", but you did not initialize it. You should give it a value first.

This is a pretty simple error to fix. Most likely, you just forgot to give your variable its default starting value. This error only occurs for local variables (with global variables *Processing* will either not care, and assume the value is zero, or else throw a *NullPointerException*).

```
int myVar;
line(0, myVar,0,0);                ERROR! myVar does not have a value.

int myVar = 10;
line(0, myVar,0,0);                OK! myVar equals ten.
```

This error can also occur if you try to use an array before allocating its size properly.

```
int[] myArray;
myArray[0] = 10;                   ERROR! myArray was not created properly.


int[] myArray = new int[3];
myArray[0] = 10;                   OK! myArray is an array of three integers.
```

___

Error:

java.lang.NullPointerException

Translation:

I have encountered a variable whose value is null. I can't work with this.

The *NullPointerException* error can be one of the most difficult errors to fix. It is most commonly caused by forgetting to initialize an object. As mentioned in Chapter 8, when you declare a variable that is an object, it is first given the value of *null*, meaning nothing. (This does not apply to primitives, such as integers and floats.) If you attempt to then use that variable without having initialized it (by calling the Constructor), this error will occur. Here are a few examples (that assume the existence of a class called "Thing").

```
Thing thing;
void setup() {

}
```

```
void draw() {
  thing.display();
}
```

ERROR! "thing" was never initialized and therefore has the value null.

Corrected:

```
Thing thing;
void setup() {
  thing = new Thing();
}

void draw() {
  thing.display();
}
```

OK! "thing" is not null because it was initialized with the constructor.

Sometimes, the same error can occur if you do initialize the object, but as a local variable by accident.

```
Thing thing;
void setup() {
  Thing thing = new Thing();
}

void draw() {
  thing.display();
}
```

ERROR! This line of code declares and initializes a different "thing" variable (even though it has the same name). It is a local variable for only **setup()**. The global "thing" is still null!

The same goes for an array as well. If you forget to initialize the elements, you will get this error.

```
Thing[] things = new Thing[10];
for (int i = 0; i < things.length; i++) {
  things[i].display();
}
```

ERROR! All the elements on the array are null!

Corrected:

```
Thing[] things = new Thing[10];
for (int i = 0; i < things.length; i++) {
  things[i] = new Thing();
}

for (int i = 0; i < things.length; i++) {
  things[i].display();
}
```

OK! The first loop initialized the elements of the array.

Finally, if you forget to allocate space for an array, you can also end up with this error.

```
int[] myArray;

void setup() {
  myArray[0] = 5;
}
```

ERROR! myArray is null because you never created it and gave it a size.

Corrected:

```
int[] myArray = new int[3];
void setup() {
  myArray[0] = 5;
}
```

> OK! myArray is an array of three integers.

Error:
Type "Thing" was not found.

Translation:
You are trying to declare a variable of type Thing, but I do not know what a Thing is.

This error occurs because you either (a) forgot to define a class called "Thing" or (b) made a typo in the variable type.

A typo is pretty common:

```
intt myVar = 10;
```

> ERROR! You probably meant to type "int" not "intt."

Or maybe you want to create an object of type Thing, but forgot to define the thing class.

```
Thing myThing = new Thing();
```

> ERROR! If you did not define a class called "Thing."

This will work, of course, if you write:

```
void setup() {
  Thing myThing = new Thing();
}

class Thing {
  Thing() {
  }
}
```

> OK! You did declare a class called "Thing."

Finally, the error will also occur if you try to use an object from a library, but forget to import the library.

```
void setup() {
  Capture video = new Capture(this,320,240,30);
}
```

> ERROR! You forgot to import the video library.

Corrected:

```
import processing.video.*;
void setup() {
  Capture video = new Capture(this,320,240,30);
}
```

> OK! You imported the library.

Error:

Perhaps you wanted the overloaded version "type function (type $1, type $2, …);" instead?

Translation:

You are calling a function incorrectly, but I think I know what you mean to say. Did you want call this function with these arguments?

This error occurs most often when you call a function with the incorrect number of arguments. For example, to draw an ellipse, you need an *x* location, *y* location, width, and height. But if you write:

```
ellipse(100,100,50);
```

ERROR! *ellipse()* requires four arguments.

You will get the error: "Perhaps you wanted the overloaded version 'void ellipse(float $1, float $2, float $3, float $4);' instead?" The error lists the function definition for you, indicating you need four arguments, all of floating point. The same error will also occur if you have the right number of arguments, but the wrong type.

```
ellipse(100,100,50,"Wrong Type of Argument");
```

ERROR! *ellipse()* can not take a String!

Error:

No method named "fnction" was found in type "Temporar y_9938_7597". However, there is an accessible method "function" whose name closely matches the name "fnction".

Translation:

You are calling a function I have never heard of, however, I think I know what you want to say since there is a function I have heard of that is really similar.

This is a similar error and pretty much only happens when you make a typo in a function's name.

```
elipse(100,100,50,50);
```

ERROR! You have the right number of arguments, but you spelled "ellipse" incorrectly.

Error:

No accessible method with signature "function (type, type, …)" was found in type "Temporary_3018_2848".

Translation:

You are calling a function that I have never heard of. I have no idea what you are talking about!

This error occurs if you call a function that just plain does not exist, and *Processing* can't make any guess as to what you meant to say.

ERROR! Unless you have defined this function, *Processing* has no way of knowing what it is.

```
functionCompletelyMadeUp(200);
```

Same goes for a function that is called on an object.

```
Capture video = new Capture(this,320,240,30);

video.turnPurple();
```
ERROR! There is no function called **turnPurple()** in the Capture class.

Error:
java.lang.ArrayIndexOutOfBoundsException: ##

Translation:
You tried to access an element of an array that does not exist.

This error will happen when the index value of any array is invalid. For example, if your array is of length 10, the only valid indices are zero through nine. Anything less than zero or greater than nine will produce this error.

```
int[] myArray = new int[10];

myArray[-1] = 0
```
ERROR! −1 is not a valid index.

```
myArray[0] = 0;
myArray[5] = 0;
```
OK! 0 and 5 are valid indices.

```
myArray[10] = 0;
myArray[20] = 0;
```
ERROR! 10 is not a valid index.

ERROR! 20 is not a valid index.

This error can be a bit harder to debug when you are using a variable for the index.

```
int[] myArray = new int[100];
myArray[mouseX] = 0;
```
ERROR! **mouseX** could be bigger than 99.

```
int index = constrain(mouseX,0,myArray.length-1);

myArray[index] = 0;
```
OK! **mouseX** is constrained between 0 and 99 first.

A loop can also be the source of the problem.

```
for (int i = 0; i < 200; i++) {
  myArray[i] = 0;
}
```
ERROR! *i* loops past 99.

```
for (int i = 0; i < myArray.length; i++) {
  myArray[i] = 0;
}
```
OK! Using the length property of the array as the exit condition for the loop.

```
for (int i = 0; i < 200; i++) {
  if (i < myArray.length) {
  myArray[i] = 0;
  }
}
```
OK! If your loop really needs to go to 200, then you could build in an if statement inside the loop.

Index